THE GLOSSARY OF
ADVERTISEMENT

Compiled & Edited By:
Mrs. Banaja Sethi

Rhythm

Independent
Publication

THE GLOSSARY OF ADVERTISEMENT

Compiled & Edited By:
Mrs. Banaja Sethi

ISBN:9798862445541

9798862445541

Published by:

Rhythm Independent Publication,

Jinkethimmanahalli, Varanasi, Bengaluru, Karnataka, India - 560036

For all types of correspondence, send your mails to the provided address above.

The information presented herein has been collated from a diverse range of sources, comprehensive perspective on the subject matter.

AIDA Model

The AIDA model is a marketing framework that is used to describe the stages that a customer goes through when interacting with an advertisement. AIDA stands for Attention, Interest, Desire, and Action, which represent the sequential steps in the customer journey. The first stage of the AIDA model is Attention, which involves capturing the customer's attention and making them aware of the advertisement. This can be achieved through eye-catching visuals, compelling headlines, or attention-grabbing slogans. The goal is to stand out from the competition and pique the customer's curiosity. The second stage is Interest, where the advertisement seeks to generate interest and engage the customer. This is done by providing information about the product or service in a way that is relevant and appealing to the customer's needs and desires. The advertisement should highlight the unique selling points and benefits of the product, creating a sense of curiosity and desire to know more. The third stage, Desire, aims to create a strong desire or want in the customer for the product or service. The advertisement should showcase how the product can solve a problem or fulfill a need, while also evoking emotional triggers such as happiness, success, or acceptance. Testimonials, success stories, or demonstrations can be effective in building desire and convincing the customer that the product is worth investing in. The final stage of the AIDA model is Action, which involves encouraging the customer to take a specific action, such as making a purchase, signing up for a newsletter, or requesting more information. The call-to-action should be clear and compelling, using urgency or scarcity to motivate the customer to act immediately. It should also provide easy and accessible ways for the customer to take action, such as clickable links, phone numbers, or online forms.

Ad Agency

An advertising agency, or ad agency, is a company that provides services in creating, planning, and executing advertisement campaigns for various businesses or organizations. Their primary goal is to help their clients effectively communicate and promote their products or services to their target audience. The ad agency acts as an intermediary between the client and the various media platforms where the advertisements will be published or displayed. They work closely with the client to understand their marketing objectives, target audience, and budget constraints. Based on this information, the agency develops a comprehensive advertising strategy that aligns with the client's goals and objectives. The agency's team of professionals includes account executives, creative directors, copywriters, art directors, media planners, and researchers, among others. Each member plays a crucial role in the development and execution of the advertising campaign. The initial phase of the process involves conducting thorough market research and analysis to identify the target audience, their interests, and their preferred media channels. This information helps the agency determine the most effective advertising platforms and create compelling messages that resonate with the target audience. Once the strategy is finalized, the agency's creative team works on designing the advertisements. This includes developing visually appealing graphics, writing captivating copy, and selecting appropriate fonts and colors that align with the client's brand identity. The creative team collaborates closely with the account executives to ensure that the advertisements meet the client's expectations and objectives. After the advertisements are created, the agency's media planning team determines the best media channels to reach the target audience. This may include television, radio, print, outdoor advertising, or digital platforms such as websites, social media, and online video streaming services. Throughout the campaign, the agency monitors and analyzes the performance of the advertisements. They use various metrics and data analysis techniques to measure the effectiveness of the campaign and make necessary adjustments to maximize its impact. In conclusion, an advertising agency is a specialized company that helps businesses and organizations create and execute effective advertising campaigns. They work closely with clients to understand their goals and objectives, develop creative and strategic advertising

1

solutions, and ensure the advertisements are delivered to the right audience through the most appropriate media channels.

Ad Auction Platforms

An ad auction platform is a digital platform that allows advertisers to bid on and purchase ad space in real-time. These platforms typically operate through an automated bidding process where advertisers set a maximum bid for their ads. When a user visits a website or mobile app that is part of the ad network, an auction is triggered, and the platform determines which advertiser's ad to display based on the bids and relevance to the user. Ad auction platforms use advanced algorithms and targeting capabilities to match ads with the right audience. These algorithms take into account various factors such as the user's demographics, browsing behavior, and interests to deliver personalized and relevant ads. This personalized approach helps advertisers maximize their return on investment by reaching the most relevant audience.

Ad Blocker Detection Tools

Ad Blocker Detection Tools are software or scripts used by advertisers and website publishers to identify if a user visiting their website is using an ad blocker. Ad blockers are browser extensions or plugins that block or filter advertisements displayed on websites. These tools are designed to detect the presence of ad blockers and provide data that can be used for various purposes. Ad Blocker Detection Tools work by checking if certain relevant elements of a webpage (such as banner ads, pop-ups, or tracking scripts) are blocked from loading. They use various techniques to detect the presence of ad blockers, such as analyzing the structure of the web page, comparing the expected and actual behavior of advertising elements, or examining network requests. The detection process usually involves sending requests for specific resources or executing JavaScript code that is likely to be blocked by ad blockers. The response from these requests or the success/failure of the executed code can indicate if an ad blocker is active. Ad Blocker Detection Tools provide feedback to the website publisher or advertiser about the status of ad blocking on the user's browser. The information obtained from these tools can be used for different purposes. Website publishers may use it to determine the number of users who are blocking ads on their website and to implement strategies to mitigate the impact of ad blocking, such as encouraging users to disable their ad blockers or offering alternative ways to generate revenue, such as subscriptions or native advertising. Advertisers can use this information to assess the effectiveness of their advertising campaigns and make adjustments accordingly. Overall, Ad Blocker Detection Tools play a crucial role in the advertising ecosystem by providing insights into the prevalence of ad blocking and allowing publishers and advertisers to adapt their strategies accordingly. By understanding the extent of ad blocking and adjusting their approach, publishers and advertisers can continue to reach their target audience effectively while maintaining a sustainable revenue model.

Ad Blocker

An ad blocker is a software or browser extension that is designed to prevent advertisements from displaying on web pages or mobile apps. It works by detecting and blocking the code that is responsible for loading and displaying ads, thereby preventing them from being seen by the user. The primary purpose of an ad blocker is to improve the user experience by eliminating annoying and distracting ads. This can include banner ads, pop-up ads, video ads, and other types of advertising that may disrupt the user's browsing or decrease the loading speed of the page.I am sorry for making mistake, here is the correct answer: An ad blocker is a utility tool used to censor and remove advertising content from being displayed on web pages or in mobile apps. It operates by identifying and intercepting the code responsible for loading and presenting ads, effectively obstructing their visual appearance for the end user. The primary aim of an ad blocker is to enhance the user's browsing experience by preventing intrusive and distracting advertising materials from appearing on the screen. These unwanted advertisements can take various forms, including banner ads, pop-up ads, video ads, and other types of promotional content that may hinder the user's engagement or interfere with the page's loading speed. Ad blockers ultimately serve as a means to regain control over the browsing environment, providing individuals with the choice to selectively view or avoid certain advertisements while navigating the internet.

Ad Blocking Software Detection

Ad Blocking Software Detection refers to the identification and tracking of software or browser extensions that block advertisements from being displayed to users. It involves methods and techniques used by online advertisers and publishers to determine whether an ad-blocking software is being used by a website visitor. Ad blocking software has gained popularity among internet users who prefer to browse the web without interruptions caused by ads. These software tools remove or prevent advertisements from loading on web pages, resulting in a faster and cleaner browsing experience. However, this poses a challenge to advertisers and publishers who rely on revenue generated from displaying ads on their websites. There are several ways in which ad blocking software can be detected. One common method is by checking for the presence of certain files or extensions that are typically associated with ad blockers. Advertisers and publishers can use JavaScript or server-side scripts to determine if such files or extensions are present in the user's browser. Another approach is to analyze the behavior and performance of a user's browser. Ad blocking software often interferes with the loading and rendering of ads, so advertisers and publishers can detect its presence by monitoring the loading times and performance metrics of ads. If ads are not being loaded or displayed as expected, it is a strong indication that an ad blocker is in use. Some ad blocking software also modifies the HTML and CSS of web pages to remove or hide ads. In such cases, advertisers and publishers can use script-based detection methods to scan the HTML and CSS code of a webpage and identify any changes or modifications made by ad blockers. Once ad blocking software is detected, advertisers and publishers can take appropriate actions. This may include displaying alternative content or messages to users who have ad blockers enabled, encouraging them to disable the ad blocker or whitelist the website. It may also involve employing different ad formats or delivery methods that are less likely to be blocked by ad blockers. Overall, ad blocking software detection plays a crucial role in understanding and addressing the impact of ad blockers on online advertising. By detecting and responding to ad blockers, advertisers and publishers can optimize their advertising strategies, maintain revenue streams, and ensure a better user experience on their websites.

Ad Blocking Software

Ad Blocking Software refers to computer applications or browser extensions that are used to prevent or block advertisements from being displayed on websites or mobile apps. These software tools typically work by filtering or blocking the code that.is responsible for displaying ads, thereby preventing the ads from being shown to the user.The main purpose of Ad Blocking Software is to improve the user experience by eliminating unwanted or intrusive advertisements. With the proliferation of online advertising, many users find themselves overwhelmed with intrusive pop-up ads, video ads, or banner ads that hinder their browsing experience and consume significant amounts of bandwidth. Ad Blocking Software helps users regain control over their online experience by allowing them to browse websites without being continuously bombarded by advertisements.

Ad Campaign Analytics

Ad Campaign Analytics refers to the process of measuring and analyzing the performance and effectiveness of advertising campaigns. It involves the collection, interpretation, and reporting of data to determine the impact and success of various marketing initiatives. Ad Campaign Analytics helps advertisers and marketers make informed decisions, optimize their campaigns, and achieve their advertising goals. The key objective of Ad Campaign Analytics is to track, measure, and evaluate the performance of advertisements across different channels and mediums. It enables advertisers to monitor the reach, engagement, conversions, and return on investment (ROI) of their advertising efforts. By analyzing various metrics and key performance indicators (KPIs), such as click-through rate (CTR), conversion rate, cost per acquisition (CPA), and customer lifetime value (CLV), advertisers can determine the effectiveness of their campaigns and identify areas for improvement. Ad Campaign Analytics involves the use of various tools and technologies to collect and analyze data. These may include web analytics platforms, ad tracking software, social media analytics tools, and customer relationship management (CRM) systems. By integrating data from multiple sources, advertisers can gain a comprehensive view of their advertising performance and derive actionable insights. The data collected through Ad Campaign Analytics can provide valuable insights into customer behavior,

3

preferences, and demographics. It helps advertisers understand which advertising channels, messages, and creative elements are most effective in driving customer engagement and conversions. This information can be used to optimize future campaigns, allocate budgets more effectively, and target specific audience segments more accurately. In summary, Ad Campaign Analytics is a crucial tool for advertisers and marketers to measure and evaluate the performance of their advertising campaigns. It helps them understand how their advertisements are performing and provides insights to improve future campaigns. By leveraging data and analytics, advertisers can make data-driven decisions, optimize their advertising efforts, and achieve their marketing goals.

Ad Campaign Management Software Tools

Ad Campaign Management Software Tools refer to a set of digital applications and platforms designed to assist advertisers and marketers in creating, organizing, monitoring, and optimizing their advertising campaigns across various channels and media types. These software tools provide a centralized platform for managing all aspects of ad campaigns, including planning, execution, analysis, and reporting. They often offer a range of features and functionalities that enable users to streamline their entire campaign lifecycle, from setting goals and budgeting to creative development, targeting, distribution, and performance measurement.

Ad Campaign Management Software

Ad Campaign Management Software is a powerful tool that helps businesses effectively plan, execute, and track their advertising campaigns. It enables organizations to streamline their advertising efforts by providing a centralized platform where they can create, monitor, and optimize campaigns across various advertising channels. The software offers a range of features and functionalities that simplify and automate the entire ad campaign process. With this software, businesses can easily set campaign objectives, define target audiences, select appropriate advertising channels, create and manage ad creatives, and allocate budgets. It also allows users to schedule ad placements and track key campaign metrics such as impressions, clicks, conversions, and return on investment (ROI). One of the key advantages of using ad campaign management software is its ability to facilitate cross-channel advertising. It allows businesses to execute campaigns across multiple platforms such as search engines, social media platforms, websites, mobile apps, and email marketing. The software provides a unified interface where users can manage campaigns across these channels, enabling them to reach a wider audience and maximize campaign effectiveness. Furthermore, ad campaign management software offers robust targeting and personalization capabilities. It allows businesses to segment their target audience based on various criteria such as demographics, interests, and behaviors. This enables organizations to deliver tailored and personalized advertisements that resonate with their target audience, increasing the chances of engagement and conversion. The software also provides in-depth analytics and reporting functionalities. Users can access real-time data on campaign performance, allowing them to monitor progress and make data-driven decisions. The analytics tools provided by the software enable businesses to gain insights into audience behavior, identify trends, and optimize their campaigns for better results. In conclusion, ad campaign management software is an essential tool for businesses looking to streamline their advertising efforts. It simplifies the process of planning, executing, and tracking ad campaigns, enabling organizations to optimize their advertising efforts, reach a wider audience, and drive better results.

Ad Campaign Management

Ad Campaign Management refers to the process of planning, creating, implementing, and monitoring advertising campaigns for a specific product, service, or brand. It involves strategizing and executing various marketing activities that aim to promote and sell a product to a target audience. Effective ad campaign management can help businesses achieve their marketing objectives and drive customer engagement and sales. This process typically begins with thorough research and analysis of the target market and competitors. The advertising team then develops a comprehensive plan that outlines the campaign's goals, target audience, messaging, and media channels to be used. Creative elements such as ad design, copywriting, and artwork are also created during this stage. Once the campaign plan is finalized, it is implemented through various advertising channels such as print, television, radio, online

4

platforms, and social media. Ad placement and scheduling are carefully strategized to reach the intended audience effectively. During the campaign's execution, metrics and data are continuously monitored and analyzed to evaluate its performance and make any necessary adjustments. Ad Campaign Management also involves budgeting and financial considerations. The campaign is typically allocated a specific budget, and the advertising team works within this budget to achieve the desired results. They closely track expenses and assess the return on investment (ROI) to ensure that the campaign remains cost-effective and delivers value to the business. Furthermore, ad campaign management requires effective communication and collaboration among team members and stakeholders. Clear communication is crucial to ensure that everyone is aligned on the campaign's objectives, messaging, and timeline. Collaboration is essential to bring together various creative elements and execute the campaign seamlessly. In conclusion, Ad Campaign Management is a comprehensive process that involves planning, executing, and evaluating advertising campaigns. It requires thorough research, strategic planning, creative development, effective implementation, budgeting, and ongoing monitoring. Successful campaign management can help businesses promote their products or services, reach their target audience, and achieve their marketing goals.

Ad Campaign Performance

An ad campaign performance is a measure of the effectiveness and success of an advertising campaign. It assesses the impact and outcomes of various advertising activities, such as the creation and dissemination of advertisements, across different channels and platforms. The goal of an ad campaign is to promote a product, service, or brand by reaching the target audience and influencing their behavior or perception. Evaluating the campaign's performance helps advertisers and marketers determine if their efforts are meeting the desired objectives and if any adjustments or optimizations are necessary. Several key performance indicators (KPIs) are commonly used to measure ad campaign performance. These include: - Reach: the total number of people who have been exposed to the ad campaign, either through impressions or actual views. - Impressions: the number of times an advertisement has been displayed, regardless of whether it has been viewed by the target audience. - Click-through rate (CTR): the percentage of people who click on an ad after seeing it, indicating their interest and engagement. - Conversion rate: the proportion of people who take the desired action, such as making a purchase or filling out a form, after clicking on an ad. - Return on investment (ROI): the overall profitability of the ad campaign, comparing the cost of the campaign to the revenue generated. Ad campaign performance can be measured and analyzed using various tools and techniques. These include tracking pixels, cookies, and analytics platforms that provide data on user behavior, engagement, and conversions. A comprehensive analysis may involve conducting A/B testing, where different versions of an ad or campaign are tested against each other to determine the most effective approach. By assessing ad campaign performance, advertisers can gain insights into their target audience's preferences, interests, and responses. This information helps in refining and optimizing future campaigns to ensure better results and return on investment. Additionally, evaluating the performance of different campaigns allows advertisers to allocate resources effectively, making data-driven decisions on where to invest their advertising budget.

Ad Campaign

An advertising campaign refers to a series of coordinated and strategic activities designed to promote a product, service, or brand to a specific target audience. It involves the creation and execution of various advertisements through different media channels to convey a compelling message that captures the attention and interest of the target market. The primary objective of an ad campaign is to raise awareness, generate interest, and ultimately drive consumer behavior towards the desired action, whether it is purchasing a product, subscribing to a service, or changing perceptions about a brand. It aims to create a strong and memorable brand image, establish a unique selling proposition, and communicate the benefits and value of the product or service offered. An effective advertising campaign typically begins with a thorough understanding of the target audience and their preferences, needs, and behaviors. This enables marketers to tailor their messages and choose appropriate media channels to reach and engage the target market effectively. The campaign message should resonate with the target audience, evoke emotions, and provide a clear and compelling call to action. The success of an ad campaign relies on careful planning, creative execution, and continuous monitoring and evaluation. Marketers need to set clear and measurable goals, establish key performance indicators, and track the campaign's performance to assess its effectiveness and make any necessary adjustments. This may involve conducting market research, analyzing consumer feedback, and measuring campaign metrics such as reach, engagement, and conversion rates.

Ad Click Fraud Prevention

Ad click fraud prevention refers to the strategies and techniques employed by advertisers and advertising platforms to defend against fraudulent clicks on online advertisements. Click fraud occurs when someone intentionally clicks on an ad for malicious purposes, such as increasing costs for the advertiser or artificially inflating the click-through rate. There are several methods used to prevent ad click fraud. One approach is to employ sophisticated algorithms and machine learning models to detect and flag potentially fraudulent clicks. These algorithms analyze various data points, such as user behavior, click patterns, and IP addresses, to identify suspicious activity. If a click is deemed fraudulent, it can be automatically filtered out or flagged for further investigation.

Ad Click-Through Rate (CTR)

The Ad Click-Through Rate (CTR) is a measurement used in online advertising to evaluate the effectiveness of an advertisement. It is the ratio of the number of clicks an ad receives to the number of times it is displayed, expressed as a percentage. The formula to calculate the CTR is: CTR = (Number of Clicks / Number of Impressions) x 100 Impressions refer to the total number of times an ad is shown to users. Clicks represent the number of times users interact with the ad by clicking on it. By dividing the clicks by the impressions and multiplying by 100, we get the CTR as a percentage value. The CTR is a crucial metric in digital advertising as it provides insights into the level of engagement an ad generates among its target audience. A high CTR indicates that a significant number of users are clicking on the ad, which can lead to increased website traffic, conversions, and ultimately, revenue. Advertisers use CTR to gauge ad performance and make data-driven decisions on campaign optimization. A low CTR may indicate that the ad is not resonating with the audience, and adjustments may be needed in terms of targeting, messaging, or creative elements. A high CTR, on the other hand, suggests that the ad is relevant, compelling, and capturing the attention of users. Advertisers may consider scaling up such ads or developing similar ones to maximize their return on investment. It is important to note that CTR alone does not provide a complete picture of an ad's success. Conversion rate, bounce rate, and other metrics should also be evaluated in conjunction with CTR to gain deeper insights into an ad campaign's performance. In summary, the Ad Click-Through Rate (CTR) is a percentage that represents the number of clicks an ad receives compared to the number of times it is shown. It is a vital metric in measuring the effectiveness of online advertising and plays a crucial role in optimizing ad campaigns for better performance.

Ad Clicks

Ad Clicks refer to the action of users clicking on an advertisement displayed on a website, mobile app, or any other online platform. It is a metric used to measure the engagement or interest of users in an advertisement. When a user clicks on an ad, they are redirected to a landing page or a specific destination determined by the advertiser. Ad clicks are tracked using various tracking mechanisms, such as click-through URLs or event tracking codes.

Ad Conversion Rate

The Ad Conversion Rate refers to the percentage of viewers or users who take a desired action after being exposed to an advertisement. It is a metric used by advertisers to measure the effectiveness of their campaigns and determine the return on investment (ROI) for their advertising efforts. The desired action can vary depending on the goals of the advertisement. It could be making a purchase, signing up for a newsletter, filling out a contact form, downloading an app, or any other predefined action that the advertiser considers valuable. The formula to calculate the Ad Conversion Rate is: Ad Conversion Rate = (Number of Conversions / Number of Ad Impressions) x 100 For example, if an ad campaign receives 1000 impressions and generates 50 conversions, the conversion rate would be: (50 / 1000) x 100 = 5% The higher the conversion rate, the more successful the ad campaign is considered to be. A high conversion rate indicates that the advertisement is effectively persuading viewers to take the desired action, leading to a higher return on investment for the advertiser. Tracking and analyzing the ad conversion rate is crucial for advertisers as it helps them optimize their campaigns. By identifying which advertisements or channels are performing well, advertisers can allocate their budget more effectively and make informed decisions to maximize their ROI. Factors that can affect the ad conversion rate include the relevance of the advertisement to the target audience, the clarity of the call-to-action, the design and layout of the ad, the landing page experience, and the overall effectiveness of the marketing message. In summary, the ad conversion rate is a key metric used to measure the success of an advertisement by calculating the percentage of viewers who take a desired action. It helps advertisers evaluate the effectiveness of their campaigns and make informed decisions to optimize their return on investment.

Ad Copy

Ad Copy is a concise and persuasive piece of text that aims to capture the attention and interest of potential customers and encourage them to take a specific action, such as purchasing a product or signing up for a service. It is a crucial element in advertising and serves as the main means of communication between a brand and its target audience. The primary goal of ad copy is to effectively convey the unique selling points and benefits of a product or service to the intended audience. It is typically written in a persuasive tone and uses language that resonates with the target market. Ad copy is often created by professional copywriters who possess a deep understanding of consumer psychology and advertising techniques.

Ad Creative Optimization

Ad Creative Optimization refers to the process of continuously improving and refining ad content in order to maximize its effectiveness and drive better performance. It involves analyzing the performance data and making data-driven changes to the creative elements of an advertisement, such as the copy, visuals, and call-to-action (CTA), to improve its relevance and appeal to the target audience. The goal of Ad Creative Optimization is to capture the attention of the audience, generate interest, and ultimately drive desired actions, whether it is making a purchase, signing up for a newsletter, or downloading an app. By constantly testing and refining various elements of the ad, marketers aim to find the most compelling combination that resonates with their target audience and generates the highest conversion rates. Ad Creative Optimization encompasses several key stages. Firstly, it involves conducting thorough market research and audience analysis to gain insights into the preferences, needs, and behaviors of the target audience. This helps in understanding what type of content will resonate with them and drive engagement. Once the initial ad creative is developed, it is important to establish clear conversion goals and set up tracking mechanisms to measure the performance of the ad. This involves collecting data on various metrics such as click-through rates, conversion rates, engagement rates, and return on ad spend (ROAS). With the performance data in hand, the next step is to analyze the results and identify areas for improvement. This can involve A/B testing, where different versions of the ad are tested simultaneously to determine which performs better. By comparing the performance of different variations, marketers can gain insights into what resonates with their target audience and make data-driven decisions on which creative elements to optimize. Based on the analysis, changes can be made to the ad copy, visuals, headline, CTA, or even the overall layout of the ad. These changes are then tested and compared again to measure their impact on performance. The process is iterative, with continuous monitoring and optimization to ensure that the ad performs at its best. In conclusion, Ad Creative Optimization is a crucial component of successful advertising campaigns. By constantly refining and improving the creative elements of an ad, marketers can increase its effectiveness, maximize engagement, and drive better results.

Ad Creative Testing

Ad creative testing refers to the process of evaluating and comparing different versions of an advertisement in order to determine which variation is most effective in achieving the desired marketing objectives. It involves testing various elements of the ad, such as the headline, visuals, copy, and call-to-action, to understand their impact on the target audience. The purpose of ad creative testing is to optimize advertising campaigns by identifying the most compelling and persuasive ad version that resonates with the target audience, generates higher engagement, and ultimately drives desired actions, such as clicks, conversions, or purchases. By conducting systematic testing, advertisers can make informed decisions based on data-driven insights rather than relying on intuition or assumptions.

Ad Creative

An ad creative, in the context of advertising, refers to the visual or textual content that is designed to capture the attention and interest of the target audience and persuade them to take a desired action. It is the culmination of various elements such as copywriting, design, and imagery that are strategically combined to convey a specific message and evoke a desired response from the viewers or readers. The primary objective of an ad creative is to communicate the unique value proposition of a product or service in a compelling and memorable way. It aims to differentiate the advertised offering from competitors and create an emotional connection with the audience. The creative execution may involve various formats, including print ads, radio spots, television commercials, online banners, social media posts, and more. Effective ad creatives are tailored to resonate with the target audience by considering their demographics, psychographics, and preferences. The messaging and visuals are crafted in a way that aligns with the audience's needs, desires, and aspirations. The content must be relevant, relatable, and engaging to capture and sustain their attention amidst the clutter of ads they are exposed to. Copywriting plays a crucial role in ad creatives, as it involves the art of persuasive writing. The copy should be concise, clear, and impactful, conveying the key benefits of the offering and addressing any pain points or objections of the audience. A well-crafted headline can grab attention and generate interest, while the body copy provides more detailed information and builds the case for why the audience should consider the advertised product or service. In addition to effective copywriting, the design and imagery in ad creatives are essential for visual appeal. Colors, fonts, layout, and graphics are strategically chosen to evoke the desired emotions and associations. Whether it's a striking visual or a clever illustration, the design elements should support and enhance the messaging, creating a cohesive and aesthetically pleasing composition. Ultimately, a successful ad creative is one that drives the desired action from the target audience, whether it's making a purchase, subscribing to a service, visiting a website, or engaging with the brand in some way. It combines persuasive messaging, captivating visuals, and relevant context to create a powerful and memorable impression on the target audience.

Ad Creativity

Ad Creativity refers to the innovative and imaginative approach used in designing and developing advertisements. It involves the ability to generate fresh, unique, and compelling ideas that capture the attention and interest of the target audience. Ad Creativity plays a crucial role in the success of advertising campaigns as it helps differentiate brands, products, and services from competitors. It aims to break through the clutter of other advertisements and deliver the message in a memorable and impactful way.

Ad Display Frequency Analysis

Ad display frequency analysis refers to the process of analyzing the number of times an advertisement is shown to a user within a specific time period. It helps marketers understand the frequency at which their ads are being displayed to users and the impact it has on user engagement and conversion rates. The analysis involves monitoring and capturing data related to ad impressions and user interactions. Ad impressions refer to the number of times an ad is displayed on a webpage or mobile app, while user interactions include actions such as clicks, conversions, and purchases. By analyzing this data, marketers can gain insights into the effectiveness of their ad campaigns. One key metric that is commonly used in ad display frequency analysis is the frequency cap. A frequency cap is a limit set by advertisers on the number of times an ad can be shown to a user within a specific time frame. This ensures that users are not bombarded with the same ad repeatedly, which can lead to ad fatigue and decreased user engagement. By analyzing the frequency cap, marketers can identify the optimal number of times an ad should be displayed to a user to maximize its impact. They can also identify any instances of overexposure, where an ad is shown to a user too frequently, leading to decreased effectiveness. In addition to analyzing the frequency cap, ad display frequency analysis also involves examining user behavior metrics such as click-through rates (CTR),

8

conversion rates, and bounce rates. These metrics provide insights into how users are responding to the ad and help marketers optimize their campaigns for better results. Overall, ad display frequency analysis plays a crucial role in helping marketers make informed decisions about their ad campaigns. By understanding how often an ad should be shown to a user and monitoring user interactions, marketers can maximize the effectiveness of their ads and improve overall campaign performance. Ad display frequency analysis is the process of analyzing the number of times an advertisement is shown to a user within a specific time period. It involves monitoring and capturing data related to ad impressions and user interactions. By analyzing this data, marketers can gain insights into the effectiveness of their ad campaigns and optimize them for better results.

Ad Display Frequency

Ad display frequency refers to the number of times an advertisement is shown to a user within a specific time period while they are browsing online. It is a metric used by advertisers and marketers to measure the frequency at which their ads are displayed to a target audience. The ad display frequency is typically managed through advertising platforms or ad servers, which allow advertisers to control how often their ads are shown to a user. Advertisers can set a frequency cap, which limits the number of times an ad is displayed to an individual user. This helps to prevent ad fatigue and irritation among users who may become annoyed by seeing the same ad repeatedly. Ad display frequency is an important factor in advertising campaigns as it can impact the effectiveness and performance of the ads. If an ad is shown too frequently, it may lead to ad blindness, where users become immune to the message and no longer pay attention to the ad. On the other hand, if an ad is shown too infrequently, it may not reach a wide enough audience to generate the desired results. By managing the ad display frequency, advertisers can optimize their campaigns for maximum impact. They can ensure that their ads are seen by the right audience without overwhelming them with excessive ad exposure. Advertisers can also use frequency capping to manage costs and prevent budget wastage by only showing ads to users who are likely to convert. It is important for advertisers to monitor and analyze the ad display frequency to understand its impact on campaign performance. By tracking metrics such as click-through rates, conversions, and engagement, advertisers can assess whether the frequency is too high or too low, and make adjustments accordingly. Advertisers can also use A/B testing to experiment with different ad frequencies and determine which frequency yields the best results.

Ad Engagement

Ad engagement refers to the level of interaction and involvement that users have with an advertisement. It goes beyond simply viewing or clicking on an ad and focuses on how users actively engage with and respond to the content. Ad engagement can be measured through various metrics such as the number of likes, shares, comments, and retweets, as well as the amount of time spent on the ad or the click-through rate. These metrics provide insights into the effectiveness and impact of an advertisement, indicating whether it successfully captures the attention and interest of the target audience.

Ad Exchange Platforms Assessment

An ad exchange platform is an online marketplace that connects advertisers and publishers for the buying and selling of digital advertisement inventory. It serves as a central hub where advertisers can bid on and purchase ad space, and publishers can sell their ad space to the highest bidder. Ad exchange platforms use real-time bidding (RTB) technology to automate the buying and selling of ad inventory. Advertisers can set their targeting parameters and bid on impressions in real-time, allowing them to reach their ideal audience with precision and efficiency. Publishers, on the other hand, can maximize their revenue by selling their ad space to the highest bidder. Ad exchanges provide a transparent and efficient way for advertisers to reach their target audience and for publishers to monetize their website or app. They offer a wide range of targeting options, including demographic, geographic, and behavioral targeting, to help advertisers reach the right audience at the right time. Advertisers can also leverage data from third-party providers to further refine their targeting. Ad exchange platforms also provide tools and analytics to help advertisers and publishers optimize their campaigns and maximize their ROI. Advertisers can track the performance of their ads and make data-driven decisions to improve their campaign effectiveness. Publishers can analyze the performance of their ad inventory and make informed decisions to optimize their revenue. Overall, ad exchange platforms play a crucial role in the digital advertising ecosystem by connecting advertisers and publishers in a transparent and efficient marketplace. They enable advertisers to reach their target audience with precision and scale, while helping publishers monetize their digital assets. With the use of RTB technology and advanced targeting options, ad exchanges have transformed the way digital advertising is bought and sold.

Ad Exchange Platforms

An ad exchange platform is a digital marketplace that facilitates the buying and selling of online advertising space. It acts as a mediator between advertisers who want to display their ads and publishers who own websites or mobile apps where these ads can be displayed. Ad exchange platforms operate in an automated and real-time bidding environment. They enable advertisers to bid for ad space in real-time based on various targeting parameters such as audience demographics, browsing behavior, and geographic location. Publishers, on the other hand, can make their ad space available for bidding to multiple advertisers simultaneously. When a user visits a website or app, the ad exchange platform uses sophisticated algorithms to determine which ad to display based on factors such as the ad relevance, bid price, and historical performance of the ad. The winning ad is then instantly delivered to the user's device, ensuring a seamless and personalized advertising experience. Ad exchange platforms provide several benefits to both advertisers and publishers. For advertisers, they offer a wide range of targeting options and control over their ad campaigns. Advertisers can reach their desired audience more effectively and efficiently, maximizing the return on their advertising investment. Ad exchange platforms also provide real-time analytics and reporting, allowing advertisers to track the performance of their ads and make data-driven optimizations. For publishers, ad exchange platforms offer a way to monetize their websites or apps by selling their ad inventory to the highest bidder. They provide access to a large pool of advertisers, increasing the chances of finding relevant and high-paying ads. Publishers can also optimize their ad revenue by setting floor prices and implementing ad quality controls to ensure a positive user experience.

Ad Exchange

An ad exchange is an online marketplace where advertisers and publishers come together to buy and sell digital advertising inventory in real-time. It acts as a intermediary between advertisers, who want to display their ads, and publishers, who have available ad space on their websites or mobile apps. Here's how it works: 1. Advertisers submit their ads to the ad exchange with specific targeting criteria, such as demographics, location, interests, or keywords. They can also set a maximum bid they are willing to pay for each ad impression. 2. Publishers provide information about their available ad inventory, including the number of impressions and the types of ads they can display. 3. When a user visits a website or app that is part of the ad exchange network, the ad exchange conducts an auction in real-time to determine which ad will be displayed. This process takes milliseconds. 4. The ad exchange considers factors such as the advertiser's bid, the relevance of the ad to the user, and the available ad space on the publisher's site. The highest bidder with the most relevant ad is selected to be displayed to the user. 5. The selected ad is immediately delivered to the user's device, appearing within the website or app they are using. 6. The ad exchange tracks and records the impression, ensuring that advertisers only pay for actual ad views. Through the ad exchange, advertisers have access to a wide range of publishers and can reach their target audience more effectively. Additionally, publishers can maximize their ad revenue by monetizing their available ad inventory. Overall, an ad exchange enables efficient and transparent trading of digital advertising, benefiting both advertisers and publishers in the advertising ecosystem.

Ad Fatigue

Ad Fatigue is a term used in the context of advertising to describe the phenomenon where consumers become tired, annoyed, or unresponsive to repeated exposure to the same advertisement or a high frequency of advertisements. It refers to the diminishing effectiveness of an advertising campaign or specific ad due to its overexposure. When individuals are bombarded with the same ad multiple times or see a particular ad too frequently, they may develop a sense of annoyance, indifference, or even hostility towards that advertisement. This can result in lower engagement, decreased brand recall, and reduced advertising effectiveness overall.

Ad Fraud

Ad Fraud refers to the practice of falsely representing online advertisement metrics, intentionally deceiving advertisers and publishers, and ultimately resulting in fraudulent activity within the advertising ecosystem. In the context of online advertising, ad fraud involves the generation of illegitimate or non-human traffic with the goal of exploiting advertisers for financial gain. This deceitful activity misleads advertisers into believing that their ads are being viewed by actual humans, when in reality, they are being shown to bots, fraudulent websites, or invisible ad placements.

Ad Group Management

Ad Group Management refers to the process of organizing and controlling a group of advertisements within an advertising campaign. It involves the strategic grouping of ads that target a specific audience and align with specific marketing goals and objectives. The main purpose of Ad Group Management is to ensure that advertisements are displayed to the right audience, at the right time, and in the right context. This helps to maximize the effectiveness of the advertising campaign and improve the overall return on investment (ROI). Ad Group Management involves several key activities: 1. Keyword Research: This involves identifying relevant keywords or phrases that are commonly used by the target audience when searching for products or services. These keywords form the basis for ad targeting and optimization. 2. Ad Creation: Ad Group Management includes the creation of compelling and relevant ads that are tailored to the specific keywords and target audience. The ads should be clear, concise, and enticing to encourage users to click on them. 3. Ad Group Segmentation: The ads within an advertising campaign are organized into different ad groups based on specific criteria such as product category, geography, or targeted demographic. This allows for better control and optimization of the ads. 4. Bidding and Budgeting: Ad Group Management involves setting bids for each ad group to determine the maximum amount an advertiser is willing to pay for a click on their ads. It also includes managing the budget allocated to each ad group to ensure that the campaign stays within the set limits. 5. Performance Monitoring: Ad Group Management requires regular monitoring of ad performance and making necessary adjustments. This includes analyzing data on impressions, clicks, conversions, and other key metrics to identify areas of improvement and optimize ad performance. Overall, Ad Group Management plays a crucial role in ensuring that advertisements reach the right audience at the right time. It requires careful planning, organization, and optimization to drive successful advertising campaigns and achieve desired marketing outcomes.

Ad Group

An ad group is a collection of advertisements that share a similar theme, targeting, and budget within an advertising campaign. It is a fundamental component of online advertising, allowing advertisers to organize and manage their ads effectively. Within an ad group, advertisers can create multiple ads, each with its own unique message and creative elements. These ads can be customized to target specific audiences, locations, demographics, or interests, ensuring they reach the right people at the right time. Ad groups serve as containers for ads, enabling advertisers to allocate budgets and set bids that align with their marketing objectives. By grouping ads together, advertisers can monitor their performance, make adjustments, and optimize their campaigns accordingly. An ad group typically consists of a set of keywords or phrases that trigger the display of the ads. These keywords are carefully selected based on their relevance to the products, services, or topics being advertised. Advertisers can bid on these keywords to determine the ad's position in search engine result pages or social media platforms. Furthermore, ad groups allow advertisers to control the display network, ad placements, and scheduling of their ads. They can choose to display their ads on specific websites, mobile apps, or social media platforms that are relevant to their target audience. Advertisers can also decide when their ads should be shown, ensuring they reach their audience when they are most likely to engage. By structuring their ads into ad groups, advertisers can effectively manage their advertising campaigns, track their performance, and make data-driven decisions. They can test different ad variations, monitor their click-through rates, and evaluate conversion rates to optimize their campaigns for maximum effectiveness. In summary, an ad group is a key component of an advertising campaign, allowing advertisers to group related ads together and control their targeting, budget, and performance. Its purpose is to organize and manage ads effectively, ensuring they reach the desired audience and generate the desired results.

Ad Impression Share

Ad impression share refers to the percentage of times an advertisement is displayed to users in relation to the total number of ad opportunities available. It is a metric used by advertisers and marketers to measure the effectiveness and reach of their ad campaigns. In the context of online advertising, an ad impression is counted each time an advertisement is shown on a web page or mobile app. Ad impression share is calculated by dividing the number of ad impressions by the total number of ad opportunities, and then multiplying by 100 to get a percentage. Ad impression share provides insights into the ad performance and visibility. A high impression share indicates that the ad is being shown frequently to users, increasing the chances of it being seen and potentially clicked on. On the other hand, a low impression share suggests that the ad is not being displayed as often, which may impact its overall effectiveness. By monitoring ad impression share, advertisers can identify areas for improvement and optimize their campaigns. For example, if the impression share is low, it may be an indication that the targeting parameters or ad placement need adjustments. Advertisers can then make changes to ensure that their ads are being shown to the right audience at the right time and in the right context. Ad impression share can also be used to benchmark against competitors or industry averages. By comparing impression shares, advertisers can gauge their ad campaign's performance relative to others in the market. This information can help inform strategic decisions and identify areas where adjustments could lead to better results. In summary, ad impression share is a metric that measures the percentage of times an advertisement is displayed to users relative to the total number of ad opportunities. It provides insights into ad performance and visibility, allowing advertisers to optimize their campaigns and make data-driven decisions.

Ad Impression Tracking

Ad impression tracking refers to the process of measuring and monitoring the number of times an advertisement is viewed by users. It helps advertisers and publishers gather valuable data about the effectiveness and reach of their ads.When an ad is displayed on a website or a mobile app, an impression is counted. Ad impression tracking systems collect this data and provide insights into the performance of the advertisement campaigns.

Ad Impressions

Ad Impressions refer to the number of times an advertisement is displayed or shown on a webpage or platform. It is a metric used to measure the exposure of an advertisement to potential viewers or visitors. Ad impressions can vary depending on the advertising model being used. In the case of traditional display advertising, the number of ad impressions is typically calculated by the number of times an ad loads on a webpage. Each time the ad is loaded and displayed, it counts as one ad impression. This metric helps advertisers understand the reach and potential audience size for their campaigns.

Ad Inventory Management

Ad Inventory Management refers to the process of effectively managing and optimizing the available advertising space or inventory on a website or digital platform. It involves the strategic allocation, tracking, and monetization of ad space to maximize revenue and ensure optimal performance for advertisers. The main objective of ad inventory management is to strike a balance between meeting advertiser demands and delivering a positive user experience. It involves various activities such as forecasting, pricing, targeting, and optimization to ensure that the right ads are served to the right audiences at the right time.

Ad Inventory Marketplace Evaluation

An ad inventory marketplace is a platform where advertisers and publishers come together to buy and sell advertisement placements. It serves as a central hub that connects advertisers who want to promote their products or services with publishers who have available ad space on their websites or other digital platforms. At its core, an ad inventory marketplace works by facilitating the buying and selling of ad impressions. Ad impressions refer to the number of times an advertisement is displayed to users. Advertisers bid for these impressions, based on targeting criteria such as demographics, interests, and geographic location. Publishers, on the other hand, offer their available ad inventory to the marketplace, specifying details such as the size and location of ad placements, as well as the desired price. Advertisers use ad inventory marketplaces to reach their target audience more effectively and efficiently. By using targeting options provided by the marketplace, advertisers can ensure that their ads are displayed to users who are more likely to be interested in their offerings. This helps increase the chances of conversions and maximizes the return on investment for advertisers. Publishers, on the other hand, benefit from ad inventory marketplaces by monetizing their digital properties. They can sell their available ad space to advertisers, helping generate revenue from their websites or other platforms. By participating in an ad inventory marketplace, publishers can also gain access to a wide range of advertisers, increasing the competitiveness of their ad inventory and ultimately maximizing their earning potential. The success of an ad inventory marketplace relies on its ability to match advertisers with the most relevant and high-quality ad inventory. This requires sophisticated targeting algorithms and a comprehensive understanding of both advertisers' needs and publishers' ad inventory. The marketplace must also provide transparent reporting and analytics to both parties, allowing them to track the performance of their advertisements and make informed decisions.

Ad Inventory Marketplace

An ad inventory marketplace is a platform or a digital marketplace where publishers or website owners can sell their available ad space to advertisers or media buyers. Publishers can list their ad space inventory and set prices, while advertisers can search and buy available ad placements that align with their advertising goals. This marketplace serves as a central hub where sellers (publishers) and buyers (advertisers) can come together, facilitating the buying and selling of ad space. It provides a convenient and efficient way for publishers to monetize their websites and for advertisers to reach their target audience through different websites.

Ad Inventory Optimization

Ad Inventory Optimization refers to the process of maximizing the efficiency and profitability of advertising inventory. It involves strategic planning and implementation to ensure that ad space is effectively utilized and generates optimal revenue for publishers or advertisers. The objective of ad inventory optimization is to match the right ad with the right audience at the right time, maximizing the chances of conversion and generating higher revenue for publishers. This process typically involves analyzing various factors such as audience demographics, website traffic, historical performance data, and market trends to make informed decisions about ad placement and targeting.

Ad Inventory

Ad Inventory refers to the available advertising space or slots on a website, mobile app, or any other digital platform that can be used for displaying advertisements. It represents the total number of ad placements that are available for sale or allocation to advertisers. Ad inventory is typically managed by publishers or advertising platforms, who are responsible for selling or allocating these advertising spaces to advertisers. It can encompass various types of ad placements, such as banner ads, video ads, native ads, pop-up ads, and more. The availability and diversity of ad inventory play a crucial role in the success of digital advertising campaigns. Advertisers often seek high-quality and targeted ad inventory that matches their campaign objectives and target audience. They aim to reach their intended audience by placing ads in the relevant and engaging ad spaces. Ad inventory management involves keeping track of the different types, sizes, and formats of available ad placements. Publishers or advertising platforms employ various techniques to effectively manage their ad inventory. This includes optimizing the allocation of ad spaces, implementing ad rotation, and controlling the frequency and placement of ads. Ad inventory can be classified into two main categories: guaranteed inventory and non-guaranteed inventory. Guaranteed inventory refers to ad spaces that are pre-booked or reserved by advertisers for a specific time period and at a fixed price. It offers a higher level of certainty and control for advertisers. Non-guaranteed inventory, on the other hand, is available for purchase on a real-time or auction basis, often through programmatic advertising platforms. It allows advertisers to bid for ad placements and ensures more flexibility and cost efficiency. In conclusion, ad inventory represents the available advertising space on digital platforms. It is managed by publishers or advertising platforms and encompasses various types of ad placements. Advertisers aim to find suitable ad inventory to reach their target audience effectively, while publishers strive to optimize the allocation and management of their ad spaces.

Ad Monetization

Ad monetization refers to the process of earning revenue by displaying advertisements on a website, app, or any other digital platform. This revenue is generated by allowing advertisers to promote their products or services to the audience of the platform. Ad monetization is an essential aspect of digital advertising and plays a crucial role in supporting the sustainability and profitability of online platforms. It enables publishers to make money from their digital assets and resources, such as websites, mobile apps, or videos, by partnering with advertisers. Through ad monetization, publishers can effectively capitalize on their digital audiences and content to generate income.

Ad Network

An ad network, in the context of advertising, is a platform that connects advertisers with publishers for the purpose of displaying ads on websites, mobile apps, or other digital media. It acts as an intermediary between advertisers who want to reach their target audience and publishers who have available ad space on their platforms. Ad networks provide a wide range of services to both advertisers and publishers. For advertisers, they offer a centralized platform to manage their ad campaigns, target specific demographics or interests, and track the performance of their ads. Ad networks also provide access to a large network of publishers, allowing advertisers to reach a wider audience and maximize their ad exposure. On the other hand, publishers benefit from ad networks by gaining access to a pool of advertisers who are willing to pay for ad space on their platforms. Ad networks enable publishers to monetize their websites or apps by displaying relevant ads to their audience. Ad networks often use advanced targeting algorithms and bidding systems to ensure that publishers receive the highest possible revenue for their ad space. One of the key advantages of ad networks is their ability to deliver targeted ads to specific audiences. Advertisers can choose to display their ads to users based on factors such as demographics, location, interests, or browsing history. This targeting capability helps advertisers reach the right audience, resulting in higher conversion rates and return on investment. In addition, ad networks provide various ad formats to cater to different marketing objectives. These may include display ads, video ads, native ads, or mobile ads. Ad networks also offer different pricing models, such as cost per click (CPC), cost per thousand impressions (CPM), or cost per action (CPA), allowing advertisers to choose the most suitable option for their campaign goals. In conclusion, an ad network is a crucial component of the digital advertising ecosystem, enabling advertisers to connect with publishers and display targeted ads to their desired audience. By facilitating efficient ad campaigns and optimizing ad monetization for publishers, ad networks play a significant role in the success of online advertising.

Ad Operations Optimization

Ad operations optimization refers to the process of maximizing the efficiency and effectiveness of advertising operations to achieve desired outcomes. It involves the management and improvement of various elements within the advertisement ecosystem to enhance performance and reach campaign goals. Ad operations optimization encompasses multiple components, including ad delivery, ad targeting, ad placements, ad formats, and ad creative. By analyzing data and making data-driven decisions, advertisers and publishers can optimize these elements to increase advertising performance and ensure higher returns on investment.

Ad Operations

Ad Operations, also known as Ad Ops, is the department responsible for the implementation, optimization, and management of online advertising campaigns. It involves the technical and

14

logistical aspects of delivering advertisements to their intended audience. The primary goal of Ad Operations is to ensure that ads are delivered accurately and efficiently, maximizing their effectiveness and return on investment. This process includes various tasks such as ad trafficking, creative management, targeting, tracking, and reporting. Ad trafficking is the process of setting up and launching ad campaigns. It involves receiving ad creatives from advertisers, reviewing and approving them, and then deploying them to ad servers or placements. Ad Ops teams are responsible for ensuring that ads are correctly coded, implemented, and targeted to the desired audience. Creative management is an important aspect of Ad Operations. It involves working with advertisers and creative agencies to optimize ad creatives for various ad formats and sizes. Ad Ops teams ensure that ads meet technical specifications, are visually appealing, and comply with industry standards and guidelines. Targeting is another key task of Ad Operations. It involves selecting the right audience for each ad campaign to maximize its impact. Ad Ops teams use various targeting parameters such as demographics, interests, behavior, and location to reach the desired audience effectively. They also employ data-driven strategies, leveraging user data and insights to optimize targeting and improve campaign performance. Tracking and reporting are integral parts of Ad Operations. It involves monitoring ad performance, analyzing data, and generating comprehensive reports for advertisers and stakeholders. Ad Ops teams track key metrics such as impressions, clicks, conversions, and engagement to evaluate the success of ad campaigns. They provide insights and recommendations for optimizing campaigns based on data analysis. In summary, Ad Operations encompasses the technical and logistical processes involved in managing online advertising campaigns. It plays a crucial role in ensuring that ads are delivered accurately, targeted effectively, and optimized for maximum results. Ad Ops teams work closely with advertisers, creative agencies, and stakeholders to implement, optimize, and measure the performance of ad campaigns.

Ad Optimization

Ad optimization refers to the process of maximizing the performance and effectiveness of advertising campaigns by strategically modifying various ad elements. It involves analyzing data, making data-driven decisions, and implementing changes to enhance key performance metrics such as click-through rates (CTR), conversion rates, and return on investment (ROI). The primary goal of ad optimization is to ensure that advertisements generate the desired outcomes, such as generating leads, driving sales, or increasing brand awareness. It is a continuous process that requires ongoing monitoring, testing, and refining of ad campaigns. To optimize ads, marketers typically employ various techniques and strategies. These include: 1. Target audience analysis: Marketers need to understand their target audience's demographics, interests, and preferences. This information helps in crafting relevant and compelling ad content that resonates with the intended viewers. 2. A/B testing: Advertisers create multiple versions of an ad, each with slight variations in elements such as headlines, images, or call-to-action buttons. These variations are then tested against each other to determine which version performs better. 3. Landing page optimization: The landing page is the webpage where users are directed after clicking on an ad. Optimizing the landing page involves improving its design, layout, and content to ensure that it aligns with the ad and encourages users to take the desired action. 4. Ad placement and targeting: Advertisers need to select the most appropriate platforms, websites, or channels to display their ads. They can use targeting options to display ads to specific audiences based on factors such as location, demographics, interests, or browsing behavior. 5. Ad scheduling and budget allocation: Advertisers can optimize ad campaigns by scheduling them to run during peak hours or specific times when their target audience is most likely to be active. They can also allocate their ad budget more efficiently by identifying high-performing ad placements and reallocating funds accordingly. By consistently monitoring and analyzing performance metrics, advertisers can identify areas that require improvement and make data-driven optimizations to achieve their advertising goals. Ad optimization is an iterative process, and marketers need to continuously adapt and refine their strategies to stay ahead in the competitive advertising landscape.

Ad Personalization Techniques

Ad personalization techniques refer to the methods used to tailor advertisements to specific individuals based on their demographics, preferences, and behaviors. By utilizing data and technology, marketers can create personalized advertisements that are more relevant and engaging for their target audience. One common technique used in ad personalization is demographic targeting. Marketers can target their advertisements to specific demographics such as age, gender, location, and income level. This allows them to show relevant ads to people who are more likely to be interested in their products or services. Another technique is interest-based targeting. Marketers collect data on individuals' browsing history, search patterns, and social media activity to determine their interests and preferences. This information is then used to deliver ads that align with their interests, increasing the likelihood of engagement and conversion. Behavioral targeting is another effective technique in ad personalization. By tracking users' online behavior, marketers can gain insights into their purchasing habits, browsing history, and preferences. This information is then used to deliver ads that are tailored to each individual's specific interests and behaviors. For example, if a user frequently visits travel websites, they may be shown ads for vacation packages or flight discounts. Dynamic creative optimization is a technique that involves creating multiple versions of ads and dynamically selecting and delivering the most relevant version to each user. This can be based on factors such as their location, browsing history, or recent interactions with the brand. By delivering personalized and relevant ads, marketers can increase the chances of capturing the user's attention and driving conversions.

Ad Personalization

Ad personalization refers to the practice of tailoring advertisements to specific individuals based on their personal preferences, browsing history, demographic information, and other relevant data. This approach is used to optimize the effectiveness and relevance of advertisements by delivering customized content to each user. Ad personalization involves the collection and analysis of user data to create individual profiles that reflect their preferences, interests, and behavior. This includes information such as search history, online purchases, social media activity, and location data. By leveraging this data, advertisers can create targeted advertisements that are more likely to resonate with the specific audience they are trying to reach.

Ad Placement Analysis Tools

Ad Placement Analysis Tools refer to the tools and methodologies used to analyze and evaluate the effectiveness and suitability of ad placements in advertising campaigns. These tools provide valuable insights and metrics to advertisers and marketers in order to optimize their ad placements and maximize their return on investment. The primary goal of ad placement analysis tools is to determine the impact and performance of ad placements across various media channels, such as television, radio, print, outdoor, and digital platforms. These tools enable advertisers to identify the most effective placements and make informed decisions on their ad placement strategies.

Ad Placement Analysis

Ad Placement Analysis refers to the process of evaluating and assessing the effectiveness and efficiency of the placement and display of advertisements. It involves analyzing various factors and metrics to determine the impact and success of ad placements in reaching the target audience and achieving the desired objectives. Ad placement plays a crucial role in the success of an advertisement campaign. The strategic placement of ads can make a significant difference in capturing the attention of the target audience and influencing their buying decisions. Therefore, analyzing and understanding the performance of different ad placements is essential for advertisers and marketers to optimize their campaigns and maximize their return on investment. There are several key metrics that are typically considered in ad placement analysis. One such metric is reach, which quantifies the number of unique individuals who are exposed to the advertisement. This metric helps advertisers determine the potential audience size and evaluate the effectiveness of their ad placements in terms of the number of people reached. Another important metric is engagement, which measures the level of interaction and response generated by the ad placement. This can include metrics such as click-through rates, conversions, or social media shares. By analyzing the level of engagement, advertisers can assess the effectiveness of the ad content and its ability to captivate and engage the target audience. Ad placement analysis also considers factors such as visibility and context. Visibility refers to the prominence and visibility of the ad placement within a particular platform or

16

medium. Advertisers need to ensure that their ads are positioned in locations where they are likely to be noticed and have a strong impact. Context is another critical factor in ad placement analysis. It involves evaluating the relevance and appropriateness of the ad placement in relation to the target audience and the surrounding content. Ads that are placed in relevant contexts are more likely to resonate with the audience and generate positive responses. In conclusion, ad placement analysis involves evaluating the effectiveness and efficiency of the placement and display of advertisements. By analyzing metrics such as reach, engagement, visibility, and context, advertisers can optimize their ad campaigns and increase their chances of reaching and engaging with their target audience. Ad Placement Analysis refers to the process of evaluating and assessing the effectiveness and efficiency of the placement and display of advertisements. It involves analyzing various factors and metrics to determine the impact and success of ad placements in reaching the target audience and achieving the desired objectives. Ad placement plays a crucial role in the success of an advertisement campaign. The strategic placement of ads can make a significant difference in capturing the attention of the target audience and influencing their buying decisions. Therefore, analyzing and understanding the performance of different ad placements is essential for advertisers and marketers to optimize their campaigns and maximize their return on investment.

Ad Placement

Ad placement refers to the strategic positioning of advertisements to maximize their visibility and impact on the intended audience. It involves identifying the most suitable platforms, channels, and media outlets for displaying the ads in order to reach the target market effectively. A well-thought-out ad placement strategy takes into consideration various factors, including the target audience's preferences, interests, and behavioral patterns. By understanding the target market, advertisers can select the most appropriate platforms where potential customers are likely to engage with the ads. Placement can vary based on the advertising medium, such as print, television, radio, outdoor signage, or digital channels like websites, social media platforms, and mobile apps. Each medium offers unique opportunities and challenges for ad placement. In print media, ad placement involves determining the optimal page or section within a magazine or newspaper where the ad will receive maximum exposure. For example, placing an ad for luxury watches in a fashion magazine targeting affluent readers can lead to more effective results. In television and radio advertising, ad placement refers to scheduling commercials at specific times when the target audience is likely to be tuned in. This can include prime time slots, popular TV shows, or during specific events or programming related to the target market's interests. For outdoor advertising, ad placement focuses on selecting high-traffic areas or locations that align with the target audience's demographics and behaviors. Billboards, transit advertisements, and signage in strategic locations can capture the attention of passersby and generate brand awareness. In the digital realm, ad placement involves targeting specific websites, social media platforms, or mobile apps that attract the desired audience. This can be done through programmatic advertising, targeting specific demographics, interests, or behaviors to deliver relevant ads to potential customers. Effective ad placement requires careful consideration of the target audience, market research, and a deep understanding of the advertising medium's strengths and limitations. By selecting the right placement and reaching the intended audience with impactful ads, advertisers can enhance brand visibility, increase customer engagement, and drive desired actions or conversions.

Ad Position Analysis

An ad position analysis refers to the process of evaluating and determining the placement of advertisements on a webpage or digital platform. It involves analyzing various factors to determine the most optimal position for an ad in order to maximize its visibility, engagement, and effectiveness. During an ad position analysis, advertisers consider several key factors, including the layout of the webpage, the content being displayed, the target audience, and the specific goals of the advertising campaign. By carefully assessing these factors, advertisers can make informed decisions about where to place their ads to capture the attention of potential customers and drive desired actions.

Ad Positioning

Ad Positioning refers to the placement or location of an advertisement within a specified medium or platform, such as a website, newspaper, or television screen. It involves strategically selecting the position where the ad will be displayed to maximize its visibility, reach, and impact on the target audience. The objective of ad positioning is to grab the attention of the audience and effectively convey the message or promote a product or service. The chosen position should be able to attract the viewers' attention and create a favorable impression that ultimately leads to the desired action, such as making a purchase or visiting a website. Ad positioning can vary depending on the medium or platform being used. For example, in online advertising, the most common ad positions are the banner ads at the top of a webpage, the sidebar ads, and the ads that appear in-between content. These positions are considered strategic because they are easily visible to the user and have a higher chance of being noticed. In print media, such as newspapers or magazines, ad positioning options include the front page, back cover, or the middle pages. Advertisers often prefer these prime positions to ensure that their ad receives maximum exposure as readers tend to focus on these areas. The choice of the ad position is crucial as it can significantly impact the effectiveness of the advertising campaign. Advertisers often rely on market research, audience demographics, and the objectives of the campaign to determine the most suitable position for their ads. They may also consider factors such as the competition within the platform and the budget available. Effective ad positioning also involves considering the context and relevance of the ad placement. For example, placing a sports-related ad during a live sports event or a food advertisement in a cooking magazine can increase its impact and engagement with the target audience. In summary, ad positioning is the strategic placement or location of an advertisement within a specific medium or platform. It aims to capture the attention of the audience, create a positive impression, and encourage the desired action. By understanding the medium, the target audience, and the objectives of the campaign, advertisers can make informed decisions regarding the ad positioning that will yield the best results.

Ad Quality Score Monitoring

The Ad Quality Score Monitoring refers to the process of tracking and evaluating the performance of advertisements based on various predefined metrics and indicators. It involves constantly monitoring and analyzing the quality and effectiveness of advertisements to ensure optimal results and return on investment. The primary goal of Ad Quality Score Monitoring is to assess the overall performance of advertisements and identify areas for improvement. This includes analyzing factors such as relevance, engagement, click-through rates, conversion rates, and other key performance indicators (KPIs) to determine the effectiveness of the advertising campaign. By continuously monitoring the Ad Quality Score, advertisers can gauge the success of their ad campaigns and make necessary adjustments to improve performance. This involves closely monitoring the metrics and data gathered from various advertising platforms such as Google Ads, Facebook Ads, and other digital advertising channels. Ad Quality Score Monitoring helps advertisers identify underperforming ads and make data-driven decisions to optimize their campaigns. It provides insights into which ads are generating the most conversions, clicks, and engagement, allowing advertisers to allocate their budgets more effectively and focus on the most successful advertisements. Furthermore, Ad Quality Score Monitoring allows advertisers to identify and address any potential issues or problems that may be affecting the performance of their ads. This can include issues such as low ad relevance, poor ad targeting, ineffective messaging, or issues with the landing page experience. By identifying and resolving these issues, advertisers can improve the overall quality and performance of their advertisements.

Ad Quality Score

An Ad Quality Score refers to a metric that is used by advertisers to assess and measure the effectiveness of their advertisements. It provides insights into the relevance and performance of an ad, helping advertisers optimize their campaigns and improve their return on investment (ROI). The Ad Quality Score takes into account various factors such as the content and design of the ad, its targeting parameters, and its overall user experience. A higher Ad Quality Score indicates that an ad is more relevant and engaging to its target audience, thus increasing the likelihood of users taking the desired action, such as clicking on the ad or making a purchase.

Ad Reach Measurement

Ad Reach Measurement is a quantitative analysis and evaluation of the number of unique individuals who have been exposed to a particular advertisement or campaign within a specified period. It is a vital metric in the world of advertising as it helps advertisers and marketers understand the potential reach and impact of their ad campaigns. By measuring ad reach, advertisers can assess the overall effectiveness of their marketing efforts and make data-driven decisions to optimize future campaigns.

Ad Reach

Ad reach refers to the total number of unique individuals or households who have seen or been exposed to a particular advertisement. It is a key metric used to measure the effectiveness and the potential audience size of an advertisement campaign. Ad reach can be assessed through various channels such as television, radio, print media, online platforms, and social media. It takes into account the number of individuals reached across different demographics, including age, gender, location, and interests.

Ad Recall Test Design

Ad Recall Test Design refers to the process of creating a structured and systematic approach to measuring the effectiveness of an advertisement in terms of how well it is remembered by viewers. This test is commonly used in the field of market research to evaluate the impact and success of advertising campaigns. The design of an ad recall test typically involves selecting a representative sample of the target audience and exposing them to the advertisement. The exposure can be in the form of watching a commercial, viewing a print ad, or any other relevant medium. After the exposure, the participants are engaged in a recall task where they are asked to remember specific details about the advertisement. The primary goal is to measure how well the advertisement is remembered, including key message points, brand information, and other essential elements.

Ad Recall Test

The ad recall test is a quantitative research method used to measure the effectiveness of an advertisement by assessing the audience's ability to recall the ad after exposure. It is a widely used tool in the advertising industry to gauge the impact and memory retention of an advertisement on the target audience. The test typically involves showing the ad to a representative sample of the target audience and then asking them, after a specified time interval, if they can remember seeing the ad. The recall is measured by recording the number and percentage of respondents who can accurately recall key elements of the ad, such as the brand, message, visuals, or any other specific details that are deemed important by the advertiser.

Ad Retargeting

Ad retargeting is a digital advertising strategy that involves targeting potential customers who have previously interacted with a brand or website. It aims to display relevant ads to these individuals in order to encourage them to complete a desired action, such as making a purchase or signing up for a newsletter. The process of ad retargeting begins with the placement of a tracking pixel on a website. This pixel tracks the behavior of visitors, including the pages they visit, the products they view, and any actions they take, such as adding items to a cart. The data collected from these interactions is then used to create personalized ads that are displayed to the same visitors when they visit other websites. This targeting is made possible through the use of cookies, which are small text files that are stored on a user's browser. These cookies allow advertisers to track user activity and serve them with relevant ads based on their browsing history. For example, if a user visits a clothing website and views a specific dress but does not make a purchase, ad retargeting can show them ads for that dress on other websites they visit, reminding them of their interest and encouraging them to return and make a purchase. Ad retargeting can be an effective strategy for increasing brand awareness, driving conversions, and maximizing the return on investment (ROI) of advertising campaigns. By reaching out to individuals who have already shown interest in a brand or product, advertisers can deliver more personalized and targeted messages, increasing the likelihood of conversion. However, it is important for advertisers to exercise caution and respect user privacy when implementing ad retargeting strategies. Clear and transparent communication about data collection and user privacy is essential to maintain trust and ensure users feel comfortable with the retargeting process.

Ad Revenue Model

An ad revenue model refers to a strategy or framework that outlines how a company or platform generates income through advertising. It involves charging advertisers for the placement of their ads on a website, app, or other digital platforms, with the revenue generated directly proportional to the number of ad impressions or user engagements. The ad revenue model is widely adopted by various online platforms, including search engines, social media networks, and content websites. These platforms offer advertisers the opportunity to reach their target audience by displaying ads alongside relevant content or search results. In return, they charge advertisers for every interaction or exposure their ads receive, such as clicks, impressions, conversions, or a fixed fee for a specific period of time.

Ad Revenue Models

Ad Revenue Models refer to the different ways in which advertisements generate revenue for publishers or platforms. These models determine how advertisers pay for ad placements or how publishers earn income through advertisements. One common ad revenue model is the Cost Per Click (CPC) model. In this model, advertisers pay for each click their ad receives. The cost per click is often determined through bidding, where advertisers compete for ad placements by offering the highest amount they are willing to pay per click. Publishers, on the other hand, earn revenue based on the number of clicks their ads receive. This model provides an incentive for advertisers to create compelling ads that generate clicks, as they only pay when users engage with their ads. Another popular ad revenue model is the Cost Per Mille (CPM) model. Here, advertisers pay for every thousand impressions their ads receive. Impressions refer to the number of times an ad is viewed by users, regardless of whether they interact with it. Advertisers typically negotiate a fixed rate they are willing to pay per thousand impressions, and publishers earn revenue based on the number of impressions their ads generate. This model is suitable for advertisers who want to increase brand awareness by ensuring their ads are seen by a large audience.

Ad Scheduling

Ad scheduling, also known as dayparting, is a technique used in advertising to determine the specific times and days when an advertisement will be displayed to the target audience. It involves strategically scheduling ad placements based on consumer behavior patterns, audience preferences, and other relevant factors. The primary objective of ad scheduling is to optimize the impact and efficiency of advertising campaigns. By carefully selecting the most suitable times and days for ad display, advertisers can maximize their reach and increase the likelihood of engaging with their target audience. It allows businesses to allocate their advertising budget more effectively by ensuring that ads are shown at times when they are most likely to generate desired customer responses, such as clicks, conversions, or sales.

Ad Server Technology

An ad server is a technology platform used in the advertising industry to manage and serve advertisements to online users. It acts as an intermediary between advertisers (or their agencies) and publishers (website owners or app developers) by matching ads with available ad spaces on digital platforms. The primary purpose of an ad server is to deliver targeted advertisements to specific audiences at the right time and on the right platforms. It allows advertisers to reach their desired target market by displaying their ads to users who are more likely to be interested in their products or services. Ad servers use various targeting methods such as demographic data, user behavior, and contextual relevance to ensure that ads are delivered to the most relevant audiences. Ad servers also play a crucial role in optimizing the performance of ad campaigns. They track and collect data on ad impressions, clicks, conversions, and other relevant metrics to measure the effectiveness of advertisements. This data is then used to analyze and optimize campaigns, making adjustments to improve performance and maximize return on investment (ROI). Furthermore, ad servers offer advanced targeting and delivery capabilities, such as frequency capping, which limits the number of times an ad is shown to the same user to avoid ad fatigue. They also support various ad formats, including display banners, video ads, native ads, and mobile ads, allowing advertisers to utilize different creative formats to engage with their target audience. Overall, ad server technology simplifies the complex process of managing and delivering ads by providing a centralized platform for advertisers and publishers. It enables precise targeting, efficient delivery, and effective measurement, ultimately helping advertisers achieve their marketing goals and publishers monetize their digital assets.

Ad Server

An ad server is a technology platform that delivers and manages online advertisements for publishers, advertisers, and agencies. It is a crucial component of the digital advertising ecosystem, providing the infrastructure necessary to serve ads to targeted audiences across various websites and devices. The main role of an ad server is to control and optimize the delivery of ads to ensure maximum effectiveness and efficiency. It acts as a central hub that stores, organizes, and delivers ads to their intended audiences based on specific targeting criteria. This includes factors such as demographics, geography, browsing behavior, and user preferences. Ad servers facilitate the process of ad trafficking, which involves the placement and rotation of ads on websites or mobile apps. They enable publishers to manage and monetize their inventory by connecting them with relevant advertisers and their campaigns. Advertisers, on the other hand, can leverage ad servers to reach their target audience and track the performance of their campaigns in real-time. One of the key functionalities of ad servers is ad serving, which involves the actual delivery of ads to the users. Ad servers ensure that ads are displayed correctly and in a timely manner, optimizing factors such as size, format, and placement. They also support various ad formats, including display ads, video ads, native ads, and mobile ads, allowing advertisers to engage users across different platforms. Furthermore, ad servers offer comprehensive reporting and analytics capabilities, providing valuable insights into the performance of ad campaigns. They track and measure key metrics such as impressions, clicks, conversions, and revenue, enabling advertisers to evaluate the effectiveness of their ads and make data-driven decisions for future campaigns. Overall, an ad server plays a crucial role in the advertising ecosystem by facilitating the efficient delivery, management, and optimization of online advertisements. It enables publishers to monetize their inventory, advertisers to reach their target audience, and agencies to effectively manage and track ad campaigns.

Ad Slogan Creation

A slogan is a concise and memorable phrase used in advertising to capture attention, convey a message, and promote a brand or product. It serves as a powerful tool to create brand recognition, build brand loyalty, and differentiate a company or product from its competitors. In the world of advertising, where capturing the audience's attention is crucial, a well-crafted slogan can make all the difference. With limited time and attention spans, consumers need to be quickly intrigued and persuaded to consider a product or brand. A good slogan helps achieve this by summarizing the key benefits, values, or unique selling points in a few words. A successful slogan is one that is instantly recognizable, easy to understand, and resonates with the target audience. It creates a connection and evokes emotions or associations that are positive and memorable. An effective slogan should also be adaptable and flexible, allowing it to be used across different advertising platforms and campaigns. The creation of a slogan involves careful consideration of the brand's positioning, target audience, and key message. It should align with the brand's identity and values, while also addressing the needs and desires of the target market. A successful slogan encapsulates the essence of the brand or product, communicates its core benefits, and leaves a lasting impact on the audience. To create a strong slogan, advertisers often use various techniques such as rhyming, alliteration, puns, or metaphors. These techniques help make the slogan catchy, memorable, and distinct. However, it is important to balance creativity with clarity and avoid any confusion or misinterpretation. In conclusion, a slogan is a powerful advertising tool that plays a crucial role in capturing attention, conveying a message, and promoting a brand or product. Through concise and memorable phrases, slogans help create brand recognition, build loyalty, and differentiate from competitors. A well-crafted slogan resonates with the target audience, evokes emotions and associations, and leaves a lasting impact.

Ad Slogan

An ad slogan is a short phrase or slogan that is used in advertising to capture the attention of the target audience and communicate a particular message or idea about a product, brand, or company. It is often a memorable and catchy phrase that is repeated consistently throughout a campaign to create brand recognition and recall. The primary purpose of an ad slogan is to create brand awareness and differentiate a product or brand from its competitors. It plays a crucial role in forming a connection with the target audience and influencing their perception and purchase decisions. A well-crafted ad slogan can effectively convey the unique selling proposition of a product or brand, evoke positive emotions, and build brand loyalty.

Ad Space Monetization Strategies

Ad space monetization strategies refer to the methods and approaches used by advertisers and publishers to generate revenue from advertising space or inventory. In the digital advertising world, ad space refers to the available slots or locations on websites, apps, or other platforms where ads can be displayed. There are several common strategies employed to monetize ad space: 1. Direct Selling: One of the simplest strategies is to sell advertising space directly to advertisers. This can be done through a direct sales team or by leveraging ad networks and exchanges. Publishers can negotiate rates and terms directly with advertisers, ensuring more control over the pricing and content of the ads displayed. 2. Programmatic Advertising: Programmatic advertising involves the use of automated systems and algorithms to buy and sell ad space in real-time. Publishers can connect their inventory to ad exchanges or supply-side platforms (SSPs), which then facilitate the purchasing process. Programmatic advertising allows for more efficient and targeted ad placements, often leading to higher revenue for publishers. 3. Cost-Per-Impression (CPM) Pricing: CPM pricing is a widely used strategy where advertisers pay a fixed rate for every thousand impressions their ads receive. Publishers can optimize their revenue by focusing on delivering high-quality content and attracting a large number of visitors who engage with the ads, thus increasing the number of impressions. 4. Cost-Per-Click (CPC) Pricing: With CPC pricing, publishers earn revenue each time a visitor clicks on an ad. This strategy incentivizes publishers to place ads in prominent positions and create engaging content that encourages users to click. CPC advertising is often used with search engine advertising, where ads are displayed based on relevant search queries. 5. Native Advertising: Native ads are designed to blend seamlessly with the content of a website or app, providing a more organic and less disruptive user experience. Publishers can monetize native ad space by incorporating sponsored or promoted content within their platform, generating revenue while maintaining a cohesive user interface. By employing these ad space monetization strategies, advertisers and publishers can effectively generate revenue from the valuable ad inventory available to them. The choice of strategy depends on factors such as the target audience, platform type, and overall advertising goals.

Ad Space Monetization

Ad Space Monetization refers to the process of generating revenue by selling or leasing advertising space on a website, mobile app, or any other digital platform. It involves utilizing available advertising inventory to attract advertisers and earn money through the placement of their ads. The concept of ad space monetization revolves around the principle of supply and demand. Website owners or publishers have space available for advertisements, which they can offer to advertisers looking to promote their products or services. This available ad space is essentially a valuable commodity, which can be utilized to generate income. When a website or digital platform has a significant user base, it becomes an attractive platform for advertisers. They are willing to pay a certain amount in exchange for utilizing the ad space provided by the publisher. The amount of revenue generated through ad space monetization varies depending on factors such as the popularity of the platform, the target audience, and the relevance of the ads to the users. Publishers can monetize their ad space through various methods, including direct sales, programmatic advertising, and ad networks. Direct sales involve establishing direct relationships with advertisers, negotiating rates, and selling ad space directly. Programmatic advertising refers to the use of automated processes and algorithms to buy and sell ad space in real-time through ad exchanges. Ad networks play a significant role in ad space monetization by acting as intermediaries between publishers and advertisers. They aggregate ad inventory from multiple publishers and offer it to advertisers, simplifying the process for both parties. Ad networks facilitate the buying and selling of ad space, often using targeting and optimization techniques to maximize revenue for publishers. Effective ad space monetization requires careful consideration of factors such as ad placement, ad formats, and targeting options. Publishers need to strike a balance between generating revenue and maintaining a positive user experience. Intrusive or irrelevant ads can negatively impact user satisfaction and, in turn, affect the long-term success of ad space monetization efforts. In conclusion, ad space monetization is a crucial aspect of the advertising industry. By leveraging available ad inventory, publishers can generate revenue by selling or leasing their advertising space to advertisers. It involves utilizing various methods, including direct sales, programmatic advertising, and ad networks. Publishers need to prioritize user experience while optimizing revenue generation through ad space monetization.

Ad Spend

Ad spend refers to the amount of money a company or individual invests in advertisements. It is the total expenditure incurred on advertising activities in order to promote a product, service, or brand. Ad spend can include various forms of advertising such as TV commercials, radio ads, print advertisements, online banners, social media promotions, and search engine marketing. The goal of ad spend is to reach a target audience, increase brand visibility, generate leads, and ultimately drive sales.

Ad Sponsorship Management

Ad Sponsorship Management refers to the process of overseeing and coordinating the sponsorship activities related to advertisements. It involves managing the relationships between advertisers and sponsors, ensuring that their objectives align and that both parties benefit from the partnership.Ad Sponsorship Management includes various tasks, such as identifying potential sponsors, negotiating sponsorship deals, and monitoring the progress and effectiveness of the sponsored advertisements. The goal is to create mutually beneficial partnerships that enhance the visibility and reach of the advertisements while providing value to the sponsors.

Ad Sponsorship

An ad sponsorship is a form of advertising where a company or individual pays to have their advertisement featured or promoted in a particular context. This can range from placing ads on websites or blogs to sponsoring events or content, such as videos or articles. With ad sponsorship, the advertiser typically pays a fee to the publisher or platform owner for the opportunity to have their ad displayed or promoted to a specific audience. This fee is often based on various factors, such as the number of impressions (the number of times the ad is displayed) or clicks the ad receives. The purpose of ad sponsorship is to increase brand awareness, drive traffic, and generate leads or sales. By sponsoring content or events that align with their target audience's interests or demographics, advertisers can reach potential customers in a more targeted and effective way. Ad sponsorship can take various forms, including: 1. Display ads: These are visual ads that appear on websites, blogs, or mobile apps. They can be static images, animated banners, or even videos. Advertisers can choose to target specific websites or use ad networks that automatically place their ads on relevant platforms. 2. Sponsored content: This involves sponsoring articles, blog posts, videos, or other forms of content created by publishers. The advertiser's brand is integrated into the content, either subtly or explicitly, to promote their products or services. 3. Event sponsorship: Companies often sponsor events, such as conferences, trade shows, or sports competitions, to gain exposure to a specific audience. This can include having their logo displayed on promotional materials, booths or signage at the event, or even the naming rights for the event. Overall, ad sponsorship provides an effective way for advertisers to target and reach their desired audience by leveraging existing platforms, websites, or events. It allows them to promote their brand, products, or services in a relevant and engaging manner, ultimately driving awareness, traffic, and potential sales.

Ad Tagging Solutions

Ad Tagging Solutions refer to the technology and tools used by advertisers and publishers to manage and optimize online advertising campaigns. It involves the process of assigning specific tags or code snippets to advertisements, which enables tracking and measurement of various advertising metrics. Ad tags are typically small pieces of HTML or JavaScript code that are inserted into web pages or ad servers. These tags contain information about the ad creative, targeting options, and other parameters that help in delivering targeted and relevant ads to the right audience. Ad tagging solutions provide a centralized platform for managing these tags and ensure that they are implemented correctly across different digital advertising channels.

Ad Tagging

Ad tagging is a process used in the context of digital advertising to track and categorize advertisements for effective targeting and measurement. It involves adding specific code or tags to ad creatives and ad placements, allowing advertisers and publishers to gather data and optimize their ad campaigns. Ad tagging serves multiple purposes in the advertising ecosystem. Firstly, it enables advertisers to track the performance of their ads across various advertising platforms and networks. By assigning a unique tag to each ad creative, advertisers can monitor its impressions, clicks, conversions, and other relevant metrics. This data helps them evaluate the effectiveness of their ad placements and make informed decisions about future ad investments. Moreover, ad tagging allows advertisers to target their ads to specific audiences or demographics. By tagging ads with relevant information such as keywords, audience interests, or location, advertisers can ensure that their ads are displayed to the right people at the right time. This increases the chances of engagement and conversion, as the ads are more likely to be relevant and personalized to the target audience. Ad tagging also facilitates the measurement of ad viewability and ad fraud detection. By including specific tags that track ad impressions and viewability metrics, such as whether the ad was actually seen by a user, advertisers can assess the visibility and impact of their ads. This information helps them optimize their ad placements to maximize visibility and minimize the risk of ad fraud. Overall, ad tagging plays a crucial role in the digital advertising landscape. It enables advertisers to track and measure the performance of their ads, target specific audiences, and optimize their ad campaigns for better results. By implementing ad tagging practices, advertisers can make data-driven decisions, improve ad relevance, and enhance the overall effectiveness of their advertising efforts.

Ad Targeting Options

Targeting options in advertising refer to specific parameters or attributes that advertisers can utilize to define and narrow down their target audience. By leveraging these options, advertisers can ensure that their ads are displayed to the most relevant and potential customers, thereby maximizing the effectiveness of their campaigns. One such targeting option is demographic targeting, which enables advertisers to focus their ads on specific demographic groups such as age, gender, and income level. This allows advertisers to tailor their messages to a particular set of consumers who are more likely to be interested in their products or services. Geographic targeting is another important option that allows advertisers to deliver their ads to users in specific locations or regions. This is particularly useful for local businesses or those with a specific target market based on geographical location. By targeting ads based on location, advertisers can reach customers in areas where their products or services are available or where there is high demand. Interest-based targeting is yet another option that enables advertisers to reach users based on their interests, hobbies, or preferences. These targeting options are often derived from user behavior data, such as online searches, browsing history, or interactions with specific websites or apps. By utilizing interest-based targeting, advertisers can showcase their ads to users who have expressed interest in similar products or services, increasing the chances of conversion. Behavioral targeting is another powerful option that allows advertisers to display their ads to users based on their previous online behavior, such as past purchases, website visits, or interactions with specific ads. By targeting users with relevant ads based on their behavior, advertisers can create personalized and tailored advertising experiences, enhancing the likelihood of engagement and conversion. Finally, contextual targeting is a targeting option that allows advertisers to display ads on websites or platforms that align with their products or services. By analyzing the content and context of webpages or platforms, advertisers can ensure that their ads are shown to users who are likely to be interested in what they offer. This option allows advertisers to reach a relevant and engaged audience, which can lead to higher click-through rates and conversions. In conclusion, targeting options in advertising provide advertisers with the ability to deliver their ads to specific audiences based on demographic attributes, geographic location, interests, behaviors, and contextual relevance. By leveraging these options, advertisers can optimize their ad campaigns, increase engagement, and drive higher conversions.

Ad Targeting Strategies

Ad targeting strategies refer to the methods and techniques used by advertisers to identify and reach their desired audience segments with relevant advertisements. These strategies involve analyzing various data points and characteristics of potential consumers in order to tailor and deliver advertisements that are more likely to resonate with and engage the target audience. There are several ad targeting strategies that advertisers commonly utilize to refine their targeting and optimize their advertising campaigns: 1. Demographic targeting: This strategy involves segmenting the target audience based on demographic variables such as age, gender, income, education, and occupation. Advertisers can use this information to ensure that their ads reach the appropriate demographic groups who are more likely to be interested in their products or services. 2. Geographic targeting: With geographic targeting, advertisers focus on reaching consumers in specific geographical areas. This allows them to tailor their advertisements to local preferences, cultural nuances, and regional needs. Geographic targeting is particularly useful for businesses that operate in specific locations or target customers in certain regions. 3. Behavioral targeting: Behavioral targeting is based on tracking and analyzing users' online behavior, such as their browsing history, search queries, website visits, and content consumption. This strategy aims to understand users' interests, preferences, and habits in order to deliver personalized advertisements that align with their behaviors and interests. 4. Psychographic targeting: This strategy involves segmenting the target audience based on psychological and lifestyle characteristics, such as personality traits, values, opinions, interests, and hobbies. Advertisers use psychographic targeting to create ads that resonate with the target audience's motivations, aspirations, and beliefs. 5. Contextual targeting: Contextual targeting relies on analyzing the content of websites or digital platforms where ads will be displayed. Advertisers select specific keywords or topics related to their products or services, and their ads are then displayed on platforms that feature relevant content. This strategy ensures that ads are shown in contexts that are relevant to the target audience's interests or needs. By employing effective ad targeting strategies, advertisers can increase the likelihood of their ads being seen by the right audience, enhance ad engagement, and maximize the return on their advertising investment.

Ad Targeting

Ad targeting refers to the process of selecting a specific audience or group of individuals for advertising purposes, based on various demographic, psychographic, and behavioral characteristics. It involves tailoring advertising content and delivery to reach the intended audience more effectively, increasing the chances of achieving the desired marketing objectives. Advertisers use ad targeting to ensure their advertisements are shown to individuals who are more likely to be interested in their products or services, thus optimizing their advertising budgets and improving the overall performance of their campaigns. By reaching the right audience, ad targeting helps increase the relevancy and impact of advertisements, leading to higher engagement and conversion rates.

Ad Tracking

Ad tracking is the process of monitoring and analyzing the performance of advertisements in order to measure their effectiveness and make informed decisions for future advertising campaigns. It involves the collection and analysis of various data points related to ads, such as impressions, clicks, conversions, and revenue generated. One of the primary objectives of ad tracking is to gain insights into how well an advertisement is performing and whether it is achieving its desired goals. By tracking key metrics, advertisers can determine the reach of their ads, the engagement levels they are generating, and the return on investment (ROI) they are delivering. This information allows them to optimize their advertising strategies, target their audience more effectively, and allocate their budget wisely. Ad tracking provides advertisers with valuable data that can be used to refine their ads and make data-driven decisions. It enables them to track the performance of their ads across different channels, platforms, and devices. This allows advertisers to identify which channels are driving the most traffic or conversions and make adjustments accordingly. Furthermore, ad tracking helps advertisers understand their target audience better. By analyzing the data collected, advertisers can identify the demographics, interests, and behaviors of their audience, which in turn allows them to create more targeted and relevant advertisements. This leads to higher engagement and conversion rates. Overall, ad tracking plays a crucial role in the success of advertising campaigns. It provides advertisers with insights into the performance and impact of their ads, allowing them to optimize their strategies, reach their target audience effectively, and maximize their ROI. By continuously monitoring and analyzing ad performance, advertisers can make data-driven decisions that result in more effective and efficient advertising campaigns.

Ad Verification Services

Ad Verification Services refer to a set of tools, technologies, and processes utilized to ensure the accuracy, quality, and legitimacy of online advertisements. These services are designed to protect advertisers, publishers, and consumers from fraudulent activities, malicious practices, and inappropriate content. In the rapidly growing digital advertising industry, ad verification services play a crucial role in maintaining brand safety, improving campaign performance, and mitigating risks associated with online advertising. These services aim to verify that advertisements are displayed on genuine and legitimate platforms, reaching the intended audience, and adhering to industry standards and guidelines.

Ad Verification

Ad Verification is the process of ensuring that online advertisements are displayed in the intended manner and reach the intended audience. It involves the use of technological tools and solutions to monitor, track, and authenticate the delivery and performance of digital ads. One of the primary goals of ad verification is to protect advertisers from fraudulent activities such as ad fraud and brand safety issues. Ad fraud refers to any attempt to generate fake ad impressions, clicks, or conversions, leading to wasted ad spend and misleading performance metrics. Brand safety concerns, on the other hand, relate to the placement of ads on inappropriate or unsafe websites that could harm the advertiser's reputation. Ad verification solutions use various techniques to combat ad fraud and ensure brand safety. They often employ advanced algorithms and machine learning models to detect and prevent fraudulent activities in real-time. This includes identifying invalid traffic, suspicious clicks, and bot-generated impressions. By detecting and blocking these fraudulent activities, advertisers can optimize their ad spend and achieve better ROI. In terms of brand safety, ad verification tools employ website categorization and content analysis to assess the quality and safety of ad placements. They check the context of the website where the ad is served to determine if it aligns with the advertiser's brand guidelines and values. This helps to prevent ads from appearing on websites that contain inappropriate content or engage in malicious activities. Ad verification also plays a crucial role in ensuring ad viewability and placement transparency. Ad viewability refers to the measurement of whether an ad is actually seen by users or if it is hidden or placed below the fold. By monitoring viewability metrics, advertisers can ensure that their ads are being delivered effectively and reaching the desired audience. Placement transparency, on the other hand, involves verifying that ads are displayed on the intended platforms and are not being redirected or served on unauthorized websites. In conclusion, ad verification is a vital process in the world of online advertising. It helps advertisers to protect their investments, prevent ad fraud, maintain brand safety, and achieve optimal ad viewability and placement transparency.

Ad Viewability Measurement

Ad Viewability Measurement is a metric used in the context of online advertising to assess the extent to which an advertisement is actually seen by users. It measures the visibility and exposure of an ad to the target audience, and helps advertisers determine the effectiveness of their ad campaigns. The concept of ad viewability arose due to concerns about wasted ad spend on impressions that were never actually seen by users. Advertisers need assurance that their ads are being displayed in a manner that allows users to see and engage with them. Therefore, ad viewability measurement plays a crucial role in evaluating the success of an advertising campaign.

Ad Viewability Rate

Ad Viewability Rate refers to the percentage of ads that are actually seen by users, out of the total ads that are available for viewing. It is a metric used in the advertising industry to measure the effectiveness of an ad campaign and the reach of the ads. In online advertising, ads are often served to webpages or mobile apps, and their viewability determines whether users have the opportunity to see them. A high ad viewability rate indicates that a larger percentage of ads are visible to users, which in turn suggests better chances of user engagement and ad effectiveness.

Ad Viewability Standards Compliance

Ad Viewability Standards Compliance refers to the level of adherence to industry-defined criteria for measuring the viewability of online advertisements. Viewability is the extent to which an ad is actually seen by users, rather than simply being loaded on a webpage. It is an important metric for advertisers to determine the effectiveness of their campaigns and ensure that their ads are being seen by the intended audience. The Interactive Advertising Bureau (IAB) and Media Rating Council (MRC) have established guidelines for ad viewability standards to provide consistency and transparency in the measurement and reporting of viewability metrics. These standards help advertisers, publishers, and ad technology vendors to assess the performance and value of ad impressions. According to the IAB and MRC guidelines, an ad is considered viewable if at least 50% of its pixels are in the user's view for a minimum of one continuous second. This duration varies for different ad formats, such as display ads, video ads, and mobile ads. Ad viewability is typically measured using specialized viewability measurement tools and technologies that capture data on ad impressions and user interactions. Ad viewability standards compliance is crucial for advertisers as it helps them determine the effectiveness of their ad campaigns and make informed decisions about their advertising strategies and investments. Advertisers can use the viewability metrics to optimize their campaigns, identify underperforming ads or placements, and adjust the creative elements or targeting parameters to improve viewability and engagement. Publishers also benefit from ad viewability standards compliance as it allows them to demonstrate the quality and value of their ad inventory. By ensuring that their ads meet the viewability standards, publishers can attract advertisers who are confident in reaching their target audience effectively. It also helps reduce discrepancies between ad viewability measurements from different vendors or platforms, providing a consistent basis for evaluating campaign performance. In conclusion, ad viewability standards compliance refers to the adherence to industry-defined guidelines for measuring the viewability of online advertisements. It helps advertisers and publishers assess the visibility of their ads and make data-driven decisions to improve campaign performance and maximize the value of ad impressions.

Ad Viewability Standards

Ad viewability standards refer to a set of criteria and measurements used to determine whether an advertisement has been seen by users, and to what extent it was visible on a webpage. These standards aim to provide transparency and assurance to advertisers that their ad impressions are being properly served and can be effectively viewed by the intended audience. In order for an ad to be considered viewable, it must meet certain predefined criteria. One commonly accepted standard is the Media Rating Council (MRC) standard, which states that at least 50% of the ad must be visible on the screen for a minimum of one continuous second. This means that if an ad is served but only a small portion of it is visible or it appears for less than one second, it would not be counted as a viewable impression. Ad viewability is typically measured through the use of specialized tracking technologies, such as ad servers or third-party viewability measurement tools. These tools can track and monitor various metrics, including the amount of time an ad is displayed on the screen, the percentage of the ad that is visible, and the position of the ad on the webpage. Advertisers can use these metrics to evaluate the effectiveness of their ad campaigns and make informed decisions regarding their media buying strategies. The importance of ad viewability standards lies in providing advertisers with a common language and framework for evaluating ad placements. By establishing clear guidelines, advertisers can have a better understanding of what they are paying for and can compare different advertising opportunities more accurately. Viewability standards also help to promote accountability within the advertising industry, as publishers and ad networks are encouraged to optimize their ad placements to increase viewability rates. Furthermore, ad viewability standards also help to enhance the user experience by ensuring that ads are not intrusive or misleading. When ads are not viewable, users may be exposed to ads that they are not aware of or cannot engage with, leading to frustration and negative perceptions of the brand. By adhering to viewability standards, advertisers can ensure that their ads are being displayed in a way that is fair and transparent to users, contributing to a more positive and engaging online advertising ecosystem.

Ad Viewability

Ad viewability refers to the extent to which an advertisement is actually seen by users. It measures the visibility of an ad and determines whether it meets industry standards for being considered "viewable". In the context of online advertising, viewability is an important metric for advertisers and publishers to assess the effectiveness of their campaigns. It addresses the concern that impressions may not always be seen by users due to issues such as ad fraud, ad blocking software, or the placement of ads on a webpage. Advertisers want to ensure that their ads are being viewed by their target audience to maximize the return on their investment, while publishers want to demonstrate the value of their ad inventory to attract advertisers.

AdSense

AdSense is an advertising program offered by Google that allows website owners or content creators to monetize their online platforms by displaying targeted ads. It serves as a platform connecting advertisers with publishers, enabling businesses to promote their products or services and generate revenue for website owners through ad clicks or impressions. With a straightforward integration on websites, AdSense provides a simple and efficient means for publishers to earn money by displaying relevant advertisements. The program operates on the basis of contextual targeting, where ads are automatically matched to the content of the web page they appear on, ensuring that they are relevant to the audience.

AdWords Quality Score Optimization

AdWords Quality Score Optimization refers to the process of improving the quality score of an advertisement in Google AdWords. Quality Score is a metric used by Google to determine the relevance and quality of an ad, keywords, and landing page. It has a direct impact on ad position, ad rank, and cost per click (CPC) in the ad auction. The primary goal of Quality Score Optimization is to increase the quality score of an advertisement, which in turn can improve its performance and lower its cost. A higher quality score means that the advertisement is more relevant to the search query and offers a better user experience. This leads to higher ad positions and lower CPCs, as Google rewards advertisers who provide a positive and valuable experience to users. There are several factors that influence the quality score of an advertisement. The relevance of ad copy and keywords, the click-through rate (CTR), the landing page experience, and the historical performance of the ad account all play a role in determining the quality score. By optimizing these elements, advertisers can improve their quality scores and maximize the effectiveness of their ad campaigns. Some strategies for AdWords Quality Score Optimization include: 1. Keyword Research and Selection: Choosing relevant and targeted keywords that align with the ad copy and landing page can improve the quality score. 2. Ad Copy Optimization: Creating compelling and relevant ad copy that encourages clicks and matches the user's search intent can increase the quality score. 3. Landing Page Optimization: Designing user-friendly and optimized landing pages that provide a seamless experience and relevant content can improve the quality score. 4. Negative Keyword Management: Adding negative keywords to the ad campaign can prevent irrelevant searches and improve the quality score. 5. Campaign Structuring: Organizing ad groups and campaigns in a logical and structured manner can enhance relevance and improve quality scores. In conclusion, AdWords Quality Score Optimization aims to improve the quality score of advertisements in Google AdWords by focusing on relevance, user experience, and performance. By optimizing various elements such as keywords, ad copy, landing pages, and campaign structure, advertisers can increase the quality score, improve ad performance, and potentially lower advertising costs.

AdWords Quality Score

AdWords Quality Score is a metric used by Google to assess the relevance and effectiveness of advertisements displayed on its search engine results pages (SERPs). It is a numerical rating given to each keyword in an advertiser's campaign, ranging from 1 to 10, with 1 being the lowest score and 10 being the highest. The Quality Score is calculated based on three main factors: click-through rate (CTR), ad relevance, and landing page experience. CTR measures the percentage of users who click on an ad after seeing it on the SERPs. A higher CTR indicates that the ad is relevant and appealing to users, which in turn increases the Quality Score. Ad relevance refers to how well the keywords in an ad match the user's search query. The more relevant the ad, the higher the Quality Score. Landing page experience evaluates the user's experience after clicking on the ad and landing on the advertiser's website. Factors considered include page load speed, mobile-friendliness, and the relevance of the landing page content to the user's search query. A higher Quality Score is beneficial for advertisers in several ways. It can lead to higher ad rankings, meaning the ad will appear higher on the SERPs, increasing visibility and the likelihood of attracting clicks. Additionally, a higher Quality Score can lower the cost per click (CPC) for an advertiser. Google rewards advertisers with high-quality ads by offering lower bidding costs and a potential boost in ad position, even if their competitors have higher bids. This means that advertisers with a better Quality Score can achieve a higher Ad Rank with a lower CPC, resulting in a more cost-effective advertising campaign. The AdWords Quality Score is an essential metric for advertisers using Google's advertising platform. By focusing on improving CTR, ad relevance, and landing page experience, advertisers can increase their Quality Score, leading to more effective and efficient advertising campaigns.

AdWords

AdWords is a pay-per-click (PPC) advertising platform developed by Google. It allows businesses to create and display ads on Google Search results pages, as well as on websites and apps that are part of the Google Display Network. AdWords offers a variety of targeting options, ad formats, and bidding strategies, making it a versatile and powerful tool for online advertising. With AdWords, businesses can reach potential customers who are actively searching for products or services on Google. Ads are shown to users based on their search queries, ensuring that the advertisement is relevant to the user's needs and interests. This targeted approach increases the chances of engaging with potential customers and driving conversions. AdWords operates on a PPC model, which means that businesses only pay when their ad is clicked on. This cost-effective system ensures that businesses can control their advertising budget and allocate it towards the most effective campaigns. Advertisers can set a maximum bid for their ads, and Google's auction-based system determines the ad's position and cost per click. One of the key features of AdWords is its extensive targeting options. Advertisers can choose to target specific geographic areas, languages, devices, and even demographics and interests. By tailoring ads to specific audiences, businesses can optimize their advertising efforts and increase the chances of reaching potential customers. AdWords also offers various ad formats, including text ads, image ads, video ads, and app promotion ads. This allows businesses to choose the format that best suits their goals and target audience. AdWords provides advertisers with advanced analytics and reporting tools, allowing them to track the performance of their ads and make data-driven decisions to optimize their campaigns. In conclusion, AdWords is a powerful advertising platform that allows businesses to create and display ads on Google's search results pages and across the Google Display Network. With its targeting options, ad formats, and flexible bidding strategies, AdWords enables businesses to reach potential customers, increase brand visibility, and drive conversions.

Adaptive Advertising Platforms

An adaptive advertising platform is a technological solution that enables advertisers to dynamically adjust their advertisements on various digital channels based on the context, user behavior, and other relevant data. It uses advanced algorithms, machine learning, and artificial intelligence to deliver personalized and relevant advertising messages to target audiences. These platforms collect and analyze large amounts of data from various sources such as user demographics, browsing behavior, purchasing history, and social media activities to understand the preferences and interests of individual users. By leveraging this data, adaptive advertising platforms can automatically optimize and tailor ads to maximize the chances of engagement and conversion.

Adaptive Advertising

Adaptive advertising refers to a targeted advertising strategy that aims to deliver personalized content and experiences to individual consumers based on their preferences, behaviors, and demographics. It involves dynamically tailoring advertisements to suit the unique needs and interests of each user in order to enhance engagement and maximize the effectiveness of the advertising campaign. This approach relies on the collection and analysis of vast amounts of data related to consumer behavior and preferences. Various sources of data, including browsing history, demographics, social media activity, and past interactions with advertisements, are used to build individual profiles for each user. These profiles are continuously updated and refined to ensure that the advertisements delivered to each user are as relevant and appealing as possible.

Advertainment Campaigns

Advertainment campaigns refer to advertising campaigns that incorporate entertainment value in order to capture the attention and engage the audience. These campaigns aim to entertain, inform, and persuade consumers, using creative and engaging content to deliver a brand's message. Traditional advertising methods often struggle to cut through the clutter and capture the attention of consumers who are increasingly bombarded with advertisements. Advertainment campaigns, on the other hand, offer a unique approach that combines entertainment and advertising to create a more memorable and effective marketing strategy. These campaigns often take the form of videos, online content, or interactive experiences that are designed to entertain and engage consumers. By incorporating elements such as humor, storytelling, or interactive features, advertainment campaigns are able to create a more positive and enjoyable experience for the audience. One of the key benefits of advertainment campaigns is their ability to build brand awareness and generate buzz. When audiences are entertained by a piece of content, they are more likely to share it with others, increasing its reach and exposure. This word-of-mouth marketing can be incredibly powerful in building brand recognition and attracting new customers. Advertainment campaigns can also help brands establish an emotional connection with their audience. By creating content that resonates with consumers on a personal or emotional level, brands are able to foster a deeper sense of loyalty and engagement. This emotional connection can lead to increased brand advocacy, as consumers are more likely to recommend and support brands that they have a positive emotional association with. Overall, advertainment campaigns offer a fresh and engaging approach to advertising that can help cut through the noise and capture the attention of consumers. By incorporating entertainment value into their campaigns, brands are able to create a more memorable and impactful marketing strategy that resonates with their audience on a deeper level.

Advertainment

Advertainment is a term used to describe the integration of advertising and entertainment in order to create engaging and attention-grabbing advertisements. It refers to the practice of blending promotional messages with entertaining content to capture the audience's interest and hold their attention. This form of advertising aims to break through the clutter and noise of traditional advertisements by providing consumers with entertaining and enjoyable content that they are more likely to engage with. By combining elements of entertainment, such as storytelling, humor, or compelling visuals, with advertising messages, advertainment seeks to create a unique and memorable experience for the viewer.

Advertisement Fraud Detection Tools

Advertisement fraud detection tools refer to the software and technology solutions designed to identify and prevent fraudulent activity in the context of online advertisements. These tools utilize various techniques and algorithms to analyze and monitor ad campaigns, detecting any signs of fraudulent behavior or manipulation. Advertisers invest substantial resources in online advertising campaigns with the goal of reaching and engaging their target audience. However, the digital advertising landscape is plagued by fraudulent practices such as click fraud, impression fraud, and bot traffic. These fraudulent activities not only waste advertisers' budgets but also undermine the effectiveness and efficiency of online advertising efforts. Advertisement fraud detection tools aim to tackle these challenges by providing real-time monitoring and analysis of ad campaigns. They integrate with advertising platforms, websites, and ad networks to collect data on ad impressions, clicks, conversions, and other relevant metrics. By analyzing this data, these tools can identify irregular patterns, unusual behavior, and indicators of fraudulent activity. These tools employ various techniques to detect advertisement fraud. Some rely on machine learning algorithms that learn from historical data to identify patterns and anomalies associated with fraud. They can determine if a click, impression, or conversion is genuine or fraudulent by comparing it to established patterns and models. Other fraud detection tools utilize IP address analysis to identify suspicious sources of traffic. They can detect traffic originating from known fraudulent IPs or identify patterns of behavior that indicate illegitimate activity. Furthermore, advertisement fraud detection tools often integrate with ad verification services that provide additional layers of protection. These services can verify the quality and legitimacy of ad impressions, ensuring that ads are shown to real users and not bots or automated scripts. In conclusion, advertisement fraud detection tools play a critical role in protecting advertisers from fraudulent activities in their online advertising campaigns. By utilizing advanced algorithms, machine learning, and data analysis techniques, these tools help identify and prevent click fraud, impression fraud, and other fraudulent practices. This enables advertisers to optimize their ad spend, reach real audiences, and maximize the return on their advertising investment.

Advertisement Fraud Detection

Advertisement fraud detection refers to the process of identifying and preventing fraudulent activities in the world of digital advertising. With the rise of online advertising, fraudulent practices have also increased, leading to significant financial losses for advertisers and publishers. In the context of advertisement, fraud can occur in various forms, including but not limited to click fraud, impression fraud, and conversion fraud. Click fraud involves artificially inflating the number of clicks on an ad, misleading advertisers into believing that their ads are generating more traffic and engagement than they actually are. Impression fraud, on the other hand, occurs when ads are served to non-existent or fraudulent websites or bots, resulting in fake impressions and wasted campaign budgets. Lastly, conversion fraud refers to fraudulent activities that manipulate the conversion process, leading to falsely inflated conversion rates and misleading advertisers about the success of their campaigns. To detect and combat advertisement fraud, advanced technologies and techniques are employed. These may include machine learning algorithms, artificial intelligence, and data analysis. Advertisers and publishers use fraud detection systems to track and analyze ad performance data, such as click-through rates, impressions, conversions, and user behavior patterns. By comparing this data with known fraudulent patterns and behaviors, these systems can identify irregularities and anomalies indicative of fraudulent activities. Common indicators of advertisement fraud include an unusually high number of clicks or impressions originating from the same IP address, suspicious user behavior like rapid clicks or short session durations, and conversion rates that are significantly higher or lower than industry averages. Additionally, advanced fraud detection systems may also consider other factors such as site reputation, traffic sources, and historical data to determine the likelihood of fraud. Once advertisement fraud has been identified, appropriate measures can be taken to mitigate its impact. This can involve blocking fraudulent IP addresses, suspending suspicious accounts, or blacklisting websites that are associated with fraud. Advertisers and publishers can also work together to share information about fraudulent activities, enabling a collaborative effort to combat ad fraud.

Advertising Appeal Analysis

Advertising appeal refers to the approach or tactic used in advertisements to capture the attention, interest, and desire of the target audience, ultimately persuading them to take a specific action, such as making a purchase or adopting a behavior. It is the underlying theme or message conveyed through various elements of an ad, including visuals, language, and emotions. There are several different types of advertising appeals that marketers employ to engage consumers and achieve their marketing objectives. One common appeal is the emotional appeal, which aims to evoke strong feelings or emotions in viewers. This can be achieved through storytelling, using relatable characters or situations, or by appealing to sentimental or nostalgic elements. Emotional appeals often rely on establishing a connection with the audience, creating empathy, or sparking a desire for happiness or fulfillment. Another popular appeal in advertising is the rational appeal, which emphasizes the logical or practical benefits of a product or service. This approach relies on presenting factual information, statistics,

31

or evidence to convince consumers that the advertised offering will meet their needs or solve a problem. Rational appeals focus on features, functionality, quality, and value for money. Some ads employ a humorous appeal, using humor or wit to grab the attention of the audience and create a positive association with the brand. Humorous appeals can be effective in breaking through the clutter of advertisements and leaving a lasting impression in consumers' minds. They can also help in increasing likability and generating word-of-mouth buzz. Celebrity endorsements are another common advertising appeal, leveraging the popularity, reputation, or expertise of a well-known person to influence consumer attitudes and behaviors. This approach aims to transfer the positive attributes or associations of the celebrity to the brand, increasing credibility and trust among consumers. Other advertising appeals include fear appeal, which highlights negative consequences or risks of not using the advertised product, and sex appeal, which uses attractive or provocative imagery to evoke desire or create a sense of allure. Additionally, adventure, exclusivity, and social appeal are often used to appeal to consumers' desire for novelty, status, or belonging.

Advertising Appeal

Advertising appeal refers to the specific tactic or approach used in an advertisement to capture the attention, interest, and desire of the target audience, ultimately persuading them to take a specific action, such as purchasing a product or service. It is the distinctive feature or attribute of an advertisement that differentiates it from others and makes it memorable. Advertising appeals can take various forms and can be based on different elements such as emotions, logic, humor, fear, social status, sex appeal, or the product's functional benefits. These appeals are carefully chosen based on the target audience's characteristics, needs, wants, and aspirations.

Advertising Benchmarking Platforms

An advertising benchmarking platform is a software or online tool that allows advertisers to measure and compare their advertising campaigns against industry standards and competitors. It provides valuable insights and data to help advertisers optimize their strategies and make more informed decisions. By using an advertising benchmarking platform, advertisers can track and analyze various key performance indicators (KPIs) of their advertising campaigns, such as reach, engagement, click-through rates, conversion rates, return on investment (ROI), and more. These platforms gather data from various sources, including social media platforms, search engines, websites, and other advertising channels, and present it in a user-friendly dashboard or report.

Advertising Benchmarking

Advertising benchmarking is a process of comparing and evaluating the effectiveness, performance, and success of an advertisement campaign against industry standards and competitors. It involves measuring various key performance indicators (KPIs) to determine the impact and efficiency of an advertisement, with the goal of identifying areas for improvement and optimizing future campaigns. Through advertising benchmarking, advertisers can assess how well their advertisements are resonating with their target audience, reaching desired objectives, and delivering the desired outcomes. It provides valuable insights into the strengths and weaknesses of different advertising strategies, helping advertisers make informed decisions and refine their approaches to maximize return on investment (ROI).

Advertising Budget Allocation Models

An advertising budget allocation model refers to a systematic approach used by businesses to determine how to allocate their resources effectively for advertising purposes. It involves analyzing various factors and making decisions on how much budget to allocate to different advertising channels or campaigns. The primary goal of an advertising budget allocation model is to maximize the return on investment (ROI) for advertising efforts. By determining the most effective use of resources, businesses can ensure that their advertising messages reach the right target audience and generate the desired outcomes, such as increased brand awareness, customer engagement, and sales. There are several types of advertising budget allocation models that businesses can consider: The percentage of sales method involves allocating a fixed percentage of total sales revenue for advertising purposes. The allocated percentage may vary depending on factors such as industry standards, competition, and the stage of the product life cycle. The objective and task method involves setting specific advertising objectives and determining the tasks required to achieve them. The budget is then allocated based on the estimated cost of performing these tasks. This method allows businesses to align their advertising efforts with their overall marketing objectives. The competitive parity method involves allocating the budget based on the spending levels of competitors. Businesses may choose to match or exceed their competitors' advertising expenditures in order to maintain or gain a competitive advantage. The affordable method involves allocating the advertising budget based on what the business can afford at a given time. This method may be suitable for businesses with limited financial resources, but it may not always result in optimal advertising outcomes. The ROI-based method involves allocating the budget based on the expected return on investment. This method requires businesses to estimate the potential revenue or other measurable outcomes that can be generated from advertising efforts and allocate the budget accordingly. Overall, an advertising budget allocation model helps businesses make informed decisions on how to allocate their advertising resources effectively. By considering factors such as sales, objectives, competition, affordability, and ROI, businesses can maximize the impact of their advertising efforts and achieve their desired marketing outcomes.

Advertising Budget Allocation

Advertising Budget Allocation refers to the process of determining how much to spend on each advertising channel or campaign in order to achieve marketing objectives and maximize return on investment. It involves dividing the total advertising budget among various media outlets, such as television, radio, print, online, and social media platforms, as well as specific campaigns or initiatives within each channel. The goal of advertising budget allocation is to allocate resources in the most efficient and effective manner, by identifying the channels and campaigns that are likely to generate the highest level of reach, engagement, and conversions. To make informed decisions about budget allocation, marketers consider factors such as target audience demographics, media consumption habits, competition, advertising goals, historical performance data, and market trends.

Advertising Budget

An advertising budget refers to the amount of money a company or organization sets aside for the purpose of promoting its products or services through various advertising channels. The advertising budget plays a crucial role in determining the reach and impact of an advertising campaign. It helps businesses strategically allocate financial resources to different advertising channels, such as television, radio, print media, online platforms, and outdoor advertising, based on their target audience, marketing objectives, and cost-effectiveness. A well-planned advertising budget involves careful consideration of both the overall budgetary constraints and the specific objectives the company aims to achieve through its advertising efforts. It is essential for companies to set realistic advertising budgets that align with their financial capabilities, marketing goals, and competitive landscape. When determining an advertising budget, companies often consider several key factors: - The nature and size of the target audience - The desired reach and frequency of the ad campaign - The competitive environment and market conditions - The company's financial resources and profitability goals - The available advertising channels and their costs - The expected return on investment (ROI) from advertising activities By setting an appropriate advertising budget, companies can efficiently allocate their resources to maximize the impact and effectiveness of their advertising campaigns. It also allows them to monitor and control their advertising spending to ensure transparency and accountability. However, it is crucial for companies to regularly evaluate and reassess their advertising budgets to adapt to changing market dynamics and consumer behavior. This allows businesses to stay competitive and make informed decisions regarding their advertising strategies. In conclusion, an advertising budget is a financial plan that outlines the amount of money allocated for advertising activities. It is a crucial component of an organization's overall marketing strategy and helps businesses allocate resources effectively to achieve their advertising objectives.

Advertising Call Center Management

Advertising Call Center Management is the process of effectively supervising and coordinating the operations of a call center that specializes in advertising-related activities. This involves overseeing all aspects of the call center's activities, including strategy development, call handling, customer support, and performance monitoring. The primary objective of Advertising Call Center Management is to optimize the call center's performance and ensure that it is aligned with the goals and objectives of the advertising campaign. This requires a deep understanding of the target audience, the advertising message, and the desired outcomes. The management team is responsible for developing strategies and tactics that maximize the effectiveness of the call center in promoting the advertised products or services. One of the key responsibilities of Advertising Call Center Management is to design and implement call scripts and guidelines for the call center agents. These scripts are carefully crafted to deliver the advertising message in a consistent and persuasive manner. The management team must ensure that agents are trained on the scripts and are capable of engaging customers in meaningful conversations that drive desired outcomes. Additionally, Advertising Call Center Management involves monitoring and evaluating the performance of call center agents. This includes assessing their adherence to scripts, their ability to handle customer objections, and their overall communication skills. The management team uses performance data to identify areas for improvement and provide targeted training to enhance agent performance. Another crucial aspect of Advertising Call Center Management is providing ongoing support and guidance to call center agents. This includes addressing any questions or concerns they may have, offering feedback and coaching, and assisting them in resolving customer issues effectively. The management team plays a vital role in motivating and empowering agents to deliver exceptional customer experiences. In summary, Advertising Call Center Management encompasses the strategic planning, operational supervision, and performance evaluation of a call center dedicated to advertising activities. It involves developing effective call scripts, monitoring agent performance, and providing ongoing support to optimize the call center's contribution to the advertising campaign's success.

Advertising Call Center

An advertising call center is a specialized customer service facility that handles inbound and outbound calls related to advertising campaigns. It serves as a central point of contact for both customers and businesses seeking marketing and promotional services. As an integral part of the advertising industry, the call center functions primarily to assist customers with product or service information, resolve inquiries or issues, and provide support throughout the purchasing process. The agents, also known as customer service representatives or sales representatives, are trained to effectively communicate the value proposition, features, and benefits of the advertised products or services.

Advertising Campaign

An advertising campaign is a coordinated series of promotional activities that are designed to achieve specific marketing objectives within a defined period of time. It involves the development and implementation of a strategic plan to communicate key messages about a company, brand, product, or service to a targeted audience. The ultimate goal of an advertising campaign is to generate awareness, build brand equity, increase sales, and ultimately drive business growth. Advertising campaigns typically include a combination of different advertising channels and mediums such as television, radio, print, outdoor, digital, and social media. These channels are carefully selected based on the target audience demographics, their media consumption habits, and the campaign objectives. The campaign may also involve the use of various creative elements such as visuals, copywriting, slogans, jingles, and spokespersons to communicate the desired messages effectively. The process of creating and executing an advertising campaign involves several stages. It starts with conducting research and identifying the target audience and their needs, preferences, and behaviors. This is followed by the development of a clear and compelling advertising message that resonates with the target audience and differentiates the brand or product from competitors. Once the message is defined, the campaign strategy is outlined, including the selection of advertising channels, mediums, and creative elements. The campaign is then launched, and the effectiveness and impact of the advertisements are continuously monitored and measured. Adjustments and optimizations may be made throughout the campaign to maximize its performance and achieve the desired results. Successful advertising campaigns require a well-defined target audience, a compelling message, creative execution, and a strategic media plan. They should be consistent, cohesive, and integrated across different channels to ensure a unified brand experience. Additionally, monitoring and analyzing key performance indicators (KPIs) such as reach, frequency, engagement, and conversion rates are essential to evaluate the campaign's effectiveness and identify areas for improvement. In conclusion, an advertising campaign is a strategic and coordinated effort to communicate messages about a company, brand, product, or service to a targeted audience using various advertising channels and mediums. Its goal is to generate awareness, build brand equity, increase sales, and drive business growth. The success of a campaign relies on effective audience targeting, compelling messaging, creative execution, and continuous monitoring and optimization.

Advertising Compliance Software

Advertising compliance software is a tool used by businesses to ensure that their advertisements and marketing campaigns adhere to the relevant laws, regulations, and industry standards. It is designed to help companies avoid legal and financial consequences, protect their brand reputation, and maintain ethical business practices. This software provides a comprehensive solution to monitor, analyze, and manage advertisements across various channels, such as print, television, radio, online platforms, and social media. It helps companies identify potential non-compliance issues, such as misleading claims, false advertising, improper disclosures, or violations of specific advertising regulations. The software typically offers features like automated monitoring and scanning of advertisements, content analysis, and comparison against legal requirements and industry guidelines. It can detect key phrases, visual elements, or claims that may be considered misleading or deceptive, and flag them for further review by compliance teams. Additionally, advertising compliance software often includes tools for managing legal disclaimers and disclosures. It helps companies ensure that mandatory information, such as terms and conditions, product disclaimers, privacy policies, or licensing information, is adequately communicated in their advertisements in a clear and conspicuous manner. The software also assists companies in generating reports and maintaining a documented history of their advertisements for compliance purposes. It allows businesses to track and record the approval processes, review cycles, and any modifications made to their advertisements, providing an audit trail for regulatory authorities and internal stakeholders. Moreover, some advertising compliance software may offer features for managing global compliance. This includes the ability to adapt to different advertising standards and legal requirements in different countries or regions. The software can help companies localize their advertisements and ensure compliance with specific local regulations, cultural sensitivities, or language requirements. In summary, advertising compliance software is an essential tool for businesses to navigate the complex landscape of advertising regulations. It simplifies the process of monitoring, analyzing, and managing advertisements, allowing companies to mitigate legal risks, maintain ethical standards, and protect their brand reputation.

Advertising Compliance

Advertising compliance refers to the adherence to guidelines and regulations set by governing bodies and laws regarding the content, presentation, and dissemination of advertisements. It encompasses various aspects, including but not limited to, truthful and accurate claims, proper disclosure of material information, and avoidance of deceptive or misleading practices. Compliance in advertising is essential to ensure that marketing communications are fair, honest, and responsible, safeguarding the interests of consumers and maintaining a level playing field for competitors. Advertisers, agencies, and media platforms need to comply with specific requirements to uphold the integrity and credibility of advertising campaigns and protect the rights of consumers. One aspect of advertising compliance is the truthfulness and accuracy of claims. Advertisers must ensure that their claims about products or services are supported by sufficient evidence and do not mislead consumers. They should avoid making exaggerated statements or false representations that could deceive or confuse the audience. Proper disclosure of material information is another crucial element of advertising compliance. Advertisements should clearly and conspicuously disclose any information that is likely to affect consumers' decision-making process, such as limitations, conditions, or risks associated with a product or offer. This includes disclosing any affiliations or relationships that may influence the credibility or objectivity of the advertisement. Another aspect of compliance is the avoidance of deceptive or misleading practices. Advertisers should refrain from using tactics or techniques that may deceive or confuse consumers. This includes avoiding false or misleading statements, images, or testimonials that could create a false impression or misrepresent the product or service being promoted. Overall, advertising compliance is essential to ensure that advertisements are fair, truthful, and transparent. It involves adhering to guidelines and regulations set by governing bodies and laws, and encompasses aspects such as accurate claims, proper disclosure, and avoidance of deceptive practices. By complying with these standards, advertisers can build trust with consumers, foster a competitive market, and contribute to the overall integrity of the advertising industry.

Advertising Copywriting

Advertising Copywriting refers to the process of creating written content for advertising materials with the purpose of promoting a product, service, or brand. This form of writing aims to capture the attention of the target audience, convey the desired message, and convince them to take action, such as making a purchase or engaging with the advertised entity. Copywriters play a crucial role in the advertising industry by crafting compelling and persuasive written content that effectively communicates the benefits, features, and unique selling propositions of the product or service being advertised. They aim to create a persuasive narrative that resonates with the target audience and prompts them to respond in a desired way. Good copywriting involves understanding the target audience and their desires, needs, and pain points. By identifying these key factors, copywriters can tailor their writing to address the audience's specific concerns and present the advertised product or service as the solution. Through the careful selection of words, tone, and style, copywriters strive to create emotional connections, evoke curiosity, and ultimately drive the consumer to take action. Copywriting for advertisements can take various forms, including print ads, radio scripts, television commercials, online banners, social media posts, emails, and website content. Each medium requires different approaches, as the space and time limitations may vary. Regardless of the medium being used, the goals of advertising copy remain the same: to captivate attention, generate interest, create desire, and ultimately lead to action. Advertisements often rely on creative and attention-grabbing headlines, concise and clear descriptions, and powerful calls-to-action to entice the audience. Alongside these elements, copywriters may employ storytelling techniques, humor, persuasive language, testimonials, and various psychological triggers to engage the reader or viewer and make the advertisement memorable. In summary, advertising copywriting is the art and skill of creating written content that effectively promotes a product, service, or brand. It requires a deep understanding of the target audience, the ability to craft persuasive narratives, and the utilization of various techniques to capture attention and drive action.

Advertising Creative Testing Tools

Advertising creative testing tools are specialized software or platforms used by advertisers to evaluate and measure the effectiveness of their advertisement campaigns. These tools help advertisers analyze and assess various aspects of their creative elements, such as visuals, copy, and messaging, to determine which elements resonate the most with their target audience. By utilizing advertising creative testing tools, advertisers can gather valuable data and insights that can inform decision-making and optimize their campaigns for better performance and impact. These tools provide a structured and systematic approach to measuring the impact of different creative variations and iterations.

Advertising Creative Testing

Advertising creative testing refers to the process of evaluating and analyzing advertisements to assess their effectiveness in achieving the desired objectives. It involves conducting research and collecting data to determine the impact of different creative elements on the target audience. The purpose of advertising creative testing is to measure the potential success of an advertisement before it is launched. By testing various aspects such as the copy, visuals, layout, and overall messaging, advertisers can identify the most compelling and persuasive elements that resonate with their target market.

Advertising Data Analytics Platforms

Advertising Data Analytics Platforms are tools or software that enable advertisers to collect, analyze, and interpret data related to their advertising campaigns. These platforms provide valuable insights and metrics that help advertisers make informed decisions and optimize their advertising strategies. Data analytics platforms gather data from various sources such as websites, social media platforms, and mobile applications. They use advanced algorithms and statistical models to process and analyze this data, providing advertisers with meaningful and actionable information. Advertisers can then use this information to measure the effectiveness of their campaigns, identify trends and patterns, and make data-driven improvements.

Advertising Data Analytics

Advertising data analytics refers to the process of collecting, analyzing, and interpreting data to gain insights into the performance and effectiveness of advertising campaigns. It involves the use of statistical methods, predictive modeling, and data visualization techniques to uncover patterns, trends, and key metrics that drive advertising success. This data-driven approach helps marketing professionals make informed decisions and optimize their advertising strategies to maximize their return on investment (ROI). By analyzing various data sources, such as customer demographics, consumer behavior, campaign reach, and engagement metrics, advertisers can measure the impact of their ads and make data-driven decisions to improve their advertising efforts.

Advertising Disclosure

Advertising Disclosure refers to the practice of clearly and prominently disclosing any relevant information regarding advertising content or sponsored partnerships within advertisements or promotional materials. The purpose of advertising disclosure is to provide transparency and ensure that consumers are aware of any commercial relationships that may influence the content or presentation of an advertisement. Advertising disclosure is particularly important in the digital age, where advertisements are often integrated seamlessly into online content. It is essential for advertisers to clearly disclose any affiliations, sponsorships, or financial incentives that may exist between the advertiser and the content creator or publisher.

Advertising Ecosystem

An advertising ecosystem refers to the interconnected network of various elements involved in the creation, distribution, and consumption of advertisements. It encompasses the entire process from the initial planning and creation of ads to their placement and delivery, and finally, their impact on the target audience. This ecosystem involves different stakeholders, each playing a unique role in the advertising process. Advertisers, such as businesses or organizations, are responsible for conceptualizing and producing the advertisements. They collaborate with advertising agencies or creative teams to develop compelling ads that effectively convey their message and objectives. Publishers, on the other hand, provide platforms or spaces to showcase these ads. They could be online platforms like websites, social media channels, or traditional mediums such as magazines, newspapers, or billboards. Publishers offer targeted audiences and extensive reach, allowing advertisers to communicate their message to the right audience at the right time. Ad networks and ad exchanges act as intermediaries between advertisers and publishers. They bring together a vast inventory of ad spaces from various publishers and connect them with advertisers seeking specific audiences. Ad networks facilitate the buying and selling of ad space, while ad exchanges use programmatic technology to automate the process of buying and selling ads in real-time auctions. Ad servers are crucial components of the advertising ecosystem as they manage and deliver ads to the intended audience. They ensure that ads are displayed correctly and track their performance to generate insights and optimize ad campaigns. Ad servers also enable targeting options, allowing advertisers to reach specific demographics or interests. Lastly, consumers form an integral part of the advertising ecosystem. They interact with ads, either consciously or subconsciously, and their responses determine the success or failure of an advertisement. Consumers may engage with ads by clicking on them, making a purchase, or simply retaining the brand message in their memory. Their actions and feedback help advertisers measure the effectiveness of their campaigns and make necessary improvements. In conclusion, the advertising ecosystem encompasses the various interconnected elements involved in the creation, distribution, and consumption of advertisements. Advertisers, publishers, ad networks, ad exchanges, ad servers, and consumers all contribute to the dynamic and evolving landscape of advertising.

Advertising Effectiveness Metrics

Advertising effectiveness metrics are quantitative measures used to assess the impact and success of advertising campaigns. These metrics provide insights into the performance and return on investment (ROI) of advertising efforts, allowing advertisers to make data-driven decisions and optimize their strategies. One commonly used effectiveness metric is reach, which measures the total number of individuals or households exposed to an advertisement. Reach indicates the potential audience size and helps advertisers determine the scale of their campaigns. Another important metric is frequency, which measures the average number of times an individual is exposed to an advertisement. By managing frequency, advertisers can control how often their message is shown to avoid overexposure or underexposure. Click-through rate (CTR) is another crucial metric, especially in digital advertising. It measures the percentage of viewers who click on an ad, indicating their level of engagement. A high CTR suggests that the ad effectively captured the audience's attention and prompted them to take action. Conversion rate is another valuable metric that measures the percentage of viewers who complete a desired action, such as making a purchase or filling out a form. Conversion rate provides insights into how well the advertisement is influencing the target audience's behavior. Return on advertising spend (ROAS) is a financial metric that assesses the revenue generated from advertising compared to the cost of the campaign. It is calculated by dividing the total revenue generated by the advertising campaign by the total cost of the campaign. ROAS helps advertisers understand the profitability of their advertising efforts and allocate resources effectively. Return on investment (ROI) is a broader metric that calculates the overall return on an advertising campaign, considering both tangible and intangible benefits.

Advertising Effectiveness Research Methods

Advertising Effectiveness Research

Advertising Effectiveness Research refers to the systematic and scientific study conducted to evaluate the impact and efficiency of advertising efforts. It involves the collection, analysis, interpretation, and presentation of data related to the advertising campaigns and their effectiveness in achieving the desired objectives. The primary objective of advertising effectiveness research is to provide valuable insights into the performance of advertising strategies and tactics. It aims to measure the extent to which advertisements influence consumer behavior, brand perception, purchase intention, and other relevant outcomes. By examining various metrics and indicators, such as brand awareness, brand recall, message comprehension, attitude change, and sales figures, researchers can determine the effectiveness of an advertising campaign.

Advertising Effectiveness

Advertising effectiveness refers to the ability of an advertisement to successfully achieve its intended purpose and generate a desirable response from its target audience. It is a measure of how well an advertisement is able to communicate its message, create awareness, generate interest, and ultimately persuade consumers to take a desired action, such as making a purchase, signing up for a service, or changing their perception about a brand or product. The effectiveness of an advertisement can be evaluated through various metrics and indicators, including reach, frequency, memorability, engagement, and conversion rates. Reach refers to the number of people exposed to the advertisement, while frequency refers to the number of times the advertisement is presented to the target audience. Memorability measures the extent to which the advertisement is remembered by the audience, and engagement measures the level of attention and interaction generated by the advertisement. Furthermore, advertising effectiveness depends on the ability of the advertisement to align with the target audience's needs, wants, and preferences. It should be able to clearly communicate the unique selling proposition of the brand or product, differentiate it from competitors, and create a meaningful connection with the audience. This entails understanding the target audience's demographic characteristics, psychographics, behaviors, and motivations. In addition, the context in which the advertisement is presented plays a crucial role in its effectiveness. The advertisement should be placed in relevant media channels that are frequented by the target audience and allow for efficient targeting. The timing of the advertisement's placement should also be strategic, ensuring that it reaches the audience when they are most likely to be receptive to the message. Ultimately, a successful advertisement is one that not only captures the attention of the target audience but also elicits the desired response and achieves the objectives set by the advertiser.

It should be able to create a positive impact on brand awareness, brand perception, and consumer behavior. Assessing the effectiveness of an advertisement allows advertisers and marketers to make informed decisions about their advertising strategies, optimize their campaigns, and allocate resources effectively.

Advertising Ethics Guidelines

Advertising ethics guidelines refer to a set of moral principles and standards that should be followed by advertisers when creating and disseminating advertisements. These guidelines aim to ensure the ethical and responsible practice of advertising, protecting the interests and rights of both consumers and society as a whole. The purpose of advertising ethics guidelines is to promote transparency, honesty, fairness, and respect in advertising practices. Advertisers are expected to adhere to these guidelines to avoid engaging in deceptive, misleading, or manipulative tactics that may harm or deceive consumers. By following these ethical principles, advertisers strive to maintain the trust and credibility of their brands and contribute to the overall well-being of the advertising industry.

Advertising Ethics

Advertising Ethics refers to the moral principles and guidelines that govern the creation, distribution, and consumption of advertisements. It encompasses the standards and practices that advertisers and marketers should adhere to in order to ensure their activities are fair, truthful, and socially responsible. These ethics apply to all aspects of advertising, including the content of advertisements, the methods used to deliver them, and the impact they have on individuals, communities, and society as a whole. Advertisers are expected to demonstrate a commitment to transparency, honesty, and integrity throughout the advertising process.

Advertising Expenditure Tracking

Advertising Expenditure Tracking refers to the process of monitoring, recording, and analyzing the financial resources spent on various advertising activities by an organization. It involves keeping a detailed record of all the expenses related to advertising and evaluating their impact on the company's marketing efforts. The purpose of advertising expenditure tracking is to gain insights into the effectiveness and efficiency of the advertising investments made by a company. By meticulously tracking and analyzing the expenses incurred on advertising campaigns, organizations can make informed decisions about their marketing strategies and allocate their resources more effectively.

Advertising Expenditure

Advertising expenditure refers to the amount of money spent on promoting a product, service, or brand through various communication channels in order to reach a target audience and generate sales or brand awareness. Advertising is an essential part of marketing strategies for businesses of all sizes. It allows companies to communicate with their target market, inform them about products or services, persuade them to make a purchase, and build brand loyalty. However, running effective advertising campaigns requires financial resources, which are allocated as advertising expenditure.

Advertising Fee Structure Evaluation

An advertising fee structure evaluation refers to the assessment and analysis of the pricing and payment mechanisms in place for advertisement services. It involves an examination of the different fee models, pricing strategies, and payment options used by advertising agencies or platforms. The evaluation aims to determine the fairness, effectiveness, and suitability of the fee structure for both the advertisers and the advertising platform. It involves considering various factors such as the target audience, advertising goals, market conditions, and competition.

Advertising Fee Structure

An advertising fee structure refers to the systematic arrangement of charges or costs associated with advertising services provided by an advertising agency, media company, or other marketing entities. It outlines the pricing model and breakdown of fees for various advertising services offered to businesses and organizations to promote their products, services, or brand. The advertising fee structure typically includes different components that contribute to the overall cost of a particular advertising campaign. These components may include: 1. Placement fees: This covers the costs associated with securing ad placements in various media channels such as television, radio, print, online platforms, or outdoor advertising spaces. The fee may vary depending on factors like the size, prominence, duration, and time slot of the ad placement. 2. Creative and production costs: This encompasses the expenses related to the development and creation of advertising materials such as graphic design, copywriting, video production, audio recording, or digital content creation. These costs can vary based on the complexity, scope, and quality of the advertising materials. 3. Media buying fees: Media buying involves procuring advertising space or time from media owners on behalf of the advertiser. The advertising fee structure may incorporate fees charged by the agency for negotiating, planning, and executing media buying strategies to reach the target audience effectively. 4. Agency commissions or markups: Some advertising agencies earn commissions or markups from media owners when they purchase advertising placements in bulk or at discounted rates. These commission fees can be included in the fee structure and may vary depending on the negotiated terms between the agency and the client. 5. Research and analytics fees: This covers costs associated with market research, audience analysis, data collection, and campaign performance tracking. The advertising fee structure may include fees for conducting surveys, focus groups, or using analytical tools to measure and optimize the effectiveness of the advertising campaign. 6. Additional services and miscellaneous fees: Apart from the core services, advertising agencies or media companies may charge additional fees for special requests, customization, rush orders, or extra services like social media management, influencer partnerships, or event activations. These miscellaneous fees can vary based on the specific requirements of the client. The advertising fee structure serves as a guideline for both the advertising provider and the client. It helps establish transparency, manage expectations, and ensure that the client understands the breakdown of costs associated with their advertising campaign. By having a clear fee structure, both parties can negotiate, agree upon, and evaluate the cost-effectiveness of the advertising services being provided.

Advertising Format Testing Procedures

Advertising Format Testing Procedures: Advertising format testing procedures refer to the methods and techniques used to evaluate and assess the effectiveness and impact of different advertising formats or layouts. Advertising plays a crucial role in promoting products, services, and brands to target audiences. However, not all advertising formats may be equally effective in conveying the intended message or generating desired consumer responses. This is where advertising format testing procedures come into play. These procedures involve systematic and controlled experiments that assess the impact of various advertising formats on consumer behavior, attitudes, and purchase intentions. The goal is to determine which format or layout is most successful in engaging the target audience and achieving the desired advertising objectives. The testing procedures typically involve a sample of individuals who represent the target market. These individuals are exposed to different advertising formats or layouts, either in a controlled experimental setting or through real-world advertising campaigns. Their responses are then measured and analyzed using various research methods, such as surveys, interviews, or observational techniques. The data collected from these procedures provide insights into the effectiveness of different advertising formats and help advertisers make informed decisions about which formats to use in their campaigns. This information can also guide them in optimizing their advertising efforts by identifying the strengths and weaknesses of each format. Advertising format testing procedures can involve a wide range of variables and factors. These may include the size and placement of visuals, the use of colors and fonts, the length and complexity of the message, the presence of endorsements or testimonials, and the overall layout and design of the advertisement. The results of these procedures can inform advertising professionals about the most effective strategies for capturing attention, increasing brand awareness, and influencing consumer behavior. By continually testing and refining advertising formats, marketers can ensure that their messages resonate with the target audience and drive desired outcomes.

Advertising Format Testing

Advertising format testing refers to the process of evaluating the effectiveness and performance of various advertisement formats. It involves conducting experiments and research to determine which format resonates best with the target audience and achieves the desired advertising objectives. During the advertising format testing, different formats of advertisements are tested, such as visual ads, audio ads, video ads, display ads, and native ads. These formats can be evaluated based on various criteria, including click-through rate (CTR), conversion rate, engagement rate, brand recall, message retention, and overall impact on consumer behavior.

Advertising Frequency Management

Advertising Frequency Management refers to the practice of controlling the number of times an advertisement is shown to a specific target audience within a given time period. It is a strategic approach used by advertisers to strike a balance between reaching their audience effectively and avoiding overexposure or annoyance. The goal of Advertising Frequency Management is to optimize the impact and effectiveness of an advertising campaign by finding the right balance between repetition and variety. By controlling the frequency at which an advertisement is shown, advertisers can ensure that their message is seen by the target audience enough times to create brand awareness and influence consumer behavior, without causing irritation or indifference. There are several factors that influence Advertising Frequency Management. These include the nature of the product or service being advertised, the target audience's characteristics and behaviors, the advertising budget, and the media channels being used. Advertisers need to carefully analyze these factors and determine the optimal frequency for their advertisements to achieve the desired objectives. When implementing Advertising Frequency Management, advertisers need to consider both reach and frequency. Reach refers to the number of different individuals exposed to the advertisement, while frequency refers to the number of times the advertisement is shown to the target audience. Finding the right balance between reach and frequency will depend on the specific communication goals of the advertising campaign. By effectively managing the frequency of advertisements, advertisers can avoid the negative consequences of underexposure or overexposure. Underexposure may result in low brand awareness and insufficient message recall, while overexposure can lead to ad fatigue and irritation, causing consumers to tune out or develop negative attitudes towards the brand. In conclusion, Advertising Frequency Management is a strategic practice that involves controlling the number of times an advertisement is shown to a specific target audience. By finding the right balance between repetition and variety, advertisers can optimize the impact and effectiveness of their advertising campaigns, leading to increased brand awareness and influencing consumer behavior.

Advertising Frequency

Advertising Frequency refers to the number of times an advertisement is displayed or aired within a specific time period. It is a critical aspect of advertising campaigns as it directly influences the reach and impact of the message being communicated to the target audience. The frequency of advertising can vary depending on several factors, including the goals of the campaign, the target audience, and the advertising budget. The main objective is to strike a balance between maintaining brand visibility and avoiding excessive repetition that may lead to ad fatigue or annoyance among consumers.

Advertising Goals

Advertising goals refer to the specific objectives that an advertiser wants to achieve through their advertising campaigns. These goals are set to guide the planning, execution, and evaluation of advertising efforts, with the aim of maximizing the desired outcomes for the advertiser. One primary advertising goal is to increase brand awareness. By exposing a brand or product to a wider audience, advertisers aim to create recognition and familiarity among consumers. Increased brand awareness can lead to an enhanced brand reputation, increased market share, and ultimately higher sales.

Advertising Grant

An advertising grant is a financial assistance provided by organizations, foundations, or government entities to support and promote advertising activities for specific businesses or projects. It is typically awarded through a competitive application process and aims to help businesses reach their target audience effectively and efficiently. The main purpose of an advertising grant is to enable businesses to create and implement marketing campaigns that they may not have been able to afford on their own. This funding can cover various aspects of advertising, including but not limited to media buying, creative development, production costs, and research and analysis. Advertising grants are commonly offered by entities that have an interest in stimulating economic growth, supporting entrepreneurship, or fostering innovation in a particular industry or region. These can include government bodies, private foundations, corporate organizations, or even public-private partnerships. Businesses seeking an advertising grant usually need to submit a detailed proposal that outlines their advertising goals, target audience, strategies, and budget. The application process may also require businesses to provide information about their financial standing, previous advertising efforts, and projected outcomes or benefits from the proposed campaign. Selection committees or boards responsible for awarding advertising grants evaluate applications based on various criteria, such as the potential impact on the target audience, alignment with the grant provider's objectives, feasibility of the proposed campaign, and the overall budget requirements. Successful applicants are then notified and provided with the grant funding to execute their advertising plans. It is important to note that advertising grants are not unlimited funds for businesses to use at their discretion. Grant recipients are generally required to adhere to certain guidelines and reporting requirements, ensuring proper use of the funds and tracking the effectiveness of the advertising campaign. In conclusion, an advertising grant is a financial support mechanism that enables businesses to implement impactful marketing campaigns by providing funds specifically allocated for advertising activities. It offers a valuable opportunity for businesses to expand their reach, promote their products or services, and ultimately drive growth and success.

Advertising Impact Assessment Techniques

Advertising Impact Assessment Techniques refer to the methods and approaches used to evaluate the effectiveness and success of advertisement campaigns. These techniques help advertisers and marketers measure the impact and outcomes of their promotional efforts and make informed decisions for future campaigns.The first technique is Surveys and Questionnaires. This method involves collecting data directly from consumers through surveys or questionnaires to assess the impact of an advertisement. Questions can be designed to measure awareness, recall, attitude, and purchase behavior among the target audience. By analyzing the responses, advertisers can gain insights into the success of their ad campaign and make necessary adjustments if needed.

Advertising Impact Assessment

Advertising Impact Assessment refers to the process of evaluating the effects and effectiveness of an advertising campaign or strategy on the target audience and overall business objectives. It involves measuring and analyzing various key performance indicators (KPIs) to determine the impact and success of the advertisement. Assessing the impact of advertising is crucial for businesses to ensure that their marketing efforts are generating the desired outcomes and contributing to the overall growth and success. It helps in identifying the strengths and weaknesses of the advertising campaign, allowing businesses to make data-driven decisions and optimize their strategies for better results.

Advertising Impact

Advertising Impact - Advertising Impact refers to the effect or influence that advertisements have on consumers, businesses, and society as a whole. It encompasses the various ways in which advertisements communicate and promote products, services, or ideas to target audiences, and how these messages are received and interpreted. Advertisements play a crucial role in shaping consumer preferences, attitudes, and purchasing behavior. They aim to create awareness about a product or service, highlight its key features and benefits, and persuade consumers to make a purchase or take a desired action. The impact of advertising can be measured through various metrics such as brand recognition, product sales, customer loyalty, and market share. For businesses, advertising impact is instrumental in building brand image and equity, driving sales and revenue growth, and gaining a competitive edge in the marketplace. Effective advertising campaigns can significantly enhance brand visibility and recognition, create a strong brand identity, and position a company as a leader or expert in its industry. Advertising can also have a broader impact on society by influencing cultural norms, values, and behaviors. Advertisements often reflect societal trends and can shape popular culture by reinforcing or challenging existing beliefs and stereotypes. They have the power to raise awareness about important social issues, promote positive messages, and inspire change. However, advertising impact is not always positive. Some advertisements may use deceptive or manipulative tactics, making false claims or presenting unrealistic expectations. Such practices can erode consumer trust, contribute to consumer skepticism, and damage brand reputation. Additionally, certain types of advertisements can perpetuate harmful stereotypes, promote materialism, or create unrealistic body ideals. In conclusion, advertising impact refers to the influence that advertisements exert on consumers, businesses, and society. It encompasses both the positive and negative effects of advertising, ranging from influencing consumer behavior and shaping brand perception to contributing to cultural norms and societal values. Understanding and managing the impact of advertising is crucial for businesses to create effective marketing strategies and for society to navigate the complex relationship between advertising and its consequences.

Advertising Industry

The advertising industry refers to the sector of the economy that is responsible for creating, planning, and executing promotional or marketing messages to reach a target audience and persuade them to take a desired action, such as purchasing a product or service. Advertising is a form of communication that aims to inform, influence, and persuade potential customers or clients about the benefits or value of a particular product or service. It is an essential component of marketing strategies and plays a crucial role in creating brand awareness, driving sales, and building customer loyalty.The advertising industry encompasses various activities and roles, including advertising agencies, media companies, marketers, advertisers, creative professionals, and market researchers. These entities work together to develop effective advertising campaigns that effectively reach and engage the target audience. The process typically involves conducting consumer research to understand the target market's needs, preferences, and behavior, and then using this information to develop compelling messages and creative content.Advertising campaigns can take various forms, such as television commercials, print ads, online banners, social media posts, influencer collaborations, and even guerrilla marketing tactics. The choice of advertising channels and mediums depends on factors such as the target audience's demographics, media consumption habits, and the objectives of the campaign. Regardless of the medium used, the primary objective of advertising is to capture the audience's attention, communicate a persuasive message, and ultimately drive desired consumer behavior.In addition to creating and executing advertising campaigns, the advertising industry also plays a significant role in measuring and evaluating the effectiveness of these efforts. This involves analyzing various key performance indicators (KPIs) such as reach, impressions, click-through rates, conversion rates, and return on investment. By assessing campaign performance, advertisers can optimize their strategies and make data-driven decisions to maximize the impact of their advertising efforts.Overall, the advertising industry plays a vital role not only in promoting products and services but also in shaping consumer perceptions, influencing buying decisions, and driving economic growth. Through strategic and creative communication, advertising provides businesses with a platform to connect with their target audience and establish a competitive advantage in the marketplace.

Advertising Innovations Exploration

Advertising Innovations Exploration refers to the process of discovering and implementing new and creative approaches to advertising with the goal of increasing customer engagement, brand awareness, and ultimately driving sales. It involves the continuous pursuit of new strategies, techniques, and platforms to effectively communicate with target audiences in a way that stands out from competitors. This exploration often involves researching and analyzing consumer behavior, market trends, and emerging technologies to identify opportunities for innovation. Advertisers constantly seek innovative ways to capture attention, engage, and hold the interest of customers amidst the ever-increasing noise and competition in the advertising landscape.

Advertising Innovations

Advertising Innovations can be defined as the creative and strategic approaches used by businesses and marketers to develop new and unique ways of promoting their products or

43

services to consumers. These innovations aim to attract attention, engage audiences, and ultimately increase brand awareness and drive sales. Advertising innovations encompass various tactics and techniques that go beyond traditional advertising methods. They involve the use of emerging technologies, unconventional media platforms, and out-of-the-box ideas to capture the target audience's interest and leave a lasting impression. This can include everything from interactive digital campaigns to experiential marketing events.

Advertising Jingle

Advertising jingles are short, catchy, and memorable musical compositions or tunes that are used in advertisements to promote a brand, product, or service. They are designed to capture the attention of the audience and leave a lasting impression. Jingles are typically accompanied by a simple and straightforward message that highlights the unique selling points or key benefits of the advertised product. The lyrics of a jingle often include a brand name or tagline, making it easier for consumers to associate the tune with a specific brand or product.

Advertising KPI Tracking

Advertising KPI Tracking refers to the process of measuring and analyzing the performance of advertising campaigns in order to evaluate their success and effectiveness. KPIs, or Key Performance Indicators, are specific metrics that are used to assess various aspects of an advertisement's performance, such as reach, engagement, and conversion rates. The tracking of advertising KPIs involves collecting data from multiple sources, such as website analytics, social media platforms, and ad-serving systems. This data is then analyzed to determine the impact of the advertising campaign on key objectives, such as brand awareness, customer acquisition, and revenue generation. Some common advertising KPIs include: - Impressions: The number of times an advertisement is displayed to potential viewers. - Click-through rate (CTR): The percentage of viewers who click on an advertisement to reach a specific landing page. - Conversion rate: The percentage of viewers who complete a desired action, such as making a purchase or filling out a form. - Return on ad spend (ROAS): The ratio of revenue generated to the amount spent on advertising. - Cost per acquisition (CPA): The average cost incurred to acquire a new customer. By tracking these KPIs, advertisers are able to measure the effectiveness of their advertising campaigns and make data-driven decisions to optimize their strategies. For example, if the CTR is low, advertisers may need to revise the ad's creative elements or targeting parameters to increase engagement. Similarly, if the conversion rate is low, advertisers can analyze the user journey to identify any obstacles that may be hindering conversions and make necessary improvements. In summary, advertising KPI tracking is a crucial component of advertising campaign management, as it provides valuable insights into the performance and impact of advertisements. By continuously monitoring and analyzing KPIs, advertisers can make informed decisions to optimize their campaigns and achieve their advertising goals.

Advertising KPIs

Advertising Key Performance Indicators (KPIs) refer to a set of measurable metrics that assess the effectiveness and success of advertising campaigns. These KPIs provide valuable insights into the performance of advertisements and help advertisers make data-driven decisions to optimize their campaigns and achieve their marketing objectives. In the context of advertising, KPIs typically include metrics such as Impressions, Click-through Rate (CTR), Conversion Rate, Return on Ad Spend (ROAS), Cost per Click (CPC), Cost per Acquisition (CPA), and Return on Investment (ROI). Each of these metrics provides specific information about different aspects of the advertising campaign. Impressions refer to the number of times an advertisement is shown to potential viewers. It helps advertisers gauge the reach and exposure of their campaign. Click-through Rate (CTR) is the ratio of users who click on the advertisement to the total number of users who view it. It indicates the level of engagement and interest generated by the advertisement. Conversion Rate measures the percentage of users who take a desired action, such as making a purchase or signing up for a newsletter, after viewing the advertisement. It reflects the effectiveness of the campaign in driving user actions. Return on Ad Spend (ROAS) measures the revenue generated in relation to the amount spent on advertising. It helps advertisers understand the profitability of their campaigns and determine their advertising budget allocation. Cost per Click (CPC) is the average cost incurred for each click on the advertisement.

It is useful in estimating the cost-effectiveness of the campaign and comparing different advertising channels or ad variations. Cost per Acquisition (CPA) measures the average cost incurred for acquiring a new customer or lead through the advertisement. It assists in assessing the efficiency of the campaign in acquiring new customers. Return on Investment (ROI) calculates the overall profitability of the advertising campaign by comparing the revenue generated to the cost of the campaign. It provides a holistic view of the campaign's financial performance. By analyzing these advertising KPIs, advertisers can identify underperforming campaigns, optimize their targeting and messaging strategies, and allocate resources effectively to achieve their marketing goals. These metrics help in measuring the success of advertising efforts and enable informed decision-making for campaign optimization. In conclusion, advertising KPIs are crucial performance indicators that quantify the effectiveness and success of advertising campaigns. Through the analysis of metrics such as Impressions, CTR, Conversion Rate, ROAS, CPC, CPA, and ROI, advertisers can gain insights and make data-driven decisions to optimize their campaigns and achieve their marketing objectives.

Advertising Language Analysis

Advertising language refers to the use of persuasive and influential techniques in promotional messages to capture the attention, evoke interest, and stimulate desire among the audience, ultimately leading to a desired action or behavior. In advertisements, language is specifically crafted to create an impact and convince consumers about the superiority, credibility, and value of a product or service. It employs various linguistic devices, rhetorical strategies, and persuasive appeals to compel individuals to purchase or engage with a particular offering.

Advertising Language

Advertising language refers to the specific choice of words, phrases, and techniques used in advertisements to persuade or influence consumers to purchase a product or service. It aims to grab the attention of the target audience, create a desire for the advertised product, and ultimately drive them towards taking action. Effective advertising language is crafted to appeal to the emotions, needs, and desires of the consumers. It often employs various rhetorical devices such as repetition, exaggeration, and emotional appeals to create a memorable and persuasive message.

Advertising Layout

An advertising layout refers to the visual arrangement or design of an advertisement, aiming to capture the attention of the target audience and effectively deliver the intended message. A well-designed advertising layout is crucial in attracting and engaging potential customers. It should be visually appealing, organized, and strategically structured to convey the brand's message in a concise and impactful manner. The layout needs to balance aesthetics with functionality, ensuring that the advertisement is easy to understand and navigate.

Advertising Media Selection Strategies

Advertising media selection strategies refer to the process of choosing the most effective and appropriate communication channels to deliver advertising messages to the target audience. This crucial decision-making process involves analyzing various factors such as the target audience, advertising objectives, budget constraints, and available media options to make informed choices and maximize the impact of advertising campaigns. The first step in media selection is understanding the target audience, including their demographics, preferences, and media consumption habits. This knowledge helps advertisers identify the most relevant media platforms that will effectively reach their target market. For example, if the target audience consists mostly of millennials who are active on social media, platforms like Instagram and Snapchat may be a more effective choice than traditional print media. Next, advertisers evaluate the advertising objectives and message. Different media have different strengths and limitations in delivering specific messages. For instance, television and video advertisements are more suitable for conveying visual and emotional messages, while radio may be more effective for delivering audio-based messages. Print media, on the other hand, can provide more detailed information and are better suited for advertisements that require in-depth explanations or specific visual details. Budget constraints also play a significant role in media selection.

45

Advertisers must assess the cost-effectiveness of various media options and determine which ones align with their budget limitations. It is important to find a balance between cost and reach, ensuring that the selected media offer sufficient exposure to the target audience while staying within the allocated budget. Additionally, the availability and accessibility of media options are considered during the selection process. Advertisers evaluate the reach and coverage of different media platforms and assess how well they align with the geographical scope of the target audience. For instance, if the target market is primarily local, using local newspapers or radio stations may offer better reach than national television networks. The media selection process also involves considering the timing and scheduling of advertisements. Advertisers analyze factors such as peak viewing/listening times, seasonal trends, and competitor's advertising schedules to determine when and how frequently to run the advertisements. By strategically timing the ads, advertisers can increase the chances of reaching their target audience at the right moments and in the most impactful manner. In conclusion, advertising media selection strategies involve carefully analyzing the target audience, advertising objectives, budget constraints, available options, and timing considerations to choose the most appropriate media platforms. By making informed decisions, advertisers can optimize the reach, effectiveness, and efficiency of their advertising campaigns.

Advertising Media Selection

Advertising media selection refers to the process of choosing the most appropriate and effective platforms or channels through which an advertisement will be presented to a target audience. It involves evaluating various media options based on their reach, frequency, cost, and other factors to determine the optimal mix of media channels for the advertisement campaign. The selection of advertising media is a critical decision for advertisers as it directly impacts the success and effectiveness of their advertising efforts. By carefully analyzing the target market, objectives, and budgetary constraints, advertisers can choose the media that will best reach and engage their intended audience. One of the primary considerations in media selection is the reach of the media channel. Reach refers to the number or percentage of the target audience that can be potentially exposed to the advertisement. Advertisers aim to maximize reach to ensure that their promotions are seen by a large number of people who are likely to be interested in their product or service. Frequency is another important factor in media selection. It refers to how often the target audience is exposed to the advertisement within a specific time frame. By selecting media channels with high frequency, advertisers can reinforce their message and create brand familiarity among the target audience. Cost is also a crucial consideration in media selection. Advertisers must assess the cost-effectiveness of different media options to ensure that they are utilizing their budget efficiently. Media with higher reach and frequency often come at a higher cost, so advertisers need to strike a balance between their desired exposure and the available budget. Apart from reach, frequency, and cost, other factors such as target audience characteristics, geographic coverage, message flexibility, and potential for engagement should also be evaluated during media selection. Advertisers may need to customize their media mix based on the unique requirements and preferences of their target market. In conclusion, advertising media selection is a strategic process that involves carefully evaluating various media options to determine the most effective channels for delivering an advertisement to the target audience. By considering factors such as reach, frequency, cost, and other relevant criteria, advertisers can make informed decisions and maximize the impact of their advertising campaigns.

Advertising Media

Advertising media refers to the various channels or platforms through which advertisements are communicated to a target audience. It includes both traditional and modern forms of media that are used to deliver promotional messages and reach potential consumers. Traditional advertising media encompass conventional channels such as television, radio, print publications (newspapers and magazines), billboards, and direct mail. These mediums have been utilized for decades and continue to play a significant role in advertising campaigns. Television commercials and radio ads reach a wide audience, enabling brands to convey their message visually or through audio. Print publications provide opportunities for advertisers to reach specific demographics and target niche markets. Billboards strategically placed in high-traffic areas attract attention and create brand awareness, while direct mail allows for personalized marketing communication. With the emergence of new technology and digital platforms, the advertising landscape has evolved, and modern advertising media have gained prominence. Digital advertising media comprise channels like websites, social media platforms, search engines, mobile apps, and email marketing. Websites serve as online platforms where companies can display their ads to attract website visitors and convert them into customers. Social media platforms enable brands to reach and engage with their target audience through organic posts, sponsored content, and influencer partnerships. Search engines utilize paid search advertising to display relevant ads to users based on their search queries. Mobile apps offer opportunities for brands to showcase ads tailored to specific user demographics and interests. Lastly, email marketing involves sending targeted promotional emails to individuals who have opted to receive communications from a particular brand.

Advertising Metrics

Advertising Metrics refers to the measurements and analysis of various parameters that are used to evaluate the effectiveness and success of advertising campaigns. These metrics play a crucial role in determining the return on investment (ROI) and the overall impact of advertising efforts. Advertising metrics can be classified into different categories, including reach, engagement, conversion, and cost. Reach metrics focus on the number of people who have been exposed to the advertisement. It includes metrics such as impressions, views, and unique visitors. These metrics help advertisers understand the potential audience they have reached and the penetration of their message. Engagement metrics measure the level of interaction and involvement of the audience with the advertisement. They gauge the effectiveness of the ad in capturing attention and generating interest. Metrics like click-through rates, time spent on the ad, likes, shares, and comments provide insights into the engagement level and audience response. Conversion metrics assess the actual outcomes and actions taken by the audience as a result of the advertisement. They analyze the behavior of users after viewing the ad, such as downloads, purchases, sign-ups, subscriptions, or any desired action. Conversion metrics help advertisers determine the effectiveness of their call-to-action and the overall impact on sales or business objectives. Cost metrics evaluate the financial aspect of advertising campaigns. They provide insights into the cost per impression, cost per click, cost per conversion, or any other relevant cost measurement. These metrics allow advertisers to optimize their advertising budget and compare the cost-effectiveness of different campaigns or channels. Overall, advertising metrics serve as a valuable tool in assessing the performance of advertising campaigns and guiding future strategies. By analyzing these metrics, advertisers can identify strengths and weaknesses, make data-driven decisions, and maximize the efficiency and effectiveness of their advertising efforts.

Advertising Network Optimization Strategies

Advertising Network Optimization Strategies refer to the tactics and techniques used to improve the effectiveness and profitability of an advertising network. An advertising network is a platform that brings together advertisers and publishers to facilitate the buying and selling of ad space. It allows advertisers to reach a wide audience by placing their ads on various websites, while publishers can monetize their websites by displaying these ads. However, in order for an advertising network to be successful, it needs to optimize its operations and make the most out of its available resources. One common strategy for advertising network optimization is target audience segmentation. By dividing the audience into specific groups based on their demographics, interests, or browsing behavior, advertisers can tailor their ads to the right people, increasing the chances of engagement and conversion. This strategy ensures that ads are seen by the most relevant audience, maximizing their effectiveness. Another important aspect of optimization is ad placement. Determining the ideal position and context for displaying ads can significantly impact their performance. Placing ads in prominent locations on high-traffic websites or within relevant content areas can increase visibility and click-through rates. This strategy involves continuous monitoring of ad performance and making adjustments to optimize placement for maximum impact. Furthermore, optimizing ad formats and creatives is crucial for successful advertising. Experimenting with different layouts, designs, and messaging can help identify the most appealing and engaging ad formats. Understanding the preferences and behavior of the target audience is essential in creating compelling ads that capture attention and drive conversions. To ensure successful optimization, it is important for advertising networks to regularly analyze and interpret data. This includes monitoring key performance indicators such as click-through rates, conversion rates, and return on investment. By analyzing this data, advertising networks can identify trends, patterns, and areas for improvement, allowing them to refine their strategies and make data-driven decisions. In conclusion, advertising network optimization strategies encompass various techniques aimed at improving the effectiveness and profitability of an advertising network. By focusing on target audience segmentation, ad placement, ad formats, and data analysis, advertising networks can maximize their revenue and provide value to both advertisers and publishers.

Advertising Network Optimization

Advertising network optimization refers to the process of improving the performance and efficiency of an advertising network by strategically optimizing various elements and factors that contribute to the network's overall effectiveness and revenue generation. This optimization process involves analyzing and adjusting key components such as ad placements, targeting criteria, bid strategies, and ad formats, among others, to maximize the network's ability to match ads with the most relevant audience and generate the highest possible return on investment (ROI) for advertisers.

Advertising Network

An advertising network is a platform or service that connects advertisers with websites or publishers for the purpose of displaying advertisements. It acts as a middleman or intermediary between advertisers and publishers, facilitating the buying and selling of advertising space. The advertising network works by aggregating a large number of websites and publishers, creating a network of available advertising inventory. Advertisers can then choose the specific websites or publishers they want their ads to be displayed on, based on factors such as the target audience, demographics, and relevance to their products or services. Once the advertisers have selected the websites or publishers, they can submit their ads to the advertising network. The network then serves these ads to the chosen websites or publishers, ensuring that they are displayed to the target audience. The ads are typically displayed in various formats, such as banner ads, text ads, or video ads. For publishers, the advertising network provides an opportunity to monetize their website by selling advertising space. Publishers can join the network and offer their available advertising inventory to advertisers. This allows them to generate revenue by displaying ads on their websites. The advertising network also handles the technical aspects of ad delivery and tracking. It ensures that the ads are delivered to the correct websites and that they are displayed correctly. It also tracks the performance of the ads, providing advertisers with data such as impressions, clicks, and conversions. In summary, an advertising network is a platform that connects advertisers with websites or publishers, allowing them to buy and sell advertising space. It provides advertisers with a wide range of websites to choose from and handles the technical aspects of ad delivery and tracking. For publishers, it offers an opportunity to monetize their website by displaying ads.

Advertising Objectives

Advertising objectives refer to the specific goals or targets that advertisers aim to achieve through their advertising campaigns. These objectives serve as guidelines for the planning, execution, and evaluation of advertisement strategies. The main purpose of advertising objectives is to enable advertisers to communicate effectively with their target audience and ultimately influence their behavior or response towards the advertised product or service. These objectives help advertisers to: 1. Create Awareness: One of the primary objectives of advertising is to generate awareness about a product, service, or brand. Advertising aims to inform and educate potential customers by creating a presence in their minds and making them aware of the benefits and features of the advertised offering. 2. Foster Interest: Once awareness is generated, advertising aims to capture the target audience's interest by presenting the advertised product or service as appealing and suitable to their needs or wants. By highlighting unique selling propositions and demonstrating value, advertising works to engage the audience and generate interest in the offering. 3. Stimulate Desire: Advertising seeks to create a desire or a sense of aspiration in the target audience, encouraging them to consider the advertised product as something they want or need. Through persuasive messaging, emotional appeals, or showcasing the product's benefits, advertising aims to create a desire for the offering among potential customers. 4. Drive Action: The ultimate objective of advertising is to drive action or encourage the target audience to take a specific action, such as making a purchase, visiting a store, requesting more information, or signing up for a service. Advertising strives to motivate potential customers to move from mere interest or desire to taking an actual step towards acquiring the advertised product or service. 5. Build and Maintain Brand Image: Advertising also plays a crucial role in building and maintaining the brand image or reputation in the market. Advertising objectives may include establishing brand authenticity, differentiating the brand from competitors, cultivating brand loyalty, or enhancing brand perception among the target audience. By setting clear and measurable advertising objectives, advertisers can align their strategies, messages, and tactics to achieve these objectives effectively. Regular evaluation and analysis of advertising campaigns against the pre-defined objectives enable advertisers to make informed decisions, optimize their strategies, and maximize the return on their advertising investments.

Advertising Package

An advertising package refers to a bundle of services, products, or promotional materials offered by a company, agency, or platform to help businesses promote their products or services effectively. This package typically includes a range of different advertising strategies, tools, and platforms designed to reach a specific target audience, increase brand awareness, and drive sales. It is a comprehensive solution that offers businesses the necessary resources and support to create and implement successful advertising campaigns.

Advertising Platform

An advertising platform is a system that allows advertisers to create, manage, and optimize their online advertisements across various channels and platforms, such as websites, social media, search engines, and mobile apps. It provides a centralized interface for advertisers to set up their ad campaigns, select specific targeting criteria, and allocate budget and resources. Advertisers can define their target audience based on demographics, interests, behaviors, and geographic location. The platform offers various ad formats, such as display ads, video ads, native ads, and sponsored content, which can be customized to align with the advertiser's branding and marketing objectives. Advertisers can create visually appealing and engaging ads that capture the attention of their target audience. Furthermore, the advertising platform provides tools and analytics to track the performance and effectiveness of ad campaigns. Advertisers can monitor key metrics like impressions, clicks, conversions, and return on investment (ROI). They can identify which channels and placements are delivering the best results and make data-driven decisions to optimize their campaigns for maximum impact. In addition, the platform facilitates the process of buying ad inventory by connecting advertisers with publishers or ad networks. Advertisers can bid for ad placements or negotiate advertising deals directly with publishers. The platform streamlines the buying process, ensuring that ads reach the right audience at the right time. Moreover, advanced targeting and personalization features of advertising platforms enable advertisers to reach their desired audience with precision. They can leverage data about consumer behavior, search intent, interests, and previous interactions to deliver highly relevant and tailored ads. This helps improve the overall customer experience and increases the likelihood of conversions. In summary, an advertising platform is a comprehensive solution that empowers advertisers to create, manage, and optimize their online advertising campaigns. It offers a range of features, including audience targeting, ad customization, performance tracking, and ad inventory management. By utilizing an advertising platform, advertisers can maximize the effectiveness of their ad campaigns, reach their target audience, and achieve their marketing goals.

Advertising ROI Calculation

Advertising Return on Investment (ROI) is a metric used to evaluate the financial performance and effectiveness of an advertising campaign. It measures the profit generated as a result of the advertising investment made by a company. ROI is a crucial measure for businesses to determine the success and efficiency of their advertising efforts. To calculate Advertising ROI, the formula used is: ROI = (Revenue - Cost of Advertising) / Cost of Advertising Revenue represents the total sales or additional revenue generated by the advertising campaign. It includes both direct and indirect sales resulting from the campaign. The Cost of Advertising includes all expenses related to advertising, such as media buying, creative production, and campaign management costs. The Advertising ROI calculation provides businesses with a clear understanding of the profitability and efficiency of their advertising investments. By comparing the revenue generated with the cost of advertising, companies can determine whether their marketing efforts are yielding positive returns or not. A positive ROI indicates that the advertising campaign has generated more revenue than the cost incurred, resulting in a profitable outcome. It demonstrates the effectiveness and success of the advertising strategy employed by the company. On the other hand, a negative ROI implies that the advertising campaign has not generated enough revenue to cover the advertising costs. This suggests that the strategy needs to be revised and optimized to improve future campaign performance. By calculating the Advertising ROI, businesses can make informed decisions regarding their advertising budgets and strategies. They can identify which campaigns are generating the highest returns and allocate resources accordingly. This helps optimize marketing efforts and maximize profitability.

Advertising Rate Card Creation

An advertising rate card is a document that outlines the costs and details of advertising options offered by a media company or platform. It serves as a pricing guide and reference tool for advertisers looking to purchase ad space or airtime. The main purpose of an advertising rate card is to provide transparency and clarity to both the media company and the advertisers. It sets the expectations and terms for advertising placements, allowing advertisers to make informed decisions about where and how to allocate their advertising budget. The rate card typically includes information such as the types of advertising options available (e.g. print, online, radio), the size or duration of the ad placements, the target audience demographics, and the associated costs. It may also include additional details such as available discounts, special packages, or premium placements. Media companies usually categorize their advertising options based on factors such as the size and prominence of the ad, the time slot or publication date, and the reach or popularity of the media platform. Each category will have its own set of rates and specifications, allowing advertisers to select the option that best suits their needs and budget. When creating an advertising rate card, media companies consider a variety of factors such as production costs, audience size, competition, and market demand. They also take into account the potential value and exposure that the ad placement can provide to the advertiser. All these factors contribute to the determination of the ad rates. By having a rate card, media companies can streamline the process of selling advertising space or airtime. It eliminates the need for negotiations on pricing and ensures that both parties are on the same page regarding the terms and conditions of the advertising agreement. Advertisers can easily compare the rates and options offered by different media platforms, allowing them to make informed decisions and maximize their return on investment. In summary, an advertising rate card is a pricing and information guide that outlines the costs, options, and specifications for advertising placements offered by a media company. It facilitates transparency and efficiency in the advertising buying process for both the media company and advertisers.

Advertising Rate Card

An advertising rate card is a document or a list that provides detailed information about the advertising options available to potential advertisers, along with the associated costs and guidelines. It is essentially a pricing guide that outlines the rates and specifications for advertising in a particular medium, such as a newspaper, magazine, website, radio station, or television channel. The purpose of a rate card is to provide transparency and clarity to both advertisers and publishers. It enables advertisers to understand the cost and scope of the various advertising options available to them, allowing them to make informed decisions about their advertising strategies. For publishers, a rate card serves as a consistent and organized reference point for communicating advertising rates to potential clients. The information included in a rate card typically includes the different types of advertisements available, such as display ads, classifieds, inserts, or sponsored content. It also outlines the different sizes and formats for each type of ad, along with any specific requirements or limitations. This ensures that advertisers have a clear understanding of the available options and can choose the format that best suits their needs and budget. In addition to the types and formats of ads, a rate card also includes the pricing structure for each option. This may include rates based on factors such as ad size, ad placement, frequency of publication, or target audience. Some rate cards may also offer discounts or special packages for advertisers who commit to long-term contracts or purchase ads in bulk. Furthermore, a rate card may include additional information such as circulation or viewership numbers, demographic data, or reach and frequency statistics. This information helps advertisers assess the potential reach and impact of their advertisements, allowing them to make strategic decisions based on their target audience. Overall, an advertising rate card serves as a comprehensive reference tool for advertisers and publishers alike. It provides a transparent and standardized overview of the advertising options available, allowing advertisers to compare prices, formats, and audience reach, and make informed decisions about their marketing campaigns.

Advertising Rate

Advertising rate refers to the cost or price that advertisers have to pay in order to display their advertisements in various media channels such as television, radio, print, online platforms, and outdoor billboards. This rate is typically determined by factors such as the media outlet's audience reach, the size and placement of the ad, the duration or frequency of exposure, and the demand for advertising space or airtime.

Advertising Recall Research

Advertising recall research refers to a method used to measure the effectiveness of advertisements and evaluate consumers' ability to remember and recall specific advertising messages. This type of research is conducted after an advertisement has been aired or published, with the aim of determining the impact of the advertisement on target consumers and gauging their brand awareness and message retention. The primary goal of advertising recall research is to assess the level of consumer engagement with the advertisement and determine whether the intended message was effectively communicated. It provides valuable insights into how well the advertisement resonates with the target audience and whether it effectively communicates the desired brand image, product benefits, or call to action. The research usually involves surveys or interviews that aim to measure consumers' recall and recognition of the advertisement. This may include asking respondents to describe the content, theme, or key message of the advertisement, or to identify the brand or product being advertised. Researchers may also inquire about the specific elements of the advertisement, such as visuals, taglines, jingles, or spokespersons, to further gauge consumer recall. In addition to measuring recall, advertising recall research often includes other metrics to evaluate the advertisement's impact. These may include assessing consumers' attitudes towards the advertisement, their perception of the brand or product, their likelihood to purchase or recommend it, or their intent to take a specific action as a result of seeing the advertisement. The findings from advertising recall research provide advertisers and marketers with valuable insights on the effectiveness of their advertising strategies and the impact of their campaigns. This information helps them make informed decisions about future advertising investments, creative messaging, media placement, and overall campaign effectiveness. It also enables them to refine and optimize their advertising efforts to better resonate with their target audience and achieve their marketing objectives.

Advertising Recall

Advertising recall refers to the ability of individuals to remember and recall an advertisement after exposure to it. It is a measure of the effectiveness of an advertisement in creating a lasting impression on consumers' minds. When evaluating advertising recall, marketers are interested in assessing how well their advertisements are remembered by their target audience. This can be measured through various techniques such as surveys, interviews, or psychological experiments. The goal is to determine whether the key elements of the advertisement, such as the brand name, tagline, or product features, are retained in consumers' memories.

Advertising Return On Investment (ROI)

Advertising Return on Investment (ROI) refers to a metric that measures the effectiveness and profitability of an advertising campaign. It is a financial indicator used to assess the return generated from an investment in advertising activities. ROI is calculated by comparing the net profit gained from advertising efforts to the cost of those efforts. It helps advertisers evaluate the performance and outcome of their campaigns, enabling them to make informed decisions regarding future investments in advertising.

Advertising Revenue Models Analysis

An advertising revenue model is a strategy or approach used by online platforms or media companies to generate income through advertisements. It outlines how the platform or company will charge advertisers for displaying their ads, and how the revenue will be generated. There are several types of advertising revenue models commonly used in the industry. One of the most common models is the cost per thousand impressions (CPM). In this model, advertisers pay a fixed rate for every thousand times their ad is displayed to users. The CPM model is often used in display advertising, where ads are shown on websites or within mobile applications. Another widely used advertising revenue model is cost per click (CPC). In this model, advertisers only pay when a user clicks on their ad. The cost per click is determined through a bidding system, where advertisers compete for ad placements based on keywords or targeting criteria. CPC is commonly used in search engine advertising, where ads are displayed alongside search results. Cost per action (CPA) is an advertising revenue model where advertisers pay when a specific action is taken by the user, such as making a purchase or filling out a form. This model is often used in affiliate marketing, where publishers earn a commission for driving conversions on behalf of advertisers. Some platforms also use a hybrid model, combining different revenue models to optimize their advertising income. For example, a platform might charge a CPM rate for premium ad placements while using a CPC model for lower-tier ad spaces. This allows the platform to maximize revenue by charging a higher rate for premium positions while still generating income from less desirable placements. In summary, an advertising revenue model is a strategy used by online platforms or media companies to generate income from advertisements. Different models, such as CPM, CPC, and CPA, offer various ways for advertisers to pay for their ads based on impressions, clicks, or specific actions taken by users. By choosing the right revenue model, platforms can effectively monetize their advertising inventory and drive revenue growth.

Advertising Revenue Models

The advertising revenue model refers to the method by which websites or other platforms generate income through the display of advertisements. Advertising is a popular revenue model for online platforms, as it allows them to offer their content or services to users for free while still generating revenue. There are several different types of advertising revenue models, each with its own characteristics and benefits. One common model is the cost-per-impression (CPM) model, where advertisers pay a certain amount for every thousand times their ad is shown to users. This model is typically used for display ads, where the goal is to reach a large number of users and generate brand awareness. With the CPM model, the revenue generated is directly proportional to the number of impressions the ad receives. Another popular advertising revenue model is the cost-per-click (CPC) model, where advertisers pay each time a user clicks on their ad. This model is commonly used for search engine advertising, as it allows advertisers to only pay for actual clicks and potential leads. The CPC model incentivizes advertisers to create compelling and relevant ads that entice users to click. The revenue generated in this model is dependent on both the number of clicks and the cost per click set by the advertisers. Additionally, there is the cost-per-action (CPA) model, where advertisers pay whenever a specific action is taken by the user, such as making a purchase or filling out a form. This model is often used in affiliate marketing, where the platform receives a commission for driving a desired action. The CPA model provides a more direct measurement of the effectiveness of the advertising campaign, as advertisers only pay when a predefined action is completed. Other advertising revenue models include the subscription model, where users pay a fee to access ad-free content or services, and the sponsored content model, where advertisers pay to have their content integrated into the platform's own content. These models offer alternative strategies for platforms to generate revenue while still providing value to users. In conclusion, the advertising revenue model is a crucial aspect of online platforms' financial sustainability. By utilizing various models such as CPM, CPC, CPA, subscription, or sponsored content, platforms can effectively monetize their user base and continue providing free or low-cost content to their users.

Advertising Sales Techniques

Advertising sales techniques refer to the methods and strategies used by advertising sales professionals to effectively sell and promote advertisement space or time to potential clients. These techniques aim to persuade and convince clients to invest in advertising opportunities by highlighting the benefits and advantages it can bring to their business or organization. The primary objective of advertising sales techniques is to increase revenue for media companies or advertising agencies by securing advertising contracts. This involves building strong relationships with clients, understanding their needs and objectives, and presenting advertising proposals tailored to their target audience and marketing goals. The first step in advertising sales techniques is prospecting. This involves identifying potential clients who would benefit from advertising their products or services. Sales professionals research and gather relevant information about these potential clients, such as their industry, target audience, and advertising budget. This enables them to make informed decisions on which clients to approach and customize their sales pitch accordingly. Once potential clients have been identified, advertising sales professionals use various communication strategies to make initial contact. This can include making phone calls, sending personalized emails, or arranging face-to-face meetings. The aim is to establish a connection and build rapport with the clients, demonstrating a genuine interest in their business and advertising needs. During the sales presentation, advertising sales professionals highlight the unique selling points of their media platform or advertising space. They emphasize the benefits of advertising with them, such as reaching a specific target audience, increasing brand awareness, or generating leads and sales. The sales professionals may use data and statistics to support their arguments and showcase the effectiveness of their advertising opportunities. In addition to showcasing the benefits, advertising sales professionals may also offer package deals or discounts to incentivize clients to secure long-term advertising contracts. This can include providing special rates or additional advertising slots at no extra cost. Negotiation skills are crucial in this stage, as the sales professionals aim to find a mutually beneficial agreement that satisfies the client's needs while maximizing revenue for their company. Finally, advertising sales professionals follow up with their clients to ensure satisfaction and address any concerns or questions. They maintain regular communication and provide ongoing support and assistance throughout the advertising campaign. This helps to build trust and long-term relationships with clients, increasing the likelihood of securing repeat business or referrals.

Advertising Sales

Advertising sales refers to the process of selling advertising space or time on various media platforms to businesses or individuals who want to promote their products or services. It involves identifying potential clients, understanding their advertising needs, and presenting them with suitable advertising options that align with their marketing goals. The goal of advertising sales is to generate revenue for the media platform by selling advertising inventory.

Advertising Schedule

An advertising schedule is a predetermined plan and timeline that outlines the specific dates and times when advertisements will be shown or aired on various platforms or media channels. It is a strategic tool used by advertisers and marketers to effectively allocate their advertising budgets and maximize the exposure and impact of their promotional messages. The purpose of an advertising schedule is to ensure that advertisements are placed in a manner that reaches the target audience at the most opportune times, when they are most likely to pay attention and respond to the message. By carefully planning and scheduling advertisements, advertisers can optimize their reach, frequency, and impact, ultimately leading to increased brand awareness, customer engagement, and sales.

Advertising Space Booking

Advertising space booking refers to the process of reserving or purchasing space in various media platforms, such as newspapers, magazines, television, radio, websites, and social media, for the purpose of promoting a product, service, or brand. It involves the strategic planning and allocation of resources to ensure that advertisements reach the desired target audience and maximize their impact. The booking process typically involves several steps. Firstly, advertisers need to identify the media platforms that are most relevant to their target audience and align with their marketing objectives. This requires careful consideration of factors such as the demographics, interests, and media consumption habits of the target market. Once the appropriate media platforms are identified, advertisers can proceed to the next step. The next step in the booking process is to negotiate and secure the advertising space. This involves contacting the media owners or advertising agencies responsible for managing the space and discussing the available options, including the duration, size, placement, and cost of the advertisements. Advertisers may need to consider factors such as the reach and frequency of the media platform, as well as any additional features or services offered, such as ad design or production assistance. After the negotiation, advertisers finalize the booking by signing a contract or agreement that outlines the terms and conditions of the advertisement placement. This includes details such as the start and end date of the campaign, the payment terms, any cancellation or modification policies, and any other relevant information. Advertisers may also be required to provide the necessary artwork or content for their ads, adhering to the specifications provided by the media platform. Once the booking is confirmed, advertisers need to track and monitor the performance of their advertisements. This involves analyzing data and metrics, such as impressions, click-through rates, conversions, and return on investment, to evaluate the effectiveness of the advertising campaign. Advertisers can then make informed decisions regarding future bookings and adjust their strategies accordingly to optimize results.

Advertising Space Rates Negotiation

Advertising space rates negotiation refers to the process of discussing and reaching an agreement on the cost and terms of placing advertisements in a specific space. This negotiation typically occurs between the advertiser or their representative and the media owner or publisher who sells the advertising space. The negotiation of advertising space rates is an essential aspect of the advertisement industry, as it allows both parties to establish a fair and mutually beneficial agreement. The rates for advertising space can vary significantly depending on factors such as the publication or media platform's popularity, target audience, circulation or viewership, and the location and size of the ad space. During the negotiation, the advertiser aims to secure the best possible rate, considering their budget, marketing objectives, and the value they perceive in the advertising opportunity. They may negotiate for discounts, bonuses, or favorable terms that can enhance the effectiveness of the advertising campaign. The media owner, on the other hand, seeks to maximize their revenue by setting rates that reflect the value of their media space and the potential reach and impact it can provide to the advertiser. The negotiation process often involves a series of discussions, presentations, and counteroffers between the advertiser and the media owner. It may involve analyzing and comparing rates offered by different media outlets, negotiating volume discounts for multiple advertisements, or exploring special promotions and packages. The negotiation may also delve into details such as ad placement, timing, duration, and any additional services or features included in the advertising agreement. Successful negotiations result in an agreement that satisfies both parties, where the advertiser secures desirable advertising space at a reasonable cost, and the media owner obtains fair compensation for their advertising inventory. The finalized agreement may be documented in a contract or a formal agreement that outlines the agreed-upon rates, terms, and conditions.

Advertising Space Rates

Advertising space rates refer to the cost that advertisers must pay to place their advertisements in various media outlets, such as newspapers, magazines, television, radio, websites, and social media platforms. These rates are determined based on several factors, including the type of media, the size and placement of the advertisement, the target audience, the duration of the campaign, and the popularity and reach of the media outlet.

Advertising Space

Advertising space refers to the area or time slot provided by a media platform for the purpose of displaying or broadcasting advertisements. It is a designated section or slot within a medium where advertisements can be placed, targeting a specific audience for promotional purposes. This space can be available in various forms, such as print media (newspapers, magazines), electronic media (television, radio), outdoor advertising (billboards, posters), and online platforms (websites, social media). It provides businesses and organizations with an opportunity to showcase their products, services, or messages to a wide range of potential customers.

Advertising Spending

Advertising Standards Compliance

Advertising Standards Compliance refers to the practice of ensuring that advertisements meet legal, ethical, and industry standards set by regulatory bodies. It involves ensuring that advertisements are truthful, not misleading, and do not contain offensive or deceptive content. The purpose of advertising standards compliance is to protect consumers from false or harmful claims made by advertisers and to maintain the integrity of the advertising industry. Advertisements, whether they are displayed on TV, print media, or online platforms, are required to comply with these standards to promote fair competition and to safeguard the interests of the general public.

Advertising Standards

Advertising standards refer to a set of guidelines and regulations that govern the creation, content, and delivery of advertising messages. These standards are put in place to ensure that advertisements are accurate, truthful, and not misleading to the consumer. The primary goal of advertising standards is to protect consumers from dishonest or deceptive advertising practices. They promote fair competition in the marketplace, ensure ethical behavior among advertisers, and maintain trust between businesses and consumers.

Advertising Strategy Consulting Services

Advertising Strategy Consulting Services refers to the professional support and guidance provided by experts in the field of advertising to assist businesses with developing effective advertising strategies. These services aim to help companies create and execute advertising campaigns that are aligned with their objectives, target audience, and budget. Advertising strategy consultants work closely with businesses to understand their unique needs, challenges, and goals. They conduct comprehensive research, analyze market trends, and evaluate competitors to identify opportunities and potential risks. Based on this information, they develop strategic plans that outline the best approach for promoting a company's products or services.

Advertising Strategy Consulting

Advertising strategy consulting refers to the practice of providing expert advice and guidance to businesses in developing, implementing, and improving their advertising strategies. This type of consulting involves analyzing a company's advertising goals, target audience, competition, and market trends to create a strategic plan that effectively promotes its products or services. The primary objective of advertising strategy consulting is to help businesses optimize their advertising efforts and achieve their marketing objectives. Consultants in this field work closely with clients to understand their business objectives and identify the most effective advertising channels and messaging to reach their target audience. They provide valuable insights on how to best allocate advertising budgets, create compelling advertising campaigns, and track and measure the success of these efforts. Advertising strategy consultants are experts in the field of advertising and marketing. They stay up-to-date with the latest industry trends, technological advancements, and consumer behavior patterns to develop innovative and efficient advertising strategies. These consultants have a deep understanding of various advertising platforms, such as print, television, radio, digital, and social media, and can recommend the most suitable channels based on the client's target audience and budgetary constraints. Through advertising strategy consulting, businesses can gain a competitive edge by effectively positioning their products or services in the market. Consultants help businesses differentiate themselves from their competitors and create memorable advertising campaigns that resonate with the target audience. They assist in developing creative concepts, designing visual elements, and crafting persuasive messaging to captivate consumers and drive them towards the desired action. Furthermore, advertising strategy consulting is an ongoing process that involves constant evaluation and adjustment. Consultants regularly monitor the performance of advertising campaigns and provide recommendations for improvement based on the data and insights gathered. They conduct market research, analyze consumer behavior, and keep a close eye on competitors to ensure that the client's advertising strategy remains relevant and effective. In conclusion, advertising strategy consulting is a specialized service that helps businesses develop and optimize their advertising strategies to effectively reach their target audience and achieve their marketing objectives. This type of consulting involves deep expertise in advertising and marketing, as well as a thorough understanding of the client's business goals and the competitive landscape.

Advertising Strategy Development

Advertising Strategy Development refers to the process of planning and implementing a series of strategic activities to promote a product, service, or brand to a target audience in order to achieve specific marketing objectives. An advertising strategy is a comprehensive plan that outlines the overall approach, goals, and tactics to be employed in advertising campaigns. It involves analyzing the target market, defining the messaging and positioning, selecting the appropriate advertising channels, setting a budget, and measuring the effectiveness of the campaigns. The first step in advertising strategy development is conducting market research to understand the target audience and their preferences, needs, and behaviors. This research helps in identifying the target market segments and developing buyer personas to tailor the advertising messages and creative content to resonate with the audience. Once the target audience is defined, the next step is to determine the advertising goals and objectives. These objectives can range from increasing brand awareness, driving sales, generating leads, promoting a new product, or establishing thought leadership. The goals should be specific, measurable, attainable, relevant, and time-bound (SMART). After setting the goals, the next stage involves developing the messaging and positioning of the advertising campaigns. This includes creating a unique selling proposition (USP) that differentiates the product or service from competitors and appeals to the target audience's needs and desires. The messaging should be clear, concise, and compelling to grab the audience's attention and evoke the desired response. Selecting the appropriate advertising channels is another critical aspect of advertising strategy development. This involves choosing the platforms, media, and formats that will effectively reach the target audience. The channels can include traditional advertising mediums such as television, radio, print, outdoor, as well as digital platforms such as social media, search engines, websites, and mobile apps. Determining the budget is an essential step in advertising strategy development. The budget should be allocated based on the advertising goals, target audience, and selected channels. It should take into account the costs of creative development, media buying, production, and measurement. The final step in advertising strategy development is measuring the effectiveness of the campaigns. This involves tracking key performance indicators (KPIs) such as reach, engagement, conversion rates, and return on investment (ROI). The data collected helps in evaluating the success of the campaigns and making informed decisions for future advertising activities. In summary, advertising strategy development is a systematic process of planning and executing advertising campaigns to achieve marketing objectives. It involves understanding the target audience, setting goals, creating compelling messaging, selecting appropriate channels, setting a budget, and measuring the results of the campaigns.

Advertising Strategy

Advertising strategy refers to the overall approach and plan that a company or organization develops to promote its products or services to its target audience. It involves determining the most effective and efficient methods to reach potential customers and persuade them to take a desired action, such as making a purchase or visiting a website. Advertising strategies typically begin with a thorough analysis of the target market, including demographic and psychographic characteristics, as well as their preferences, needs, and behaviors. This information helps companies identify the most relevant and compelling messages that will resonate with their audience. The next step in developing an advertising strategy is setting clear objectives and goals. These objectives should be specific, measurable, achievable, relevant, and time-bound (SMART). For example, an objective might be to increase brand awareness by 30% within the next six months. Once the objectives are established, companies can determine the most appropriate advertising channels and media to reach their target audience. This can include traditional channels such as television, radio, print, and outdoor advertising, as well as digital channels such as social media, search engine marketing, display advertising, and email marketing. The messaging and creative elements of an advertising campaign are also crucial components of the strategy. Companies must develop compelling and persuasive messages that differentiate their products or services from competitors. Creative elements, such as images, videos, and slogans, are used to grab attention and communicate the key selling points. Measurement and analysis are essential parts of any advertising strategy. Companies must track and evaluate the effectiveness of their campaigns to make informed decisions about future investments. Key performance indicators (KPIs), such as reach, frequency, click-through rates, conversion rates, and return on investment (ROI), are used to assess the success of the advertising efforts.

Advertising Tactics Execution

An advertising tactics execution refers to the implementation and deployment of various strategies, methods, and activities aimed at promoting a product, service, or brand to a target audience. It involves the practical implementation of the advertising plan and the execution of specific tactics to reach and engage with potential customers. During the execution phase, advertising professionals work on translating the overall advertising strategy into actionable tactics. This involves developing and implementing various forms of promotional activities such as television or radio advertisements, print media placements, digital marketing campaigns, social media promotions, and other communication channels to deliver the intended advertising messages. The execution of advertising tactics requires careful planning and coordination to ensure that the chosen tactics align with the overall marketing objectives and target audience. It often involves collaboration with various stakeholders, such as creative teams, media planners, copywriters, graphic designers, and digital marketers, to ensure a cohesive and impactful advertising campaign. Effective execution of advertising tactics involves a thorough understanding of the target audience and their preferences, as well as the identification of relevant communication channels to reach them. This may include leveraging data and insights to determine the most effective platforms, timing, and messaging for the advertising campaign. Furthermore, evaluation and analysis of the executed advertising tactics are crucial to measure the effectiveness of the campaign and make informed decisions for future iterations. This may involve tracking key performance indicators, such as reach, engagement, conversion rates, and return on investment, to assess the success and impact of the advertising efforts. In conclusion, advertising tactics execution encompasses the overall process of implementing and deploying various strategies, activities, and campaigns to promote a product, service, or brand. It involves the practical implementation of advertising plans, the coordination of various stakeholders, and the evaluation of campaign effectiveness to drive desired outcomes.

Advertising Tactics

Advertising tactics refer to the strategic techniques and methods used by businesses and marketers to promote their products or services to their target audience. These tactics are designed to capture the attention of potential customers and persuade them to take action, such as making a purchase or visiting a website. There are various advertising tactics that businesses can employ to effectively reach their target market. One common tactic is the use of persuasive language and compelling messaging to create a sense of urgency or desire in the minds of consumers. This can be achieved through persuasive words, catchy slogans, and compelling storytelling. Another common advertising tactic is the use of visual elements to capture attention. This includes the use of eye-catching images, vibrant colors, and visually appealing designs. Visual elements can be used to convey the benefits or unique features of a product, as well as to create a memorable brand identity. Additionally, many businesses use promotional offers and discounts as advertising tactics to incentivize consumers to make a purchase. These can include limited-time offers, exclusive discounts for new customers, or bundled packages that provide added value. Furthermore, advertising tactics often involve targeting specific audiences through various channels and mediums. This can include traditional advertising channels such as television, radio, and print media, as well as digital platforms such as social media, search engine marketing, and email marketing. By targeting specific demographics, interests, or behaviors, businesses can maximize the effectiveness of their advertising efforts. In conclusion, advertising tactics are the strategic techniques and methods used by businesses to promote their products or services. These tactics involve the use of persuasive language, visual elements, promotional offers, and targeting specific audiences through various channels and mediums. By employing effective advertising tactics, businesses can increase brand awareness, generate leads, and ultimately drive sales.

Advertising Target Audience Profiling

Advertising Target Audience Profiling refers to the process of identifying and analyzing the characteristics, preferences, behaviors, and needs of a specific group of individuals who are most likely to be interested in the advertised product or service. In the context of advertising, target audience profiling plays a crucial role in ensuring that marketing efforts are directed towards the right group of people, increasing the chances of successful customer conversion and brand loyalty. By understanding the demographics, psychographics, and purchasing habits of the target audience, advertisers can create tailored messages and campaigns that resonate with their desired consumers.

Advertising Target Audience

An advertising target audience refers to the specific group of individuals or demographic that an advertisement is intended to reach. It is the segment of the population that the ad is designed to appeal to and influence. The target audience is determined based on various factors such as age, gender, income, location, interests, and behaviors. Advertisers focus on identifying and understanding their target audience in order to create effective and engaging campaigns that resonate with them.

Advertising Techniques Testing

Advertising techniques testing refers to the process of evaluating and analyzing various promotional strategies and methods used in advertisements to gauge their effectiveness and impact on the target audience. It involves conducting research and experiments to determine which techniques are most successful in capturing attention, building brand awareness, and influencing consumer behavior. The primary objective of advertising techniques testing is to assess the efficiency of different advertising approaches and measure their ability to achieve desired goals. This testing process helps advertisers and marketers identify which techniques yield the highest return on investment (ROI) and generate the greatest response from the intended audience.

Advertising Techniques

Advertising techniques refer to the various methods and strategies used by advertisers to engage and persuade consumers to buy their products or services. These techniques aim to create a favorable and lasting impression of the brand in the minds of the target audience, ultimately stimulating demand and increasing sales. One popular advertising technique is emotional appeal, which taps into consumers' emotions to create a connection with the product or brand. Advertisers often depict heartwarming or inspiring stories that evoke feelings of joy, nostalgia, or empathy in the audience. By associating these emotions with their products, advertisers hope to build positive associations and increase the likelihood of purchase. Another common technique is persuasive language, which involves the use of strong and compelling words to convince consumers of the product's benefits. Advertisers carefully choose language that emphasizes the value, quality, and superiority of their offerings. They may employ superlatives, such as "the best," "the most effective," or "the ultimate," to convey a sense of exclusivity, desirability, and superiority. Testimonials and endorsements are also frequently used techniques, leveraging the credibility and influence of well-known individuals or satisfied customers. By featuring these individuals in their advertisements, businesses aim to gain trust and credibility, as consumers may be more likely to trust the opinions and experiences of others like themselves or respected figures. Scarcity and urgency are techniques that play on consumers' fear of missing out. Advertisers emphasize limited availability, time-limited promotions, or exclusive offers to create a sense of urgency and persuade consumers to take immediate action. This technique aims to capitalize on consumers' desire to possess something before it's too late. Visual appeal is another key technique, particularly in print and digital advertising. Advertisers use eye-catching visuals, colors, and designs to create attractive and visually appealing advertisements that capture consumers' attention. Visual elements can evoke emotions, convey product benefits, and reinforce brand identity. In summary, advertising techniques encompass a wide range of strategies used by advertisers to persuade and engage consumers. Emotional appeal, persuasive language, testimonials, scarcity and urgency, and visual appeal are just a few examples of these techniques. By understanding and utilizing these techniques effectively, advertisers can create impactful and successful advertising campaigns that resonate with their target audience and drive business growth.

Advertising Time

Advertising is a form of communication intended to persuade and inform an audience about a product, service, or idea. It is a marketing strategy that aims to increase brand awareness, drive sales, and create a favorable perception of the advertised entity. Advertisements are typically paid messages delivered through various media channels, such as television, radio, print publications, digital platforms, and outdoor signage. The content of an advertisement is carefully crafted to capture attention, generate interest, and ultimately influence consumer behavior.

Advertising Tracking Software Selection

Advertising tracking software refers to a tool or program used to monitor, analyze, and track the effectiveness and performance of advertising campaigns. It is an essential component of the advertising process, as it provides insights and data that help advertisers make informed decisions and optimize their marketing efforts. The primary purpose of advertising tracking software is to measure and evaluate the impact of advertisements on target audiences. It tracks various metrics and key performance indicators (KPIs) such as impressions, clicks, conversions, cost per acquisition (CPA), return on investment (ROI), and customer engagement. By monitoring these metrics, advertisers can assess the effectiveness of their ad campaigns and determine areas for improvement.

Advertising Tracking Software

Advertising tracking software refers to a tool or program used by advertisers to monitor and analyze the performance of their advertising campaigns. It allows advertisers to track and measure key metrics such as impressions, clicks, conversions, and return on investment (ROI). This software typically works by placing a tracking pixel or code on advertisements, landing pages, or websites. When a user interacts with an ad, the tracking pixel is triggered, collecting data about the user's actions and behavior. This data is then used to generate reports and insights that inform the optimization and targeting of future ad campaigns.

Advertising Trends Analysis

Advertising trends analysis refers to the process of examining and evaluating the current and emerging patterns, strategies, and techniques used in advertising campaigns. It involves studying the various elements of advertising, such as mediums, messaging, targeting, and delivery methods, to identify the changes and developments occurring in the industry. By analyzing advertising trends, businesses can gain insights into consumer behavior, market dynamics, and competition, which can help them make informed decisions about their own advertising efforts. It allows companies to stay updated with the latest advancements and adapt their strategies accordingly, ensuring maximum reach and impact on their target audience.

Advertising Trends

Advertising trends refer to the patterns and shifts in the strategies, tactics, and techniques used in advertising to communicate and promote products, services, or ideas to consumers. These trends are influenced by various factors such as changes in technology, consumer behavior, market dynamics, and cultural shifts. One of the prominent advertising trends is the growth of digital advertising. With the increasing prominence of internet-connected devices and platforms, advertisers are allocating a significant portion of their advertising budgets towards online channels. This includes display ads, social media advertising, search engine marketing, and video advertising. Digital advertising offers greater targeting capabilities, real-time data tracking, and the ability to personalize content, providing advertisers with more effective and efficient ways to reach their target audience. Social media advertising is another advertising trend that has gained significant traction in recent years. Platforms like Facebook, Instagram, Twitter, and LinkedIn have become popular channels for advertisers to engage with consumers. With the ability to target specific demographics, interests, and behaviors, social media advertising allows advertisers to deliver personalized messages to their intended audience, increasing the likelihood of engagement and conversions. Native advertising is also an emerging trend in the advertising industry. It involves creating content that seamlessly blends with the platform or medium it appears on, providing users with a non-disruptive and more engaging advertising experience. Native ads can take the form of sponsored articles, videos, or social media posts that match the look and feel of the platform they are placed on, making them less intrusive and more likely to be consumed by users.Additionally, influencer marketing has become a popular strategy in the advertising landscape. Brands collaborate with influential individuals, such as celebrities, bloggers, or social media personalities, to promote their products or services. By leveraging the influencer's followers and credibility, advertisers can effectively reach their target audience and generate brand awareness or drive sales.

Advertising Vehicle

An advertising vehicle refers to a specific medium or platform that is used to convey promotional messages or advertisements to the target audience. It serves as a channel through which businesses or organizations can communicate their marketing messages, raise brand awareness, and promote their products or services. The main purpose of an advertising vehicle is to reach the largest possible number of potential customers or consumers in order to generate interest, drive sales, or achieve other marketing objectives. Various advertising vehicles are available, each with its own unique characteristics, advantages, and limitations.

Advertising Volume

Advertising volume refers to the amount or quantity of advertisements being produced and disseminated within a specific period of time or across a particular platform or medium. It is a measurement of the scale or extent of advertising activities. The advertising volume can be measured in different ways, depending on the specific context and objectives. It can be quantified by the number of ad units or impressions, the total duration of advertisement content, or the overall advertising expenditure. For instance, in digital advertising, the volume can be expressed in terms of impressions, clicks, or conversions, while in traditional media, it can be measured by the number of pages, minutes, or spots allocated for advertisements. The advertising volume is a key metric that reflects the saturation level of advertising within a given market or industry. It provides insights into the intensity and competitiveness of advertising campaigns, as well as the overall investment and strategic focus of advertisers. A high advertising volume may indicate a thriving industry with intense competition, while a low advertising volume may suggest a lack of promotional activities or market opportunities. Monitoring and analyzing advertising volume can be crucial for various stakeholders, including advertisers, marketers, media agencies, and publishers. It helps them understand the market dynamics, identify trends, and make informed decisions regarding their advertising strategies. By comparing the advertising volume among different competitors or time periods, companies can assess their market share, evaluate the effectiveness of their advertising efforts, and optimize their resource allocation. Furthermore, the advertising volume can also impact the audience's perception and response to advertising messages. When the volume of advertisements becomes excessive or overwhelming, it may lead to ad fatigue and desensitization among viewers, causing a decline in attention or engagement. Therefore, advertisers need to strike a balance between maximizing the advertising volume and maintaining the quality, relevance, and impact of their advertisements.

Advertorial

An advertorial is a form of advertisement that is designed to resemble editorial content or news articles. It is a combination of the words "advertisement" and "editorial," and it is intended to deliver a promotional message in a more subtle and engaging way. The purpose of an advertorial is to capture the attention of the audience and persuade them to take a desired action, such as purchasing a product, signing up for a service, or visiting a website. Unlike traditional advertisements, advertorials are often longer in length and provide more detailed information about the product or service being promoted. They may also include personal stories, testimonials, or case studies to establish credibility and build trust with the audience.

Adware Prevention Solutions

Adware prevention solutions refer to measures and strategies implemented to protect against the infiltration and spread of adware, a form of malicious software designed to display unwanted advertisements on users' devices. These solutions aim to detect, block, and remove adware to ensure a safe and uninterrupted digital experience for individuals and businesses. Adware, short for advertising-supported software, typically enters users' devices through deceptive practices such as software bundling or disguised downloads. Once installed, it monitors users' online activities, collects information about their browsing habits, and displays intrusive advertisements. These advertisements can appear in various forms, including pop-up windows, banners, and in-text ads, disrupting users' browsing experience, slowing down their devices, and posing potential privacy and security risks. Adware prevention solutions employ a range of techniques to counter the threats posed by adware. One common approach is the use of anti-malware software equipped with adware detection and removal capabilities. These programs scan users' devices, identify known adware patterns, and quarantine or delete any detected malicious code. To keep up with the ever-evolving adware landscape, these solutions also rely on regular updates to their virus databases and detection algorithms. Furthermore, web browsers often incorporate built-in ad blocking functionality or allow users to install ad-blocking extensions. These tools block unwanted ads from being displayed, neutralizing the impact of adware infections. Additionally, browser settings can be adjusted to restrict pop-ups, disable third-party cookies, and block auto-redirects, reducing the likelihood of adware infiltration. Education and user awareness play a vital role in adware prevention. Users should be cautious while downloading and installing software, ensuring that it is from trusted sources. They should also carefully read through software license agreements, avoiding any applications that request excessive or unnecessary permissions. Regularly updating operating systems, software, and browsers, along with the use of strong and unique passwords, can also enhance adware protection. In summary, adware prevention solutions encompass a combination of tools, software, and best practices aimed at safeguarding against adware infections. By utilizing anti-malware software, leveraging ad-blocking features, adjusting browser settings, and practicing safe online habits, users can mitigate the risks associated with adware and enjoy a more secure and uninterrupted browsing experience.

Adware Prevention

Adware prevention refers to the measures taken by individuals and organizations to protect against the intrusion of unwanted and potentially malicious advertising software, commonly known as adware. Adware is a type of software that displays advertisements on a user's device, often without their consent or knowledge. Adware can be installed on a device through various methods, such as downloading and installing free software that comes bundled with adware, clicking on malicious ads or links, or visiting infected websites. Once installed, adware displays advertisements in various forms, including pop-up windows, banners, and in-text ads, often disrupting the user's browsing experience and potentially compromising their privacy and security. To prevent adware, individuals and organizations can take several steps. Firstly, it is important to exercise caution when downloading and installing software from the internet. It is recommended to only download software from trusted sources, preferably from the official website of the software provider. Additionally, carefully read the terms and conditions and the installation screens for any bundled software, as adware often hides within these installation processes. Another important prevention measure is to avoid clicking on suspicious ads or links. By refraining from clicking on ads that appear too good to be true or those that redirect to unfamiliar websites, the risk of adware infection can be significantly reduced. It is also advisable to enable pop-up blockers in web browsers, as these can help prevent unwanted pop-up adware from appearing. Regularly updating operating systems, web browsers, and security software is crucial for adware prevention. Updates often include security patches that address vulnerabilities that adware can exploit. By keeping software up to date, users can benefit from enhanced security measures and reduced risk of adware infection. Lastly, it is recommended to use reputable antivirus and anti-malware software. These programs can detect and remove adware from a device, as well as provide real-time protection against future adware infections. Performing regular scans with such software can help identify and eliminate any adware that may have slipped through other prevention measures.

Adware

Adware refers to a type of software that displays advertisements to users, typically in the form of pop-up windows or banners, while they are browsing the internet or using specific applications on their devices. Unlike other forms of advertising, adware software is often installed on users' devices without their explicit consent or knowledge. Adware is generally designed to generate revenue for its creators by displaying targeted advertisements based on users' browsing habits, online activities, or personal information. This often involves tracking users' behavior and

61

collecting data on their browsing patterns, search queries, and interests. This information is then used to deliver relevant ads with the intention of increasing the likelihood of user engagement or click-through rates. While adware may be seen as an annoyance by many users, it is typically not considered to be malicious software such as viruses or malware. However, adware can sometimes have negative effects on users' devices and browsing experiences. It can slow down system performance, consume network bandwidth, and disrupt the normal functioning of websites or applications. In addition to its impact on user experience, adware raises privacy concerns, as it often tracks and collects sensitive user data without their explicit consent. This data may be shared with third-party advertisers or used for targeted advertising purposes, which can lead to privacy breaches or unwanted exposure to personalized advertisements. The installation of adware often occurs without users' direct consent, often bundled with free software or downloads. It might also be unknowingly installed when visiting certain websites or clicking on suspicious links. Therefore, it is essential for users to be cautious about the sources of software they download and regularly update their antivirus or anti-adware tools to prevent adware infections.

Affiliate Advertising Program Management

Affiliate Advertising Program Management refers to the process of overseeing and managing the various aspects of an affiliate marketing program. It involves the strategic planning, implementation, and optimization of the program to ensure maximum effectiveness and success. An affiliate advertising program is a business model where companies partner with independent affiliates or publishers who promote their products or services in exchange for a commission on each sale or lead generated. The management of such a program involves various activities: 1. Recruitment and selection of affiliates: The program manager identifies potential affiliates who have the right audience, reach, and promotional capabilities to effectively promote the company's products or services. They review applications, conduct interviews, and negotiate terms to onboard the most suitable affiliates. 2. Affiliate onboarding and training: Once selected, affiliates need to be properly onboarded and provided with all the necessary resources and information to promote the company's offerings effectively. The program manager ensures that affiliates understand the program's guidelines, marketing materials, tracking mechanisms, and commission structure. 3. Program monitoring and evaluation: The program manager continuously monitors the performance of affiliates, tracking key metrics such as clicks, conversions, sales, and ROI. They analyze data to identify top-performing affiliates and opportunities for improvement. Regular reporting and feedback sessions are conducted to keep affiliates motivated and aligned with the program objectives. 4. Commission and payment management: The program manager handles commission calculations, ensuring that affiliates are accurately compensated for their promotional efforts. They establish payment terms, track sales attribution, and process payments in a timely manner. Disputes and inquiries related to commissions are addressed promptly. 5. Program optimization and growth: To achieve better results, the program manager continuously optimizes the program by testing different strategies, offers, creative assets, and promotional channels. They explore new affiliate partnerships and negotiate better commission structures. Additionally, the program manager stays updated with industry trends and competitor activities to keep the program competitive. Effective affiliate advertising program management requires a thorough understanding of the company's goals, target audience, products, and industry. It demands strong analytical, communication, and negotiation skills to build and maintain successful relationships with affiliates. By efficiently managing the program, companies can leverage the power of affiliate marketing to increase brand reach, drive sales, and achieve their marketing objectives.

Affiliate Advertising Programs

Affiliate advertising programs refer to a type of online marketing strategy where an affiliate, also known as a publisher or an advertiser, promotes products and services of a business in exchange for earning a commission on every sale or lead generated through their efforts. These programs rely on partnerships between businesses and individuals or other companies to drive traffic and customers to their websites. In an affiliate advertising program, the affiliate typically receives a unique tracking link or code that they can use to promote the products or services of the business. This link or code helps track the performance of the affiliate's marketing efforts and ensures that they are properly rewarded for their work.

Affiliate Advertising

Affiliate advertising is a form of online marketing where a company, referred to as the advertiser, pays a commission to another website, known as the affiliate, for driving traffic, generating leads, or making sales. The affiliate places advertisements or links on their website, promoting the advertiser's products or services. When a visitor clicks on these ads and makes a purchase or completes a desired action, the affiliate earns a percentage of the revenue or a predetermined flat fee. Affiliate advertising relies on a performance-based model, as the affiliate only receives compensation when specific actions are taken by users referred from their website. This makes it a cost-effective and efficient way for advertisers to reach a wider audience and for affiliates to monetize their traffic. The success of affiliate advertising is heavily dependent on building and maintaining mutually beneficial relationships between advertisers and affiliates.

Agency Commission

Agency commission in the context of advertisement refers to the fee or percentage that an advertising agency receives from a media owner for the services provided in the creation, planning, and implementation of an advertising campaign. An advertising agency acts as an intermediary between the client (the advertiser) and various media channels such as television, radio, print, or digital platforms. They help the client to develop an effective advertising strategy, create engaging content, and select the appropriate media channels to reach the target audience. The agency commission is usually negotiated between the agency and the media owner. It is commonly calculated as a percentage of the total media spend or the advertising space purchased on behalf of the client. This commission serves as a source of revenue for the agency and compensates them for their expertise, time, and effort in executing the campaign. The agency commission can vary depending on several factors such as the complexity of the campaign, the size of the media budget, and the bargaining power of the agency. In some cases, the media owner may offer a discounted rate or provide additional incentives to the agency for bringing in a client with a substantial advertising budget. The agency commission is an important aspect of the agency-client relationship as it helps to align the interests of both parties. The client benefits from the agency's industry knowledge, relationships with media owners, and their ability to negotiate favorable rates. On the other hand, the agency is motivated to deliver the best possible results for the client as their commission is directly tied to the success of the campaign. However, it is worth noting that the traditional agency commission model has evolved in recent years due to the changing dynamics of the advertising industry. With the rise of digital advertising, the concept of commission-based compensation has been supplemented by alternative pricing models such as retainer fees, project-based fees, or performance-based fees. In conclusion, agency commission in the context of advertisement refers to the fee or percentage that an advertising agency receives from a media owner for their services in planning, creating, and implementing an advertising campaign. It serves as a source of revenue for the agency and incentivizes them to deliver successful campaigns for their clients.

Agency Fee

An agency fee in the context of advertisement refers to the payment made by a client to an advertising agency for the services it provides. The agency fee is typically a percentage of the total advertising budget or a fixed monthly retainer fee agreed upon between the client and the agency. The agency fee covers various aspects of the advertising process, including strategic planning, creative development, media buying, campaign execution, and performance analysis. It compensates the agency for its expertise, resources, and efforts in delivering effective advertising campaigns that meet the client's objectives.

Agency Of Record (AOR)

An Agency of Record (AOR) is a term commonly used in the advertising industry to refer to a company or agency that is responsible for managing and coordinating all aspects of a client's advertising and marketing campaigns. The AOR acts as the primary point of contact between the client and the various advertising and media agencies involved in the campaign. They are responsible for developing and implementing the client's overall advertising strategy, as well as overseeing the execution of individual advertising projects. In order to fulfill their role, the AOR typically employs a team of professionals with expertise in various areas of advertising and marketing, including account management, creative development, media planning and buying, and digital marketing. This team works closely with the client to understand their objectives, target audience, and brand positioning, and then develops customized advertising solutions to meet these requirements. One of the key responsibilities of the AOR is to manage the client's advertising budget. They work with the client to establish a budget that aligns with their objectives and then allocate the funds across different advertising channels and campaigns. Throughout the campaign, the AOR closely monitors the performance of each advertising initiative and makes adjustments as necessary to optimize results and ROI. Additionally, the AOR is responsible for coordinating the efforts of various advertising agencies and vendors involved in the campaign. They ensure that all materials and deliverables are produced on time and meet the client's quality standards. They also facilitate communication and collaboration among the different agencies to ensure a cohesive and integrated advertising strategy. In summary, an Agency of Record is a company or agency that manages and coordinates all aspects of a client's advertising and marketing campaigns. They are responsible for developing the client's advertising strategy, managing the budget, overseeing the execution of advertising projects, and coordinating the efforts of various agencies and vendors.

Agile Advertising Approaches

Agile advertising approaches refer to a flexible and adaptable methodology used in the development and execution of advertisement campaigns. This approach emphasizes collaboration, iteration, and open communication between all stakeholders involved, such as marketers, advertisers, and clients. Unlike traditional advertising methods that follow a linear and rigid process, agile advertising allows for continuous feedback and adjustment throughout the campaign. It prioritizes delivering valuable and relevant ad content to target audiences by responding quickly to changing market dynamics and consumer preferences.

Agile Advertising Campaigns Execution

Agile advertising campaigns execution refers to the practice of implementing advertising strategies and initiatives in a flexible and adaptive manner, allowing for quick response and adjustment based on real-time data and customer feedback. This approach embraces the principles of the agile methodology, which emphasizes collaboration, iterative development, and continuous improvement. Unlike traditional advertising campaigns that are carefully planned and executed over a fixed period of time, agile advertising campaigns are characterized by their ability to adapt and respond to changing market conditions and customer preferences. This flexibility enables advertisers to make timely adjustments to their messaging, targeting, and creative execution to optimize campaign performance.

Agile Advertising Campaigns

Agile advertising campaigns refer to a dynamic and flexible approach to planning, executing, and evaluating advertising strategies and tactics. This methodology is inspired by agile software development principles and emphasizes adaptability, collaboration, and continuous improvement. Unlike traditional waterfall campaign management, which follows a linear and sequential process, agile advertising campaigns are iterative and responsive to rapidly changing market dynamics. The core principles of agile advertising campaigns include: 1. Flexibility: Agile campaigns are designed to quickly adapt to changes in consumer behavior, market trends, and competition. This allows advertisers to pivot their strategies based on real-time data and insights, enabling them to stay relevant and effective in reaching their target audience. 2. Collaboration: Agile campaigns foster close collaboration between different stakeholders, such as advertisers, creative teams, media buyers, and data analysts. Regular and open communication ensures that all team members are aligned on goals, objectives, and strategies, leading to more cohesive and impactful campaigns. 3. Iterative Planning: Rather than following a fixed schedule or rigid plan, agile campaigns embrace an iterative planning process. This involves breaking down the campaign into smaller, manageable tasks or experiments, setting short-term goals, and constantly evaluating and adjusting strategies based on performance data. 4. Constant Learning: With the help of data analytics and feedback mechanisms, agile campaigns prioritize continuous learning and improvement. Advertisers gather insights from campaign results, customer feedback, and market data to inform future planning and optimize campaign performance. By adopting an agile approach, advertisers can maximize their campaign's effectiveness in a fast-paced and ever-changing advertising landscape. They can respond quickly to emerging opportunities or threats, optimize their strategies based on real-time data, and deliver more personalized and relevant messages to their target audience.

Agile Advertising Strategies Frameworks

Agile Advertising Strategies Frameworks refer to a set of methodologies and techniques used in the context of advertisement to plan, develop, and execute advertising campaigns in a dynamic and iterative manner. Derived from the Agile software development approach, these frameworks emphasize flexibility, collaboration, and responsiveness to changing market conditions, consumer behavior, and feedback to drive effective advertising strategies. The Agile Advertising Strategies Frameworks typically involve the following key principles and practices: 1. Iterative Planning: Unlike traditional advertising approaches that follow a linear process, Agile Advertising Strategies Frameworks encourage iterative planning, where campaigns are broken down into smaller, more manageable chunks called sprints. This allows advertisers to stay adaptable and make adjustments as necessary to optimize the campaign's performance. 2. Cross-functional Collaboration: Effective communication and collaboration amongst cross-functional teams, including advertisers, marketers, creatives, and strategists, are essential in Agile Advertising. Regular meetings, such as daily stand-ups, help ensure everyone's alignment and progress towards campaign goals. 3. Continuous Improvement: Continuous improvement is a core aspect of Agile Advertising Strategies Frameworks. This involves analyzing campaign performance data and customer feedback to identify opportunities for optimization and make data-driven decisions for future iterations. 4. Data-Driven Decision Making: The use of data and analytics is integral in Agile Advertising. Advertisers monitor key performance indicators (KPIs) and leverage real-time data to measure campaign success, identify bottlenecks, and make informed decisions to enhance advertising strategies and tactics. 5. Rapid Prototyping: Agile Advertising Strategies Frameworks encourage the rapid prototyping of advertisements. This involves creating and testing multiple variations of ads across different channels and target audiences to determine the most effective approach, which can then be iteratively refined. 6. Flexibility and Adaptability: The ability to be flexible and adapt to changing market trends, consumer preferences, and competitor activities is crucial in Agile Advertising. By continuously monitoring and evaluating campaign performance, advertisers can quickly respond and adjust their strategies accordingly. 7. Emphasis on Customer Feedback: Customer feedback plays a significant role in Agile Advertising. Advertisers actively seek customer input to gain insights into their preferences, behaviors, and needs. This feedback informs campaign iterations and helps advertisers deliver more personalized and targeted advertisements. 8. Agile Campaign Execution: Agile Advertising Strategies Frameworks advocate for a nimble and efficient campaign execution process. Campaign elements, such as creative assets, messaging, targeting strategies, and media placements, can be adjusted and optimized based on real-time insights and customer feedback. Overall, the Agile Advertising Strategies Frameworks provide a collaborative and data-driven approach to advertising, enabling advertisers to quickly adapt to market changes, optimize campaign performance, and drive meaningful results.

Agile Advertising Strategies

Agile advertising strategies refer to a flexible and iterative approach to creating and implementing advertising campaigns. This methodology is based on the agile principles used in software development and project management, which emphasize adaptability, collaboration, and continuous improvement. In the context of advertising, an agile approach involves quickly responding to changing market conditions, consumer preferences, and emerging trends. It prioritizes the delivery of value to customers while also maximizing the return on investment for advertisers. Agile advertising strategies typically involve the following key elements: 1. Collaboration: Agile advertising teams promote cross-functional collaboration, bringing together individuals with diverse expertise, such as marketers, creatives, and data analysts. This collaborative approach facilitates the sharing of ideas, knowledge, and skills, leading to more effective advertising campaigns. 2. Iterative planning and execution: Instead of following a linear and rigid planning process, agile advertising uses iterative cycles. Campaigns are divided into smaller increments, allowing for regular feedback and adjustments. This iterative approach enables advertisers to adapt their strategies based on real-time data and insights. 3. Data-driven decision making: Agile advertising relies heavily on data analysis and insights. Advertisers continuously collect and analyze data to gain a deeper understanding of their target audience, campaign performance, and market trends. This data-driven approach helps inform decision making, enabling advertisers to optimize their strategies for better results. 4. Rapid prototyping and testing: Rather than spending long periods developing an advertising concept, agile advertising encourages rapid prototyping and testing. By creating and testing multiple iterations of ads or campaign elements, advertisers can quickly determine what resonates best with their target audience and make necessary adjustments. Overall, agile advertising strategies enable advertisers to be more responsive, adaptable, and customer-centric. By embracing an iterative and data-driven approach, advertisers can continuously refine their campaigns to better meet the evolving needs and preferences of their audience.

Agile Advertising

Agile advertising refers to a flexible and adaptive approach to creating and launching ad campaigns. It is a marketing strategy that emphasizes quick iterations, frequent client collaboration, and data-driven decision making. In agile advertising, the traditional linear process of creating advertisements is replaced with a more dynamic and iterative workflow. Instead of spending months on extensive planning and development, agile advertising focuses on delivering small, measurable results in short periods of time. The key principles of agile advertising are: 1. Collaboration: Agile advertising encourages frequent and open communication between all stakeholders involved in the advertising process. This includes the advertising team, the client, and other relevant parties. By working closely together, they can quickly adapt to changes, incorporate feedback, and ensure that the final output aligns with the client's goals and expectations. 2. Iterative Approach: Rather than creating an entire ad campaign at once, agile advertising divides the work into smaller, manageable tasks called sprints. Each sprint focuses on delivering a specific component of the campaign, such as a single ad banner or a social media post. This iterative approach allows for continuous improvement and adjustments based on real-time data and feedback. 3. Data-Driven Decision Making: Agile advertising heavily relies on data and analytics to make informed decisions. By continuously monitoring the performance of ads and collecting customer insights, advertising teams can quickly identify what works and what doesn't. This enables them to make data-driven adjustments to optimize campaign performance and maximize return on investment. 4. Adaptability: One of the main advantages of agile advertising is its ability to adapt to changing market conditions and consumer trends. With traditional advertising methods, making significant changes mid-campaign can be costly and time-consuming. However, agile advertising allows for quick pivots and adjustments, ensuring that campaigns stay relevant and effective. In conclusion, agile advertising is a modern marketing strategy that emphasizes collaboration, iteration, data-driven decision making, and adaptability. By embracing this approach, advertisers can create and launch campaigns that are more responsive to client needs, more efficient, and more likely to yield positive results.

Alternate Media

Alternate media refers to various forms of non-traditional advertising channels that are employed by businesses to reach and engage their target audiences. Unlike traditional media such as television, radio, and print, which have been used for decades, alternate media takes advantage of newer technologies and platforms to deliver messages in unique and innovative ways. One common form of alternate media is digital advertising, which includes various online channels such as websites, search engines, social media platforms, and mobile applications. Digital advertising offers businesses the opportunity to target specific demographics, tailor their messages, and track the effectiveness of their campaigns through analytics and data. With the increased usage of the internet and mobile devices, digital advertising has become a crucial component of any comprehensive advertising strategy. In addition to digital advertising, another form of alternate media is experiential marketing. This type of advertising focuses on creating immersive and memorable experiences for consumers. By engaging multiple senses and eliciting emotional responses, businesses aim to establish a deeper connection with their target audience. Examples of experiential marketing include pop-up stores, interactive installations, and branded events. Furthermore, out-of-home advertising is another category of alternate media that encompasses various formats such as billboards, transit ads, and street furniture. Out-of-home advertising allows businesses to reach consumers when they are outside of their homes and typically targets high-traffic areas. With advancements in technology, out-of-home

66

advertising has also evolved to include dynamic digital signage and interactive displays. In recent years, influencer marketing has emerged as a popular form of alternate media. This type of advertising involves collaborating with individuals who have a large following and influence over a specific target audience. Through sponsored content, product placements, and endorsements, businesses can leverage the credibility and reach of influencers to promote their products or services. Overall, alternate media provides businesses with a diverse range of options to advertise and communicate with their target audiences. By utilizing digital channels, creating experiential marketing campaigns, leveraging out-of-home advertising, and collaborating with influencers, businesses can enhance brand awareness, engage consumers, and drive sales in today's competitive advertising landscape.

Ambient Advertising Campaigns Execution

Ambient advertising campaigns execution refers to the implementation and implementation of advertising strategies that aim to create a non-traditional and unconventional brand presence in the everyday environment of consumers. These campaigns take advantage of ambient media, which includes various physical elements and spaces, such as billboards, buildings, sidewalks, public transportation, and even natural surroundings, to communicate messages to the target audience. Ambient advertising campaigns often involve using creative and captivating visual designs, installations, or experiential activations to catch people's attention and engage them in an interactive and memorable way. Instead of relying solely on traditional media channels, such as print, television, or online ads, ambient advertising campaigns leverage the immediate surroundings and contexts of individuals to convey brand messages and create brand associations.

Ambient Advertising Campaigns

Ambient advertising campaigns are a form of advertisement that seeks to engage with the target audience by creating an immersive and unexpected experience within their everyday environment. Unlike traditional forms of advertising, ambient campaigns do not rely on traditional media channels such as television, radio, or print. Instead, they use unconventional spaces and objects to captivate the audience's attention and deliver the brand's message. One of the key features of ambient advertising campaigns is their ability to seamlessly blend into the environment in which they are placed. By doing so, they can surprise and delight the audience, creating a memorable experience that not only grabs their attention but also leaves a lasting impression. These campaigns often leverage the element of surprise to create a strong emotional response, making them highly effective in generating brand recall and word-of-mouth publicity.

Ambient Advertising Tactics Evaluation

Ambient advertising is a strategic approach in the field of advertising that aims to create brand awareness and promote products or services through unconventional and unconventional means. This advertising tactic involves integrating advertisements within a person's environment, making use of ambient elements and spaces that are part of their everyday routines. The goal is to capture their attention in a subtle and non-intrusive way, so they become aware of the brand or message without feeling overwhelmed or disrupted. Ambient advertising takes advantage of various physical, social, and cultural elements to engage with the target audience. It can utilize public spaces such as walls, floors, buildings, and vehicles, as well as objects and everyday items that are commonly found in people's surroundings. By creatively incorporating the advertisements into these elements, the brand can seamlessly become part of the consumer's environment. Some common tactics used in ambient advertising include guerilla marketing, 3D street art, projections, interactive installations, and ambient media. Guerilla marketing involves executing unconventional and imaginative campaigns that generate buzz and surprise the target audience. 3D street art uses optical illusions to create visually striking images on pavements or walls, capturing the attention of passersby. Projections can be used to display dynamic and captivating visuals on the surfaces of buildings or other structures. Interactive installations allow people to physically engage with the advertisement, creating a memorable and interactive experience. Ambient media encompasses various methods such as scented posters, cling wrap advertising, or even branded items placed in unexpected locations. Overall, ambient advertising aims to create an immersive and memorable experience for the target audience, providing a unique and unconventional way of promoting products or services. By incorporating advertisements into people's everyday environments, this tactic seeks to achieve effective brand awareness and recall while avoiding the traditional methods of advertising that may be perceived as intrusive or disruptive.

Ambient Advertising Tactics

Ambient advertising tactics refer to a set of strategic and creative techniques used in advertising to integrate promotional messages seamlessly into the environment or context in which they are placed. This approach aims to capture the attention and engage the target audience in a non-intrusive and unobtrusive manner. In ambient advertising, various unconventional and out-of-home mediums are utilized to communicate the brand message effectively. These could include public spaces, transportation facilities, streets, parks, elevators, washrooms, and even personal belongings. The goal is to create a unique and memorable experience that resonates with the audience and leaves a lasting impression.

Ambient Advertising

Ambient advertising refers to a form of advertisement that aims to create a lasting impact on the target audience by promoting a brand or message in a non-traditional and unexpected manner. It involves integrating advertisements into the environment where the target audience is likely to be present, such as public places, transportation vehicles, or even virtual spaces. This type of advertising relies on the element of surprise and uses creative techniques to engage and captivate the audience. The advertisements are designed to blend seamlessly with the surroundings, making them harder to ignore and more likely to leave a lasting impression.

Area Of Dominant Influence (ADI)

The Area of Dominant Influence (ADI) in the context of advertisement refers to the geographic region in which a particular media outlet, such as a television station or radio station, has the highest concentration of viewers or listeners. It is a market research term used to define the reach and impact of media in a specific area. The ADI is determined by collecting data on viewer or listener habits through surveys or other research methods. This data is then analyzed to identify the primary and secondary markets of the media outlet, taking into account factors such as population size, media consumption patterns, and competition from other media. The aim is to understand where the media outlet has the greatest potential to reach and influence its target audience.

Artwork

Artwork in the context of advertisement refers to any visual or graphic representation created to promote a product, service, or brand. It is a form of creative expression that visually communicates messages or information to a target audience.Artwork in advertisements can take various forms, including illustrations, photographs, paintings, graphics, or a combination of these elements. The purpose of including artwork in advertisements is to attract attention, evoke emotions, and convey the desired message or concept.Artwork in advertisements plays a crucial role in capturing the audience's attention and creating a memorable impression. It helps to differentiate the advertisement from competitors and establish a unique brand identity. By using compelling visuals, advertisers can communicate complex ideas or concepts in a concise and visually appealing way.Artwork selection for advertisements requires careful consideration of the target audience, brand image, and campaign objectives. The chosen artwork should align with the brand's values and evoke the desired emotions or associations. The style, colors, and composition of the artwork should resonate with the target audience and effectively convey the intended message.In addition to aesthetics, artwork in advertisements should also be functional and practical. It should be easily comprehensible, legible, and visually pleasing. The placement of artwork within the advertisement should consider factors such as eye-catching positions, hierarchy of information, and overall layout design.Advancements in digital technology have expanded the possibilities for artwork creation in advertisements. Computer-generated imagery (CGI), animation, and interactive elements are commonly used to create engaging and immersive visual experiences. These techniques allow for greater customization, interactivity, and personalization of artwork in advertisements.In conclusion, artwork in the context of

68

advertisement refers to the visual or graphic representation created to promote a product, service, or brand. It is a vital component that captures attention, conveys messages, and helps create a memorable impression. The chosen artwork should align with the target audience, brand image, and campaign objectives while being visually appealing and practical.1. Artwork in the context of advertisement. 2 . A form of creative expression that visually communicates messages or information. 3 . Various forms, including illustrations, photographs, paintings, graphics, or a combination. 4. Function: attracting attention, evoking emotions, and conveying desired messages or concepts. 5. Differentiates advertisement, establishes brand identity, and communicates complex ideas. 6 . Considerations: target audience, brand identity, campaign objectives. 7 . Importance of aesthetics, functionality, comprehensibility, and legibility. 8. Advancements in digital technology allow for greater customization and interactivity.

Attraction

Attraction in the context of advertisement refers to the ability of an advertisement to capture the attention and interest of the target audience. It is the quality that compels individuals to engage with the advertisement, explore the product or service being promoted, and ultimately take action. An attractive advertisement has the power to stand out from the clutter of other promotions and create a memorable impression on the audience. It involves various elements such as visuals, design, copy, and message that work together harmoniously to draw the viewer's attention and evoke a positive response. Visual appeal plays a crucial role in attraction. A visually appealing advertisement utilizes eye-catching colors, shapes, and imagery that immediately catch the audience's eye. The use of striking visuals not only piques curiosity but also creates a sense of desire or aspiration within the viewer. In addition to visuals, the design of an advertisement also contributes to its attraction. Clean and balanced layouts with clear hierarchy help guide the viewer's eye and ensure the message is communicated effectively. The use of whitespace and proper typography further enhances the advertisement's overall appeal. Another factor that contributes to attraction is the copy or text used in the advertisement. Well-crafted headlines and compelling ad copy can pique the viewer's interest and persuade them to explore further. The language used should be simple, concise, and resonate with the target audience, effectively communicating the benefits or unique selling points of the product or service. Moreover, the message conveyed by the advertisement should be relevant and relatable to the audience. It should address their needs, desires, or pain points, offering a solution or fulfilling a specific want. A strong and relevant message helps create an emotional connection, which can lead to increased attraction towards the advertisement. Lastly, the placement and timing of the advertisement are crucial in attracting the target audience. Placing the advertisement where the target audience is most likely to see it, such as popular websites, social media platforms, or specific print publications, increases the chances of attracting their attention. Additionally, timing the advertisement to coincide with relevant events or trends can also enhance its attraction by making it more contextually relevant.

Audience Accumulation

Audience accumulation refers to the process of gradually building a group of individuals who are exposed to a specific advertisement or marketing campaign over time. This concept is essential in advertising as it allows businesses to expand their reach and increase the likelihood of achieving their marketing objectives. Creating an effective audience accumulation strategy involves identifying the target audience and implementing various tactics to attract and retain their attention. One of the primary goals of audience accumulation is to generate awareness and interest in the advertised product or service, ultimately leading to higher conversion rates and increased sales.

Audience Analysis

Audience analysis in the context of advertisement refers to the systematic process of gathering and interpreting information about the target audience for a specific advertisement campaign. During audience analysis, advertisers aim to understand the characteristics, needs, preferences, and behaviors of their target audience in order to create effective and impactful advertisements. This analysis helps them tailor their messaging, design, and delivery channels to appeal to the intended audience and achieve their communication objectives.

Audience Composition

Audience composition, in the context of advertising, refers to the demographic and psychographic characteristics of a specific group of individuals who are targeted by an advertisement or marketing campaign. It involves a detailed analysis and understanding of the audience's age, gender, income level, education, lifestyle, interests, values, and attitudes. By examining the audience composition, advertisers gain insights into their target market and can tailor their messages and strategies accordingly. This segmentation helps to ensure that the advertisement reaches the right people, with the right message, at the right time.

Audience Duplication

Audience duplication in the context of advertisement refers to the occurrence when the same individual or group of individuals is exposed to the same marketing message multiple times through different channels or touchpoints. Effective advertising campaigns aim to reach a wide and diverse audience to maximize their brand exposure and potential customer base. However, it is counterproductive and inefficient to repeatedly target the exact same individuals with the same marketing message. This is where audience duplication becomes a concern.

Audience Flow

Audience flow refers to the movement of viewers or users through different stages or steps within an advertisement or marketing campaign. It describes how individuals interact with a particular advertisement and the journey they take from initial exposure to desired action or conversion. The concept of audience flow is crucial in analyzing the effectiveness of an advertisement and identifying any potential bottlenecks or barriers that hinder the desired flow of users. By understanding the patterns and behaviors of the audience, marketers can optimize their campaigns to improve engagement, increase conversions, and achieve desired objectives.

Audience Fragmentation

Audience fragmentation refers to the phenomenon in advertising where the target audience becomes divided into smaller, more specialized groups. This division occurs as a result of various factors such as the proliferation of media channels, technological advancements, and changes in consumer behavior. In the past, advertisers had a relatively straightforward task of reaching a broad, homogeneous audience through a few traditional media channels such as television, radio, and print. However, with the advent of the internet and the subsequent rise of social media, streaming platforms, and other digital channels, people now have a plethora of choices when it comes to consuming content. Consequently, their attention is divided among multiple platforms and their interests and preferences become more specialized. This fragmentation presents both opportunities and challenges for advertisers. On the positive side, it allows them to target specific audience segments with precision, tailoring their messages to suit individual preferences and behaviors. This enhances the chances of capturing the attention of a particular group and increasing the effectiveness of the advertising campaign. Advertisers can leverage data and analytics to identify the fragmented segments within their target audience and design personalized advertisements that resonate with these subgroups. However, audience fragmentation also poses challenges for advertisers. With a fragmented audience, it becomes increasingly difficult to achieve mass reach and engage a wide range of consumers simultaneously. Advertisers must allocate their budgets across multiple channels and platforms to ensure optimal coverage, which can be a complex and resource-intensive task. Furthermore, the fragmented nature of the audience requires a deeper understanding of each subgroup's characteristics, interests, and media consumption habits. In conclusion, audience fragmentation refers to the division of a target audience into smaller, more specialized groups due to various factors such as media proliferation and changing consumer behavior. While it presents opportunities for advertisers to deliver personalized messages and increase campaign effectiveness, it also poses challenges in terms of achieving mass reach and engaging a diverse audience.

Audience Measurement

Audience measurement in the context of advertisement refers to the process of assessing and quantifying the number and characteristics of individuals or households exposed to advertising messages. It aims to provide advertisers, agencies, and media companies with a better understanding of their target audience and the effectiveness of their advertising campaigns. By measuring the audience, advertisers can evaluate the reach and frequency of their advertisements, determine the demographics and behaviors of the people exposed to their messages, and assess the impact and ROI of their campaigns. This information is crucial for making informed decisions regarding media planning, targeting, and optimization.

Audience Profile

Audience Profile refers to a description or analysis of the target audience that an advertiser is trying to reach with their advertisements. It involves identifying and understanding the key characteristics, demographics, and behaviors of the intended audience in order to tailor the advertising message and delivery to effectively engage and resonate with the target audience. The audience profile helps advertisers to better understand who their target customers are, what they want, and how to effectively communicate with them. It provides insights into the specific traits and preferences of the audience, allowing advertisers to create more relevant and compelling advertisements that are likely to generate greater response and engagement.

Audience Rating Points (ARPs)

Audience Rating Points (ARPs) are a metric used in the field of advertising to measure the reach and effectiveness of a specific advertising campaign. It provides valuable insights into the target audience reached by the advertisement and helps advertisers make informed decisions about their marketing strategies. ARPs are calculated by multiplying the reach of an advertisement by the frequency with which it is viewed by the target audience. Reach refers to the total number of individuals or households exposed to the advertisement. Frequency, on the other hand, represents the average number of times each member of the target audience views the advertisement. By combining these two factors, ARPs provide a comprehensive measure of the overall impact of an advertisement. For example, an advertisement with a high reach but low frequency may indicate that the message is being seen by a large number of people, but not often enough to make a lasting impression. Conversely, an advertisement with low reach but high frequency may suggest that the message is being seen repeatedly by a small group of people, potentially leading to audience fatigue. Advertisers use ARPs to evaluate the cost-effectiveness and efficiency of their campaigns. By comparing the ARPs of different advertisements or different media channels, advertisers can determine which strategies are yielding the best results and adjust their marketing budgets accordingly. ARPs can also help advertisers identify any gaps in their target audience and make adjustments to improve the overall effectiveness of their campaigns. ARPs are particularly useful when planning media buys and negotiating ad placements. Advertisers can assess the potential reach and frequency of different media channels and determine which ones align best with their target audience. This allows for more strategic decision-making regarding budget allocation and optimizing the return on investment. It's important to note that ARPs are just one piece of the puzzle when evaluating the success of an advertising campaign. Other factors such as brand awareness, engagement metrics, and sales impact should also be taken into consideration. However, ARPs provide a quantitative measure that serves as a valuable benchmark for advertisers to assess and compare the effectiveness of their advertising efforts.

Audience Segmentation Tools

Audience segmentation tools refer to the technological solutions or methods used in advertisement to divide or categorize a target audience into distinct groups based on various demographic, psychographic, or behavioral attributes. These tools enable advertisers to create more effective and personalized marketing campaigns by tailoring their messages and offerings to specific audience segments. By utilizing audience segmentation tools, advertisers can gather and analyze a wide range of data points, such as age, gender, location, interests, browsing habits, purchase history, and more. This information helps identify similarities and differences among the target audience, allowing advertisers to customize their messaging, select appropriate channels, and optimize their ad spend.

Audience Segmentation

Audience segmentation in the context of advertising refers to the process of dividing a target market into distinct groups or segments based on specific characteristics or behavior patterns. This segmentation allows advertisers to tailor their marketing messages and strategies to effectively reach and engage with different audience segments. The purpose of audience segmentation is to better understand the diverse needs, preferences, and motivations of different groups within the target market. By identifying and analyzing these segments, advertisers can develop targeted advertising campaigns that resonate with specific audience segments, increasing the effectiveness of their messages and ultimately driving better results.

Audience Share

Audience share refers to the portion of the total audience that a particular advertisement or marketing campaign reaches. It is commonly used in the advertising industry to gauge the effectiveness and reach of an advertisement. The audience share is usually expressed as a percentage and can be calculated by dividing the number of people who were exposed to the advertisement by the total number of people in the target audience. This information is crucial for advertisers as it helps them determine the reach and impact of their campaigns.

Augmented Reality (AR) Advertising

Augmented Reality (AR) Advertising refers to a marketing strategy that utilizes computer-generated sensory inputs, such as graphics, video, or sound, to enhance the interactive experience between the user and a real-world environment. It aims to create a powerful and immersive advertisement experience by blending virtual elements seamlessly into a physical environment. AR Advertising is based on the concept of augmentation, where digital content overlays physical reality, allowing consumers to engage with products, brands, or services in a more interactive and meaningful way. Unlike traditional advertising, which is primarily passive, AR Advertising actively involves users, making them an integral part of the advertisement experience.

Awareness

Awareness in the context of advertisement refers to the level of familiarity and recognition that consumers have with a particular brand, product, or service. It is the extent to which a target audience is aware of the existence and attributes of a brand or product, and whether they can recall or recognize it when prompted. Advertisement plays a crucial role in creating and increasing awareness among consumers. It acts as a medium to introduce a brand or product to potential customers, educate them about its features and benefits, and influence their perception and consideration. Through various advertising channels such as television, print media, radio, online platforms, and social media, companies strive to raise awareness and build a strong brand presence.

B2B Advertising

B2B Advertising refers to the marketing and promotion of products or services from one business to another business. It is a form of advertising that specifically targets and caters to the needs and preferences of business entities and professionals, rather than individual consumers. In B2B advertising, the aim is to establish and maintain a strong business-to-business relationship by effectively showcasing the value, benefits, and unique selling propositions of the offered products or services. The primary objective is to attract and capture the attention of potential business clients and convince them to engage in a business transaction.

B2C Advertising

B2C advertising refers to the practice of creating and disseminating promotional messages or content to consumers in order to stimulate interest in and drive sales of a company's products or services. The term B2C stands for business-to-consumer, which indicates that the advertising is aimed at individual consumers rather than businesses or organizations. In B2C advertising, the focus is on reaching and engaging a large and diverse audience of individual consumers. The goal is to persuade consumers to choose the advertised products or services over those of competitors, and ultimately to make a purchase. B2C advertising campaigns often utilize a variety of channels and mediums to reach consumers, such as television, radio, print media, online platforms, and social media. One key aspect of B2C advertising is understanding the target audience and tailoring the message to resonate with their needs, desires, and preferences. This involves conducting market research to identify consumer behaviors, interests, and demographics, and using this information to create targeted and relevant advertisements. B2C advertisers may also use tactics such as segmentation and personalization to further refine their messages and reach specific subsets of consumers. Another important element of B2C advertising is creating compelling and persuasive content that grabs the attention of consumers and motivates them to take action. This can include using visual imagery, storytelling, emotional appeals, and catchy slogans or jingles. The content should highlight the unique selling points and benefits of the product or service and clearly communicate why it is superior to alternatives. Tracking and measuring the effectiveness of B2C advertising campaigns is also crucial. This involves analyzing key performance indicators such as reach, engagement, click-through rates, conversions, and return on investment. By monitoring these metrics, advertisers can gain insights into which strategies and tactics are most effective and make data-driven decisions to optimize future campaigns.

Back-End Analytics

Back-End Analytics in the context of Advertisement refers to the process of collecting, organizing, and analyzing data related to the performance and effectiveness of advertisements on a website or digital platform. It involves examining the data generated by user interactions with the ads to gain insights and make informed decisions to optimize future ad campaigns. The main goal of back-end analytics in advertising is to measure the success of ad campaigns and determine the return on investment (ROI) for advertisers. By tracking various key performance indicators (KPIs), such as click-through rates (CTR), conversion rates, engagement metrics, and revenue generated, advertisers can assess which ads are most effective in reaching their target audience and driving desired actions, such as purchases or sign-ups.

Banner Ad

A banner ad is a type of advertisement that appears on a web page, typically in the form of a rectangular or square graphic display. It is designed to attract the attention of the viewer and encourage them to click on it, leading them to the advertiser's website or landing page. Banner ads are commonly found on websites and are an important part of online advertising. They are typically placed in prominent positions on web pages, such as the top, side, or bottom, where they are highly visible to the viewer. The purpose of a banner ad is to capture the viewer's attention and entice them to take action, such as clicking on the ad.

Banner Advertising Networks Evaluation

Banner Advertising Networks are platforms that connect advertisers and publishers for the purpose of displaying banner advertisements on websites. These networks provide a marketplace where advertisers can display their banners on a wide range of websites, while publishers can earn revenue by hosting these advertisements. Advertisers benefit from banner advertising networks as they allow them to reach a large audience across various websites. These networks provide advertisers with tools to manage their campaigns, including targeting options to reach specific demographics or interests. They also offer analytics and reporting to track the performance of their advertisements. Publishers, on the other hand, can monetize their websites by joining banner advertising networks. These networks provide publishers with a platform to easily display banner advertisements on their websites without having to directly negotiate with advertisers. Publishers earn revenue either through a pay-per-click (PPC) model, where they receive a commission for each click on the advertisement, or a cost-per-impression (CPM) model, where they earn a fixed amount for every thousand impressions of the advertisement. Banner advertising networks serve as intermediaries between advertisers and publishers, facilitating the buying and selling of banner advertisement space. They streamline the process by providing a centralized platform where advertisers can find relevant websites to display their banners, and publishers can easily integrate the advertisements into their websites. These networks often use targeting technologies to ensure that advertisements are displayed to the most relevant audience. Advertisers can specify their target audience based on various criteria such as location, age, interests, and browsing behavior. This helps advertisers optimize

73

their campaigns by reaching the right audience and increasing the chances of a click or conversion. In conclusion, banner advertising networks are platforms that connect advertisers and publishers, allowing advertisers to display their banners on various websites and publishers to earn revenue by hosting these advertisements. These networks simplify the process of buying and selling banner ad space, provide targeting options, and offer analytics to track campaign performance.

Banner Advertising Networks

Banner advertising networks are online platforms that connect advertisers with publishers to facilitate the display of banner advertisements on websites. These networks act as intermediaries, helping advertisers reach their target audience by leveraging the publishing capabilities of various websites. Advertisers typically create banner ads in various formats (e.g., images, animations) and sizes (e.g., leaderboard, skyscraper) that are visually appealing and strategically designed to capture users' attention. The banner advertising networks offer a platform where these ads can be displayed on participating websites.

Behavioral Advertising Insights Analysis

Behavioral advertising is a form of online advertising that uses data collected from individuals' online activities to target them with specific advertisements. It involves analyzing user behavior and preferences to deliver personalized and relevant ads. The process of behavioral advertising starts with the collection of data through various tracking mechanisms, such as cookies, pixel tags, and mobile device identifiers. These tools monitor an individual's online activities, including websites visited, searches made, and content viewed. The data collected reveals valuable information about the individual's interests, preferences, and purchasing behaviors. After data collection, the information is analyzed and categorized into different user segments based on their common behaviors and interests. These segments can be created using various factors, such as demographics, geographic location, and browsing patterns. Advertisers can then target specific user segments with advertisements that are most likely to resonate with them. Behavioral advertising offers several benefits for both advertisers and consumers. For advertisers, it allows them to reach their target audience more effectively and increase the chances of conversion. By tailoring ads to individuals' specific interests and preferences, advertisers can deliver more relevant and engaging content, leading to higher click-through rates and conversions. For consumers, behavioral advertising can enhance their online shopping experience by showing ads that are more personalized and relevant to their needs. Instead of being bombarded with generic advertisements, consumers are presented with products and services that align with their interests and preferences. This results in a more enjoyable browsing experience and increases the chances of discovering products or services they may be interested in. However, behavioral advertising raises concerns regarding privacy and data security. The collection and use of personal data can be seen as an invasion of privacy, and there is a risk of data breaches or misuse. Additionally, some individuals may find targeted ads intrusive or manipulative, and they may prefer to browse the internet without being tracked. In conclusion, behavioral advertising is a targeted advertising approach that uses data from individuals' online activities to deliver personalized and relevant ads. It helps advertisers reach their target audience more effectively and enhances consumers' online shopping experience. However, it also raises concerns regarding privacy and data security.

Behavioral Advertising Insights

Behavioral advertising refers to the practice of collecting and analyzing user data in order to personalize and target advertisements to individual users based on their online behavior and interests. Through the use of various tracking technologies, such as cookies and pixels, advertisers are able to track users' online activities, such as the websites they visit, the searches they make, and the content they engage with. This data is then used to segment users into different audience groups and serve them relevant advertisements. The main goal of behavioral advertising is to increase the effectiveness of advertising campaigns by delivering ads that are more likely to be relevant and engaging to individual users. By tailoring advertisements to users' specific interests and preferences, advertisers can enhance user engagement and increase the likelihood of conversions and sales.

Behavioral Advertising Platforms Assessment

Behavioral Advertising Platforms, within the context of advertisement, refer to online advertising platforms that utilize user behavior data to deliver targeted and relevant ads to individuals. These platforms analyze and track various aspects of user behavior such as browsing history, search queries, and interactions with online content to understand the interests, preferences, and purchasing patterns of users. By collecting and analyzing user data, Behavioral Advertising Platforms aim to deliver personalized advertising experiences to individuals, increasing the effectiveness of ad campaigns and minimizing wasted impressions. These platforms leverage advanced data analytics techniques and machine learning algorithms to segment users into specific audiences or user profiles based on their demonstrated interests, demographics, and online behaviors.

Behavioral Advertising Platforms

Behavioral advertising platforms are advanced software systems used in the advertising industry to personalize and deliver targeted advertisements to individual users based on their online behavior and preferences. These platforms utilize various data sources, such as browsing history, search queries, social media interactions, and purchase patterns, to build a comprehensive profile of each user. By analyzing this data, the platforms can identify the user's interests, demographics, and other relevant characteristics. Once the user's profile is established, behavioral advertising platforms can then match the user with relevant advertisements from advertisers. This matching process involves algorithms that consider the user's preferences, browsing habits, and other behavioral data to determine the most suitable ad for that individual. These platforms use sophisticated targeting techniques to ensure that the right advertisements are shown to the right people at the right time. They take into account factors such as the user's location, device, and browsing context to optimize the ad delivery and improve the chances of engagement. The primary goal of behavioral advertising platforms is to increase the effectiveness of online advertising by delivering personalized content that is more likely to resonate with the individual user. This personalized approach can lead to higher click-through rates, conversion rates, and overall return on investment for advertisers. However, it is important to note that behavioral advertising platforms must adhere to privacy regulations and obtain explicit user consent for data collection and targeting. Users should have control over their data and the ability to opt-out of personalized advertising if they wish. In summary, behavioral advertising platforms leverage user data and algorithms to deliver personalized and targeted advertisements based on individual preferences and online behavior. These platforms aim to maximize the relevance and effectiveness of ads, ultimately benefiting both advertisers and users in the online advertising ecosystem.

Bill Insert

A bill insert is a form of advertising that is typically included with a bill or invoice to promote a product or service to the recipient. It is a printed or digital document that is specifically designed to fit within the same envelope or package as the bill, ensuring that it is seen and read by the customer. The purpose of a bill insert is to grab the attention of the customer and encourage them to take action, such as making a purchase or signing up for a service. It is an effective way for businesses to reach their target audience because the customer is already engaged with the billing process, making them more likely to pay attention to the insert. Bill inserts are often used by utility companies, financial institutions, and other businesses that regularly send bills or invoices to their customers. They are an additional marketing opportunity for these companies to promote their own products or services, or to partner with other businesses for co-branded offers. Bill inserts can take various forms, depending on the company and the advertising campaign. They can be simple flyers or brochures that provide information about a product or service, or they can be more interactive, such as including a QR code or a tear-off coupon that the customer can redeem. When creating a bill insert, it is important to consider the design and messaging. The insert should be visually appealing and eye-catching, with a clear and concise message that highlights the benefits of the product or service. It should also include a strong call to action, encouraging the customer to take the next step, whether that is visiting a website, calling a phone number, or visiting a physical location. In conclusion, a bill insert is a form of advertising that is included with a bill or invoice. It is a targeted marketing opportunity for businesses to promote their products or services to customers who are already engaged with the billing process. Bill inserts can vary in form and should be visually appealing, with a clear message and a strong call to action.

Billboard Ad Design Software

A billboard ad design software refers to a digital tool or program that allows users to create visually appealing and professional advertisements specifically designed for billboard displays. This software provides a platform for advertisers, designers, and marketers to transform their ideas and concepts into eye-catching billboard ads that effectively communicate their brand message to a wide audience. Utilizing a billboard ad design software, users are able to leverage various features and functionalities to create compelling visuals and graphics. These tools typically offer a wide range of customizable templates, fonts, colors, and shapes, enabling users to experiment and customize their ads according to their specific requirements and brand identity. Moreover, this software often includes image editing capabilities, allowing users to enhance and manipulate their visuals to create a polished and professional look. Users can resize, crop, adjust colors, and add filters to their images to ensure they are visually striking and effectively convey the intended message. Typography is another crucial aspect of billboard ad design, and the software usually provides a vast selection of fonts and text effects to choose from. Users can easily create attention-grabbing headlines and compelling taglines that are easily readable from a distance. The ability to adjust text size, alignment, and spacing ensures that the message remains clear and impactful even on large outdoor displays. Additionally, a billboard ad design software may offer advanced features such as layers, transparency, and gradient effects, enabling users to add depth and dimension to their designs. This allows for the creation of visually engaging advertisements that stand out among the clutter of other billboards. Once the design process is complete, the software typically enables users to export their creations in various formats, including printable files optimized for large-scale printing. This ensures that the final design can be easily transferred to a printing company, guaranteeing a seamless transition from the digital design phase to the physical billboard display. In summary, a billboard ad design software provides a user-friendly and comprehensive platform for creating visually appealing and engaging advertisements tailored specifically for outdoor billboard displays. By offering a range of customization options and advanced features, this software empowers users to design impactful and memorable billboard ads that effectively convey their brand message to a large audience.

Billboard Ad Design

A billboard ad design refers to the visual representation and layout of an advertisement that is displayed on a billboard, typically located in high-traffic areas such as roadsides, city centers, or popular landmarks. It is a form of outdoor advertising that aims to capture the attention of passersby and communicate a message effectively within a limited space. The design of a billboard ad plays a crucial role in grabbing the attention of the target audience and conveying the intended message. It involves the careful selection of visuals, colors, typography, and layout to create a visually appealing and impactful advertisement.

Billboard Advertisements

Billboard advertisements refer to large outdoor displays that are typically found along highways, busy streets, or in prominent locations visible to a wide range of audiences. These advertisements are designed to attract attention and communicate a specific message or promote a product, service, or event. Billboard ads are traditionally printed on large sheets of paper or vinyl and mounted on billboards or other structures specifically designed for outdoor advertising. In recent years, digital billboards have become more popular, displaying dynamic and interactive content that can be changed frequently. The primary purpose of billboard advertisements is to create brand awareness and capture the attention of passersby. By employing striking visuals, bold colors, and concise messages, these advertisements aim to make a lasting impression in a short amount of time. Since billboard advertisements are often seen by people driving or walking by, they need to be easily readable and easily understood from a distance. In terms of design, billboard advertisements usually follow certain principles to ensure their effectiveness. They often feature eye-catching graphics or images, minimal text, and a strong call-to-action. The use of bright colors, large fonts, and simple but impactful designs can help grab the viewer's attention and convey the intended message quickly. Effective

76

billboard advertisements utilize a combination of visual and verbal elements to create a memorable and compelling message. They may use slogans, taglines, or clever wordplay to reinforce the brand or product being advertised. Additionally, the use of imagery that resonates with the target audience and reflects the brand's identity can help create a strong connection and leave a lasting impression. While billboard advertisements are proven to be an effective advertising medium, they do have limitations. Due to their size and location, they have a brief exposure time to capture the attention of viewers. Therefore, it is crucial for advertisers to create visually appealing and attention-grabbing advertisements that can be easily understood in a short period. In conclusion, billboard advertisements are large outdoor displays that are strategically placed to reach a wide audience. They utilize visually striking designs, concise messages, and strong calls-to-action to create brand awareness and promote products, services, or events. By employing effective design principles and taking advantage of their high visibility, billboard advertisements aim to make a lasting impact on viewers in a short amount of time.

Billboard Advertising Strategies Development

A billboard advertising strategy is a plan developed to effectively utilize billboards as a means of promoting a product, service, or brand to a target audience.It involves identifying the objectives of the advertisement, selecting strategic locations for billboards, designing impactful visuals and messaging, and engaging with the audience to maximize the impact and effectiveness of the campaign.

Billboard Advertising Strategies

Billboard advertising strategies refer to the techniques and methods used to create effective and impactful advertisements on billboards. Billboards are large outdoor advertising displays that are typically placed in high-traffic areas such as highways, busy streets, and commercial areas. These strategies aim to capture the attention of passersby and convey a memorable message that resonates with the target audience. The first key strategy in billboard advertising is to ensure that the message is concise and easily understandable. Due to the limited time and space for viewers to absorb the information, the advertisement should convey its message quickly and clearly. This can be achieved through the use of bold and attention-grabbing headlines, as well as visually appealing graphics or images. The goal is to capture the viewer's interest within a few seconds and leave a lasting impression. Another vital strategy is to consider the location and placement of the billboard. Choosing high-traffic areas where the target audience is likely to pass by ensures maximum exposure and reach. Factors such as traffic flow, pedestrian footfall, and visibility from different angles should be taken into account when selecting the location. Additionally, considering the demographics and preferences of the target audience is crucial in tailoring the message and design of the billboard to resonate with their interests and needs. Utilizing eye-catching visuals and creative designs is also an essential strategy in billboard advertising. Advertisements should be visually appealing, with attention-grabbing colors, fonts, and images. The use of reputable and recognizable brands or endorsements can help to establish credibility and trust with the audience. However, it is essential to strike a balance between creativity and simplicity to ensure that the message is not overshadowed by excessive visuals or clutter. Lastly, incorporating a call-to-action is a strategy that encourages viewers to take action after seeing the billboard. This can be achieved through the use of clear and concise instructions, such as "visit our website," "call now," or "get a free sample." Including contact information or a unique website link can help to track the effectiveness of the advertisement and measure the response from the target audience.

Billboard Advertising

Billboard advertising refers to the practice of using large outdoor advertising structures, commonly known as billboards, to display promotional messages or advertisements. These billboards are typically placed in high-traffic areas, such as along highways, in urban centers, or near major intersections, with the intention of capturing the attention of a wide audience. Billboard advertising has been a popular form of advertising for many years due to its ability to reach a large number of people. The messages displayed on billboards are often simple and visually appealing, utilizing eye-catching graphics, bold colors, and concise text to quickly convey the intended message to passing motorists or pedestrians.

Bing Ads

Bing Ads is an advertising platform offered by Microsoft, allowing businesses to create and manage online advertisements. It provides a means for businesses to display their ads on the Bing search engine, as well as other Microsoft-owned platforms and partner websites. With Bing Ads, businesses can target their ads based on keywords, demographics, and location, ensuring that their ads reach the right audience. Advertisers can set a budget for their campaigns, controlling how much they are willing to spend on each click or impression. They can also track the performance of their ads using the built-in analytics tools, making it easier to measure the effectiveness of their advertising efforts.

Blind Testing

Blind Testing, in the context of advertisement, refers to a research technique used to evaluate the performance and effectiveness of different advertisements without disclosing the identity of the brands or the intentions behind the advertisements to the participants. This technique involves presenting a group of individuals with different advertisements and gathering their feedback and reactions. The participants are typically unaware of which brand or product the advertisement is promoting. This ensures that their responses are unbiased and not influenced by their preconceived notions or brand preferences.

Bounce Rate

Bounce Rate is a metric used in the context of online advertising to measure the percentage of visitors who leave a website after only viewing one page. When an advertisement directs users to a website, the bounce rate indicates the number of visitors who do not engage with the website beyond the initial landing page. A high bounce rate suggests that the advertisement and the landing page may not be effectively capturing and retaining the attention of the target audience.

Brand Advertising

Brand advertising refers to the promotion of a specific brand or product through various marketing channels. It aims to create awareness, establish a positive perception, and build a strong identity for the brand among consumers. The primary goal of brand advertising is to differentiate the brand from its competitors and create a distinct image in the minds of the target audience. This is often achieved by highlighting a unique selling proposition, which sets the brand apart and demonstrates its value and benefits. Brand advertising typically involves the use of creative and compelling messaging, visuals, and storytelling techniques to capture the attention and engage the emotions of consumers. It leverages various media platforms, such as television, print, radio, outdoor signage, digital channels, and social media, to reach a wide audience and reinforce the brand message. Effective brand advertising not only seeks to attract new customers but also aims to retain existing ones by fostering brand loyalty. It helps to establish a strong connection between the brand and its customers, making them more likely to choose and recommend the brand over its competitors. Moreover, brand advertising plays a crucial role in building brand equity, which refers to the intangible value and perception associated with a brand. By consistently delivering a compelling brand message and reinforcing it through different touchpoints, brand advertising helps to enhance brand equity over time. In summary, brand advertising is a strategic and creative approach to promote a brand or product. It involves crafting a unique brand identity, communicating the brand message effectively, and building a strong emotional connection with consumers. By doing so, it aims to create brand awareness, differentiate the brand from competitors, foster brand loyalty, and enhance brand equity.

Brand Ambassador Marketing Programs

A brand ambassador marketing program is a promotional strategy implemented by a company to leverage the influence and popularity of an individual or group of people to promote their brand and increase brand awareness. The selected brand ambassadors are typically individuals who have a strong following and a positive image, and who are aligned with the values and target audience of the brand. Brand ambassador marketing programs involve creating a partnership or collaboration between the company and the brand ambassadors, with the aim of utilizing their credibility and reach to promote the brand to a wider audience. The ambassadors are typically engaged in various marketing activities, such as attending events, creating social media content, participating in ad campaigns, and endorsing products or services. The primary objective of brand ambassador marketing programs is to enhance brand visibility and create a positive brand perception among consumers. By associating the brand with well-known and respected individuals, companies aim to build trust and credibility, and to establish an emotional connection with their target audience. Through the ambassadors' endorsement or recommendations, consumers are more likely to perceive the brand as trustworthy and reliable. In addition to increasing brand awareness, brand ambassador marketing programs can also help drive sales and customer loyalty. The ambassadors' positive association with the brand can influence their followers to try the brand's products or services, leading to increased sales. Moreover, ongoing collaborations with brand ambassadors can strengthen the brand-consumer relationship, as the ambassadors serve as relatable figures that customers can connect with on a more personal level. Overall, a brand ambassador marketing program is a strategic approach that leverages the influence and popularity of individuals or groups to promote a brand and improve brand perception among consumers. By selecting brand ambassadors who align with the brand's values and target audience, and by engaging them in various marketing activities, companies can effectively increase brand visibility, drive sales, and foster customer loyalty.

Brand Ambassador Marketing

A brand ambassador is an influential individual who is hired by a company to represent and promote its brand to a specific target audience. They are typically well-known personalities or industry experts who have a large following and strong influence over their followers. The role of a brand ambassador is to create awareness, generate interest, and build positive associations with the brand. They act as the face and voice of the company, embodying its values and personality. Through their credibility and authenticity, they aim to establish a strong connection between the brand and the audience.

Brand Associations Research

Brand associations in the context of advertisement refer to the mental connections that consumers form with a particular brand based on their experiences, perceptions, and interactions with it. These associations can be positive or negative and they play a crucial role in influencing consumer behavior and decision-making. When consumers see an advertisement for a brand, they often recall their past experiences and knowledge about that brand. These associations can include various elements such as the brand's logo, packaging, tagline, spokesperson, and overall brand image. For example, a person who sees an ad for a luxury car brand may associate it with sophistication, exclusivity, and high performance based on their previous exposure to the brand's advertisements, reviews, or personal interactions. Brand associations are formed through a process of cognitive learning and are influenced by factors such as advertising, word of mouth, social media, and personal experiences. Effective advertisements aim to create positive brand associations by strategically communicating the brand's message, values, and unique selling propositions to the target audience. Advertisers use various techniques to establish and reinforce brand associations in their advertisements. They may use emotional appeals, storytelling, imagery, music, and other creative elements to evoke specific emotions, attitudes, or beliefs associated with the brand. For example, a soft drink advertisement may feature a group of friends having a great time on a sunny beach to create a positive association between the brand and fun, enjoyment, and socializing. Brand associations are important for advertisers because they can influence consumer perceptions, attitudes, and buying decisions. Positive brand associations can enhance brand loyalty, increase brand equity, and result in repeat purchases and positive word of mouth. On the other hand, negative brand associations can lead to brand avoidance, loss of customers, and damage to the brand's reputation.

Brand Associations

Brand associations refer to the mental connections and associations that consumers have with a particular brand. These associations are formed through various marketing activities, such as advertising, packaging, and product experiences, and they influence consumers' perceptions and attitudes towards the brand. Advertisement plays a crucial role in shaping brand associations by strategically creating and reinforcing certain associations in consumers' minds. Different advertising techniques and messages are used to establish and enhance these associations, ultimately influencing consumer behavior and purchase decisions.

Brand Awareness

Brand awareness is a crucial concept in the realm of advertisement, referring to the extent to which a target audience is able to recognize and recall a particular brand. It encompasses the level of familiarity and knowledge that individuals have about a brand's existence, characteristics, values, and offerings. When it comes to advertising, building and maintaining brand awareness is of utmost importance for businesses. By increasing brand awareness, companies aim to establish a strong and recognizable presence in the minds of consumers. This presence enables a brand to differentiate itself from competitors and helps to cultivate trust and loyalty among its target audience.

Brand Content Partnerships Negotiation

Brand Content Partnerships Negotiation refers to a strategic process in the field of advertising where two or more parties negotiate and collectively develop a partnership agreement for creating and distributing branded content. This type of negotiation involves discussions and agreements on various aspects such as content creation, distribution channels, target audience, and financial terms. During the negotiation process, both parties aim to reach a mutually beneficial agreement that enables them to achieve their marketing and branding objectives. The negotiations typically include the following key steps: 1. Identifying Objectives: In the initial stage of negotiation, the involved parties clarify their goals and objectives for the partnership. This may include increasing brand awareness, reaching new audiences, promoting specific products or services, or enhancing brand reputation. 2. Assessing Capabilities and Resources: Each party assesses their respective capabilities and resources that can contribute to the partnership. This includes evaluating their expertise in content creation, access to distribution channels, audience insights, and financial resources. 3. Defining Roles and Responsibilities: The negotiation process involves determining the roles and responsibilities of each party in the partnership. This includes specifying who will be responsible for content creation, distribution, analytics, and performance evaluation. 4. Determining Financial Terms: The negotiation also focuses on determining the financial aspects of the partnership. This includes discussions on the budget allocation, payment terms, revenue sharing models, and any other monetary considerations. 5. Setting Content Guidelines: Both parties collaborate to establish content guidelines that align with their brand values and marketing objectives. This includes defining the tone, style, messaging, and other specifications for the branded content. 6. Establishing Performance Metrics: The negotiation process involves agreeing on key performance indicators (KPIs) that will be used to evaluate the success of the partnership. These metrics may include reach, engagement, conversion rates, return on investment, brand sentiment, and other relevant measurements. 7. Agreement Finalization: Once all the negotiations have taken place, the final step is to document the partnership agreement in a legally binding contract. This agreement outlines all the terms and conditions agreed upon by the parties, including the duration of the partnership, termination clauses, and any other relevant provisions.

Brand Content Partnerships

Brand content partnerships refer to collaborative agreements between a brand and another entity, such as a publisher, influencer, or media outlet, to create and distribute content that promotes the brand and its offerings. These partnerships are typically formed to enhance brand visibility, engage the target audience, and ultimately drive business objectives.In the context of advertising, brand content partnerships involve the creation of branded content or influencers, seamlessly integrates the brand's messaging and values into the partner's platform. This content can take various forms, including articles, videos, podcasts, social media posts, and more.The primary goal of brand content partnerships is to leverage the partner's existing audience and credibility to reach and influence consumers. By collaborating with established platforms or influencers, brands can tap into their followers or subscribers, who are already receptive to the partner's content, to expand their own reach and connect with potential customers in a more authentic and engaging manner.Brand content partnerships often provide mutual benefits for both the brand and the partner. The brand gains access to the partner's audience and the partner's

80

expertise in creating engaging content that resonates with their followers. Meanwhile, the partner benefits from the brand's resources, financial support, and potential exposure to a wider audience.These partnerships allow brands to create content that aligns with the partner's tone, style, and values, making it more appealing and relatable to the target audience. By providing valuable and high-quality content, brands can establish themselves as thought leaders, gain credibility, and foster a positive perception among consumers.Successful brand content partnerships require careful collaboration and open communication between the brand and the partner. It is crucial for both parties to establish shared goals, define the target audience, and outline the key messages and brand guidelines to ensure a cohesive and effective content strategy.In conclusion, brand content partnerships are strategic collaborations between a brand and another entity to produce and distribute content that promotes the brand. By harnessing the partner's platform and expertise, brands can create engaging and authentic content to reach and influence their target audience.

Brand Equity

Brand equity refers to the perceived value and strength of a brand in the eyes of consumers. It represents the level of consumer awareness, loyalty, and preference towards a particular brand compared to its competitors. Brand equity is built through consistent and effective advertising strategies that create a positive brand image, foster emotional connections, and provide a unique and superior brand experience. It encompasses various elements such as brand identity, brand reputation, brand awareness, and brand loyalty.

Brand Image Research Methods

Brand Image research methods refer to the various strategies and techniques used to gather information and insights on how a brand is perceived by its target audience in the context of advertisement. It involves conducting research to understand the image that consumers have of a brand, including their attitudes, perceptions, associations, and emotions towards the brand. There are several methods that can be employed to conduct brand image research in the context of advertisement. One such method is through surveys and questionnaires. This involves collecting data from a representative sample of consumers through structured surveys or questionnaires. The questions in these surveys are designed to measure various dimensions of brand image, such as brand awareness, brand associations, brand loyalty, and perceived quality. Surveys can be conducted through various channels, including online, phone, or in-person interviews.

Brand Image Research

Brand image research in the context of advertising refers to the systematic and comprehensive study of the perceptions, attitudes, and beliefs that consumers hold towards a particular brand. It involves conducting research to gain insights into how consumers perceive the brand, what associations they have with it, and what emotions or feelings it evokes in them. The purpose of brand image research in advertising is to understand how the brand is perceived in the minds of consumers and to assess whether the brand's positioning and messaging align with the intended image. It helps advertisers and marketers evaluate the effectiveness of their advertising campaigns and make informed decisions about branding strategies.

Brand Image

Brand Image refers to the perception and overall impression that consumers have of a particular brand. It is the sum of all the thoughts, feelings, and opinions that consumers associate with a brand, based on their experiences, interactions, and exposure to the brand's marketing communications. A strong brand image is crucial for the success of any advertisement campaign as it helps in building trust, credibility, and loyalty among consumers. It is an intangible asset that sets a brand apart from its competitors and acts as a promise of quality and satisfaction to the consumers.

Brand Loyalty

Brand Loyalty is a consumer's strong preference for a particular brand or product, often resulting in repeated purchases and a reluctance to switch to competitor brands. It is a measure of customer satisfaction and trust, indicating a successful relationship between the brand and the consumer.Advertisements play a crucial role in developing and maintaining brand loyalty. Through effective advertising campaigns, brands aim to establish a positive emotional connection with consumers, influencing their purchasing decisions and fostering long-term loyalty. Advertisements are designed to communicate the unique value proposition of a brand, differentiate it from competitors, and build a strong brand image in the minds of consumers.Advertisers employ various strategies to cultivate brand loyalty. They emphasize the key features and benefits of their products or services, highlighting their superior quality, convenience, or affordability. Advertisements also leverage emotional appeals, associating the brand with positive emotions and desirable experiences. By creating a sense of trust and familiarity, these advertisements strengthen the bond between the brand and the consumer.Moreover, advertisers use repetition and consistency in their messaging to reinforce brand loyalty. Consistent branding across multiple ad placements helps consumers recognize and remember the brand, even when they are exposed to a vast array of advertising messages. This consistency builds credibility and trust, as consumers perceive the brand as reliable and dependable.Additionally, effective advertisements foster a sense of belonging and community among consumers. By showcasing satisfied customers and user-generated content, brands create a sense of social proof, indicating that others trust and prefer the brand. This social influence encourages consumers to align themselves with the brand and become loyal advocates.In conclusion, brand loyalty is a consumer's inclination to repeatedly choose a particular brand over its competitors. It is influenced by effective advertising campaigns that establish a positive emotional connection, communicate the unique value proposition, and maintain consistency in messaging. Advertisements play a crucial role in building and nurturing brand loyalty by creating trust, familiarity, and a sense of belonging among consumers.

Brand Personality

Brand personality refers to the set of human characteristics, traits, and values that are attributed to a brand in order to create a distinctive and unique identity in the minds of consumers. It helps to establish a brand's position, differentiate it from competitors, and build a strong emotional connection with its target audience. By personifying a brand, marketers aim to create a relatable and likable persona that consumers can identify with and align themselves with. A brand's personality is communicated through various elements of its advertising, including the tone of voice, visual aesthetics, messaging, and overall brand experience. It is essential for advertisers to carefully craft and maintain a consistent brand personality that resonates with their target market, aligns with their brand values, and supports their overall marketing objectives.

Brand Recognition

Brand recognition refers to the extent to which a target audience is able to identify and associate a specific brand with its products or services. It is a vital aspect of advertising as it plays a crucial role in creating consumer preference and loyalty. Brand recognition is achieved through various marketing strategies and communication efforts, such as advertising campaigns, sponsorships, product placements, and public relations activities. The ultimate goal is to create a strong and positive brand image in the minds of consumers, leading to increased brand recall and familiarity. Successful brand recognition relies on the consistent and effective use of brand elements, such as logos, slogans, jingles, and packaging. These visual and auditory cues help consumers identify and differentiate a brand from its competitors. By repeatedly exposing consumers to these brand elements, marketers aim to establish a strong brand presence in the market. Furthermore, brand recognition is closely tied to brand recall. When consumers encounter a brand stimulus, such as an advertisement or a logo, their ability to remember and retrieve the brand from their memory is known as brand recall. Brand recognition serves as a foundation for brand recall, as it enhances the likelihood of consumers recalling the brand when making purchasing decisions. Effective brand recognition leads to numerous benefits for a company. Firstly, it creates familiarity and trust among consumers, making them more likely to choose a familiar brand over unknown alternatives. Additionally, brand recognition helps to differentiate a brand from its competitors, allowing it to secure a unique market position. This can lead to increased market share, customer loyalty, and long-term profitability.

Brand-Integrated Content Planning

Brand-Integrated Content Planning refers to the strategic process of identifying and incorporating a brand's messaging and values into a content campaign or advertisement. It involves aligning the brand's objectives, target audience, and unique selling proposition with the content creation and distribution plan. The concept of brand-integrated content planning recognizes that content and advertising are most effective when they seamlessly integrate with the overall brand strategy. This means that the content should not only be engaging and informative but also reflect the brand's identity and values. By doing so, brand-integrated content creates a consistent and cohesive experience for the audience, strengthening brand awareness and brand recall.

Brand-Integrated Content

Brand-Integrated Content refers to the form of advertising where a brand seamlessly incorporates its message or products into the content of a specific medium. This approach aims to create a cohesive and unobtrusive brand experience for the audience.Unlike traditional advertising methods that interrupt the content flow, brand-integrated content integrates the brand's message or products in a natural and authentic way. It could be in the form of product placements, sponsored content, or endorsements by influencers or celebrities.

Branded Content

Branded content in the context of advertisement refers to content that has been created or sponsored by a brand with the intention of promoting a product, service, or brand itself. It is a form of advertising that involves the integration of brand messaging or associations in the content itself, usually in a subtle or non-promotional way. This type of content is typically designed to be entertaining, informative, or engaging, with the aim of capturing and retaining the attention of the target audience. It can take various forms, including articles, videos, social media posts, podcasts, and more, and is often distributed through various channels such as websites, social media platforms, or traditional media outlets.

Branded Entertainment Creation

Branded Entertainment Creation refers to the process of developing and producing content that combines entertainment and advertisement to promote a brand or product. It involves the integration of brand messaging and values into various forms of entertainment, such as movies, TV shows, web series, music videos, and video games. The purpose of branded entertainment creation is to engage the audience in a compelling and immersive storytelling experience while subtly promoting the brand. Unlike traditional advertising, which interrupts the audience's consumption of entertainment, branded entertainment aims to seamlessly integrate the brand into the narrative, making it a part of the content itself.

Branded Entertainment

Branded entertainment refers to a form of advertising that seamlessly integrates a brand or product into the content of a television show, film, video game, or any other form of entertainment media. This type of advertising is intended to be subtle and non-intrusive, allowing the audience to experience and engage with the branded content in a natural way. Rather than interrupting the entertainment experience with traditional advertisements, branded entertainment aims to create an immersive and enjoyable experience for the audience.

Branded Merchandise Creation

Branded merchandise creation, in the context of advertising, refers to the process of designing and producing promotional products that carry a company's logo or brand identity. These products, commonly known as branded merchandise or promotional items, serve as tangible marketing tools used to increase brand awareness, attract new customers, and reinforce brand loyalty. Branded merchandise can encompass a wide range of products, including but not limited to pens, apparel, tech accessories, bags, drinkware, and stationery. These items are often customized with a company's logo, slogan, or specific branding elements, such as color schemes or taglines, to create a cohesive and memorable representation of the brand. The creation of branded merchandise involves several steps. First, a company needs to define its objectives and target audience for the promotional products. This information helps determine the type of merchandise that will best align with the brand's identity and resonate with its intended recipients. Once the objectives and target audience are identified, the next step is the design phase. Designers, either in-house or hired externally, create artwork that incorporates the brand's logo and messaging in an aesthetically pleasing and cohesive manner. The artwork needs to be adaptable to various merchandise sizes and materials while maintaining brand consistency. After the design is finalized, the production phase begins. Manufacturers or suppliers are responsible for producing the branded merchandise in large quantities, ensuring quality control throughout the process. Depending on the complexity and type of products, production lead times may vary. The final step in branded merchandise creation is distribution. Companies distribute the promotional items through various marketing channels, such as trade shows, events, corporate gifting, or inclusion in product packaging. The distribution process is an opportunity for the brand to make a lasting impression on its target audience and generate positive brand associations. Overall, branded merchandise creation is an effective and tangible marketing strategy that allows companies to connect with their target audience in a physical way. By offering useful and visually appealing products that carry their branding, companies can increase brand visibility, create positive brand associations, and engage customers on a deeper level.

Branded Merchandise

Branded Merchandise refers to promotional products that are customized with a company's logo or messaging and distributed to target audiences to increase brand visibility and awareness. These products serve as tangible reminders of the company and its offerings, helping to create a lasting impression and foster brand loyalty. By using branded merchandise in their advertising strategy, companies aim to achieve multiple goals. Firstly, they seek to enhance their brand recognition by placing their logo on everyday items such as t-shirts, pens, or tote bags. These items serve as walking billboards, exposing the brand to a wider audience as they are used or worn in public. This increased exposure helps to build familiarity and establish the brand as a trusted and recognizable entity. Secondly, branded merchandise serves as an effective promotional tool during events, trade shows, or conferences. By offering free branded products to event attendees, companies can generate interest and engagement with their brand. Free merchandise creates a positive brand association, leaving a lasting impression in the minds of potential customers. Moreover, branded merchandise can also encourage customer loyalty and increase repeat business. By offering customized products as gifts or rewards to their existing customers, companies nurture a sense of appreciation and reciprocity. Customers who receive these branded gifts are more likely to become brand ambassadors, promoting the company through word of mouth or by proudly using and displaying the merchandise. Furthermore, branded merchandise can be strategically used as part of a larger marketing campaign. Companies can incorporate these products into their promotional efforts, such as by offering them as incentives for specific actions, running contests or giveaways, or including them in gift bags or welcome kits. This integrated approach ensures that the brand and its messaging are consistently reinforced across various touchpoints, increasing the chances of brand recall and recognition. In summary, branded merchandise plays a vital role in advertising by effectively showcasing a company's logo and message on various products. It not only enhances brand visibility and recognition but also creates a positive brand association, fosters customer loyalty, and serves as a memorable promotional tool. Ultimately, branded merchandise helps companies establish a strong brand presence and build long-term relationships with their target audience.

Branding Strategy

A branding strategy is a marketing technique that focuses on creating a unique and favorable identity for a product, service, or company. It involves developing a distinct brand image and message that resonates with the target audience and sets the product or company apart from competitors. The main objective of a branding strategy is to establish a strong and recognizable brand that evokes positive associations and emotions among consumers. This enables the brand to stand out in a saturated market and build long-term customer loyalty.

Branding

Branding in the context of advertisement refers to the process of creating a unique and recognizable identity for a product, service, or company. It involves establishing a set of tangible and intangible attributes that differentiate the brand from its competitors and leave a lasting impression on consumers. A successful branding strategy incorporates various elements such as a distinct logo, tagline, visual design, and consistent messaging to convey the brand's personality, values, and promise to the target audience. It includes careful consideration of the target market, competition, and overall marketing objectives.

Broadcast Advertising Time Slots Allocation

Broadcast advertising time slots allocation refers to the process of determining and assigning specific time periods during which advertisements will be aired on television or radio. This allocation is crucial for advertisers and media planners to reach their target audiences effectively and maximize the impact of their advertising campaigns. The allocation of advertising time slots involves various considerations and factors, including audience demographics, viewing or listening habits, program genres, and advertising budgets. Advertisers aim to place their commercials in time slots that attract the highest number of their target audience, ensuring maximum exposure and engagement.

Broadcast Advertising Time Slots

Broadcast Advertising Time Slots refer to specific time periods during which advertisements are broadcasted on television or radio. These time slots are typically divided into different categories based on their audience reach, cost, and effectiveness in reaching the target market. Television and radio stations sell these time slots to advertisers, allowing them to reach their target audience through the broadcast medium. The duration of these time slots can vary, ranging from a few seconds to several minutes.

Broadcast Advertising

Broadcast advertising refers to the promotion and marketing of products or services through television or radio platforms. It is a form of mass communication that targets a wide audience by using audio or visual cues to convey messages. In broadcast advertising, companies or individuals purchase airtime on television or radio networks to showcase their products or services. These advertisements are typically created by advertising agencies or creative teams with the goal of capturing the attention of viewers or listeners and persuading them to take a specific action, such as making a purchase or visiting a website.

Broadcast Media Planning Tools

Broadcast media planning tools refer to the various techniques and strategies used by advertisers and marketers to effectively plan and optimize the placement of advertisements on broadcast media platforms such as television and radio. These tools are essential in ensuring that advertisements reach the desired target audience, maximize reach and frequency, and ultimately achieve the marketing objectives of the advertiser. The primary purpose of broadcast media planning tools is to assist advertisers in making informed decisions regarding their media buying and placement strategies. These tools provide valuable insights and data on audience demographics, viewing habits, programming schedules, and other relevant factors that can impact the success of an advertising campaign. By analyzing and interpreting this data, advertisers can determine the most appropriate media platforms, time slots, and programs to maximize the impact and effectiveness of their advertisements.

Broadcast Media Planning

Broadcast media planning refers to the strategic process of determining how and when an advertisement will be aired on television or radio in order to reach the intended target audience and achieve specific advertising objectives. It involves careful analysis and decision-making to maximize the effectiveness and impact of the advertisement. The first step in broadcast media planning is identifying the target audience. This requires understanding the demographics, psychographics, and media consumption habits of the target audience. By knowing who the advertisement is intended for, advertisers can choose the right channels and time slots to reach the desired viewers or listeners. Once the target audience is determined, the next step is selecting the appropriate media channels. This involves considering factors such as the reach, frequency, and cost of different television or radio stations. Advertisers may also consider the program content and audience composition of each channel to ensure alignment with the target audience. After selecting the media channels, the media planner needs to decide on the desired time slots for airing the advertisement. This can involve analyzing ratings data to determine when the target audience is most likely to be tuned in. Advertisers may choose to air the advertisement during prime time or specific programs that attract the target audience. Another important consideration in broadcast media planning is budgeting. The media planner needs to allocate the available budget across different channels and time slots in a way that optimizes reach and frequency. This may involve negotiating with media vendors to secure the best possible rates and deals. Finally, the media planner monitors the performance of the advertisement once it is aired. They track metrics such as reach, frequency, and audience response to assess the effectiveness of the media plan. This feedback can inform future media planning decisions and help improve the overall success of advertising campaigns.

Bumper Ads Campaigns

Bumper Ads Campaigns refer to a type of digital advertising strategy that involves the creation and distribution of short, non-skippable video ads. These ads are typically 6 seconds or less in duration and appear before or in between longer videos on various online platforms. The aim of Bumper Ads Campaigns is to capture the attention of viewers quickly and deliver the key message or brand image in a concise and impactful manner. By leveraging the limited duration of these ads, advertisers are compelled to convey their message effectively and efficiently, maximizing the impact of their campaigns.

Bumper Ads

Bumper ads refer to short and concise advertisements that are typically displayed before or after online video content. These ads are designed to capture viewers' attention within a short span of time, typically lasting no more than six seconds. With the rise of online video platforms and the increasing trend of consumers watching videos on their mobile devices, bumper ads have become an effective way for advertisers to reach their target audience. They allow advertisers to convey their message quickly and concisely, making them ideal for delivering impactful and memorable brand messages. Bumper ads are commonly used to create brand awareness, generate interest, and drive specific actions. Due to their brevity, these ads are often used in conjunction with longer-form video ads or as part of a broader advertising campaign. For example, advertisers may use bumper ads to tease or preview longer video content, encourage viewers to take a specific action such as signing up for a newsletter or following a social media account, or simply to increase brand exposure. When creating bumper ads, advertisers must carefully consider the limited time frame and ensure that their message is clear, concise, and visually appealing. Since bumper ads lack the luxury of delivering complex narratives or detailed product information, advertisers must focus on capturing viewers' attention through clever storytelling, strong visuals, and compelling calls-to-action. Due to their short duration, bumper ads are often unskippable, meaning viewers are unable to skip or fast-forward through them. This ensures that advertisers have a captive audience and increases the likelihood that their message will be seen and remembered. Additionally, bumper ads are typically designed to be non-intrusive, allowing viewers to seamlessly transition between video content and advertisements.

Buzz Marketing Strategies Planning

Buzz marketing strategies planning refers to the process of developing and implementing innovative techniques to generate excitement and buzz around a product, service, or brand. It involves creating a captivating and compelling message that resonates with the target audience, thus encouraging them to spread the word and create a sense of anticipation and curiosity. This approach requires careful research and analysis of the target market to identify their needs, interests, and preferences. By understanding their motivations and behaviors, marketers can design strategies that will evoke a strong emotional response and create a buzz-worthy experience.

Buzz Marketing Strategies

Buzz marketing is a strategic advertising technique used to generate excitement and create a buzz around a product or service. It is a form of word-of-mouth marketing that relies heavily on the power of social influence and consumer recommendations. The main goal of buzz marketing is to create a sense of anticipation and curiosity among target consumers, which ultimately leads to increased brand awareness, customer engagement, and ultimately sales. This is achieved through various strategies that aim to engage and captivate the audience, stimulating conversations and interactions both online and offline.

Buzz Marketing Tactics Implementation

Buzz marketing tactics refer to strategic promotional activities that aim to create a buzz or generate excitement and interest around a product or brand. This form of advertising relies on word-of-mouth and viral marketing techniques to increase awareness and generate a strong positive buzz among consumers. Unlike traditional advertising methods, which are often focused on reaching a wide audience through mass media channels, buzz marketing tactics primarily target specific groups of influential individuals, known as "mavens" or "influencers." These individuals are seen as trendsetters or opinion leaders in their social circles and have the ability to shape the opinions and purchasing decisions of others. Buzz marketing often involves the use of unconventional and attention-grabbing strategies to capture the attention of consumers and spark conversations. Some common buzz marketing tactics include: 1. Guerrilla marketing: This involves creating unexpected and memorable experiences in public spaces to generate buzz and create a lasting impression on consumers. 2. Product seeding: Companies provide free products or samples to influencers in the hopes that they will try and promote them to their network, generating positive buzz and word-of-mouth recommendations. 3. Viral marketing: This involves creating and sharing engaging content, such as videos or memes, that have the potential to spread rapidly across social media platforms, generating buzz and exposure for a product or brand. 4. Stunt marketing: This involves organizing attention-grabbing events or stunts that capture public interest and generate media coverage, creating buzz and raising awareness for a product or brand. 5. Social media campaigns: Companies leverage social media platforms to create buzz by engaging with consumers, running contests or giveaways, and encouraging user-generated content. By implementing buzz marketing tactics, companies aim to create a sense of excitement and anticipation around their products or brands, leading to increased consumer interest, enhanced brand image, and ultimately, higher sales and customer loyalty. Buzz marketing is particularly effective in industries where consumer opinions and recommendations play a significant role in purchasing decisions, such as fashion, food, and technology. However, it is important for companies to carefully plan and execute buzz marketing campaigns to ensure they resonate with the target audience and align with the overall brand strategy.

Buzz Marketing Tactics

Buzz marketing tactics refer to strategic actions and techniques employed by advertisers to generate excitement, curiosity, and conversations surrounding a product, service, or brand. The primary objective of buzz marketing is to create a buzz or viral effect, where consumers become actively engaged and spread awareness through word-of-mouth and social media platforms. Buzz marketing tactics often involve the use of unconventional and attention-grabbing promotional activities that are designed to captivate the target audience and generate a strong emotional response. These tactics aim to create a sense of anticipation, exclusivity, and desirability among consumers, making them eager to share their experiences with others. Social media platforms play a significant role in buzz marketing, as they provide a powerful and cost-effective means for advertisers to reach a massive audience quickly. By leveraging the influence of social media influencers, brands can amplify their message and garner a wider reach. This tactic often includes creating compelling and shareable content, such as engaging videos, captivating images, or interactive campaigns that encourage user participation. Another popular buzz marketing tactic is the use of product seeding, where advertisers distribute free samples or exclusive access to influential individuals, such as celebrities, bloggers, or industry experts. This strategy aims to create excitement and buzz around a product or service through positive endorsements and reviews from credible sources. Event sponsorships and experiential marketing are also frequently employed buzz marketing tactics. By associating a brand with exciting events, festivals, or experiential activations, advertisers can create memorable and share-worthy experiences for consumers. This generates a sense of curiosity and encouragement for individuals to discuss and share their experiences with others. In summary,

87

buzz marketing tactics involve strategic actions and techniques used by advertisers to generate excitement and generate conversations surrounding a product, service, or brand. Through attention-grabbing promotions, social media engagement, product seeding, event sponsorships, and experiential marketing, advertisers aim to create a buzz or viral effect that results in increased awareness and customer engagement.

Buzz Marketing

Buzz Marketing is a strategy employed in advertising that aims to generate significant attention and hype around a product, brand, or campaign. It involves creating a buzz or excitement through various marketing techniques in order to capture the attention and interest of the target audience. The main objective of Buzz Marketing is to create a viral effect, where people become so enthusiastic and excited about a product or brand that they willingly spread the message to their friends, family, and colleagues. This word-of-mouth marketing can be incredibly powerful, as it comes from trusted sources and can lead to increased brand awareness, customer engagement, and ultimately, sales.

Buzzword

A buzzword in the context of advertisement refers to a trendy or popular term or phrase that is used to capture the attention of the audience and create a sense of excitement or interest around a product, service, or campaign. Buzzwords are often highly impactful and persuasive, as they tap into current cultural trends or address specific consumer needs and desires. Marketers and advertisers strategically incorporate buzzwords into their advertisements to attract attention and generate buzz or hype around their offerings. These buzzwords are carefully chosen to resonate with the target audience and build a positive perception of the product or brand. By leveraging buzzwords, advertisers can create a sense of curiosity and anticipation, driving consumers to engage with the advertisement and ultimately make a purchase decision.

CPA Advertising Campaigns

CPA advertising campaigns, also known as cost per action campaigns, are a form of online advertising in which advertisers pay a fee only when a specific action is completed by the target audience. This action can vary depending on the goals of the campaign and may include actions such as filling out a form, signing up for a newsletter, making a purchase, or downloading an app. Unlike other forms of online advertising where advertisers pay for ad impressions or clicks, CPA campaigns provide a more direct way for advertisers to measure the effectiveness of their ads and ensure they are only paying for desired results. Advertisers can set specific goals or actions they want their target audience to take and only pay when those actions are completed.

CPM Advertising Networks

A CPM (Cost per Mille) advertising network is a platform that connects advertisers with website publishers, allowing them to display targeted ads on their web pages. CPM is a pricing model in which advertisers pay a set amount for every thousand impressions (views) their ads receive. The goal of CPM advertising networks is to help advertisers reach their target audience effectively and efficiently, while also providing publishers with an opportunity to monetize their website traffic. By utilizing CPM advertising networks, advertisers can easily promote their products or services to a large number of potential customers. These networks typically offer tools and features that allow advertisers to target specific demographics, interests, or locations to ensure their ads are shown to the most relevant audience. Advertisers can also track the performance of their ads by analyzing metrics such as click-through rates, conversion rates, and return on investment (ROI). Publishers, on the other hand, can benefit from CPM advertising networks by earning revenue from displaying ads on their websites. These networks provide publishers with ad code that they can integrate into their web pages, allowing relevant ads to be displayed to their visitors. Publishers earn money based on the number of ad impressions their website generates, regardless of whether or not visitors actually click on the ads. The more traffic a website receives, the higher the potential earnings for the publisher. CPM advertising networks act as intermediaries between advertisers and publishers, managing the entire process of ad serving and monetization. They use advanced algorithms and technologies to match relevant ads with suitable websites, maximizing the chances of ad engagement and generating higher revenue for both parties. These networks typically offer a wide range of ad formats, including display ads, video ads, native ads, and more, to cater to different advertiser preferences and publisher website layouts. In conclusion, CPM advertising networks provide a mutually beneficial platform for advertisers and publishers, allowing them to connect and collaborate in the display of targeted ads. Advertisers can effectively promote their products or services, while publishers can monetize their website traffic by displaying relevant ads. By leveraging CPM pricing and targeting capabilities, these networks help optimize ad performance and maximize revenue for both parties involved.

CRO Techniques

CRO Techniques, in the context of advertising, refer to a set of strategies and tactics employed to effectively optimize the conversion rate of website visitors into desired actions, such as making a purchase, filling out a form, or subscribing to a service. The ultimate goal of CRO techniques is to maximize the return on investment (ROI) by increasing the number of conversions without necessarily increasing the number of website visitors. These techniques involve analyzing and understanding user behavior and preferences, and then implementing changes to the website design, layout, content, and functionality to encourage visitors to take the desired action. CRO techniques rely heavily on data analysis and testing to identify the most effective approaches for improving conversions.

CRO Tools For Conversion Optimization

CRO Tools for Conversion Optimization are helpful resources that are used in the context of advertisement to improve the conversion rates and overall performance of a website or an advertisement campaign. These tools provide necessary data, insights, and functionalities to analyze, optimize, and measure the effectiveness of advertisements and marketing strategies with the aim of increasing customer engagement, conversion, and revenue. Conversion Optimization is a process that involves identifying areas of improvement in an advertisement campaign and making data-driven decisions to enhance its performance and increase conversions. CRO Tools play a crucial role in this process by offering various features and functionalities that support marketers and advertisers in achieving their goals.

CTR Optimization Tools

CTR Optimization Tools, also known as Click-Through Rate Optimization Tools, refer to various digital tools and software that help advertisers maximize the effectiveness of their online advertisements by improving the click-through rate (CTR). CTR is a metric that measures the number of times an advertisement is clicked on, divided by the number of times it is shown. These optimization tools provide advertisers with valuable insights and data to make informed decisions. They offer features and functionalities to analyze, monitor, and improve CTR, leading to more successful ad campaigns and higher ROI. CTR optimization tools typically offer the following capabilities: 1. Performance Analysis: These tools provide in-depth analysis and reporting on the performance of advertisements. They track metrics such as impressions, clicks, conversions, and CTR, allowing advertisers to identify patterns and trends in their campaign results. 2. A/B Testing: A critical feature of CTR optimization tools is the ability to conduct A/B testing. This involves creating multiple versions of an ad and testing them against each other to determine the most effective copy, design, or call-to-action (CTA). Advertisers can compare the CTRs of different variations and make data-driven decisions on which elements to optimize. 3. Ad Creative Optimization: These tools assist advertisers in optimizing their ad creatives to enhance CTR. They offer recommendations and best practices on design, format, visuals, and ad placements. Advertisers can modify and iterate their creatives based on these insights to maximize CTR. 4. Ad Placement Analysis: CTR optimization tools enable users to analyze the performance of ads across different platforms, websites, or placements. This helps advertisers identify high-performing channels and optimize their ad placements accordingly, ensuring they reach their target audience effectively. 5. Audience Targeting: CTR optimization tools often include features to target specific demographics, interests, or behaviors. Advertisers can refine their audience targeting to increase the likelihood of attracting users who are more likely to click on their ads, thereby improving CTR. Overall, CTR optimization tools empower advertisers to make data-driven decisions to improve the effectiveness of their online advertisements. By analyzing performance, conducting A/B testing, optimizing ad creatives, analyzing ad placements, and refining audience targeting, advertisers can maximize their CTR and generate more successful ad campaigns.

Cable Television Advertising

Cable Television Advertising refers to the practice of promoting products or services through commercials that are broadcasted on cable television networks. It is a form of marketing where advertisers pay for airtime on specific cable channels to reach a targeted audience. Cable television advertising offers businesses the opportunity to reach a wide range of viewers through channels that are available on cable networks. These channels can be categorized into various genres such as news, sports, entertainment, lifestyle, and more. Advertisers can choose the channels that align with their target market to maximize the effectiveness of their advertisements. Commercials aired during cable television programming typically range in duration from a few seconds to a couple of minutes. Advertisers use this time to create visually appealing and engaging content that captures the attention of viewers. The goal is to convey key messages about the product or service and persuade viewers to take action, such as making a purchase or visiting a website. One of the advantages of cable television advertising is its ability to target specific demographics. Advertisers can select channels that appeal to their desired audience based on factors such as age, gender, interests, and geographical location. This targeting capability helps businesses minimize wasted ad spend by reaching viewers who are more likely to be interested in their offerings. Another advantage of cable television advertising is its reach. Cable networks have a wide viewership, and advertisements are exposed to a large number of potential customers. This increased reach can contribute to generating brand awareness and increasing sales for businesses. In addition, cable television advertising provides the opportunity for repetitive exposure. Advertisers can choose to air their commercials multiple times during popular shows or at specific times of the day, reinforcing the message and increasing the likelihood of viewer recall. This repetition can play a crucial role in establishing brand familiarity and driving consumer action. Overall, cable television advertising is a marketing strategy that enables businesses to promote their products or services through commercials on cable television networks. It allows for targeted messaging, broad reach, and repetitive exposure, making it an effective tool for reaching and influencing potential customers.

Call To Action (CTA) Optimization Techniques

A Call to Action (CTA) is a key element in an advertisement that encourages and motivates the audience to take a specific action. CTA optimization techniques refer to the various strategies used to make the CTA more effective in achieving its desired goal. One important technique in CTA optimization is creating clear and concise messaging. The CTA should use straightforward language that clearly states what action the audience should take. This helps eliminate any confusion or ambiguity, making it easier for the audience to understand and follow through with the desired action. A well-optimized CTA also utilizes persuasive language to create a sense of urgency or value. By highlighting the benefits or exclusive offers associated with taking action, the CTA can entice the audience to act immediately. Using words like "limited time," "exclusive," or "act now" can help create a sense of urgency and encourage immediate response. In addition to persuasive language, CTA optimization often involves using attention-grabbing design elements. The CTA should stand out from the rest of the advertisement, with visually appealing colors and fonts that draw the audience's attention. The CTA button or link should be easily distinguishable and visually enticing, making it more likely that the audience will notice and click on it. Another effective technique is placing the CTA in a strategic location. It should be positioned prominently within the advertisement, where it is easily visible and accessible to the audience. Placing the CTA above the fold or near the main focal point of the ad can increase its visibility and effectiveness. Furthermore, optimizing the CTA involves aligning it with the overall goals and message of the advertisement. The CTA should be relevant to the content of the ad, offering the audience a logical next step or action to take. The language and design of the CTA should be consistent with the overall branding and messaging of the advertisement, ensuring a cohesive and seamless user experience.

Call To Action (CTA) Optimization

A Call to Action (CTA) is a compelling statement or phrase used in advertisements to prompt and motivate the audience to perform a specific action. It is a crucial element in advertising campaigns as it helps convert potential customers into actual buyers or leads. The optimization of a Call to Action entails refining and improving its effectiveness in order to achieve higher conversion rates and better campaign results. This process involves various strategies and techniques to maximize the impact of the CTA and encourage more customer engagement. An essential aspect of CTA optimization is its placement within the advertisement. It should be strategically positioned in a prominent and easily noticeable location to capture the attention of viewers. Placing the CTA above the fold, which refers to the upper area of a web page visible without scrolling, can significantly improve its visibility and increase the chances of users taking the desired action. Another crucial factor in CTA optimization is the use of clear and concise language. The statement or phrase should be straightforward, using simple but persuasive words to convey the intended message effectively. The CTA should clearly inform the audience about the action they need to take, whether it is making a purchase, subscribing to a newsletter, or signing up for a service. In addition to the language, the design and appearance of the CTA also play a significant role in its optimization. The use of contrasting colors, bold fonts, and compelling visuals can help draw attention and make the CTA visually appealing. It is important to ensure that the CTA stands out from the rest of the advertisement and is easily identifiable. Furthermore, CTA optimization involves creating a sense of urgency or excitement to prompt immediate action. Phrases like "limited time offer," "exclusive discount," or "reserve your spot today" can instill a sense of urgency and encourage users to act promptly. Including time-sensitive offers or limited availability can help drive higher engagement and conversion rates. Lastly, CTA optimization also entails proper testing and analysis. Conducting A/B tests, where different versions of the CTA are compared, can provide valuable insights on which approach resonates better with the target audience. Analyzing metrics such as click-through rates, conversion rates, and bounce rates can help identify areas for improvement and guide the optimization process.

Call To Action (CTA)

A Call to Action (CTA) in the context of advertisement refers to a specific prompt that is used to encourage or persuade the viewer to take a desired action. It is typically presented in a concise, compelling and visually appealing manner to attract the attention of the target audience. The main purpose of a CTA is to drive immediate action from the viewer, whether it is to make a purchase, sign up for a newsletter, download an app, request a quote, or engage in any other desired action. It serves as a direct invitation that motivates the viewer to take the next step in the advertising journey.

Campaign Attribution Models Evaluation

An advertisement campaign attribution model is a method used to determine the effectiveness of different marketing channels and touchpoints in contributing to the success of an advertising campaign. It helps businesses understand which marketing efforts are generating the most impact and driving desired actions, such as conversions or sales. The evaluation of campaign attribution models involves analyzing and assigning credit or value to the various marketing touchpoints that a customer encounters along their journey. These touchpoints can include online and offline channels, such as search ads, social media ads, display ads, email marketing, and more. There are multiple attribution models available, each with its own approach to distributing credit. Some of the common attribution models include: 1. First-click attribution: This model attributes all the credit to the first touchpoint or channel that a customer interacts with. It assumes that the initial touchpoint is solely responsible for driving the conversion or action. 2. Last-click attribution: In contrast to the first-click model, the last-click attribution model assigns all the credit to the final touchpoint before the conversion or action takes place. It assumes that the last touchpoint is the most influential in driving the desired outcome. 3. Linear attribution: This model distributes credit equally across all touchpoints encountered during the customer journey. It assumes that each touchpoint played an equal role in leading to the conversion or action. 4. Time-decay attribution: This model gives more credit to the touchpoints that are closer in time to the conversion or action. It assumes that the touchpoints closer to the conversion had a greater impact on the customer's decision-making process. 5. Position-based attribution: Also known as U-shaped attribution, this model gives more credit to the first and last touchpoints, with the remaining credit distributed evenly among the touchpoints in between. It assumes that the first and last touchpoints are the most crucial in driving the customer's decision. These attribution models provide businesses with insights into the effectiveness of their advertising campaigns and help them make data-driven decisions on allocating their marketing budget and optimizing their campaign strategies. Understanding the strengths and limitations of each attribution model is essential to ensure accurate evaluation and interpretation of campaign performance.

Campaign Attribution Models

A campaign attribution model is a framework used in the field of digital advertising to track and assign credit to various marketing touchpoints within a campaign, with the goal of understanding the impact and effectiveness of each touchpoint on the overall campaign performance. It provides insights into which channels, advertisements, or interactions contribute to desired outcomes, such as conversions or sales. There are several types of campaign attribution models, each with its own approach to assigning credit. The most commonly used models include: 1. First touch attribution: This model gives credit for a conversion or sale to the first touchpoint a user interacts with, regardless of subsequent touchpoints. It focuses on the initial introduction of a user to a campaign. 2. Last touch attribution: In contrast to the first touch model, the last touch model attributes all credit for a conversion or sale to the final touchpoint the user interacts with before taking the desired action. It emphasizes the touchpoint that immediately precedes the conversion. 3. Linear attribution: This model evenly distributes credit among all touchpoints within a campaign, giving each touchpoint an equal share of the credit for a conversion or sale. It ensures that every interaction is considered equally influential. 4. Time decay attribution: This model assigns greater credit to touchpoints that occur closer in time to the conversion or sale, recognizing that interactions closer to the point of conversion are typically more impactful than earlier ones. 5. Position-based attribution: Also known as U-shaped attribution, this model assigns 40% of the credit to the first touchpoint, 40% to the last touchpoint, and distributes the remaining 20% among the touchpoints in between. It recognizes both the initial introduction and the final interaction as significant contributors to the conversion. Choosing the right campaign attribution model depends on the specific goals and objectives of the advertising campaign. It is important to analyze the customer journey, understand the interaction patterns, and consider the influence of each touchpoint on driving desired actions. The selected model can provide valuable insights for optimizing marketing strategies, allocating budgets, and maximizing the return on investment.

Campaign Message

A campaign message in the context of advertisement refers to a concise and targeted statement or slogan that encapsulates the key message or theme of a marketing campaign. It is designed to capture the attention of the target audience and convey a persuasive and memorable message that encourages them to take a specific action or make a desired decision. The primary goal of a campaign message is to effectively communicate the unique selling proposition (USP) of a product, service, or brand in a way that resonates with the target audience and differentiates it from competitors. It should be clear, concise, and compelling, taking into consideration the needs, desires, and pain points of the target market.

Campaign Monitoring Tools Selection

Campaign monitoring tools, in the context of advertisement, refer to software or applications used to track, measure, and analyze the performance of advertising campaigns. These tools enable advertisers and marketers to obtain actionable insights and make data-driven decisions to optimize their campaigns. The primary purpose of campaign monitoring tools is to provide a comprehensive overview of various advertising efforts across different channels, such as print, digital, social media, and television. These tools collect and compile data related to impressions, clicks, conversions, and other relevant metrics. By analyzing this data, advertisers can assess the effectiveness and return on investment (ROI) of their campaigns.

Campaign Monitoring Tools

Campaign monitoring tools are software applications that allow advertisers to track and analyze the performance and success of their advertising campaigns. These tools provide comprehensive data and visualizations, enabling advertisers to make informed decisions and optimize their marketing strategies. By monitoring key metrics such as impressions, clicks, conversions, and engagement, advertisers can gain valuable insights into the effectiveness of their campaigns.

Campaign Strategy

A campaign strategy in the context of advertisement refers to the overall plan and approach devised to achieve specific marketing goals and objectives through targeted advertising efforts. It involves the careful selection and integration of various advertising elements and channels in order to effectively reach and engage the target audience. A successful campaign strategy encompasses both the creative and tactical aspects of advertising, aiming to deliver the desired message to the right audience at the right time. The first step in developing a campaign strategy is to clearly define the objectives. These may include raising brand awareness, increasing sales, launching a new product, or promoting a specific offer. Once the objectives are established, the next step is to identify the target audience and understand their needs, preferences, and behavior patterns. This information helps in designing the campaign message and selecting the most appropriate advertising channels to reach the target audience effectively. The campaign strategy typically involves the creation of compelling and relevant advertising content that resonates with the target audience. This content could take various forms, such as written copy, visuals, audio, or video. The messaging should be consistent and aligned with the overall brand image, values, and positioning. It should also clearly communicate the unique selling proposition (USP) of the product or service being advertised. In addition to creating the right content, the selection of advertising channels is crucial in a campaign strategy. These channels could include traditional media such as television, radio, print, and outdoor advertising, as well as digital platforms such as social media, search engines, websites, and mobile apps. The choice of channels depends on factors such as the target audience's media consumption habits, the budget, and the campaign objectives. Integration across multiple channels is often necessary to create a cohesive and impactful campaign. Once the campaign is launched, continuous monitoring and evaluation are essential to gauge its effectiveness and make adjustments if needed. This involves tracking key performance indicators (KPIs) such as reach, engagement, conversions, and return on investment (ROI). By analyzing the campaign's performance data, marketers can identify strengths, weaknesses, and opportunities for improvement, enabling them to refine the strategy and optimize future campaigns.

Campaign

A campaign in the context of advertisement refers to a structured and coordinated set of activities designed to promote a specific product, service, or idea to a targeted audience within a given time period. It is a strategic approach used by businesses, organizations, or individuals to communicate their message effectively and influence consumer behavior. A successful advertising campaign typically involves careful planning, creative execution, and precise implementation of various marketing techniques. The primary objective is to raise awareness, generate interest, and ultimately drive sales or achieve a desired outcome. This may involve a combination of different advertising channels, such as television, radio, print media, social media, and online platforms. Before launching a campaign, extensive research and analysis are conducted to identify the target audience, understand their preferences and needs, and determine the most effective way to reach them. This includes market research, competitor analysis, and consumer insights. Based on this information, a campaign strategy is developed, outlining the key messages, positioning, and overall theme. Once the strategy is in place, creative materials are designed and developed to communicate the messages effectively. This may include advertisements, taglines, slogans, visuals, jingles, and other promotional materials. The creative elements should resonate with the target audience, create a memorable impression, and differentiate the product or service from competitors. After the creative development, the campaign is executed by implementing the planned activities across the chosen advertising channels. This may involve negotiating media placements, scheduling advertisements, managing social media accounts, conducting public relations activities, and monitoring the campaign's progress. To evaluate the effectiveness of the campaign, analytics and performance metrics are measured and analyzed. This allows for continuous monitoring of the campaign's impact, identifying areas for improvement, and making necessary adjustments to optimize results. The success of a campaign is typically measured by key performance indicators (KPIs) such as reach, engagement, conversion rate, and return on investment (ROI). In summary, an advertising campaign is a strategic and coordinated effort to promote a product, service, or idea by utilizing various marketing techniques and channels. It involves careful planning, creative execution, implementation, and evaluation, with the ultimate goal of influencing consumer behavior and achieving desired outcomes.

Cannibalization Avoidance

Cannibalization Avoidance refers to the strategic approach taken by advertisers to prevent or minimize the negative impact of cannibalization on their advertising efforts. Cannibalization occurs when a company's own advertisements or marketing campaigns inadvertently compete against each other for the same target audience, resulting in decreased effectiveness and efficiency. This phenomenon is particularly relevant in today's multi-channel and multi-platform advertising landscape, where companies utilize various channels, such as television, radio, print, digital, and social media, to reach their target customers. The main goal of cannibalization avoidance is to ensure that advertising campaigns complement each other rather than compete. This involves careful planning and coordination among different advertising channels and campaigns to optimize their performance and avoid duplicative efforts. There are several strategies and tactics advertisers employ to avoid cannibalization. One common approach is to carefully segment the target audience based on demographic, psychographic, or behavioral characteristics and tailor advertising messages accordingly. By understanding the different preferences and needs of various customer segments, advertisers can create distinct campaigns that resonate with each segment without overlapping or competing against each other. Another strategy is to carefully schedule and coordinate advertising campaigns across different channels to avoid overlapping timeframes or conflicting messages. This requires close collaboration among different teams or agencies responsible for managing various advertising channels to ensure a seamless and integrated approach. Furthermore, advertisers often leverage data and analytics to gain insights into the performance of different campaigns and channels. By monitoring key metrics such as reach, frequency, engagement, and conversion rates, advertisers can identify potential cannibalization issues and make data-driven decisions to optimize their advertising efforts. In conclusion, cannibalization avoidance is a critical aspect of effective advertising. By carefully planning, coordinating, and analyzing advertising campaigns, advertisers can maximize their reach, engagement, and conversion rates while minimizing the negative impact of cannibalization.

Cannibalization

Cannibalization refers to a phenomenon in the field of advertising where the introduction of a new product or advertising campaign negatively impacts the sales of an existing product or campaign within the same company or brand. This occurs when the new product or campaign attracts customers who would have otherwise purchased the existing product or engaged with the existing campaign. As a result, the company or brand ends up competing with itself, leading to a decrease in overall sales or effectiveness.

Captive Audience

A captive audience, in the context of advertisement, refers to a group of individuals who are unable to avoid or escape exposure to a particular marketing message or promotional content. This audience is "captive" in the sense that they have limited or no choice in whether they encounter the advertisement, making it more likely for the message to be absorbed and retained. Typically, a captive audience is found in situations where individuals are confined or have limited control over their surroundings. This can include various settings such as waiting rooms, public transportation, elevators, cinemas, or even certain online platforms. In these environments, individuals may find themselves compelled to pay attention to advertisements due to factors such as boredom, lack of alternative distractions, or the necessity to pass time.

Car Wrap Advertising Programs

Car wrap advertising programs are marketing initiatives that involve wrapping a vehicle with a vinyl graphic advertisement. This form of advertisement allows businesses to promote their products and services by turning a car, truck, or other vehicle into a mobile billboard. The process of car wrap advertising typically involves designing a custom vinyl graphic that is then printed onto high-quality adhesive vinyl. This vinyl is then applied to the vehicle's exterior, covering the existing paint job and creating a visually striking advertisement. The vinyl wrap can be produced in various sizes and shapes, allowing for a customized fit on different vehicle types and models. Car wrap advertising programs offer businesses several advantages. Firstly, they provide a cost-effective advertising solution compared to traditional methods such as billboards or television commercials. Wrapping a vehicle is a one-time investment that can generate exposure for a prolonged period, making it a cost-efficient long-term strategy. Moreover, car wrap advertising programs offer a high level of visibility. The mobile nature of the advertisement allows businesses to reach a wider audience as the wrapped vehicle travels throughout various locations. It effectively turns a company's fleet of vehicles into mobile billboards, maximizing brand awareness and exposure. Car wrap advertising programs also offer flexibility in terms of targeting specific demographics or geographic areas. Businesses can choose to wrap specific vehicles that are frequently seen in their target market or select routes that pass through areas where their target audience resides. This targeted approach ensures that the advertisement reaches the intended audience effectively. Furthermore, car wrap advertising programs allow for easy customization and updates. Businesses can modify the vinyl graphic to include promotions, sales, or new product launches. The advertisement can evolve along with the business's marketing strategy, ensuring it remains relevant and engaging. Overall, car wrap advertising programs provide businesses with a unique and eye-catching way to promote their products and services. With their cost-effectiveness, high visibility, and flexibility, they offer an attractive alternative to traditional forms of advertisement.

Car Wrap Advertising

Car wrap advertising refers to a form of advertisement in which a vehicle, such as a car, truck, or van, is partially or completely covered with vinyl graphics or decals that display promotional messages, logos, or other branding elements. This method of advertising transforms vehicles into mobile billboards, allowing businesses to promote their products or services to a wide audience while the vehicle is in motion or parked in high-traffic areas. Car wrap advertising offers several advantages compared to traditional advertising methods. Firstly, it provides high visibility as wrapped vehicles capture the attention of pedestrians, motorists, and passersby, creating a lasting impression. The eye-catching and colorful designs make it easier for the audience to remember and recall the brand or message being advertised. Additionally, since the vehicle is constantly on the move in different locations, car wrap advertising extends the reach of the advertisement beyond a fixed location, ensuring a larger exposure to potential customers. Moreover, car wrap advertising is cost-effective and delivers a high return on investment. Wrapping a vehicle is often more affordable than other forms of advertising, such as billboards or TV commercials, and the message displayed on the vehicle can be seen by thousands of individuals daily. This makes it a cost-efficient option for businesses, especially small and local ones, that aim to generate brand awareness and increase their customer base without breaking the bank. In terms of flexibility, car wrap advertising allows businesses to customize the design, colors, and content of the vehicle wrap to align with their brand identity and marketing objectives. Whether it is promoting a specific product, a limited-time offer, or simply enhancing brand recognition, the design and message can be tailored to suit the specific goals of the campaign. Additionally, the vinyl wraps can be easily removed or replaced, providing businesses with the flexibility to update their advertisement as needed. Overall, car wrap advertising is an effective and versatile strategy to gain exposure and increase brand awareness. It combines the benefits of outdoor advertising with the mobility and flexibility of vehicles, ensuring a wide reach and constant presence in the target market. By utilizing car wrap advertising, businesses can effectively communicate their message and engage potential customers in a unique and impactful way.

Casual Research

Advertisement is a form of communication that aims to promote a product, service, or idea to a target audience. It is typically a paid message, delivered through various media channels, with the intention of influencing and persuading potential customers or clients. The primary purpose of an advertisement is to create awareness and generate interest in the advertised offering. By presenting information about the features, benefits, and advantages of the product or service, advertisements seek to convince the audience of its value and encourage them to take a desired action, such as making a purchase or seeking further information. Advertisements can take different formats depending on the medium used, such as print, broadcast, online, or outdoor advertising. They can be displayed as text, images, audio, video, or a combination of these elements. The content and design of an advertisement are carefully crafted to capture attention, invoke emotions, and convey the desired message effectively. Effective advertisements commonly utilize various persuasive techniques, such as appealing to logic, emotions, or credibility. They may employ storytelling, humor, testimonials, endorsements, or comparisons to differentiate the advertised offering from competitors and create a memorable impression in the minds of the target audience. Advertisers also consider factors like target audience demographics, psychographics, and media habits to ensure that their message reaches the right people through the most appropriate channels. They often conduct market research and consumer analysis to gain insights into customer behavior and preferences, enabling them to tailor advertisements accordingly. Regulations and ethical guidelines govern advertisement practices to protect consumers from false or misleading claims. Advertisements are expected to be truthful, transparent, and responsible, without intentionally deceiving or manipulating the audience. In conclusion, advertisements are a paid form of communication that aims to promote products, services, or ideas. They seek to create awareness, generate interest, and persuade the target audience to take a desired action. Through careful crafting of content and design, advertisements use persuasive techniques and various media channels to effectively convey their message to the intended audience.

Channel Advertising

Channel advertising refers to the strategic placement of advertisements on various channels or platforms to reach a specific target audience. It involves the selection and utilization of different channels such as television, radio, print media, online platforms, and social media to promote a product, service, or brand. With the proliferation of media channels and the increasing fragmentation of audiences, channel advertising has become essential for businesses to create awareness, generate interest, and drive sales. By leveraging different channels, advertisers can reach a wide range of consumers through their preferred medium of communication.

Cinema Advertising Strategy

Cinema advertising strategy refers to the plan and approach used by advertisers to promote their products or services in movie theaters. It involves the selection of the appropriate films, timing, and placement of advertisements to effectively reach and engage the target audience. The primary goal of cinema advertising is to capture the attention of moviegoers and create brand awareness or drive sales. Advertisers leverage the immersive and captivating cinema environment to deliver impactful messages that resonate with the audience. By strategically placing ads before feature films, during the pre-show, or through sponsored content, cinema advertising allows brands to connect with a captive audience in a unique and memorable way.

Cinema Advertising

Cinema advertising refers to the practice of promoting products or services through advertising messages that are screened before or during a movie in a cinema hall. It is a form of out-of-home advertising that targets a captive audience of moviegoers who are waiting for the movie to begin or during the intermission. This type of advertising offers several advantages compared to other forms of media. Firstly, cinema advertising allows advertisers to reach a large audience in a confined and controlled environment. Unlike television or online advertising, where viewers can skip or ignore ads, cinema audiences are typically more attentive as they are there specifically to watch a movie. This means that advertisers have a higher chance of their messages being seen and heard. Furthermore, cinema advertising has the advantage of being displayed on a larger-than-life screen, creating a more immersive and impactful experience for the audience. The combination of visuals and sound in a cinema environment can be highly engaging, capturing the attention of viewers and leaving a lasting impression. Another benefit of cinema advertising is its ability to target specific demographics. Advertisers can choose to have their ads screened before movies that appeal to their target audience. For example, a car manufacturer might choose to advertise their latest model before an action-packed blockbuster, targeting young and adventurous moviegoers. Cinema advertising can take various forms, including traditional commercials, product placements within movies, interactive advertisements, or even experiential marketing campaigns. Advertisers have the flexibility to choose the format and duration of their ads based on their objectives and budget. In conclusion, cinema advertising is a highly effective advertising strategy that utilizes the captive audience of moviegoers to promote products or services. It offers advantages such as reaching a large, captive audience, creating an immersive experience, and targeting specific demographics. By leveraging the power of the big screen and captivating visuals, cinema advertising has the potential to leave a lasting impact on viewers.

Click Fraud Detection Solutions

Click Fraud Detection Solutions refer to the technology and tools utilized by advertisers to identify and prevent fraudulent or illegitimate clicks on online advertisements. Click fraud occurs when individuals or automated bots purposely click on ads with malicious intent, such as generating false click counts, driving up advertising costs, or misleading advertisers about the effectiveness of their campaigns. These solutions typically employ sophisticated algorithms and machine learning techniques to analyze click patterns, user behavior, and other relevant data points to identify fraudulent activity. They aim to differentiate between genuine clicks from potential customers and fraudulent clicks generated by malicious actors.

Click Fraud Detection Tools Selection

Click Fraud Detection Tools are software or algorithms used to identify and prevent fraudulent activities in online advertising campaigns. These tools analyze various data points and patterns to determine the legitimacy of clicks on advertisements. Click fraud refers to the fraudulent clicking of online ads with no genuine interest in the product or service being advertised. This activity may be carried out by competitors, bots, or individuals with the intention to exhaust the advertiser's budget or gain a competitive advantage. Click fraud can lead to wasted ad spend, inaccurate performance metrics, and diminished trust in online advertising. Click Fraud Detection Tools utilize sophisticated algorithms and machine learning techniques to identify patterns and anomalies that indicate fraudulent clicks. These tools monitor and analyze multiple metrics such as IP addresses, click-through rates, click timestamps, and user behavior to detect patterns associated with click fraud. By continuously monitoring and analyzing these metrics, the tools can identify suspicious activities in real-time and take appropriate actions to mitigate the impact of click fraud. Some of the common features provided by Click Fraud Detection Tools include: - IP address monitoring: Detecting multiple clicks from the same IP address can indicate click fraud. - Geolocation analysis: Analyzing the geographic location of clicks can help identify fraudulent activities originating from certain regions or countries. - User behavior analysis: Evaluating user behavior patterns can reveal discrepancies that indicate non-human interactions with ads. - Conversion tracking: Monitoring conversions and attributing them to specific clicks can help identify fraudulent clicks that do not lead to any meaningful engagement. - Real-time alerts: Sending notifications or alerts in real-time when suspicious activities are detected, allowing advertisers to take immediate action. Click Fraud Detection Tools are essential for advertisers to ensure the effectiveness and integrity of their online advertising campaigns. By identifying and preventing click fraud, these tools help advertisers optimize their ad spend, improve ROI, and maintain trust in the digital advertising ecosystem.

Click Fraud Detection Tools

Click Fraud Detection Tools are software applications or services designed to identify and prevent fraudulent activities in online advertising campaigns. These tools use advanced algorithms and techniques to analyze and monitor the clicks generated by ad impressions, determining whether they are genuine or fraudulent. The primary purpose of click fraud detection tools is to protect advertisers from wasting their budget on fraudulent clicks, which can significantly impact the effectiveness and ROI of their ad campaigns. Click fraud occurs when individuals or automated systems repeatedly click on ads with malicious intent, such as generating revenue for website owners or depleting competitors' ad budgets.

Click Fraud Prevention Measures

Click fraud prevention measures refer to the strategies and techniques implemented by advertisers and ad networks to detect, prevent, and mitigate fraudulent activities in online advertising campaigns. Click fraud occurs when individuals or automated bots purposely click on advertisements with the intention of inflating the number of clicks and generating fraudulent advertising revenue. This fraudulent activity can have negative implications for both advertisers and publishers, as it can result in wasted ad spend, decreased campaign performance, and mistrust in the online advertising industry.There are several click fraud prevention measures that advertisers and ad networks can employ to safeguard their online advertising investments:1. IP Monitoring and Filtering: Ad networks and advertisers can track and analyze IP addresses associated with click fraud and block or filter out suspicious IPs to prevent fraudulent clicks.2. User Behavior Analysis: By examining user behavior patterns, such as excessive clicking, repeated clicking, or irregular clicking intervals, advertisers can identify and mitigate fraudulent activities.3. Ad Fraud Detection Tools: Utilizing advanced technology and machine learning algorithms, ad fraud detection tools can identify and flag suspicious activities, such as click farms or bot traffic, in real-time.4. Click Validation: Implementing click validation systems can help verify the legitimacy of clicks by cross-referencing various data points, such as IP addresses, user agents, and session durations.5. Geolocation Targeting: Advertisers can target specific geographic regions, effectively reducing the exposure to click fraud from different countries or regions known for fraudulent activities.6. Ad Fraud Audits: Conducting regular audits on advertising campaigns can help identify any suspicious or abnormal click patterns and take appropriate actions to prevent further fraudulent activities.7. Collaboration with Anti-Fraud Organizations: Advertisers can collaborate with industry associations and organizations dedicated to combating ad fraud, sharing insights and best practices to collectively fight against click fraud.By implementing these click fraud prevention measures, advertisers and ad networks can minimize the impact of click fraud, protect their advertising investments, and ensure fair and accurate measurement of campaign performance.

Click Fraud Prevention

Click Fraud Prevention refers to the measures taken in the field of online advertising to mitigate and deter the occurrence of click fraud. Click fraud is a fraudulent practice where individuals or automated systems generate fake or illegitimate clicks on online advertisements with the intention of inflating the costs for advertisers or manipulating the advertising metrics. Efficient click fraud prevention entails the implementation of various technological solutions, analytical techniques, and monitoring mechanisms to detect and combat fraudulent clicks. These preventive measures aim to maintain the integrity of online advertising campaigns, ensure accurate performance metrics, and protect advertisers from financial losses.

Click Fraud

Click fraud refers to the deceptive practice of generating invalid clicks on online advertisements with the intent of inflating advertising costs or manipulating the pay-per-click (PPC) model. It involves repetitive clicking on ads intentionally by individuals or automated scripts, rather than genuine interest or intention to engage with the advertised content. This fraudulent activity aims to exploit the advertiser's budget by driving up the number of clicks without generating any real conversions or value. Click fraud can be carried out through various means, including but not limited to: - Manual clicking by individuals or dedicated teams solely focused on generating fraudulent clicks. - The use of automated bots or scripts that simulate human-like behavior to repeatedly click on ads. - Practices such as click farms, where individuals are paid to perform clicking tasks in large numbers. - Utilizing malicious software or malware to force clicks on ads without the user's knowledge or consent. The motivations behind click fraud can vary. Competitors may engage in click fraud to deplete a rival's advertising budget, reduce their ad visibility, or negatively impact their return on investment. Publishers or website owners participating in ad revenue sharing programs may also resort to click fraud to boost their earnings by generating false traffic and clicks. Additionally, fraudulent clicks can be aimed at manipulating and distorting advertisement performance metrics, misguiding advertisers in their decision-making processes. In response to click fraud, advertisers and ad platforms employ various methods and technologies to detect and prevent it. These measures typically involve sophisticated fraud detection systems that analyze patterns, user behavior, and other relevant data to identify potentially fraudulent clicks. Ad platforms may also track IP addresses, session durations, and other metrics to flag suspicious activity. Additionally, advertisers often rely on click fraud monitoring tools and third-party services to enhance their fraud detection efforts. Click fraud poses significant challenges for advertisers, as it can drain advertising budgets, diminish ad effectiveness, and distort performance metrics. Effective prevention and detection mechanisms are crucial to combat this fraudulent practice and ensure a fair and trustworthy online advertising ecosystem.

Click Rate

Click Rate, also known as Click-Through Rate (CTR), is a metric commonly used in the advertising industry to measure the effectiveness of an online advertisement. It refers to the percentage of users who click on a specific link or advertisement, out of the total number of impressions or views it receives. The formula to calculate Click Rate is: Click Rate = (Number of Clicks / Number of Impressions) * 100 This metric is crucial for advertisers as it helps them determine the success of their campaigns and optimize their marketing strategies. A high Click Rate indicates that the ad is engaging and compelling to the audience, resulting in a higher interaction and potential conversions. On the other hand, a low Click Rate may suggest that the ad is not resonating well with the target audience, requiring adjustments to be made in the ad content, design, or placement. Furthermore, Click Rate is not solely an indicator of ad effectiveness, but also an important factor for ad platforms and publishers. Platforms that display advertisements typically charge advertisers based on the number of impressions or clicks their ads receive. Therefore, Click Rate plays a significant role in determining the cost and value of advertising space. It's important to note that Click Rate is just one of the many metrics used to assess the performance of an advertisement. Other important metrics include Conversion Rate, Cost per Click (CPC), and Return on Investment (ROI). These metrics together provide a comprehensive understanding of the advertisement's impact on the target audience and its effectiveness in achieving the desired goals. In conclusion, Click Rate is a vital metric in the advertising industry as it measures the percentage of users who click on an advertisement or link. It helps both advertisers and ad platforms gauge the effectiveness of their campaigns and make informed decisions about optimizing their strategies.

Click-Through Rate (CTR) Optimization

Click-Through Rate (CTR) Optimization refers to the process of enhancing the performance of online advertisements by increasing the percentage of users who click on the ads to visit the advertised webpage. CTR is calculated as the number of clicks an ad receives divided by the number of impressions (or views) it gets. It is commonly used as a key performance indicator (KPI) in digital advertising campaigns, as it helps measure the effectiveness of ads in generating user engagement and driving traffic to the advertiser's website. CTR optimization involves implementing various strategies and tactics to improve the click-through rate of ads. These strategies may include: 1. Crafting Compelling Ad Copy: Creating persuasive and engaging ad content that grabs the audience's attention and entices them to click on the ad. 2. Targeting the Right Audience: Identifying and targeting the most relevant audience for the ad to increase the likelihood of attracting interested users who are more likely to click on the ad. 3. A/B Testing: Conducting split tests with different ad versions to determine which performs better in terms of CTR. This helps advertisers optimize their ads by making data-driven decisions based on the test results. 4. Optimizing Ad Placement: Positioning ads strategically on websites, search engine result pages, or social media platforms to increase visibility and maximize the chances of attracting user clicks. 5. Ad Format Optimization: Experimenting with different ad formats, such as text, image, video, or interactive ads, to determine which formats drive higher CTR and resonate better with the target audience. 6. Ad Campaign Monitoring and Adjustments: Regularly monitoring the performance of ad campaigns, analyzing the data, and making necessary adjustments to optimize CTR. This may involve tweaking ad targeting, adjusting bidding strategies, or refining ad content. By optimizing CTR, advertisers aim to improve the overall effectiveness and performance of their advertising campaigns. Higher CTR not only indicates that the ad is capturing user interest and attention but also leads to increased click-throughs and potentially higher conversion rates, ultimately contributing to a better return on investment (ROI) for the advertiser.

Click-Through Rate (CTR)

Click-Through Rate (CTR) is a metric used in the context of online advertising to measure the effectiveness of an ad campaign by calculating the percentage of users who click on a specific advertisement to the total number of users who viewed the ad. CTR serves as an important indicator of how successful an advertisement is in generating user engagement and driving traffic to the advertiser's website. It helps advertisers assess the relevance, attractiveness, and overall performance of their ads. Advertisers strive to achieve a high CTR as it signifies that the advertisement is reaching and resonating with its target audience.

Clickbait

Clickbait refers to a type of advertisement that uses sensationalized headlines or images to attract people's attention and entice them to click on the ad. It is designed to generate high click-through rates and drive traffic to a specific website or landing page. Clickbait often employs misleading or exaggerated claims to create curiosity and intrigue. The goal is to make people curious about the content behind the headline or image, leading them to click on the advertisement. Once users click on the ad, they are directed to a website or landing page where they may find the promised information, but often accompanied by additional advertising or promotional content. Clickbait can take various forms, such as articles, videos, quizzes, or images. It frequently leverages emotional triggers, controversial topics, or popular trends to grab the attention of potential viewers or readers. The use of provocative headlines, enticing phrases, or shocking images is common in clickbait advertisements. Advertisers use clickbait as a strategy to increase website traffic, promote products or services, and generate revenue through advertising or affiliate marketing. By attracting a large number of users to click on their ads, they can potentially increase the visibility of their brand, increase ad revenue, or boost sales. However, clickbait has received criticism for misleading users and providing them with content that does not live up to the initial promise. Users may feel disappointed or deceived after clicking on a clickbait ad, leading to negative user experiences and reduced trust in advertisements in general. Overall, clickbait is a form of advertisement that utilizes sensationalized headlines or images to attract users' attention and entice them to click. While it can be an effective strategy to drive traffic and generate revenue, it is important for advertisers to prioritize transparency and deliver on the promises made in their clickbait ads.

Co-Branded Advertising Initiatives

Co-branded advertising initiatives refer to collaborative marketing efforts between two or more brands or companies, with the goal of combining their respective brand equity, resources, and target audiences to create a mutually beneficial promotional campaign. In this type of advertising, two or more brands come together to create a promotion or advertisement that features both their brand names or logos, highlighting the partnership between them. These initiatives are typically implemented to achieve various objectives, such as increasing brand awareness, expanding customer reach, and driving sales. By leveraging the strengths and customer bases of multiple brands, co-branded advertising initiatives enable each participant to tap into new audiences and enhance their overall marketing impact. Co-branded advertising initiatives can take various forms, including joint product launches, co-sponsored events or promotions, cross-promotional campaigns, and shared advertising channels. For example, two fashion brands might collaborate on a limited-edition clothing line and create joint advertisements featuring both brand names. Alternatively, a beverage company may partner with a popular music artist to produce a co-branded commercial that appeals to both their target demographics. Through co-branded advertising, brands can benefit from each other's reputation, customer loyalty, and expertise. This collaborative approach allows companies to access new markets, gain credibility, and differentiate themselves from competitors. Additionally, co-branded advertising initiatives can help brands save costs by sharing marketing expenses and resources. However, successful co-branded advertising initiatives require careful planning, alignment of objectives, and effective communication between the partnering brands. It is crucial for both parties to maintain a strong brand fit and ensure that the collaboration enhances rather than dilutes each brand's image.

Co-Branded Advertising

Co-Branded Advertising refers to a marketing strategy where two or more brands collaborate to create a promotional campaign or advertisement. In this approach, two distinct brands partner to combine their resources, expertise, and customer bases to create a mutually beneficial advertising campaign that promotes both brands simultaneously. The objective is to leverage the strengths and brand equity of each partner to increase brand awareness, reach a larger audience, and ultimately drive sales. Co-Branded Advertising offers several advantages for the participating brands. By aligning with another reputable and complementary brand, companies can enhance their brand perception and credibility. The collaboration allows the brands to tap into each other's customer base, expanding their reach and increasing the likelihood of attracting new customers. Additionally, co-branded advertisements provide an opportunity to share advertising costs, saving both brands money. This allows the partners to invest in high-quality campaigns or explore advertising channels that may have been cost-prohibitive if executed individually. To create successful co-branded advertisements, brands must ensure that there is a strong alignment between their values, target audience, and marketing objectives. The partnership should be strategic and mutually beneficial, with each brand bringing something unique to the table. The advertisement should effectively communicate the shared values and benefits of both brands, while also highlighting the individual qualities that make each brand distinct. Co-branded advertising can take various forms, including joint television commercials, social media campaigns, print ads, events, or product collaborations. The key to a successful co-branded advertisement lies in finding innovative ways to integrate both brands in a seamless and authentic manner. By effectively leveraging the strengths, expertise, and customer loyalty of each brand, co-branded advertising can create a powerful synergy that resonates with consumers and drives positive brand associations. In conclusion, co-branded advertising is a dynamic marketing strategy that involves the collaboration of two or more brands to create a promotional campaign. By combining resources, expertise, and customer bases, co-branded advertising aims to increase brand awareness, reach a larger audience, and drive sales for the participating brands. It provides an opportunity for brands to enhance their credibility, expand their reach, and share advertising costs. Effective co-branded advertisements align the values and marketing objectives of the partnering brands and effectively communicate their unique qualities to consumers.

Co-Branding Agreements Management

Co-Branding Agreements Management in the context of advertisement refers to the strategic collaboration between two or more brands to create a joint marketing campaign or product. This type of agreement allows brands to leverage each other's reputation, customer base, and resources to achieve mutual benefits. Co-branding agreements are typically formed between brands that have complementary products or target markets. The purpose is to increase brand awareness, reach a wider audience, and enhance the overall value proposition. In this arrangement, the brands involved often share the costs, risks, and rewards associated with the co-branded venture.

Co-Branding Agreements

Co-Branding Agreements refer to a formal arrangement between two or more brands to promote and market their products or services together. This collaboration allows the brands to leverage each other's reputation, customer base, and resources to create a mutually beneficial advertising campaign. In the context of advertisement, co-branding agreements are formed to achieve certain objectives such as increasing brand awareness, expanding market reach, gaining a competitive edge, or tapping into new target segments. By joining forces, the collaborating brands can pool their resources, expertise, and budgets to create impactful advertising campaigns that grab the attention of consumers and create a lasting impression.

Co-Branding Strategy Development

Co-Branding Strategy Development refers to the process of collaboration between two or more brands to create a combined product, service or advertising campaign in order to leverage each brand's equity and reach a wider audience. Co-branding is a marketing strategy that aims to increase brand awareness, enhance brand image and create value by aligning two or more brands that share similar values or target the same customer segment. It is a mutually beneficial partnership where brands combine their resources, expertise and customer base to promote and sell a product or service, while sharing the risks and rewards.

Co-Branding Strategy

Co-Branding Strategy refers to a marketing approach in which two or more brands collaborate to create a unique product or service, leveraging each other's strengths and reputation to enhance brand equity and reach a wider target audience. This strategy involves combining resources, expertise, and market presence to create a mutually beneficial partnership that can lead to increased sales and brand awareness for both parties. Co-branding is commonly used in advertising to create a positive association between the participating brands, allowing them to tap into each other's customer base and market segments. By aligning their values, objectives, and target audience, the collaborating brands can create a compelling proposition that attracts consumers and differentiates the co-branded product or service from competitors. Co-branding can take various forms, including product co-branding, where two or more brands collaborate to create a new product or service, such as Adidas and Porsche teaming up to design a limited-edition sneaker. Another approach is promotional co-branding, where brands join forces to promote a specific campaign or event together, such as Coca-Cola and McDonald's partnering for a joint summer promotion. This strategy has several advantages for advertisers. Firstly, co-branding allows brands to tap into each other's customer loyalty and trust, benefiting from shared brand reputation and credibility. Secondly, it enables brands to access new markets or target audience segments that they may not have been able to reach individually. Thirdly, it can lead to cost-sharing, as both brands contribute resources, reducing the overall marketing expenses and financial risks associated with launching a new product or campaign. However, implementing a co-branding strategy requires careful planning and consideration. It is essential to find a partner brand that complements your brand's values, target audience, and market positioning to ensure a successful collaboration. The partnership should align with the strategic objectives of both brands and create a value proposition that resonates with consumers.

Co-Branding

Co-Branding, in the context of advertisement, refers to the collaboration between two or more brands to promote a product or service. It involves the strategic alliance of companies that have complementary brand identities and target markets, with the aim of achieving mutual benefits and increased market share. The essence of co-branding lies in leveraging the strengths of each participating brand to create a unique value proposition for the consumers. By associating themselves with a well-established and trusted brand, companies can enhance their own brand image and credibility in the market. This can lead to increased consumer trust, brand loyalty, and ultimately, higher sales and revenue.

Commercial Advertisement

A commercial advertisement is a promotional message that is paid for and placed by businesses or organizations with the purpose of persuading and influencing target audiences to take specific actions, such as purchasing a product, using a service, or supporting a cause. Commercial advertisements can take many forms, including television commercials, radio spots, print advertisements in newspapers and magazines, online banner ads, social media posts, and even billboards. These advertisements are typically created by advertising agencies or in-house marketing teams and are strategically crafted to capture the attention of potential customers and differentiate the advertised product or service from its competitors.

Commercial Break

A commercial break is a designated period of time during a television or radio program that is specifically intended for airing advertisements. It is a scheduled interruption of the program's content in order to promote products, services, or brands. Commercial breaks are typically implemented to generate revenue for the broadcasting network or station by selling advertising slots to companies or individuals who wish to advertise their offerings to the program's audience. During a commercial break, the regular programming is temporarily halted and replaced with a series of advertisements. These ads can vary in length, with some lasting as short as a few seconds and others lasting several minutes. The content of the advertisements can also vary widely, as they may focus on different products or services, utilize various advertising techniques, and target different audience demographics. The structure and frequency of commercial breaks may vary depending on the broadcasting regulations and the specific content provider. In general, however, commercial breaks are strategically placed at predetermined intervals within the program to avoid interrupting the flow of the content too frequently or disruptively. In television, for example, commercial breaks are often scheduled before, in the middle of, and after specific segments or scenes to provide natural breaks in the storytelling or to align with the program's pacing. Commercial breaks serve several purposes. First and foremost, they provide a means for advertisers to reach a large, captive audience. By leveraging the popularity and viewership of a particular television or radio program, advertisers can maximize their exposure and potentially influence consumer behavior. Furthermore, commercial breaks enable broadcasters to generate revenue that can be reinvested into the production of high-quality content, as well as cover operational costs such as salaries and infrastructure. In conclusion, a commercial break is a scheduled interruption during a television or radio program, allowing for the airing of advertisements. Through these breaks, advertisers can reach a wide audience, while broadcasters can generate revenue to support their programming.

Comparative Advertising

Comparative advertising is a marketing strategy in which a company promotes its products or services by directly comparing them to those of its competitors. It involves highlighting the advantages or superior qualities of one's own brand over others in order to convince consumers to choose their product instead. This type of advertising often involves mentioning specific competitors by name, demonstrating side-by-side product comparisons, or presenting statistical data to support the claims. The purpose of comparative advertising is to differentiate a brand from its competitors and create a perception of superiority or better value in the minds of consumers. By highlighting the unique features, benefits, or performance of their products, companies aim to influence consumer choices and gain a competitive edge in the marketplace.

Competitive Advertising Analysis

Competitive advertising analysis refers to the process of studying and evaluating the advertisements and marketing strategies used by direct competitors in a specific industry or market. It involves identifying and analyzing the key messaging, positioning, and creative tactics employed by competitors to gain market share and attract customers. This analysis helps businesses understand their competitors' advertising strategies, strengths, weaknesses, and overall brand positioning to develop effective countermeasures and gain a competitive edge. By examining the advertising messages, target audience, media placement, and overall campaign execution of competitors, businesses can identify opportunities to differentiate themselves, improve their own marketing efforts, and better meet the needs and preferences of their target market.

Competitive Advertising

Competitive advertising refers to a form of marketing communication where companies directly compare the features, prices, or benefits of their products or services to those of their competitors. This type of advertising aims to differentiate a company's offerings from its rivals and influence consumers' purchase decisions in its favor. Competitive advertising typically employs various strategies to gain an edge in the market. One common approach involves highlighting unique selling points or advantages that a company's product or service possesses over its competitors. It may emphasize factors such as lower prices, superior quality, innovative features, or faster delivery. By emphasizing these advantages, the company aims to position itself as the superior choice in the consumer's mind. Another tactic frequently employed in competitive advertising is comparative advertising. This approach directly compares the company's products or services to those of its competitors, often highlighting perceived weaknesses or drawbacks of the rival offerings. The objective is to convince consumers that the company's offerings are superior and offer better value. Comparative advertising can be particularly effective when supported by evidence or data that demonstrates the superiority of the advertised product or service. In addition to highlighting advantages or conducting direct comparisons, competitive advertising may also attempt to influence consumers' perceptions of the competitor's brand. This is achieved through tactics such as creating doubt or raising concerns about the competitor's reliability, customer service, or overall reputation. By positioning the competitor negatively, the company hopes to steer consumers towards its own brand. Competitive advertising can play a critical role in shaping consumers' choices in the market. It provides information and alternative options, encourages product differentiation, and stimulates healthy competition among companies. However, it is important for advertisers to adhere to ethical standards and avoid making false or misleading claims in their competitive advertisements.

Consumer Advertising

Consumer advertising refers to the promotional activities carried out by businesses or organizations to promote their products or services directly to the general public or target consumers. It involves creating persuasive messages and using various communication channels to reach and influence potential customers. The main objective of consumer advertising is to inform, educate, persuade, and remind consumers about a particular product or service. The aim is to create awareness, generate interest, and ultimately drive consumer behavior towards the purchase of the advertised product or service. Consumer advertising typically utilizes a combination of different media platforms, including television, radio, print (e.g., newspapers, magazines), outdoor advertising (e.g., billboards, transit ads), online platforms (e.g., websites, social media), and digital media (e.g., mobile apps, email marketing). The choice of media channels depends on various factors, such as target audience demographics, budget, reach, and objectives of the advertising campaign. Effective consumer advertising strategies often involve creating compelling and memorable advertisements that capture the attention of consumers. This may involve using creative visuals, catchy slogans, storytelling, celebrity endorsements, humor, emotional appeals, or other persuasive techniques. The goal is to make the advertisement stand out and leave a lasting impression on the target audience. Consumer advertising campaigns also involve extensive market research to identify the target audience, understand their needs and preferences, and develop messages that resonate with them. By conducting market research, businesses can tailor their advertisements to specific consumer segments, increasing the chances of capturing their attention and influencing their purchasing decisions. In addition to creating brand awareness and driving sales, consumer advertising also plays a crucial role in shaping consumer perceptions and attitudes towards a company and its products. Through consistent and effective advertising, businesses can build strong brand equity and loyalty among their target consumers, leading to long-term customer relationships and repeat purchases. In summary, consumer advertising is the strategic communication and promotion of products or services directly to consumers. It involves creating persuasive advertisements and utilizing various media channels to inform, educate, and influence potential customers. Through effective consumer advertising, businesses can generate awareness, interest, and ultimately drive consumer behavior towards purchasing their advertised products or services.

Consumer Behavior

Consumer behavior in the context of advertising refers to the study of how individuals, or consumers, make decisions and take actions regarding the purchase, usage, or disposal of products or services, influenced by various factors. Consumers' behavior is a crucial aspect for advertisers to understand as it helps them tailor their advertising strategies effectively. It involves analyzing and understanding the different factors that impact consumers' decision-making processes, such as their needs, motivations, perceptions, attitudes, and cultural and social influences.

Consumer Goods

Consumer Goods are products that are purchased by individuals or households for personal use and consumption. These goods can be classified into two categories: durable goods and non-durable goods. Durable goods are long-lasting and have an average lifespan of more than three years, such as furniture, appliances, and vehicles. Non-durable goods, on the other hand, have a short lifespan and are consumed or utilized quickly, such as food, beverages, and personal care products. In the context of advertising, consumer goods play a crucial role as they are the primary focus of various marketing campaigns. Advertisements are designed to inform, persuade, and influence consumers to purchase specific consumer goods. These advertisements aim to capture the attention of the target audience, highlight the features and benefits of the product, and create a desire or need for the consumer to buy the goods.

Consumer Insight

A consumer insight in the context of advertising refers to a deep understanding of the target audience's needs, desires, motivations, and behaviors. It involves gathering and analyzing data about consumers to gain valuable insights that can inform the development of effective advertising campaigns. Consumer insights help advertisers create advertisements that resonate with the target audience, capture their attention, and drive desired actions. By understanding consumers' preferences, attitudes, and habits, advertisers can tailor their messaging, tone, and creative elements to better connect with consumers on an emotional level.

Consumer Panel

A consumer panel is a group of individuals who have been selected to participate in market research studies and provide feedback on advertisements. These participants represent a target demographic or specific consumer segment, and their opinions are used to evaluate the effectiveness of advertising campaigns. Consumer panels are often recruited by market research companies or advertising agencies to gather valuable insights about consumers' attitudes, preferences, and purchasing behaviors. They typically consist of a diverse range of individuals from different backgrounds, age groups, income levels, and locations, ensuring a broad perspective on advertising messages and their impact.

Consumer Survey

A consumer survey, in the context of advertisement, refers to a research method used to gather information and feedback from consumers regarding their preferences, opinions, and experiences related to specific products or services. This survey aims to collect data that helps advertisers and marketers gain insights into consumer behavior, attitudes, and needs, ultimately guiding the development and improvement of targeted advertising strategies. The primary purpose of conducting a consumer survey in the context of advertisement is to obtain valuable feedback that aids in understanding the target audience better. By gathering information directly from consumers, advertisers can gain insights into their preferences, purchasing behavior, and motivations. This data can then be analyzed and utilized to create more effective advertising campaigns that are tailored to meet the needs and desires of the target market.

Content Marketing Strategy Planning

Content marketing strategy planning is the process of creating a comprehensive plan to produce and distribute relevant, valuable, and engaging content with the goal of attracting, engaging, and retaining a specific target audience. It involves setting specific objectives, identifying target audience personas, developing a content strategy, and creating an editorial calendar to guide content creation and distribution Advertisement is a form of marketing communication that aims to promote a product, service, or brand to a target audience. It typically involves paid promotion through various channels such as television, radio, print media, digital platforms, and social media. Its primary goal is to generate awareness, capture attention, and persuade consumers to take a specific action, such as making a purchase or visiting a website for more information.

Content Marketing Strategy

Content marketing strategy is a structured approach implemented by businesses to create and distribute valuable and relevant content with the aim of attracting and engaging an audience, ultimately driving profitable customer action. It is a form of advertisement that focuses on providing information, entertainment, and value to consumers rather than directly selling a product or service. The main objective of content marketing strategy is to establish a relationship of trust and credibility with the target audience. Instead of bombarding consumers with traditional advertising messages, businesses use content marketing to educate, entertain, and solve problems for their potential customers. By consistently delivering high-quality content, businesses are able to build awareness, strengthen brand loyalty, and position themselves as a trusted authority in their industry. One of the key elements of content marketing strategy is identifying the target audience and understanding their needs and preferences. By creating content that resonates with the target audience, businesses are able to attract and engage the right individuals. This requires thorough research and analysis to ensure that the content addresses the target audience's pain points and provides valuable insights or solutions. Another important aspect of content marketing strategy is selecting the appropriate channels and platforms to distribute the content. This can include a wide range of mediums such as blog posts, social media, videos, podcasts, whitepapers, and more. Businesses need to carefully choose the channels that will effectively reach their target audience and align with their overall marketing goals. Measurement and analysis play a critical role in content marketing strategy. Businesses need to track and evaluate the performance of their content to determine its effectiveness in achieving the desired outcomes. This includes monitoring metrics such as website traffic, engagement levels, social media shares, conversions, and other relevant key performance indicators. In conclusion, content marketing strategy is an advertisement approach that focuses on creating and delivering valuable content to attract, engage, and retain a target audience. It is a long-term strategy that aims to build trust, establish authority, and drive profitable customer action through the distribution of high-quality and relevant content.

Content Marketing

Content marketing is an advertising technique that involves creating and distributing valuable, relevant, and consistent content to attract and engage a specific target audience. The goal of content marketing is to establish and maintain a positive brand image while ultimately driving profitable consumer action. Through content marketing, businesses can provide useful information, entertainment, or solutions to potential customers, rather than simply promoting their products or services. By offering high-quality content, businesses aim to build trust, credibility, and loyalty among their audience, positioning themselves as industry experts and thought leaders.

Content-Driven Advertising Strategies

Content-driven advertising strategies refer to marketing approaches that focus on creating and delivering valuable and relevant content to attract and engage a specific target audience. These strategies aim to deliver advertising messages in a way that is seamless and non-intrusive, while providing the audience with useful and informative content that they find interesting and beneficial. By leveraging content-driven advertising strategies, brands and advertisers can build trust and credibility with their target audience. Rather than interrupting consumers with traditional forms of advertising, such as banner ads or pop-ups, content-driven advertising aims to provide value by offering content that is entertaining, educational, or inspirational. One key aspect of content-driven advertising is understanding the target audience's interests, needs, and preferences. By conducting thorough research and analysis, advertisers can identify relevant topics and themes that resonate with their audience. This allows them to create content that aligns with their audience's interests and ultimately attracts their attention. Another important element of content-driven advertising is storytelling. By creating compelling narratives and stories, advertisers can captivate their audience and establish an emotional connection. This storytelling approach helps to humanize the brand and make it relatable to the audience, leading to increased engagement and brand loyalty. Content-driven advertising can take various forms, including articles, blog posts, videos, infographics, podcasts, and social media posts. The type of content used depends on the target audience's preferences and the platform where the content will be distributed. Additionally, content-driven advertising strategies often involve leveraging influencers and thought leaders in the industry. Collaborating with these individuals can help brands expand their reach and credibility, as well as tap into their followers' trust and loyalty. In conclusion, content-driven advertising strategies focus on delivering valuable and relevant content to target audiences, rather than interrupting them with traditional forms of advertising. By creating engaging and informative content, brands can attract and engage their target audience while building trust and credibility.

Content-Driven Advertising

Content-Driven Advertising refers to a marketing strategy that focuses on creating and delivering relevant, informative, and valuable content to target audiences. This approach aims to engage and attract consumers by providing them with useful information or entertainment, rather than directly promoting a product or service. In this form of advertising, the content itself becomes the driving force behind the message, with the objective of establishing a connection with the target audience and building brand loyalty. Through engaging and high-quality content, advertisers can establish themselves as industry experts and thought leaders while indirectly promoting their products or services.

Contextual Advertising Networks Assessment

Contextual advertising networks refer to advertising platforms that use the context of the webpage or the content being viewed by the user to deliver relevant advertisements. These networks target specific keywords, topics, or themes to match advertisements with the user's interests or the website's content. Contextual advertising networks utilize various techniques to analyze the text and context of webpages, including natural language processing, semantic analysis, and machine learning algorithms. By understanding the context of the content, these networks can display advertisements that are more likely to be of interest to the user, increasing the chances of engagement and conversion for advertisers.

Contextual Advertising Networks

Contextual advertising networks are online advertising platforms that use algorithms to display targeted advertisements to website visitors based on the content they are currently viewing. These networks analyze the textual and visual content of a webpage and match it to relevant advertisements. The goal of contextual advertising is to provide users with ads that are relevant and of interest to them, increasing the chances of user engagement and conversion. When a user visits a webpage that is supported by a contextual advertising network, the network's algorithm scans the page's content, including the text, images, and links, to determine the context or topic of the page. It then selects advertisements that are related to that context and displays them to the user. This means that if a user is reading an article about gardening, the contextual advertising network may display ads for gardening tools, plants, or landscaping services.

Contextual Advertising Platforms Assessment

Contextual advertising platforms refer to online advertising platforms that provide targeted advertisements to users based on the content they are currently viewing or the search queries they have entered. These platforms analyze the context of the webpage or the user's search query and display ads that are relevant to the topic or keywords being identified. These platforms use sophisticated algorithms to understand the meaning and intent behind the web content or search query in order to serve the most appropriate advertisements. By delivering ads that are closely related to the user's interests or needs, contextual advertising platforms aim to enhance the user experience and increase the likelihood of ad engagement.

Contextual Advertising Platforms

Contextual advertising platforms are online advertising systems that use an individual's browsing behavior and the content of the webpage they are visiting to deliver relevant advertisements. These platforms analyze the context of the webpage, including keywords and other relevant information, to determine which ads are most likely to resonate with the user. By understanding the context of the webpage, including the user's interests, preferences, and intentions, contextual advertising platforms are able to display targeted advertisements that align with the user's current needs and desires. This personalized approach helps to increase the effectiveness and engagement of the advertising campaigns.

Contextual Advertising

Contextual advertising refers to the targeted placement of advertisements on websites or other digital platforms based on the content being viewed by users. This type of advertising aims to provide relevant and personalized promotions to individuals who are likely to be interested in the advertised products or services. The process of contextual advertising involves analyzing the textual and visual content of a webpage or other online content in order to determine its topic or theme. Advertisements are then selected and displayed based on this contextual information, ensuring that the ads are highly relevant to the content and likely to capture the attention of the target audience.

Conversion Funnel Analysis Tools Selection

A conversion funnel analysis tool refers to a software or platform that helps advertisers track and optimize their marketing strategies by analyzing the customer journey from initial contact to final conversion. It provides valuable insights into how users interact with advertisements at each stage of the funnel, allowing advertisers to identify areas of improvement and make informed decisions to maximize conversions. The primary purpose of a conversion funnel analysis tool is to measure and analyze the effectiveness of advertisement campaigns by capturing and analyzing user data at various touchpoints. It helps advertisers understand the customer's journey, starting from the awareness stage, where users become aware of the advertised product or service, to the consideration stage, where users evaluate their options, and finally, the conversion stage, where users take the desired action, such as making a purchase or filling out a form. Through the use of conversion funnel analysis tools, advertisers can track critical metrics and measurements, such as click-through rates (CTRs), bounce rates, conversion rates, and exit rates. These metrics provide insights into the effectiveness of different advertisements, landing pages, and call-to-action elements. By identifying bottlenecks and areas of drop-off in the conversion funnel, advertisers can optimize their campaigns to increase conversion rates and improve return on investment. Furthermore, conversion funnel analysis tools often offer advanced features such as segmentation and cohort analysis, which allow advertisers to segment their audience and analyze specific user groups' behavior. This segmentation helps advertisers tailor their marketing strategies and optimize their campaigns for different customer segments. In conclusion, a conversion funnel analysis tool is an essential component of any advertiser's toolkit. It enables advertisers to gain valuable insights into the effectiveness of their advertisement campaigns, optimize their strategies, and maximize conversions. By tracking and analyzing the customer journey from initial contact to final conversion, advertisers can make data-driven decisions and achieve their marketing goals.

Conversion Funnel Analysis Tools

Conversion funnel analysis tools refer to the software or platforms that help businesses analyze and optimize their advertising campaigns by tracking and measuring user behavior throughout the conversion funnel. The conversion funnel represents the journey that a user takes from being aware of a product or service to becoming a paying customer. These tools track and measure key metrics at each stage of the conversion funnel, allowing advertisers to evaluate the effectiveness of their marketing efforts and make data-driven decisions to improve their advertising strategies. The analysis provided by these tools enables businesses to identify bottlenecks or areas of improvement in the conversion process and make necessary optimizations.

Conversion Funnel

The conversion funnel, in the context of advertisement, refers to the process of guiding potential customers through a series of steps or stages with the ultimate goal of converting them into paying customers. It is a strategic framework that helps marketers and advertisers optimize their campaigns to maximize conversions and increase profitability. The conversion funnel typically consists of four main stages: awareness, consideration, conversion, and retention. Each stage represents a different level of customer engagement and requires tailored marketing tactics to effectively move prospects along the funnel. The first stage, awareness, aims to attract the attention of a wide audience and make them aware of a product or service. This can be achieved through various channels such as online advertising, social media marketing, search engine optimization, and content marketing. The goal at this stage is to generate interest and drive potential customers to explore further. Once individuals are aware of the product or service, they enter the consideration stage. Here, they actively research and evaluate their options. Marketers need to provide valuable information, demonstrate the unique value proposition, and address potential objections to persuade prospects to move forward. This stage often involves tactics like targeted advertising, email marketing, customer testimonials, and comparison tools to differentiate and position the offering favorably. If a prospect decides to make a purchase or take the desired action, they enter the conversion stage. This is where the funnel narrows as the number of prospects decreases. Marketers must remove any remaining barriers to conversion and provide a seamless and easy process for customers to complete their purchase. Strategies such as personalized offers, limited-time promotions, and clear call-to-action buttons can help increase conversion rates at this stage. Finally, the retention stage focuses on retaining customers and fostering loyalty. This is crucial for maximizing customer lifetime value and generating repeat business. Marketers employ tactics such as email newsletters, loyalty programs, personalized recommendations, and excellent customer service to keep customers engaged and satisfied. The conversion funnel is a vital concept in advertising as it provides a structured framework for marketers to understand and optimize the customer journey. By identifying potential drop-off points and implementing targeted strategies at each stage, advertisers can improve conversion rates, increase customer acquisition, and ultimately drive business growth.

Conversion Rate Optimization (CRO) Tools

Conversion Rate Optimization (CRO) tools are software applications or platforms used in the context of advertising to improve the conversion rates of online campaigns. These tools analyze and optimize various elements of a website or advertisement to increase the likelihood of visitors taking a desired action, such as making a purchase or filling out a form. One key aspect of CRO tools is the ability to track and analyze user behavior. They provide insights into how visitors interact with a website or advertisement, including where they click, how long they stay, and what actions they take. This data helps advertisers identify areas of improvement and make informed decisions to optimize their campaigns.

Conversion Rate Optimization (CRO)

Conversion Rate Optimization (CRO) refers to the practice of improving the effectiveness of advertisements with the goal of increasing the number of conversions or desired actions by the target audience. Conversion rate optimization involves analyzing and optimizing various elements of an advertisement to maximize its impact and encourage users to take a specific action, such as making a purchase, subscribing to a newsletter, or filling out a form.

Conversion Rate

The conversion rate, in the context of advertising, refers to the percentage of individuals who complete a desired action or goal after being exposed to an advertisement or marketing campaign. This action or goal can vary depending on the specific objectives of the campaign, such as making a purchase, signing up for a newsletter, or filling out a form. It is an essential metric for advertisers as it directly measures the effectiveness and success of their efforts. A higher conversion rate indicates that a larger proportion of the targeted audience is taking the desired action, resulting in a more successful campaign. Conversely, a lower conversion rate suggests that the advertisement may not be resonating with the audience or that the call-to-action needs improvement.

Copywriter

An advertisement is a carefully crafted message aimed at promoting a product, service, event, or idea to a specific audience. It is a form of communication that uses various mediums, such as print, television, radio, online platforms, and social media, to reach and engage potential customers. Advertisements are designed to capture attention and create interest in the advertised offering. They often utilize persuasive techniques, such as emotional appeals, endorsements, catchy slogans, and compelling visuals, to convince individuals to take a desired action. An advertisement typically follows a strategic framework consisting of several key components. Firstly, it identifies the target audience by defining the demographics, psychographics, and behaviors of the individuals who are most likely to be interested in the product or service. This helps ensure that the message is tailored to resonate with the intended recipients. The next step in creating an advertisement involves developing a unique selling proposition (USP). The USP highlights the distinctive features, benefits, or advantages that set the advertised offering apart from competitors. It provides a compelling reason for customers to choose the product or service over alternatives. Furthermore, an advertisement includes a call to action (CTA) which prompts the audience to take a specific action, such as making a purchase, visiting a website, or contacting the company for more information. The CTA is typically clear, concise, and easy to follow, providing individuals with clear instructions on how to proceed. Lastly, an effective advertisement is often supported by strong research and analysis. Marketers conduct market research to understand consumer needs and preferences, analyze competitor strategies, and evaluate the effectiveness of different advertising channels. This data-driven approach helps refine the message, optimize the placement of ads, and maximize the overall impact of the campaign.

Copywriting

Copywriting is the art and science of creating persuasive and compelling written content for advertising purposes. It involves strategically crafting messages that capture the attention of the target audience and motivate them to take a desired action. Effective copywriting is essential in advertisements as it plays a crucial role in attracting and engaging potential customers. The main objective is to create copy that not only grabs the reader's attention but also holds their interest long enough for the message to be conveyed and the desired action to be taken.

Corporate Sponsorship

Corporate Sponsorship in the context of advertisement refers to a business arrangement where a company provides financial or other support to an event, activity, or organization in exchange for visibility and promotional benefits. In this arrangement, the sponsoring company aims to enhance its brand image, reach a specific target audience, and potentially generate increased sales or brand loyalty. When a corporation sponsors an event or organization, it typically involves the provision of funds, goods, services, or a combination of these resources. The level of sponsorship can vary, ranging from small contributions to full-scale partnerships. The sponsor's investment is often driven by the potential marketing opportunities and benefits associated with the sponsored entity. The primary objective of corporate sponsorship is to create a favorable association between the sponsor's brand and the sponsored event, activity, or organization. This association is accomplished through various promotional activities, such as displaying the sponsor's name or logo prominently on event materials, advertising campaigns, or even physical infrastructure. By doing so, the sponsor aims to increase brand recognition and visibility among the target audience. Moreover, corporate sponsorship often includes additional promotional opportunities such as product placement, exclusive branding rights, or the development of joint marketing campaigns. These initiatives further strengthen the sponsor's exposure and allow for direct engagement with the intended consumer segment. In return, the sponsored entity gains financial support as well as the potential for increased credibility and prestige. It is important to note that corporate sponsorship is different from corporate philanthropy or corporate social responsibility, as the latter is typically characterized by donations or contributions made without the expectation of direct advertising or promotional benefits. Corporate sponsorship, on the other hand, is explicitly a marketing strategy aimed at generating a return on investment. In conclusion, corporate sponsorship in the context of advertisement refers to a strategic partnership where a company provides financial or other support to an event, activity, or organization in exchange for promotional opportunities and increased brand visibility. It is a mutually beneficial arrangement, as the sponsored entity gains the necessary resources, while the sponsoring company achieves marketing objectives and strengthens its brand image.

Cost Per Acquisition (CPA)

Cost per Acquisition (CPA) is a performance-based advertising metric that measures the average cost an advertiser incurs for each desired action or conversion acquired through an advertisement campaign. CPA is widely used in the advertising industry to determine the effectiveness and success of online marketing campaigns. CPA is calculated by dividing the total cost of an advertising campaign by the number of desired actions or conversions generated. The desired action can vary depending on the advertiser's objectives and can include actions such as making a purchase, filling out a form, subscribing to a newsletter, or downloading an app. CPA provides advertisers with valuable insights into the cost-effectiveness of their marketing efforts. By analyzing the CPA, advertisers can evaluate the profitability of their campaigns and make informed decisions about the allocation of their advertising budget. An important factor in determining the CPA is the quality and relevance of the traffic generated by an advertisement. Advertisers aim to attract high-quality traffic that is more likely to convert into desired actions. This can be achieved through targeting specific demographics, geographical locations, or interests that are relevant to the advertiser's product or service. CPA is often compared with the Customer Lifetime Value (CLV) to determine the profitability of acquiring a customer. CLV represents the total value a customer brings to the advertiser over their lifetime. By comparing the CPA with the CLV, advertisers can assess the return on investment (ROI) of their marketing campaigns and determine whether they are acquiring customers at a sustainable cost. Advertisers can optimize their CPA by continuously analyzing and optimizing their advertising campaigns. This can involve testing different ad creatives, targeting strategies, landing pages, or call-to-action buttons. By identifying the most effective strategies, advertisers can reduce their CPA and maximize the value generated from their advertising efforts.

Cost Per Click (CPC)

Cost Per Click (CPC) is a metric used in the field of digital advertising to determine the cost an advertiser pays for each click on their ad. It is a pricing model commonly used in search engine advertising platforms like Google Ads and Bing Ads, as well as on social media platforms like Facebook and Twitter. CPC is calculated by dividing the total amount spent on an advertising campaign by the number of clicks generated. For example, if an advertiser spends $100 on a campaign and receives 200 clicks, the CPC would be $0.50. This means the advertiser paid $0.50 for each click on their ad.

Cost Per Impression (CPI)

Cost Per Impression (CPI) is a metric used in the field of advertising to measure the cost involved in generating one impression of an advertisement. An impression refers to the instance when an advertisement is viewed by a user on a website, app, or any other platform. CPI is commonly used by advertisers and marketers to evaluate the efficiency and effectiveness of their advertising campaigns. CPI is calculated by dividing the total cost of running an ad campaign by the number of impressions generated. It provides insights into how much an advertiser is paying for each individual viewer who sees their ad. The formula to calculate CPI is: CPI = Total Cost of Campaign ÷ Total Impressions The total cost of a campaign typically includes factors such as media buying costs, creative production expenses, and any additional fees incurred. The total impressions refer to the number of times an ad is displayed to users. It is important to note that an impression does not necessarily mean that a user has interacted with the ad, but rather that it has been visually presented to them. CPI is an essential metric as it allows advertisers to compare the costs of different advertising campaigns and channels. By calculating CPI, advertisers can determine the most cost-effective platforms and strategies to reach their target audience. It helps in optimizing advertising budgets and making informed decisions for future campaigns. Moreover, CPI is often used in conjunction with other key performance indicators (KPIs) such as click-through rate (CTR) and conversion rate to evaluate the overall success of an advertising campaign. By analyzing CPI alongside these metrics, advertisers can gain a better understanding of the return on investment (ROI) and the effectiveness of their ads in driving user engagement and conversions.

Cost Per Mille (CPM)

Cost Per Mille (CPM) is an advertising metric that measures the cost an advertiser pays for every thousand impressions of an advertisement. It is commonly used in online advertising campaigns to determine the effectiveness and efficiency of an advertising campaign. The term "mille" in CPM represents the Latin word for one thousand. CPM is calculated by dividing the total cost of an advertising campaign by the number of impressions (views) the advertisement receives, and then multiplying it by one thousand. The formula for calculating CPM is as follows: CPM = (Total Cost / Number of Impressions) * 1000 Advertisers often use CPM as a benchmark to compare the relative costs of different advertising campaigns, as well as to evaluate the cost-effectiveness of specific websites or platforms. It allows advertisers to assess the cost of reaching their target audience and determine whether the advertising investment is providing favorable returns. CPM is especially useful when comparing different advertising channels or mediums, such as television, radio, print, and online platforms. By calculating the CPM for each channel, advertisers can make informed decisions on where to allocate their advertising budget to maximize their reach and impact. However, it's important to note that CPM is just one metric used in advertising evaluations, and it has its limitations. CPM does not take into account the actual engagement or response of the viewers to the advertisement. It solely focuses on the cost of reaching a thousand viewers. Despite its limitations, CPM remains a widely used metric in online advertising due to its simplicity and easiness to compare across different platforms. Advertisers can negotiate and optimize their CPM rates by targeting specific demographics, adjusting their ad placements, and improving the quality and relevance of their ads to achieve better results.

Cost-Effective

Cost-Effective refers to the efficiency and profitability of an advertisement strategy in relation to its cost. It involves achieving the desired results or goals while minimizing expenses. A cost-effective advertisement is one that provides significant value for the money invested. In the context of advertisement, cost-effectiveness is determined by evaluating the return on investment (ROI) achieved through the campaign. The primary objective of any advertisement is to generate revenue or create a favorable perception of the product or brand. Therefore, the cost-effectiveness of an advertisement lies in its ability to generate a significant ROI.

Cost-Per-Action (CPA) Advertising

Cost-Per-Action (CPA) Advertising refers to a type of online advertising model where advertisers pay for a specific action taken by a user. Unlike other advertising models that charge based on impressions or clicks, CPA advertising charges based on a measurable outcome, such as a sale, lead, or download. CPA advertising offers advertisers a more direct and measurable way to gauge the success of their campaigns. Instead of simply tracking clicks or views, CPA advertising focuses on actual user engagement and conversion. Advertisers are only charged when a desired action is completed, ensuring that they are getting a return on their investment.

Cost-Per-Mille (CPM) Advertising

Cost-Per-Mille (CPM) Advertising is a pricing model used in the world of online advertising, where advertisers pay a predetermined amount for every thousand impressions or views of their ad. The term "mille" refers to a thousand impressions, which is derived from the Latin word for thousand. In this advertising model, the advertiser agrees to pay a specific rate for every thousand times their ad is displayed to users. This is different from other pricing models, such as Cost-Per-Click (CPC), where advertisers only pay when a user clicks on their ad. With CPM, the advertiser pays for the potential exposure and visibility their ad receives, regardless of whether or not a user engages with it.

Coverage

In the context of advertisement, coverage refers to the extent or reach of an advertising campaign in terms of how many people it reaches and how often it is seen or heard. Coverage is a crucial metric in advertising as it helps advertisers evaluate the effectiveness of their campaigns and assess the return on investment. It indicates the potential exposure of an advertisement to the target audience, which directly impacts the campaign's ability to generate awareness, build brand recognition, and ultimately drive sales.

Creative Brief

A creative brief is a document that provides a clear and concise outline of the objectives, target audience, key messaging, and visual elements for an advertisement. It serves as a roadmap for the creative team, ensuring that the final ad aligns with the overall marketing strategy and effectively communicates the desired message to the intended audience. A creative brief typically includes the following components: 1. Objectives: The brief begins by stating the specific goals the ad aims to achieve. These objectives may include increasing brand awareness, generating leads, driving sales, or promoting a new product or service. 2. Target Audience: The brief defines the intended audience for the advertisement, outlining their demographics, psychographics, and behaviors. Understanding the audience is crucial in crafting a message that resonates with them and motivates them to take action. 3. Key Messaging: This section highlights the main talking points and key messages that the ad should convey. It defines the unique selling propositions, benefits, and brand attributes that need to be communicated to the audience. The messaging should be clear, concise, and persuasive. 4. Visual Elements: The creative brief outlines the desired visual elements for the ad, including the colors, typography, imagery, and overall design style. These elements should be aligned with the brand's visual identity and evoke the desired emotions or sentiments in the audience. 5. Tone and Voice: This section defines the tone and voice that the ad should adopt. It outlines the desired style of writing, whether it should be formal, casual, humorous, or professional. The tone should reflect the brand personality and resonate with the target audience. By providing these essential details, a creative brief helps the creative team develop concepts and executions that align with the marketing objectives and effectively engage the target audience. It serves as a

112

reference throughout the creative process, ensuring that the final advertisement delivers the desired impact and successfully communicates the intended message.

Creative Strategy

Creative Strategy is an essential element in the field of advertising that encompasses the thought process and planning techniques used to develop innovative and impactful advertisements. It involves creating a clear and compelling message that resonates with the target audience and effectively communicates the brand's value proposition. The primary objective of a creative strategy is to develop advertisements that engage and captivate the audience, ultimately leading to increased brand awareness, improved brand perception, and higher customer engagement. It is the foundation upon which successful advertising campaigns are built, guiding the overall direction and approach of the creative team.

Cross-Media Campaign

A cross-media campaign in the context of advertising refers to a marketing strategy that utilizes multiple forms of media to effectively communicate with and engage a target audience. This approach involves integrating various media channels, such as print, television, radio, digital, social media, and outdoor advertising, to create a cohesive and consistent message that reaches consumers through multiple touchpoints. The goal of a cross-media campaign is to increase brand awareness, generate leads, drive customer engagement, and ultimately, achieve higher conversion rates. By leveraging different media platforms, businesses can broaden their reach and interact with potential customers in various ways, maximizing the likelihood of capturing their attention and influencing their purchasing decisions.

Cross-Promotion

Cross-promotion refers to the strategic partnership between two or more companies to promote each other's products or services. It involves the collaboration of businesses that share a similar target audience but do not directly compete with each other. Through cross-promotion, companies can leverage each other's resources, customer base, and brand equity to increase their visibility, reach a wider audience, and ultimately drive sales. This type of advertising can be done through various channels, including social media, email marketing, advertising campaigns, events, and content collaborations.

Cultural Advertising Research Methods

Cultural advertising research methods refer to the techniques and approaches used to study and analyze how advertisements relate to and influence culture. This research aims to understand the cultural context and its impact on advertising strategies and messages. Cultural advertising research methods involve various qualitative and quantitative techniques to gather data and insights. These methods are employed by researchers, marketers, and advertisers to gain a deeper understanding of the cultural aspects that influence consumer behavior and attitudes towards advertisements.

Cultural Advertising Research

Cultural advertising research is a branch of market research that focuses on understanding and analyzing the cultural aspects of a target audience in order to create effective advertising campaigns. It involves conducting in-depth studies and analysis of the cultural backgrounds, beliefs, values, and behaviors of the target audience. This research helps advertisers gain insight into the cultural context within which their target audience operates, allowing them to create advertising messages that resonate with their cultural identity.

Cultural Advertising Trends Research

Cultural advertising trends research refers to the study and analysis of current and emerging marketing practices that are influenced by cultural factors. It involves examining how advertisements are tailored to target specific consumer groups based on their cultural backgrounds, beliefs, and values. This form of research aims to understand the impact of culture on advertising messages, strategies, and tactics. It explores the ways in which advertisers adapt their campaigns to resonate with different cultural groups, taking into account their language, traditions, customs, and lifestyle preferences. Cultural advertising trends research delves into the cultural nuances that shape consumer behavior and attitudes towards brands and products. It looks at how advertising messages are crafted to appeal to and connect with diverse audiences, acknowledging that culture plays a significant role in shaping individual perceptions and preferences. By staying informed about cultural advertising trends, companies can design more inclusive and effective marketing campaigns. This research enables advertisers to avoid cultural appropriation, stereotypes, or offensive content that may negatively impact their brand reputation or alienate potential customers. Furthermore, cultural advertising trends research helps marketers identify emerging cultural shifts and new audience segments to target. It provides insights into the changing demographics, interests, and demands of different cultural groups, allowing brands to adapt their advertising strategies accordingly. In summary, cultural advertising trends research is the systematic analysis of how advertisements are influenced by culture, with the aim of developing more culturally sensitive and engaging marketing campaigns. It helps companies understand the role of culture in consumer behavior, enabling them to connect with diverse audiences and effectively communicate their brand's value proposition.

Cultural Advertising Trends

Cultural advertising trends refer to the patterns and shifts in how advertisements incorporate and reflect cultural values, beliefs, and norms. It involves considering and leveraging cultural factors such as language, symbols, traditions, and societal attitudes to effectively communicate and connect with target audiences. In today's diverse and interconnected world, cultural advertising trends have become essential for brands and marketers to engage and resonate with consumers. By understanding and respecting different cultures, advertisers can create messages and campaigns that are more relevant, relatable, and impactful.

Cultural Advertising

Cultural advertising refers to the practice of incorporating specific cultural elements, such as symbols, traditions, values, and customs, into advertisements with the aim of appealing to a particular group of people who share that culture. This form of advertising recognizes the significance of culture in shaping individuals' identities, perceptions, and behaviors. By tapping into cultural cues, advertisers can establish a connection with their target audience, evoke positive emotions, and influence consumers' purchasing decisions.

Cultural Marketing Research

Cultural Marketing

Cultural marketing, in the context of advertisement, refers to the strategic practice of targeting specific cultural groups or communities in order to better connect and resonate with them. It involves understanding the cultural values, beliefs, traditions, and preferences of the target audience and integrating them into the marketing messages and strategies. By leveraging cultural insights, marketers aim to create content and campaigns that are more relatable and appealing to the target audience. This approach recognizes the diversity within societies and acknowledges that different cultures may have distinct needs, desires, and responses to advertising messages.

Custom Ad Creatives Design

Custom Ad Creatives Design refers to the process of creating unique and tailored advertisements that effectively convey the brand message and capture the target audience's attention. It involves the use of various design elements, such as graphics, typography, colors, and layout, to craft visually appealing and compelling ad campaigns. The goal of custom ad creative design is to differentiate a brand or product from its competitors and leave a lasting impression in the minds of consumers. By customizing the design, advertisers can effectively communicate the brand's value proposition and generate interest and desire among the viewers. In custom ad creative design, each advertisement is carefully crafted to align with the brand's overall marketing strategy and campaign objectives. The design elements are chosen to resonate with the target audience's preferences, interests, and demographics. By understanding the audience's psychology and using relevant imagery, language, and design techniques, custom ad creatives can effectively engage the viewers and increase their likelihood of taking the desired action. Custom ad creatives can take various forms, such as print ads, digital banners, social media posts, video commercials, or outdoor billboards. Regardless of the medium, the design must be adaptable and optimized for the specific platform, ensuring a seamless and consistent brand experience across different channels. Moreover, custom ad creative design involves a continuous process of testing, analyzing, and refining the advertisements based on the audience's response and feedback. Advertisers monitor the performance of their ad campaigns, track key metrics, and make data-driven decisions to optimize the design elements and improve the overall effectiveness of the ads. In conclusion, custom ad creative design plays a crucial role in advertising by creating visually appealing and tailored advertisements that effectively communicate the brand's message and capture the attention of the target audience. By utilizing various design elements and continuously refining the ads based on performance data, advertisers can maximize the impact of their ad campaigns and drive desired consumer actions.

Custom Ad Creatives

A custom ad creative refers to a personalized and tailored advertising material that is specifically designed to promote a product, service, or brand in a unique and engaging way. It is a strategic approach that aims to capture the attention of the target audience and effectively convey the intended message. The concept of custom ad creatives revolves around the idea of creating visually appealing and highly persuasive advertisements that stand out from the clutter and leave a lasting impression on the viewers. These creatives are carefully crafted by professionals who possess a deep understanding of consumer behavior and market trends. One of the key purposes of custom ad creatives is to differentiate a brand from its competitors and build brand recognition and recall. By using innovative storytelling techniques, captivating visuals, and compelling copywriting, these creatives strive to evoke emotions, engage the audience, and generate interest in the advertised product or service. Custom ad creatives can take various forms, including print advertisements, television commercials, digital banners, social media posts, and interactive web experiences. Each format offers different opportunities and challenges in terms of design, layout, and presentation, requiring careful consideration and adaptation of the creative concept. Moreover, custom ad creatives often incorporate elements of personalization and interactivity to enhance the overall effectiveness of the advertising campaign. By addressing the specific needs, preferences, and demographics of the target audience, these creatives can deliver a more personalized and relevant message, which in turn improves the chances of conversion or purchase. In summary, custom ad creatives are tailor-made advertising materials designed to captivate and engage the target audience. Through creative design, storytelling, and personalization, these creatives aim to differentiate a brand, build brand recognition, and generate interest in the advertised product or service. They come in various forms and incorporate elements of interactivity to create a unique and memorable advertising experience.

Custom Ad Placements Strategy

Custom Ad Placements Strategy refers to the strategic approach used by advertisers and publishers to carefully select and place advertisements in specific locations within a website or digital platform. This approach aims to optimize the visibility, relevance, and effectiveness of ads by tailoring their placement to the target audience, content context, and user experience. The process of implementing a custom ad placements strategy involves analyzing various factors, such as the website's layout, navigation structure, and user behavior. Advertisers and publishers collaborate to identify the most appropriate ad locations within the website, taking into consideration the content type, user engagement patterns, and site performance metrics. Custom ad placements can be implemented through various methods, including manual ad placement, native advertising, and programmatic advertising. Manual ad placement involves manually selecting and placing ads in specific areas of the webpage, such as the header, sidebar, or within the content itself. This method offers more control over ad placement but requires a hands-on approach to ensure optimal results. Native advertising involves seamlessly integrating ads into the website's content, making them appear more organic and less intrusive. This method often involves collaboration between advertisers and content creators to craft ads that align with the overall user experience and provide value to the audience. Programmatic advertising utilizes automated algorithms and data-driven targeting to dynamically place ads in real-time. This method leverages machine learning and user data to identify the most suitable ad placement opportunities for each individual user. It allows for more personalized and contextually relevant ad placements, enhancing the overall user experience and increasing the likelihood of engagement. By implementing a custom ad placements strategy, advertisers and publishers can maximize the impact and effectiveness of their ads. Customization ensures that ads are strategically placed in areas that are most likely to capture the audience's attention and generate desired actions, such as clicks or conversions. It also helps to maintain a balance between user experience and monetization, ensuring that ads do not disrupt the overall browsing experience. In conclusion, a custom ad placements strategy is a strategic approach to advertisement placement within digital platforms. It involves careful analysis of website layout, user behavior, and content context to determine the most suitable locations for ads. Custom ad placements can be implemented through manual placement, native advertising, or programmatic advertising, aiming to optimize visibility, relevance, and user experience.

Custom Ad Placements

Custom ad placements refer to the strategic positioning of advertisements within various marketing channels, tailored to fit the specific needs and goals of advertisers. This approach allows advertisers to have more control and flexibility over where their ads are displayed, maximizing their reach and effectiveness. With custom ad placements, advertisers can choose specific websites, apps, or platforms where they want their ads to be showcased. This allows them to target their desired audience and optimize their ad placement for maximum visibility and engagement. By carefully selecting the right platforms, advertisers can align their ads with relevant content and context, creating a more seamless and effective advertising experience. One of the key benefits of custom ad placements is the ability to tailor the ad placement to suit the unique needs and preferences of the target audience. By understanding the interests, behavior, and demographics of their audience, advertisers can strategically place their ads where they are most likely to catch the attention of their desired customers. In addition to choosing specific platforms, custom ad placements also involve selecting the optimal placement within the chosen platform. Advertisers can choose whether they want their ads to be displayed at the top, bottom, or side of a webpage, or within a specific section or category of an app or platform. This allows advertisers to capture the attention of their audience at the right moment and in the most effective way possible. Custom ad placements can also involve the use of advanced targeting techniques, such as geo-targeting or behavioral targeting. By leveraging data and insights, advertisers can narrow down their audience based on location, interests, or past online behavior. This enables them to display their ads to a more relevant and receptive audience, increasing the chances of driving conversions and achieving their advertising goals. Overall, custom ad placements offer advertisers greater control and flexibility in displaying their ads across various marketing channels. By carefully selecting platforms and optimizing ad placements, advertisers can enhance the visibility, engagement, and effectiveness of their advertisements, ultimately driving better results for their marketing campaigns. Custom ad placements refer to the strategic positioning of advertisements within various marketing channels, tailored to fit the specific needs and goals of advertisers. This approach allows advertisers to have more control and flexibility over where their ads are displayed, maximizing their reach and effectiveness. With custom ad placements, advertisers can choose specific websites, apps, or platforms where they want their ads to be showcased. This allows them to target their desired audience and optimize their ad placement for maximum visibility and engagement.

Custom Audiences Creation

A Custom Audience is a feature provided by online advertising platforms that allows advertisers to target specific groups of users based on their previous interactions with the advertiser's website or mobile app. When creating a Custom Audience, advertisers can upload a list of customer data, such as email addresses or phone numbers, which is then matched with the respective platform's user accounts. This process ensures that the advertising platform can deliver ads to those specific individuals or users who are already familiar with the advertiser's brand. Custom Audiences are beneficial for advertisers as they enable highly targeted advertising campaigns. By focusing on a specific group of individuals who have already shown interest in the advertiser's products or services, advertisers can increase the relevancy of their ads and potentially improve their ad performance. For example, an online clothing retailer could

116

create a Custom Audience comprised of individuals who have previously made a purchase on their website. By doing so, the retailer can deliver targeted ads to these customers, showcasing new product arrivals or offering them exclusive discounts. This strategy not only helps in retaining existing customers but also encourages repeat purchases. Additionally, Custom Audiences can be used for retargeting purposes. For instance, if a user visits an e-commerce website, views a particular product, but doesn't make a purchase, the retailer can create a Custom Audience based on these website visitors. The retailer can then show ads to this specific audience, reminding them of the product they were interested in and incentivizing them to complete the purchase. Overall, the ability to create Custom Audiences represents a powerful targeting tool for advertisers. By leveraging previous customer interactions, advertisers can optimize their ad campaigns, improve their return on investment, and ultimately achieve their marketing objectives.

Custom Audiences

Custom Audiences in the context of advertisement refer to a targeting feature provided by advertising platforms, such as social media platforms or online advertising networks. It allows advertisers to create specific audience segments based on a set of predefined criteria or customer data. With Custom Audiences, advertisers can reach a more tailored and relevant audience by targeting individuals who have already shown interest or engagement with their brand, website, app, or products. This targeting approach enables advertisers to deliver personalized and targeted messages to the right people, at the right time, and in the right place.

Customer Acquisition Advertising Campaigns

Customer acquisition advertising campaigns refer to strategic marketing initiatives designed to attract and acquire new customers for a business or organization. These campaigns are focused on increasing brand awareness, generating leads, and ultimately converting those leads into paying customers. The primary goal of customer acquisition advertising campaigns is to expand the customer base and drive revenue growth. This is achieved through various channels, including print, digital, television, radio, and social media. The specific approach may vary depending on the target audience and the nature of the business.

Customer Acquisition Advertising

Customer acquisition advertising refers to the strategic and targeted marketing efforts aimed at acquiring new customers or clients for a business or organization. It involves using various advertising channels and tactics to attract and engage potential customers and persuade them to make a purchase or take a desired action. The goal of customer acquisition advertising is to increase the customer base and drive sales growth. It plays a crucial role in the overall business growth strategy by identifying and reaching out to potential customers who may have an interest in the products or services being offered.

Customer Acquisition

Customer acquisition, in the context of advertisement, refers to the process of attracting and converting new customers for a business or organization. It is a crucial aspect of marketing and sales strategies, aiming to expand the customer base and generate revenue. The customer acquisition process involves various stages and techniques to effectively reach and engage potential customers. It begins with identifying the target audience and understanding their needs and preferences. This information is then used to develop marketing campaigns and advertisements that resonate with the target market. In order to acquire customers, businesses utilize different advertising channels and platforms. This includes traditional forms of advertisement such as print media, television, radio, and outdoor advertising, as well as modern digital channels like social media, search engine marketing, email marketing, and online display ads. Once the advertisements are deployed, businesses monitor their performance through various metrics, such as click-through rates, conversion rates, and return on investment. These metrics help assess the effectiveness of the advertising strategies and make necessary adjustments to optimize customer acquisition efforts. Customer acquisition is not just about attracting new customers; it also involves building and maintaining relationships with existing customers. This is achieved through personalized marketing initiatives, customer loyalty

117

programs, excellent customer service, and consistent communication. The ultimate goal of customer acquisition is not only to acquire new customers but also to retain them and turn them into loyal advocates of the business. A successful customer acquisition strategy leads to increased brand awareness, higher sales, and overall business growth.

Customer Behavior

Customer behavior, in the context of advertisement, refers to the actions, reactions, and decision-making processes that customers go through when they encounter and interact with advertisements. It involves understanding how customers think, feel, and behave in response to marketing messages and stimuli. Customers' behavior in relation to advertisements is influenced by a variety of factors, including their needs, preferences, values, attitudes, and past experiences. These factors shape their perception, interpretation, and response to marketing communications.

Customer Insight

Customer insight, in the context of advertisement, refers to a deep understanding of the customers' needs, preferences, motivations, and behaviors. It involves gathering and analyzing data, as well as interpreting customers' actions and responses to various marketing stimuli. Customer insight aims to uncover valuable and actionable information that can guide communication strategies, product development decisions, and overall marketing efforts. By gaining customer insight, advertisers can tailor their advertisements to target specific customer segments more effectively. This insight helps advertisers understand what resonates with their customers, enabling them to create persuasive and engaging advertisements that are more likely to capture the attention and interest of their target audience.

Customer Relationship Management (CRM)

Customer Relationship Management (CRM) in the context of advertisement refers to the strategic use of technology and processes to manage and nurture relationships with customers across various touchpoints and channels. CRM allows advertisers to effectively track and analyze customer interactions and behaviors, enabling them to develop targeted advertising campaigns that resonate with their target audience. By capturing and analyzing customer data, CRM systems help advertisers gain insights into customer preferences, behaviors, and needs, which can be used to create personalized and tailored advertisements.

Customer Segmentation In Advertising Tools

Customer segmentation in advertising tools refers to the process of grouping customers into distinct segments based on specific characteristics or behaviors, in order to effectively target and tailor advertising messages and campaigns to each segment. It involves dividing a larger target audience into smaller, more homogeneous groups that share similar traits or preferences. The goal of customer segmentation in advertising is to identify and reach the most relevant audience for a particular product or service, maximizing the impact and return on investment of advertising efforts. By understanding the unique needs, interests, and preferences of different customer segments, advertisers can develop targeted strategies that resonate with specific groups, leading to higher engagement, conversion rates, and customer loyalty.

Customer Segmentation In Advertising

Customer segmentation in advertising refers to the process of dividing a broad target market into distinct groups or segments based on specific characteristics, behaviors, or preferences. The goal of customer segmentation is to better understand the needs, motivations, and preferences of different customer groups, enabling advertisers to tailor their advertising campaigns to effectively reach and engage with each segment. Segmenting customers allows advertisers to create targeted and personalized advertising messages that resonate with specific groups of consumers. By identifying and understanding the unique traits and interests of each segment, advertisers can develop highly relevant and compelling advertisements that are more likely to capture the attention and interest of the intended audience.

Customer Segmentation

Customer segmentation refers to the process of dividing a target market into distinct groups or segments based on shared characteristics or behaviors. This segmentation allows businesses to better understand and identify their customers, and then tailor their advertising strategies to effectively reach and communicate with each segment. By segmenting their customer base, businesses can gain valuable insights into the preferences, needs, and purchasing patterns of different groups of customers. This information enables businesses to create targeted advertisements that resonate with and appeal to each segment. It allows them to customize their messaging, visuals, and offers to better suit the unique interests and motivations of specific customer groups, resulting in more effective and impactful advertising campaigns.

Customer-Centric Advertising Approaches

A customer-centric advertising approach refers to a marketing strategy that places the customer at the center of all advertising efforts. This approach recognizes the importance of understanding customer needs, preferences, and behaviors in order to deliver personalized and relevant advertisements. By adopting a customer-centric advertising approach, businesses aim to build strong relationships with their target audiences and enhance the overall customer experience. This approach involves collecting and analyzing customer data to gain insights into their interests, preferences, and purchase patterns. These insights enable businesses to create customized marketing campaigns that resonate with customers and drive higher engagement and conversions.

Customer-Centric Advertising

Customer-Centric Advertising refers to a marketing strategy where advertisements are designed and tailored to meet the specific needs and preferences of the target audience. It aims to create a personalized and engaging experience for customers, placing them at the center of the advertising campaign. In customer-centric advertising, the main focus is on understanding the customers' behaviors, interests, and motivations. Through extensive market research and data analysis, advertisers gain insights into the target audience's demographics, psychographics, and purchase patterns. This information helps in crafting advertisements that resonate with customers on a deeper level.

D2C (Direct-To-Consumer) Advertising

D2C advertising, also known as Direct-to-Consumer advertising, is a marketing strategy that involves bypassing intermediaries, such as retailers or wholesalers, and directly targeting consumers with advertising messages and promotions. This approach allows brands and companies to establish a direct relationship with their target audience by delivering their marketing messages without relying on traditional distribution channels. The rise of e-commerce and digital technologies has facilitated the growth of D2C advertising, making it easier for brands to reach consumers directly through various online channels, including social media, websites, email marketing, and mobile applications. By eliminating intermediaries, companies can have more control over their brand image, pricing, and customer experience, resulting in a more personalized and tailor-made marketing approach. Moreover, D2C advertising allows brands to gather valuable data about their consumers, enabling them to make data-driven decisions and improve their overall marketing strategies. By collecting information about consumer preferences, behaviors, and buying patterns, companies can deliver more targeted and relevant advertisements, enhancing the effectiveness of their campaigns. One of the key advantages of D2C advertising is its ability to create a direct line of communication between brands and consumers. Through social media platforms and other digital channels, companies can interact with their customers in real-time, addressing inquiries, resolving issues, and building brand loyalty. This direct engagement fosters a sense of trust and strengthens the customer-brand relationship. Furthermore, D2C advertising allows brands to have greater control over their pricing and profit margins. By eliminating the need for middlemen, brands can offer their products or services at competitive prices, attracting price-sensitive consumers. Additionally, companies can allocate more resources to marketing and customer acquisition instead of paying fees or commissions to intermediaries. In conclusion, D2C advertising is a marketing strategy that enables brands to directly target consumers without relying on intermediaries. By leveraging digital technologies and online channels, brands can establish a direct line of communication, personalize their marketing messages, and gather valuable consumer data. This approach offers greater control over pricing and customer experience, allowing companies to build stronger relationships with their target audience.

Data-Driven Advertising Approaches

Data-Driven Advertising Approaches are marketing strategies that utilize data analytics and insights to create targeted and personalized advertisements for specific audiences. This approach involves collecting and analyzing large amounts of data from various sources, such as customer behavior, demographics, and preferences, to better understand the target audience and their needs. By analyzing this data, advertisers can gain valuable insights into consumer behavior and preferences, allowing them to tailor their advertising messages and content to resonate with their target audience. This not only helps to improve the effectiveness of advertising campaigns but also enhances customer engagement and overall brand experience.

Data-Driven Advertising Campaigns Implementation

Data-driven advertising campaigns implementation refers to the process of executing an advertisement strategy that utilizes data and analytics to inform and optimize decision-making. This approach leverages consumer data and insights to target specific audiences, personalize advertising messages, and measure the campaign's effectiveness. In a data-driven advertising campaign, data is collected from various sources such as customer behavior, demographics, and online activity. This information is then analyzed to identify patterns, preferences, and trends, allowing advertisers to create targeted and relevant advertisements. The implementation of data-driven advertising campaigns involves several key steps. Firstly, advertisers define their campaign objectives and target audience. They then use data analysis techniques to segment and evaluate the target market, enabling them to understand consumer behavior, interests, and preferences. Next, advertisers utilize technology and automation tools to deliver personalized messages and advertisements to the identified target audience. This can include customized content, product recommendations, or personalized offers tailored to individual consumer preferences. By using data insights, advertisers can increase the relevance and effectiveness of their advertisements, resulting in higher engagement and conversion rates. Furthermore, data-driven advertising campaigns enable advertisers to measure and evaluate the success of their strategies. By analyzing data in real-time, advertisers can monitor key performance indicators (KPIs) such as click-through rates, conversions, and return on investment (ROI). This allows them to make data-driven decisions during the campaign implementation and optimize their advertising efforts for better results. The implementation of data-driven advertising campaigns has numerous benefits for advertisers. It maximizes the return on advertisement investment by targeting the right audience with relevant messages. It also enhances customer engagement and satisfaction by delivering personalized experiences. Additionally, data-driven advertising enables advertisers to identify trends and adjust their strategies accordingly, staying ahead of the competition. In conclusion, data-driven advertising campaigns implementation involves utilizing data analysis and technology to create targeted, personalized, and effective advertisements. By leveraging consumer insights, advertisers can optimize their campaign strategies, measure performance, and achieve better results.

Data-Driven Advertising Campaigns

Data-Driven Advertising Campaigns refer to strategic marketing initiatives in which decision-making and campaign optimization are based on data analysis and insights. These campaigns are designed to target specific audiences, personalize messaging, and ensure effective use of advertising budget. Data plays a significant role in every step of a data-driven advertising campaign. It starts with collecting and analyzing relevant data about the target audience, including their demographics, preferences, and behaviors. This data is then used to identify the most suitable advertising channels, platforms, and formats for reaching the target audience effectively. Once the target audience and advertising platforms are identified, data-driven advertising campaigns focus on creating personalized and tailored messages that resonate with the target audience. This personalization is achieved by leveraging the insights gained from the data analysis, allowing advertisers to craft messages that meet the specific needs and preferences of their audience segments. Data-driven advertising campaigns also utilize data to optimize their performance and deliver better results. Advertisers continuously monitor the performance of their campaigns, track key performance indicators (KPIs), and analyze data in real-time. This allows them to make data-driven decisions and make adjustments to their campaigns to improve their effectiveness and maximize return on investment. Furthermore, data-driven advertising campaigns enable advertisers to measure the impact and success of their campaigns with greater accuracy. They can track and evaluate the performance of their advertisements by analyzing various metrics, such as click-through rates, conversion rates, and return on ad spend. This data-driven approach provides advertisers with valuable insights into the effectiveness of their campaigns and helps them refine their strategies for future campaigns. In conclusion, data-driven advertising campaigns leverage data analysis and insights to optimize decision-making, tailor messages, and improve campaign performance. By utilizing data at every stage of the advertising process, these campaigns enable advertisers to better target their audience, deliver personalized messaging, and achieve desired marketing outcomes.

Data-Driven Advertising

Data-driven advertising refers to the practice of using data and analytics to personalize and optimize advertising strategies and campaigns. It involves collecting and analyzing consumer data, both online and offline, to understand audience preferences, behaviors, and demographics. This data is then used to create targeted and relevant advertising messages that resonate with specific segments of the target market. Data-driven advertising relies on the use of various data sources, such as website analytics, social media insights, customer relationship management (CRM) systems, and third-party data providers. These sources provide valuable information about consumer interests, purchase history, browsing habits, and other relevant data points. By integrating and analyzing this data, advertisers gain insights into their audience, enabling them to deliver more personalized and effective advertising messages. The key advantage of data-driven advertising is the ability to reach the right audience with the right message at the right time. By leveraging data, advertisers can identify the most promising segments of the target market and tailor their advertising efforts accordingly. This results in higher engagement, improved conversion rates, and increased return on investment (ROI) for advertising campaigns. In addition to audience targeting, data-driven advertising also allows for optimization and measurement of advertising performance. Through continuous monitoring and analysis of data, advertisers can optimize ad placements, creative elements, and messaging to maximize campaign effectiveness. They can also track and measure the impact of their advertising efforts, providing valuable insights for future campaign planning and decision-making. Data-driven advertising also enables real-time decision-making and agility in ad campaigns. By constantly monitoring data and performance metrics, advertisers can make quick adjustments to their strategies, ensuring that advertising efforts remain relevant and effective in a dynamic and fast-paced marketing landscape.

Database Marketing Solutions Evaluation

A database marketing solution is a strategic approach to advertising that uses data and customer information to effectively target and personalize marketing campaigns. It involves the use of a comprehensive database that stores information about customers, their preferences, behaviors, and interactions with the brand. Through the database marketing solution, businesses can segment their customer base into different groups based on specific criteria, such as demographics, purchase history, or user behavior. This segmentation allows marketers to tailor their marketing messages, offers, and content to each specific customer segment, increasing the likelihood of a positive response and conversion. Database marketing solutions offer several advantages in the advertising field. Firstly, they provide businesses with a deep understanding of their customers. By analyzing the data stored in the database, marketers can gain insights into customer preferences, buying patterns, and interaction history. This knowledge enables them to create highly targeted campaigns that resonate with each individual customer. Additionally, database marketing solutions enable personalized communication with customers. By leveraging the information stored in the database, businesses can send customized messages and offers to specific customer segments, making the marketing content more relevant and engaging. This personalization increases the chances of capturing the attention and interest of customers, ultimately leading to higher conversion rates. Furthermore, database marketing solutions help optimize marketing efforts and improve efficiency. By tracking and analyzing customer responses and campaign results, marketers can measure the effectiveness of their marketing activities and make data-driven decisions. They can identify which campaigns were successful, which segments responded best, and which strategies need adjustment, allowing for continuous improvement and optimization of advertising efforts. In summary, a database marketing solution is a powerful tool in the world of advertising. It harnesses the power of data and customer information to target, personalize, and optimize marketing campaigns. By utilizing the insights and capabilities provided by a comprehensive database, businesses can create more effective and engaging advertisements, leading to better customer engagement, increased conversions, and ultimately, improved business outcomes.

Database Marketing Solutions

Database Marketing Solutions refer to the use of customer data and analytics to inform advertising decisions and strategies. This approach utilizes database management systems to collect, store, and analyze information on customers and prospects, allowing businesses to target and personalize their advertisements more effectively. By leveraging a database of customer information, businesses can gain insights into consumer behaviors, preferences, and demographics. This data can then be used to create targeted marketing campaigns that are more likely to resonate with specific customer segments, leading to improved advertising results and higher return on investment.

Database Marketing

Database marketing is a strategic approach used by businesses to manage their customer data and utilize it effectively for targeted advertising campaigns. It involves gathering and analyzing large sets of customer data from various sources and organizing it in a structured database. This data typically includes demographic information, purchase history, online behavior, and other relevant details. The primary purpose of database marketing in the context of advertising is to enhance the effectiveness of marketing campaigns by targeting specific customer segments with tailored messages. By extracting insights from the database, businesses can identify patterns, preferences, and trends among their customers, allowing them to create personalized advertisements that resonate with their target audience. Database marketing enables advertisers to segment their customer base and define precise target groups based on characteristics such as age, gender, location, interests, and buying behavior. This segmentation process ensures that advertisements are delivered to the most relevant audience, increasing the likelihood of conversions and maximizing return on investment. Furthermore, database marketing facilitates customer relationship management (CRM) by enabling businesses to build stronger connections with their customers. By understanding customer preferences and behaviors, advertisers can create personalized experiences and deliver targeted offers to enhance customer satisfaction and loyalty. In order to execute successful database marketing campaigns, businesses employ various techniques such as data mining, data cleansing, and predictive analytics. These techniques help in identifying patterns, predicting future behaviors, and optimizing marketing strategies to achieve desired outcomes. Additionally, advanced technologies such as artificial intelligence and machine learning are often utilized to process and analyze vast amounts of data efficiently. In conclusion, database marketing in the context of advertising is a data-driven approach that leverages customer information to deliver targeted and personalized advertisements. By analyzing customer data, businesses can identify specific audience segments and tailor marketing messages to maximize effectiveness. Through effective database marketing, businesses can improve customer relationships, increase conversions, and ultimately drive growth in the highly competitive advertising landscape.

Demographic Targeting Tactics

Demographic targeting tactics refer to the specific strategies and approaches used in advertising to target a specific audience based on various demographic factors such as age, gender, income, education, location, and more. This type of targeting allows advertisers to reach their intended audience more effectively and increase the chances of relevant and engaging advertisements. Demographic targeting allows advertisers to tailor their advertisements to suit the interests and preferences of their target audience. By identifying the demographic characteristics of their ideal customers, advertisers can create more personalized and relevant ad campaigns. For example, a clothing retailer may target young females aged 18-24 with their latest fashion collection, while a luxury car brand may target affluent individuals with high income levels. Demographic targeting tactics involve analyzing data and insights gathered from various sources such as customer surveys, public databases, social media platforms, and website analytics. Advertisers can use this information to better understand their target audience's demographics and tailor their messaging and ad placement accordingly. One of the common demographic targeting tactics is age targeting. Advertisers can choose to display their ads to specific age groups or exclude certain age groups to ensure their message reaches the right audience. For instance, a video game company may want to target teenagers and young adults, while a retirement planning service may target individuals above a certain age. Another demographic targeting tactic is gender targeting. Advertisers can display their ads to a specific gender or exclude a particular gender to ensure their message resonates with their intended audience. For example, a cosmetic brand may target females with their new skincare product, while a shaving razor brand may target males. Location targeting is another effective tactic used in demographic targeting. It allows advertisers to display their ads to users in specific geographic locations or exclude certain areas. This tactic is particularly useful for local businesses aiming to reach customers in their vicinity. Overall, demographic targeting tactics play a crucial role in advertising by allowing advertisers to reach the right audience with the right message. By understanding the demographic characteristics of their target audience, advertisers can create more effective and engaging campaigns that drive better results.

Demographic Targeting Tools Assessment

Demographic targeting tools assess and analyze the characteristics, preferences, and behaviors of a specific group of individuals to aid in the creation and delivery of targeted advertisements. These tools enable advertisers to narrow down their audience based on factors such as age, gender, location, income, education, and other demographic variables. By utilizing demographic targeting tools, advertisers can reach their desired audience effectively and efficiently. These tools allow advertisers to tailor their advertising content and messages to resonate with the needs and interests of specific demographic segments. This approach ensures that the right message is delivered to the right people at the right time, which can significantly improve the overall effectiveness and impact of an advertisement campaign.

Demographic Targeting Tools

Demographic targeting tools in the context of advertisement refer to the technology or systems used by advertisers to identify and reach specific segments of a population based on demographic characteristics. These tools enable advertisers to target their advertisements more precisely and effectively by tailoring their message to the specific needs, preferences, and behaviors of different demographic groups. Demographic targeting tools typically utilize data collected from various sources, including census data, public records, online behavior and purchasing data, and surveys. By analyzing this data, advertisers can identify trends and patterns that help them understand the demographic composition of their target audience. They can then use this information to create targeted advertising campaigns that are more likely to resonate with their intended audience.

Demographic Targeting

Demographic targeting in the context of advertising refers to the practice of aiming marketing campaigns at specific segments of the population based on their demographic characteristics. These characteristics may include age, gender, income level, education level, marital status, occupation, geographical location, and more. By utilizing demographic targeting, advertisers can tailor their advertisements to reach specific groups of people who are more likely to be interested in their products or services. This allows for a more efficient use of advertising resources and a greater chance of converting potential customers into actual buyers.

Demographic

Demographic refers to a specific segment of the population that shares common characteristics such as age, gender, income level, education, occupation, and geographical location. In the context of advertisement, demographic analysis is a vital tool used by businesses to identify and target their desired audience effectively. Understanding the demographics of a target audience allows advertisers to tailor their marketing messages and strategies to resonate with the specific needs, preferences, and behaviors of the individuals within that group. By doing so, advertisers can increase the likelihood of achieving favorable outcomes, such as generating more brand awareness, driving higher sales, and fostering brand loyalty.

Digital Advertising

Digital advertising refers to the practice of promoting products, services, or brands using various digital channels and platforms. These channels may include websites, search engines, social media platforms, email, mobile apps, and other online platforms. Unlike traditional forms of advertising, digital advertising leverages the power of the internet and digital technologies to reach a wider audience and engage with them in a more personalized and targeted manner. It allows advertisers to deliver their messages to the right people, at the right time, and in the right context.

Digital Billboard Advertising Design Software

A digital billboard advertising design software is a computer application that is specifically designed to create visually appealing and captivating advertisements for digital billboards. It provides users with a range of tools and features to design, customize, and display professional-grade advertisements on digital billboards. Designed for the advertising industry, this software allows users to create eye-catching and interactive ads that can attract the attention of passersby. It offers an intuitive and user-friendly interface, making it easy for both professionals and beginners to navigate and utilize its various functionalities. The primary purpose of this software is to enable users to design advertisements that effectively communicate their brand message and engage with their target audience. Users can leverage the software's diverse range of design tools to incorporate attractive visuals, animations, and multimedia elements into their ads. Additionally, this software often includes templates and pre-designed layouts to simplify the ad creation process. Users can choose from a variety of professionally designed templates or create their own designs from scratch. The software also provides access to a vast library of high-quality images, icons, fonts, and other design resources to enhance the visual appeal of the advertisements. One of the key features of a digital billboard advertising design software is its ability to preview and simulate how the ad will appear on a digital billboard. It allows users to visualize their designs in the context of a digital billboard's layout, size, and dimensions. This feature helps users optimize their designs for maximum impact and ensures that the final ad is visually optimized for the specific digital billboard it will be displayed on. Moreover, this software often includes scheduling and distribution features, allowing users to plan and manage their advertising campaigns. Users can schedule the display of their ads to ensure maximum visibility and target specific time slots or locations. They can also monitor the performance of their advertisements to measure their effectiveness and make data-driven decisions for future campaigns.

Digital Billboard Advertising Design

Digital billboard advertising design refers to the process of creating visually appealing and impactful advertisements that are displayed on digital billboards. These billboards use advanced technology such as LED screens and digital displays to showcase advertisements in a dynamic and engaging manner. Designing digital billboard advertisements requires careful consideration of various elements like color, typography, imagery, and layout to effectively convey the intended message and capture the attention of viewers. The goal is to create eye-catching visuals that instantly grab the audience's attention and leave a lasting impression. The size and proportions of digital billboards are typically larger than traditional static billboards, requiring bold and high-resolution visuals that can be easily viewed from a distance. The use of vibrant colors and contrasting tones can help create visually appealing advertisements that stand out against the backdrop of the surrounding environment. Typography plays a crucial role in digital billboard advertising design. Choosing the right fonts and font sizes is essential for legibility, especially considering the potentially fast-moving traffic that viewers may be a part of. Bold, sans-serif fonts are often preferred for their readability and impact. Imagery can be a powerful tool in digital billboard advertising design. Eye-catching visuals, such as high-resolution photographs or compelling illustrations, can help to convey the message effectively and make a lasting impression on viewers. However, it is important to ensure that the imagery used is relevant to the brand and the advertisement's message. The layout of a digital billboard advertisement should be clear and concise. A clutter-free design with minimal text and a focus on the key message is key. The message should be easy to read and comprehend within the limited viewing time that a billboard allows. Strategic use of negative space can help draw attention to the main elements of the advertisement. In conclusion, digital billboard advertising design is the art of creating visually appealing and impactful advertisements that are displayed on digital billboards. By carefully considering elements such as color, typography, imagery, and layout, advertisers can create attention-grabbing visuals that effectively convey their message and capture the audience's attention.

Digital Billboard Advertising Planning

Digital billboard advertising planning refers to the strategic process of designing and implementing advertising campaigns on digital billboards. Digital billboards are large electronic display boards that use LED technology to showcase dynamic and visually captivating advertisements. Unlike traditional billboards, digital billboards allow for real-time content updates and sophisticated targeting options, making them a highly effective advertising medium. The planning stage of digital billboard advertising involves several key steps. Firstly, advertisers must identify their target audience and define their advertising objectives. They need to understand who their ideal customers are and what message they want to convey. This helps in tailoring the content and design of the advertisement to ensure maximum impact. Once the target audience and objectives are established, advertisers must research and select the most suitable digital billboard locations. Factors such as high traffic volume, visibility from key roads or intersections, and proximity to target demographics play a crucial role in determining the effectiveness of advertising campaigns. After identifying the optimal locations, advertisers then need to create compelling advertisements that are specifically tailored for digital billboards. This includes selecting visually appealing graphics, creating concise and impactful copy, and ensuring that the overall design stands out in the highly competitive outdoor advertising landscape. In addition to the design, the planning process also involves deciding on the duration and timing of the advertisement. Advertisers must determine how long they want their message to be displayed on the digital billboard and whether they want to schedule their ads to appear during specific times of the day or week to target a specific audience. Furthermore, digital billboard advertising planning requires careful consideration of the budget. Advertisers need to assess the costs associated with renting digital billboard space, producing high-quality advertisements, and any additional expenses such as content updates or monitoring. Budgeting appropriately ensures that resources are allocated wisely and that the campaign meets its objectives within financial constraints. Overall, digital billboard advertising planning involves a strategic approach to harnessing the power of digital billboards to reach and engage target audiences effectively. By carefully considering the target audience, objectives, location selection, ad design, timing, and budget, advertisers can maximize the impact and return on investment of their digital billboard advertising campaigns.

Digital Billboard Advertising

Digital Billboard Advertising refers to the practice of displaying advertisements on digital screens located in high-traffic areas, such as major roads, highways, and shopping centers. These digital billboards are equipped with advanced technology that allows for the dynamic and interactive display of content. Unlike traditional static billboards, digital billboards offer a range of features that make advertising more engaging and effective. They are capable of displaying multiple advertisements in a rotation, allowing advertisers to target different audiences at different times. The content on digital billboards can be easily updated and changed, providing flexibility for advertisers to optimize their messaging in real-time.

Direct Mail Advertising Campaigns Management

Direct Mail Advertising Campaigns Management refers to the process of planning, executing, and evaluating promotional campaigns that use direct mail as the primary method of communication with target audiences. In this type of advertising, marketers create and send physical promotional materials, such as brochures, flyers, postcards, or letters, directly to potential customers' mailboxes. The goal is to grab their attention, generate interest in the product or service being offered, and ultimately drive them to take a desired action, such as making a purchase or requesting more information. The management of direct mail advertising campaigns involves several key steps: 1. Planning: This includes defining the campaign objectives, identifying the target audience, determining the budget, and selecting the appropriate direct mail strategies and tactics. 2. Design and Production: This step involves creating compelling and visually appealing direct mail pieces that effectively convey the marketing message and engage the recipients. It may also involve coordinating with designers, copywriters, and printers to ensure the materials are produced to the desired quality and standards. 3. Mailing List Selection: Marketers need to identify and obtain the most relevant and up-to-date mailing lists to reach their target audience. This may involve purchasing lists from data providers, leveraging existing customer databases, or utilizing data mining techniques. 4. Mailing and Distribution: Once the direct mail pieces are ready, they are mailed out to the target recipients. This step requires careful coordination of logistics, such as addressing, sorting, and ensuring timely delivery to the intended recipients. 5. Response Tracking and Analysis: It is essential to track and analyze the response rates and effectiveness of the direct mail campaigns. This can be done through various methods, such as unique phone numbers, coupon codes, or personalized URLs. The insights gained from this analysis help in refining future campaigns and optimizing return on investment. Overall, effective management of direct mail advertising campaigns requires careful planning, attention to detail, creativity in design and messaging, and systematic tracking and analysis of results. By utilizing this form of advertising, businesses can directly target and communicate with their desired audience, increasing brand awareness, customer engagement, and ultimately driving desired business outcomes.

Direct Mail Advertising Campaigns

Direct mail advertising campaigns are targeted marketing strategies that involve sending promotional materials, such as brochures, catalogs, or postcards, directly to potential customers through mail. This form of advertisement aims to reach a specific audience and generate a response or action from the recipients. Unlike other forms of advertising that rely on mass distribution or passive exposure, direct mail campaigns allow companies to selectively target individuals or groups based on various criteria, such as demographics, location, or interests. By tailoring the content and design of the promotional materials to match the recipient's preferences or needs, companies can increase the likelihood of generating a positive response and achieving their marketing objectives.

Direct Mail Advertising

Direct Mail Advertising refers to a promotional strategy used by businesses to deliver advertisements or marketing materials directly to targeted individuals or households through the postal service or other delivery methods. This method involves sending physical letters, postcards, brochures, catalogs, or other printed materials to a carefully selected audience, typically based on demographics, geographic location, or previous purchasing behavior. One of the key advantages of direct mail advertising is its ability to reach a specific target market. By using data analysis and customer segmentation, businesses can identify and target individuals who are more likely to be interested in their products or services. This helps to maximize the effectiveness of the advertising campaign and minimize any wasted distribution costs. Direct mail advertising is also known for its ability to provide a personalized and tangible experience for the recipients. Unlike digital ads that can be easily ignored or forgotten, physical mail has a higher chance of capturing the attention of the recipient, as it requires a physical action to open and read. This can lead to better brand recall and higher response rates compared to other forms of advertising. Additionally, direct mail advertising allows businesses to track and measure the effectiveness of their campaigns. By including unique codes, coupons, or special offers in the mailings, businesses can analyze the response rates and use that data to refine their future marketing strategies. While direct mail advertising can be an effective marketing tool, it does have some limitations. The cost of printing and postage can be higher compared to digital advertising methods, and there is always a possibility of the mailings being discarded without being read. Therefore, it is crucial for businesses to carefully plan and design their direct mail campaigns to ensure they are compelling and impactful.

Direct Mail Campaigns Execution

Direct mail campaigns execution refers to the process of implementing a targeted advertising strategy that involves sending promotional material directly to individuals or businesses through the mail. This form of advertising allows companies to reach a specific audience with a personalized message, usually in the form of letters, postcards, brochures, or catalogs. The execution of direct mail campaigns typically begins with identifying the target audience and compiling a mailing list. This can be done by purchasing a list from a third-party vendor or by using customer data collected by the company. The mailing list should be refined to ensure the campaign reaches the most relevant prospects. Once the mailing list is established, the next step in executing a direct mail campaign is designing the promotional material. The design should be visually appealing and attention-grabbing, with a clear call-to-action that entices recipients to respond. The message should be concise and persuasive, highlighting the benefits of the product or service being promoted. After the design is finalized, the promotional material is printed and prepared for mailing. This entails printing enough copies to reach the desired number of recipients and organizing the materials for efficient distribution. In some cases, companies may choose to outsource the printing and fulfillment process to a professional printing company. Once the promotional material is ready, it is mailed out to the targeted recipients. This can be done in-house by using a postage meter or by partnering with a postal service provider that specializes in bulk mailings. The timing of the campaign is an important consideration, as companies may choose to coordinate their direct mail efforts with other marketing channels for maximum impact. Throughout the execution of a direct mail campaign, it is important for companies to track and measure the outcomes. This can be done by including unique codes or URLs on the promotional material to track response rates. By analyzing the results, companies can determine the effectiveness of their campaign and make adjustments to improve future efforts.

Direct Mail Campaigns

Direct mail campaigns refer to targeted advertising campaigns that involve the distribution of promotional materials directly to specific individuals or households. This form of advertisement typically takes the form of physical mailings, such as postcards, letters, brochures, or catalogs, and is sent via postal mail. The goal of direct mail campaigns is to reach a specific audience in order to promote a product, service, or brand. This targeted approach allows businesses to tailor their message to a specific demographic or geographic location, increasing the likelihood of reaching potential customers who may be interested in the offering. Direct mail campaigns offer several advantages over other forms of advertising. Firstly, they allow businesses to directly engage with potential customers in a personalized manner. By addressing the recipient by name and tailoring the content to their specific needs or preferences, direct mailings can create a sense of personal connection and increase the likelihood of a response or purchase. Furthermore, direct mail campaigns provide tangible materials that recipients can hold and reference at their convenience. Unlike digital advertisements that can easily be ignored or forgotten, physical mailings have a physical presence that can be physically interacted with. This tangibility can help businesses create a lasting impression and increase brand awareness. Direct mail campaigns also offer the advantage of measurability. By including unique promotional codes, coupons, or response mechanisms in the mailings, businesses can easily track the success of their campaign and measure the return on investment (ROI). This data helps businesses evaluate the effectiveness of their messaging and make data-driven decisions for future campaigns. Despite the advantages, it is important for businesses to carefully plan and execute direct mail campaigns to ensure success. This involves identifying the target audience, creating compelling and relevant content, and accurately measuring the results. Additionally, businesses must adhere to legal regulations regarding the use of personal data and opt-out provisions to respect recipients' privacy and preferences. In conclusion, direct mail campaigns are targeted advertising campaigns that involve the distribution of physical mailings to specific individuals or households. By customizing the messaging and reaching a specific audience, businesses can create personalized connections, increase brand awareness, and measure the success of their campaigns.

Direct Mail

Direct Mail is a targeted advertising strategy that involves sending physical promotional materials, such as letters, postcards, catalogs, or brochures, directly to potential customers via mail. It is a form of direct marketing that aims to engage the recipient and generate interest in a product or service. Direct Mail allows businesses to reach a specific audience demographic, defined by factors such as location, age, income, or interests. By sending materials directly to potential customers' mailboxes, businesses can effectively deliver their message and capture the attention of recipients who may be interested in their offerings.

Direct Marketing

Direct marketing is a form of advertising that involves directly communicating with potential customers to promote products or services. It is an interactive marketing strategy that aims to generate a direct response from individuals, whether it be through a purchase, inquiry, or other desired action.This marketing approach involves reaching out to target audiences through various channels, such as email, direct mail, telemarketing, or even face-to-face interactions. It allows companies to tailor their messages and offers to specific individuals or groups, increasing the chances of getting a positive response.Direct marketing campaigns often utilize customer databases and segmentation techniques to identify and reach out to individuals who are likely to be interested in the products or services being promoted. By understanding their target audience's preferences, behaviors, and demographics, companies can create personalized messages that resonate with recipients and increase the likelihood of conversion.One significant advantage of direct marketing is its ability to provide measurable results. By tracking responses, conversions, and other key performance indicators, companies can evaluate the effectiveness of their campaigns and make data-driven decisions to optimize future efforts. This data-driven approach helps businesses refine their targeting strategies, messaging, and offers to improve overall campaign performance and return on investment.Direct marketing also enables businesses to establish direct relationships with customers, fostering loyalty and repeat business. By maintaining regular communication and providing relevant offers and information, companies can build trust, increase brand awareness, and encourage customer retention.However, it is crucial for companies engaging in direct marketing to comply with applicable laws and regulations, such as obtaining consent for email marketing or respecting do-not-call preferences. Failure to comply with these regulations can result in financial penalties and damage to the company's reputation.In conclusion, direct marketing is a targeted advertising approach that involves directly communicating with potential customers to promote products or services. It provides opportunities for personalized messaging, measurable results, and the establishment of direct customer relationships. When executed effectively and in compliance with regulations, direct marketing can be an effective tool for businesses to drive sales and build long-term customer loyalty.

Direct-Response Advertising Strategies

Direct-response advertising strategies are marketing tactics that aim to prompt immediate action from the target audience. Unlike traditional forms of advertising that focus on creating awareness or building brand image, direct-response advertising is designed to elicit a direct response or specific action from consumers, such as making a purchase, subscribing to a service, or requesting more information. These strategies typically employ persuasive and compelling messages, often combined with attractive incentives or offers, to encourage consumers to take immediate action. Such advertisements are often trackable and measurable, allowing marketers to assess their effectiveness and make data-driven decisions to optimize their campaigns.

Direct-Response Advertising

Direct-Response Advertising is a type of advertisement that is specifically designed to elicit an immediate response from the targeted audience. Unlike traditional forms of advertising, which primarily focus on building brand awareness or increasing overall sales, direct-response advertising aims to generate an immediate action, such as making a purchase, signing up for a newsletter, or requesting more information.This form of advertising typically incorporates strong calls to action, compelling offers, and a sense of urgency to encourage immediate response. It often employs specific tactics such as direct mail, email marketing, telemarketing, online advertisements, or television infomercials.

Display Advertising Metrics Tracking

Display Advertising Metrics Tracking refers to the process of measuring and analyzing the performance of display advertisements, in order to evaluate their effectiveness and make data-driven decisions for optimization and campaign improvement. This involves tracking and analyzing various metrics and key performance indicators (KPIs) related to the display ads, such as impressions, click-through rates (CTRs), conversions, and return on investment (ROI). The purpose of display advertising metrics tracking is to monitor and assess the impact and performance of display ads, enabling advertisers to gain insights and make informed decisions about their advertising strategies. By tracking and analyzing these metrics, advertisers can determine which ads are delivering the desired results and which ones need to be adjusted or discontinued.

Display Advertising Metrics

Display advertising metrics are quantitative measurements used to evaluate the performance and effectiveness of display advertisements. These metrics provide insights into how well an ad is performing in terms of visibility, engagement, and conversion, and can help advertisers make data-driven decisions to optimize their campaigns. The most commonly used display advertising metrics include: 1. Impressions: The number of times an ad is displayed on a web page. This metric gives an indication of the reach and visibility of an ad. 2. Click-through rate (CTR): The percentage of people who click on an ad after seeing it. It is calculated by dividing the number of clicks by the number of impressions. CTR is a measure of the ad's effectiveness in generating interest and driving traffic. 3. Conversion rate: The percentage of users who complete a desired action, such as making a purchase or filling out a form, after clicking on an ad. Conversion rate is a critical metric for evaluating the success of an ad in terms of achieving its intended goal. 4. Cost per thousand impressions (CPM): The cost an advertiser pays for every thousand ad impressions. CPM is used to evaluate the cost-effectiveness of an ad campaign and allows advertisers to compare different ad placements and networks. 5. Cost per click (CPC): The cost an advertiser pays for every click on an ad. CPC is a key metric for measuring the efficiency and profitability of a campaign, as it directly relates to the cost of acquiring website traffic. 6. Return on ad spend (ROAS): A metric that calculates the revenue generated from a campaign in relation to the cost of running that campaign. ROAS helps advertisers determine the profitability and overall success of their ad campaigns. By tracking and analyzing these metrics, advertisers can gain valuable insights into the performance of their display ads and make data-driven decisions to optimize their campaigns. These metrics provide a comprehensive view of the ad's reach, engagement, and effectiveness, allowing advertisers to measure the success of their advertising efforts and adjust their strategies accordingly.

Display Advertising Networks Assessment

Display Advertising Networks refer to a system in the field of advertisement that enables advertisers to place their promotional content on various websites, targeting a specific audience based on their demographics, interests, and browsing behavior. These networks facilitate the buying and selling of ad inventory across multiple websites, allowing advertisers to reach a broader audience and publishers to monetize their websites. Within the realm of display advertising networks, advertisers can opt for different formats, such as banner ads, rich media ads, video ads, and native ads, to create visually engaging and interactive campaigns that capture the attention of website visitors. The network acts as an intermediary between advertisers and publishers, offering a platform where advertisers can select specific websites or categories of websites where they want their ads to be displayed. Advertisers can also customize their campaigns by setting parameters like ad placement, frequency, duration, and targeting options.

Display Advertising Networks

Display Advertising Networks are online platforms that connect advertisers with publishers. They enable advertisers to display their ads on various websites or mobile applications, reaching a wide audience and increasing brand visibility. These networks operate on a Cost-Per-Thousand-Impressions (CPM) or Cost-Per-Click (CPC) basis, allowing advertisers to choose their preferred payment model. Advertisers create campaigns and set specific targeting parameters, such as audience demographics, interests, geographic location, and device type. This targeting ensures that their ads are displayed to the most relevant users. Publishers, on the other hand, register their websites or mobile apps with display advertising networks to monetize their digital properties. They receive payment for hosting ads and generating impressions or clicks. Publishers have the flexibility to choose the ads they want to display on their platforms based on relevance and user experience. Display advertising networks provide a variety of ad formats, including banner ads, video ads, native ads, interstitial ads, and more. These formats allow advertisers to create visually appealing and engaging advertisements that capture users' attention. The networks also offer ad tracking and analytics tools, allowing advertisers to monitor the performance of their campaigns in real-time. By using display advertising networks, advertisers can reach a larger audience compared to traditional advertising methods. They can target specific demographics or interests, ensuring that their ads are seen by the right people. Moreover, these networks offer flexibility in terms of ad placement and duration, allowing advertisers to optimize their campaigns based on performance and budget. For publishers, display advertising networks provide a steady source of income by monetizing their websites or mobile apps. They can choose the ad formats that best fit their platforms and have control over which ads are displayed to their audience. The revenue generated from these networks can be crucial for sustaining and growing online businesses.

Display Advertising

Display advertising refers to a form of advertising where visual ads, such as images, videos, or audio, are placed on websites or other online platforms to promote a product or service. These ads are typically displayed on specific sections or pages of a website that attract a particular target audience. Display advertising can be found in various formats, including banner ads, pop-up ads, interstitial ads, and native ads. Banner ads, the most common type of display ads, are rectangular or square images that are placed at the top, bottom, or sides of a web page. Pop-up ads, on the other hand, are ads that appear in separate windows or tabs while browsing a website. Interstitial ads are full-screen ads that appear between page transitions, while native ads are ads that blend in with the content of a website, resembling regular articles or posts. The objective of display advertising is to capture the attention of potential customers and encourage them to click on the ad, leading them to the advertiser's website or landing page. It is an effective way for businesses to increase brand awareness, drive traffic to their website, and generate leads or sales. Display advertising utilizes various targeting options to reach the desired audience. This includes demographic targeting, where ads are shown to specific groups based on age, gender, or location. Behavioral targeting involves showing ads to users based on their browsing history or online behavior. Contextual targeting involves displaying ads related to the content of a web page. Additionally, display advertising allows advertisers to retarget users who have previously interacted with their website or shown interest in their products or services. Display advertising is often sold on a cost per thousand impressions (CPM) basis, where advertisers pay for every thousand times their ad is shown. Alternatively, it can be sold on a cost per click (CPC) basis, where advertisers only pay when someone clicks on their ad. Some display advertising platforms also offer cost per action (CPA) pricing, where advertisers pay when a specific action, such as a purchase or form submission, is completed.

Display Network Advertising Tools

Display Network Advertising Tools refers to a set of online advertising tools provided by various platforms that allow advertisers to display their ads on a network of websites or mobile apps. These tools enable advertisers to reach a wider audience by placing their ads on relevant websites or apps that are part of the network. This helps in increasing brand visibility and attracting potential customers. One commonly used display network advertising tool is the display ad builder. This tool allows advertisers to create visually appealing and interactive ads using pre-designed templates, images, and text. Advertisers can customize the ad according to their preferences, such as choosing fonts, colors, and background images. The display ad builder simplifies the process of creating ads, especially for advertisers who may not have a background in design or coding. Another important tool is the placement targeting feature. This tool allows advertisers to select specific websites or apps where they want their ads to be displayed. Advertisers can choose websites or apps that are relevant to their target audience or industry, ensuring that their ads reach the right people. This targeting feature helps in increasing the effectiveness of the ads by reaching users who are more likely to be interested in the advertised products or services. Furthermore, audience targeting is another essential display network advertising tool. This tool allows advertisers to target specific groups of users based on various factors such as demographics, interests, or behaviors. Advertisers can define their target audience and set parameters to ensure that their ads are shown to users who are more likely to engage with the ads or convert into customers. This helps in maximizing the return on investment by increasing the relevancy and impact of the ads. Additionally, remarketing is a powerful display network advertising tool. This tool allows advertisers to show their ads to users

130

who have previously visited their website or interacted with their mobile app. By targeting these users, advertisers can remind them of their products or services, increasing the likelihood of conversions. Remarketing helps in maintaining brand awareness and encourages repeat visits or purchases. In conclusion, display network advertising tools provide advertisers with the means to effectively showcase their ads on a wide range of websites or mobile apps. These tools include the display ad builder, placement targeting, audience targeting, and remarketing. By utilizing these tools, advertisers can enhance their visibility, reach their target audience, and maximize their advertising efforts.

Display Network Advertising

Display Network Advertising refers to a type of online advertising that enables businesses to display their ads on a network of websites across the internet. These ads can take the form of banners, images, text, or videos, and are strategically placed on websites that are relevant to the advertiser's target audience. The main purpose of display network advertising is to increase brand awareness, generate leads, and drive traffic to the advertiser's website. This form of advertising allows businesses to reach a wide range of internet users who are browsing websites that align with their interests or demographics.

Distributed Advertising Content Platforms Evaluation

A distributed advertising content platform refers to a system or platform that enables the distribution and management of advertising content across multiple channels and platforms. It allows advertisers to reach a wide audience by distributing their content through various digital mediums, such as websites, social media platforms, mobile apps, and other online platforms. These platforms provide a centralized hub where advertisers can create, manage, and track their advertising campaigns. They offer features like content creation tools, audience targeting capabilities, campaign optimization options, and performance analytics. Advertisers can upload their advertising content, such as images, videos, and text, and customize their campaigns based on their goals and target audience. The key characteristic of distributed advertising content platforms is their ability to distribute the content across multiple channels and platforms simultaneously. This allows advertisers to reach their target audience in different contexts and environments, maximizing their reach and impact. For example, an advertiser can distribute their content on popular social media platforms like Facebook, Instagram, and Twitter, as well as on websites and mobile apps that are relevant to their target audience. Furthermore, these platforms often provide advanced targeting options that help advertisers deliver their content to the right audience. They utilize various targeting parameters, such as demographics, interests, online behaviors, and location, to ensure that the content reaches the most relevant audience segment. This not only improves the effectiveness of the advertising campaigns but also helps advertisers optimize their budget by focusing on the most promising audience segments. Another important aspect of distributed advertising content platforms is the ability to track and measure the performance of the campaigns. They provide real-time analytics and reporting tools that allow advertisers to monitor key metrics, such as impressions, clicks, conversions, and return on investment (ROI). This data helps advertisers understand the effectiveness of their campaigns and make data-driven decisions to optimize future campaigns.

Distributed Advertising Content Platforms

A distributed advertising content platform refers to a digital advertising system that allows businesses to distribute their promotional content across multiple channels, reaching a wider audience base. This platform facilitates the delivery of advertisements through various online channels, such as websites, social media platforms, mobile applications, and email newsletters. Unlike traditional advertising platforms that operate on a centralized model, distributed advertising content platforms leverage the power of technology to disseminate ads through a decentralized network. This decentralization enables businesses to target specific demographics, geographical locations, and online behaviors with greater precision and efficiency.

Distributed Advertising Content Strategies

Distributed advertising content strategies refer to the techniques and approaches used to

131

distribute promotional content across multiple platforms and channels in order to reach a wider audience and achieve marketing goals. These strategies are designed to maximize the visibility and impact of advertising messages by delivering them to the right audience at the right time and in the right format. The primary objective of distributed advertising content strategies is to increase brand awareness, generate leads, drive traffic, and ultimately boost sales. By utilizing various distribution channels such as social media, websites, blogs, email marketing, and online advertisements, advertisers can effectively target their desired audience and deliver their messages in a manner that is both engaging and persuasive. One key aspect of distributed advertising content strategies is the use of data and analytics to identify the most effective channels and platforms for content distribution. Through analyzing audience demographics, behavior, and preferences, advertisers can optimize their content distribution efforts and ensure that their messages are delivered to the right audience on channels where they are most likely to be seen and engaged with. In addition to data analysis, distributed advertising content strategies often incorporate elements of personalization and customization. By tailoring content to individual needs and preferences, advertisers can create a more personalized and interactive experience for their audience, thereby increasing engagement and encouraging desired actions such as clicking on links, filling out forms, or making purchases. Furthermore, distributed advertising content strategies also involve leveraging partnerships and collaborations with influencers, bloggers, and other brands to amplify the reach and impact of promotional content. By partnering with individuals or organizations that have a large and engaged following, advertisers can extend the reach of their messages to new audiences and tap into their existing trust and credibility. In summary, distributed advertising content strategies encompass the various techniques and tactics used to distribute promotional content across multiple platforms and channels. By leveraging data, personalization, partnerships, and collaborations, advertisers can optimize their content distribution efforts and maximize the impact of their advertising messages.

Distributed Advertising Content

Distributed Advertising Content refers to the practice of spreading promotional material across multiple platforms and channels in order to reach a larger and more diverse audience. It involves creating and distributing advertisements that are tailored to specific target audiences and delivered through various media channels, such as television, radio, print, online platforms, and social media. This marketing strategy aims to increase brand awareness, generate leads, and drive customer engagement by reaching consumers through multiple touchpoints. By utilizing a wide range of distribution channels, advertisers can reach their target audience wherever they may be, increasing the likelihood of capturing their attention and influencing their purchasing decisions.

Distribution Channel

A distribution channel refers to the path or route through which goods or services are delivered from the producer or manufacturer to the end consumer. In the context of advertisement, a distribution channel encompasses the various methods and channels used to promote and deliver advertisements to the target audience. In the advertising industry, distribution channels play a crucial role in ensuring that advertisements reach the intended recipients efficiently and effectively. These channels can include both traditional and digital mediums, such as print media, television, radio, outdoor advertising, social media platforms, websites, and mobile applications.

Diversity In Advertising Initiatives Monitoring

Diversity in Advertising Initiatives Monitoring refers to the process of systematically tracking and evaluating the representation, portrayal, and inclusion of diverse individuals and groups in advertising campaigns. It involves monitoring and analyzing various aspects of advertisements, such as the demographics, ethnicities, genders, ages, abilities, and body types of the individuals featured in the ads. The primary goal of Diversity in Advertising Initiatives Monitoring is to ensure that advertising accurately reflects the diversity of the target audience and society as a whole. By promoting inclusivity and representation, it aims to challenge and break down stereotypes, biases, and discriminatory practices prevalent in advertising. Furthermore, it seeks to create a more inclusive and equitable advertising landscape that reflects and respects the diverse characteristics and experiences of individuals and communities. The monitoring process includes gathering and analyzing data from different sources, such as advertisements across various media channels, consumer feedback, market research, and industry reports. This data is then examined to determine whether diverse groups are adequately represented and portrayed in commercials, print ads, online banners, and other advertising formats. Additionally, the monitoring process evaluates the quality, authenticity, and sensitivity of the portrayals to ensure they are respectful and avoid perpetuating stereotypes. Once the monitoring analysis has been conducted, the findings are used to inform and guide advertising strategists, marketers, and creative teams. This allows them to make informed decisions about the content, messaging, and casting choices in future advertising campaigns. By understanding the gaps and areas for improvement highlighted by the monitoring process, advertisers can work towards more inclusive, representative, and effective advertising content. Moreover, Diversity in Advertising Initiatives Monitoring is not a one-time activity, but an ongoing process that requires continuous evaluation and adjustment. As societal norms, perspectives, and demographics evolve, the monitoring process needs to adapt to ensure that advertising remains current and reflective of the diverse audience it seeks to engage. Therefore, regular monitoring enables advertisers to track progress, identify emerging patterns, and address any shortcomings in their efforts to promote diversity and inclusion in advertising.

Diversity In Advertising Initiatives

Diversity in advertising initiatives refers to intentional efforts made by advertisers to incorporate and represent individuals from various races, ethnicities, genders, sexual orientations, ages, abilities, and other diverse backgrounds in their advertisements. These initiatives aim to challenge and break stereotypes, increase representation, and promote inclusivity through the portrayal of a wide range of individuals, experiences, and perspectives. By embracing diversity in ads, advertisers acknowledge the importance of reflecting the reality of diverse consumer audiences and understanding their unique needs, preferences, and values.

Diversity In Advertising

Diversity in advertising refers to the representation and inclusion of individuals from various backgrounds, cultures, races, genders, and abilities in advertising campaigns. It aims to reflect the diversity of the target audience and society as a whole, promoting equal representation and inclusivity. In today's diverse and multicultural world, it is essential for advertisers to recognize and acknowledge the different identities and experiences of their audience. By incorporating diversity in advertising, brands can connect with a broader range of consumers and create a sense of belonging and acceptance.

Drip Email Campaigns Management Techniques

A drip email campaign refers to a marketing strategy that involves sending a series of pre-written, automated emails to potential customers or leads with the aim of nurturing them and eventually converting them into paying customers. This technique is commonly used in advertisement to establish a consistent and targeted communication channel with prospects. The management of drip email campaigns involves several techniques to optimize their effectiveness and maximize the chances of achieving the desired outcomes. One important technique is segmenting the target audience into different groups based on their characteristics, preferences, or behaviors. By segmenting the audience, marketers can tailor the content and timing of the emails to better suit the specific needs and interests of each group, thereby increasing the chances of engagement and conversion. Another crucial aspect of managing drip email campaigns is creating compelling and relevant content. The emails should be designed to provide value to the recipients, such as useful information, insights, tips, or exclusive offers. Engaging and informative content not only keeps the recipients interested and encourages them to continue opening the emails but also helps to build trust and credibility, which are essential for successful advertisement campaigns. Monitoring and analyzing the performance of the drip email campaign is another essential management technique. Marketers need to constantly track important metrics, such as open rates, click-through rates, conversion rates, and unsubscribe rates, to assess the effectiveness of the campaign and identify areas for improvement. By studying these metrics, marketers can make data-driven decisions and make adjustments to the content, timing, or targeting of the emails to optimize their impact. In addition, personalization is

133

a key technique in managing drip email campaigns. By leveraging data about the recipients, such as their names, preferences, or past interactions with the brand, marketers can customize the emails to create a more personalized and tailored experience. Personalization not only increases the likelihood of engagement but also helps to establish a stronger connection and rapport with the recipients.

Drip Email Campaigns Management

A drip email campaign is a method of advertising that involves sending a series of pre-written emails to a targeted group of individuals over a specified period of time. The purpose of these campaigns is to nurture leads and build relationships with potential customers or clients. In a drip email campaign, the emails are typically sent out in a predetermined sequence, with each email building upon the previous one. The content of the emails may vary depending on the goals and objectives of the campaign, but they are usually designed to provide valuable information, drive engagement, and encourage specific actions.

Drip Email Campaigns

A drip email campaign is a method of online advertising that involves sending a series of pre-written, automated emails to a targeted group of recipients. This form of email marketing is designed to nurture leads, increase engagement, and ultimately drive conversions. The term "drip" refers to the gradual release of emails over a period of time, typically spaced out at regular intervals. The purpose of this strategy is to build a relationship with potential customers by providing them with valuable content, while also guiding them through the buyer's journey. This type of campaign is often used by businesses to educate their audience, showcase their products or services, and ultimately persuade recipients to take a desired action, such as making a purchase or signing up for a newsletter. Drip email campaigns are particularly effective for businesses with longer sales cycles or complex offerings, as they allow for a more personalized and targeted approach. One of the key advantages of drip email campaigns is their automation. Once the initial setup is complete, the emails are sent out automatically based on triggers or predefined time intervals. This saves businesses time and effort, as they can set up and schedule the campaign in advance, freeing up resources for other marketing activities. Furthermore, drip email campaigns allow for segmentation and personalization. Businesses can group recipients based on certain criteria, such as their interests, demographics, or previous interactions with the brand. This enables them to tailor the content of the emails to the specific needs and preferences of each segment, increasing the chances of engagement and conversion. In addition, drip email campaigns provide valuable insights and data for analysis. By tracking the open rates, click-through rates, and conversion rates of each email in the campaign, businesses can gain a better understanding of what resonates with their audience and make data-driven decisions for future marketing efforts. In conclusion, a drip email campaign is a targeted and automated method of online advertising that involves sending a series of pre-written emails to nurture leads, increase engagement, and drive conversions. With its automation, segmentation, personalization, and data analysis capabilities, it is an effective tool for businesses to build relationships with their audience and guide them towards a desired action.

Drip Marketing

Drip marketing refers to a marketing strategy that involves sending a series of targeted, timed messages to potential customers or leads to nurture their interest and guide them through the sales funnel. This approach aims to engage with the audience consistently over time, delivering relevant and valuable content that addresses their needs and keeps the brand top of mind. The term "drip" in drip marketing conceptually reflects the idea of a steady, continuous stream of communication rather than a single heavy push. Instead of bombarding prospects with one-off promotional messages, drip marketing focuses on building relationships and establishing trust gradually by providing ongoing value.

Dwell Time

Dwell Time refers to the amount of time that a person spends viewing or engaging with an advertisement. It is a metric used to measure the effectiveness of an advertisement in capturing and maintaining the attention of the audience. With the rise of digital advertising, dwell time has become an essential factor in evaluating the success of an ad campaign. It provides insights into how well the advertisement is resonating with the target audience and whether it is able to hold their attention for a significant duration.

Dynamic Advertising

Dynamic advertising refers to the practice of creating and delivering ads that are tailored to each individual viewer or target audience based on various data points such as demographics, browsing behavior, and geographic location. Unlike traditional static advertising, which displays the same content to all viewers, dynamic ads provide a more personalized and relevant experience, increasing engagement and conversion rates. The process of dynamic advertising involves gathering data about the viewer or target audience, analyzing it in real-time, and then dynamically generating ad content that is most likely to resonate with each individual. This can include customized messages, images, offers, and calls-to-action that are specifically designed to appeal to the viewer's preferences and needs. There are several technologies and techniques that enable dynamic advertising, including data management platforms (DMPs), demand-side platforms (DSPs), and programmatic advertising. These tools allow advertisers to effectively collect, analyze, and utilize data to create highly targeted ad campaigns. Dynamic advertising offers numerous benefits for advertisers. By delivering personalized ads, companies can increase their chances of capturing the viewer's attention and driving them to take desired actions, such as making a purchase or subscribing to a service. It also helps in improving ad relevancy, mitigating ad fatigue, and maximizing advertising ROI. For viewers, dynamic advertising can enhance their overall browsing experience by providing them with content that is specifically tailored to their interests and needs. Instead of being bombarded with irrelevant ads, viewers are more likely to engage with ads that are relevant and offer value to them. Overall, dynamic advertising has revolutionized the advertising industry by allowing advertisers to deliver highly targeted and personalized ads to their audience. By leveraging data and technology, companies can create more effective ad campaigns that resonate with viewers, leading to higher engagement and conversion rates.

Dynamic Creative Optimization (DCO)

Dynamic Creative Optimization (DCO) is a data-driven approach used in advertising that leverages real-time data and machine learning algorithms to deliver personalized and highly relevant creatives to individual users. Unlike traditional static advertising, where a single creative is displayed to all users, DCO customizes ad experiences based on various user attributes such as demographics, geolocation, browsing behavior, interests, and previous interactions. DCO starts by collecting and analyzing vast amounts of data on users, including their preferences, behaviors, and online activities. This data is then used to create user profiles that help advertisers understand each user's context and preferences. Using machine learning algorithms, DCO determines the most effective combination of creative elements, such as headlines, images, copy, and call-to-action buttons, for each user. It dynamically assembles these elements into personalized ad creatives in real-time, ensuring that the content displayed is tailored specifically to each individual's preferences and needs. The real-time nature of DCO enables advertisers to respond instantly to changes in user behavior and preferences. For example, if a user abandons a shopping cart, DCO can deliver a personalized ad with a discount or offer related to the abandoned item, increasing the likelihood of conversion. DCO also allows for A/B testing, where different variations of creatives are served to different users to determine which combination performs best. This data-driven approach helps advertisers optimize their campaigns by continuously learning what works best for different segments of their target audience. Overall, DCO enhances the effectiveness of advertising campaigns by delivering relevant and engaging ad experiences that resonate with individual users. By leveraging real-time data and machine learning, DCO empowers advertisers to maximize their return on investment by delivering the right message to the right audience at the right time.

Dynamic Creative Optimization Platforms

Dynamic Creative Optimization (DCO) platforms are advanced advertising tools that automatically create and optimize personalized ads in real time. These platforms use data and algorithms to determine the most effective ad variations for each individual viewer, allowing advertisers to deliver highly relevant and engaging messages to their target audiences. DCO platforms break down the traditional one-size-fits-all approach to advertising by leveraging data on user demographics, browsing behavior, and other contextual information. They combine this data with creative assets such as images, videos, and copy to generate personalized ad variations that resonate with individual viewers. By dynamically selecting and optimizing the creative elements of an ad, DCO platforms help advertisers achieve better performance and ROI. The optimization process typically involves A/B testing different ad variations and analyzing performance metrics such as click-through rates, conversions, and engagement. The platform then uses this data to continuously refine and improve the ad creative, ensuring that the most effective versions are delivered to the right audiences. DCO platforms also offer features such as audience segmentation, real-time bidding, and automation tools to streamline ad delivery and campaign management. With audience segmentation, advertisers can target specific groups of users based on attributes such as age, gender, interests, and location. Real-time bidding capabilities enable advertisers to bid for ad placements in real time, ensuring that their ads are displayed to the most relevant audiences at the optimal time. Automation tools further simplify the process by automating tasks such as ad generation, optimization, and reporting. In summary, Dynamic Creative Optimization platforms revolutionize advertising by enabling personalized, data-driven, and automated ad delivery. These platforms empower advertisers to create highly relevant and engaging ads that maximize their campaign performance and drive better results.

Dynamic Product Ads Creation Tools

Dynamic Product Ads Creation Tools are software tools designed to help advertisers create and manage dynamic product ads for their online advertising campaigns. These tools enable advertisers to showcase a wide range of products to their target audience in a personalized and relevant way. Dynamic product ads are highly effective in capturing the attention of potential customers as they show ads with products that the customers have shown interest in or are similar to what they have previously viewed or purchased. This level of personalization helps in increasing the engagement and conversion rates of the ads. The creation tools provide a user-friendly interface where advertisers can easily upload their product catalog and define the creative elements of the ads such as images, text, and call-to-action buttons. The tools also integrate with the advertiser's website or e-commerce platform to dynamically populate the ads with the most up-to-date product information, availability, and pricing. Furthermore, these tools offer targeting options that allow advertisers to reach the most relevant audience for their products. Advertisers can use various demographic, behavioral, and interest-based targeting parameters to ensure that their ads are seen by the right people at the right time. In addition to creation and targeting, these tools also provide analytics and reporting features that enable advertisers to track the performance of their dynamic product ads. Advertisers can monitor key metrics such as click-through rates, conversion rates, and return on ad spend to optimize their campaigns and maximize their advertising ROI. Overall, dynamic product ads creation tools are essential for advertisers looking to leverage the power of personalization in their online advertising. By using these tools, advertisers can efficiently create and manage highly relevant and engaging ads that drive more conversions and revenue for their business. Dynamic Product Ads Creation Tools are software tools designed to help advertisers create and manage dynamic product ads for their online advertising campaigns. These tools enable advertisers to showcase a wide range of products to their target audience in a personalized and relevant way, increasing engagement and conversion rates.

Dynamic Product Ads Creation

Dynamic Product Ads are a type of advertisement that allows businesses to promote their products to customers who have shown interest in similar items on their website or app. These ads automatically generate personalized content, such as product images, descriptions, and prices, based on the user's browsing and purchase history. Creating dynamic product ads involves a combination of data feed management, ad creation, and audience targeting. First, businesses need to create a product catalog or data feed that contains information about their products, such as IDs, names, descriptions, images, and prices. This catalog is then uploaded to the ad platform, which uses this data to dynamically create personalized ads. When a user visits a website or app, the ad platform tracks their interactions, such as browsing products or adding items to the cart. Based on this information, the platform determines which products to display in the dynamic ad. For example, if a user viewed a specific pair of shoes on a website, the ad platform can show an ad featuring the same pair of shoes, along with other related products. Dynamic product ads can be displayed on various platforms, including social media, websites, and mobile apps. They can appear in different formats, such as carousels, single images, or collection ads. These ads often include a call-to-action button, such as "Shop Now" or "Learn More," which directs users to the business's website or app to complete their purchase. This type of advertisement is highly effective in reaching the right audience with personalized content. By showcasing relevant products to users who have already shown interest in similar items, businesses can increase their chances of converting them into customers. Dynamic product ads allow businesses to deliver a tailored advertising experience, ultimately driving sales and generating revenue.

Dynamic Product Ads

Dynamic Product Ads are a type of advertisement that are designed to automatically show personalized product ads to individual users based on their previous interactions with a website or app. These ads are dynamically generated and tailored to each user's interests and preferences, making them highly relevant and effective in driving conversions. The key feature of Dynamic Product Ads is their ability to showcase products that are specifically relevant to individual customers. These ads pull product information, such as images, titles, prices, and descriptions, from a catalog or inventory and display them to users who have expressed interest in similar products in the past. By leveraging data on user behavior, engagement, and purchase history, Dynamic Product Ads are able to deliver targeted ads that are more likely to capture the attention and interest of potential customers.

E-Commerce Advertising

E-commerce advertising refers to the practice of promoting and marketing products or services through online channels in order to drive sales and attract customers. It involves the use of various digital advertising techniques and strategies to reach a targeted audience and create brand awareness. With the increasing popularity and widespread use of the internet, e-commerce advertising has become an essential component of any online business's marketing strategy. It allows businesses to showcase their products or services to a large number of potential customers and drive traffic to their websites. E-commerce advertising can take various forms, including display ads, search engine marketing, social media advertising, email marketing, influencer marketing, and affiliate marketing.

Earned Media Analysis

Earned media analysis refers to the process of evaluating and analyzing the organic or unpaid media coverage that a brand or advertisement receives. It involves examining the reach, impact, and sentiment of the media coverage to assess its effectiveness and influence on the target audience. Earned media, also known as "free media" or "publicity," includes any mention, feature, or review of a brand, product, or advertisement that is not paid for or controlled by the brand itself. This can include news articles, blog posts, social media mentions, influencer reviews, and user-generated content. Earned media analysis involves monitoring and tracking the various channels and platforms where the brand or advertisement is being mentioned or discussed. This can be done through media monitoring tools that scan newspapers, magazines, TV broadcasts, online news sites, blogs, forums, social media platforms, and other digital channels. The analysis of earned media typically focuses on several key aspects: 1. Reach: The total number of people exposed to the earned media coverage is measured to determine the potential audience size. 2. Impressions: The number of times the earned media content was viewed or displayed is counted to gauge the overall visibility. 3. Sentiment: The tone and attitude expressed in the media coverage, whether positive, negative, or neutral, are evaluated to assess the public perception and reputation. 4. Influencers: The identification and analysis of influential individuals or entities who have mentioned or shared the brand or advertisement can help determine the impact on the target audience. 5. Virality: The extent to which the earned media content has been shared or spread across different channels or platforms is measured to gauge the level of engagement and potential amplification. Earned media analysis provides valuable insights into the overall performance and impact of a brand or advertisement in the media landscape. It helps assess the effectiveness of public relations efforts, identifies potential

137

areas for improvement, and informs future marketing strategies and campaigns.

Earned Media

Earned Media refers to the publicity and exposure that a brand receives through promotional efforts that are not paid for or directly controlled by the brand itself. It occurs when others, such as journalists, bloggers, or consumers, voluntarily and organically share information about a brand, product, or service. This form of media is often considered more credible and trustworthy than paid media because it is based on the unbiased opinions and experiences of others. Unlike paid media, which includes traditional advertising or sponsored content, earned media is the result of brand recognition and positive perception. It is a reflection of how well a brand resonates with its target audience and how effectively it communicates its value proposition. While brands cannot directly control the content or timing of earned media, they can influence it through strategic public relations initiatives, engaging social media campaigns, and outstanding customer experiences.

Eco-Friendly Advertising Practices Implementation

Eco-friendly advertising practices implementation refers to the adoption and utilization of sustainable and environmentally conscious strategies in advertising campaigns. It involves the incorporation of methods and techniques that minimize negative impacts on the environment, promote sustainability, and uphold ethical standards. Organizations that implement eco-friendly advertising practices aim to minimize resource consumption, reduce waste generation, and promote responsible consumption among their target audience. These practices typically involve the use of eco-friendly materials, energy-efficient technologies, and the reduction of harmful emissions throughout the advertising process.

Eco-Friendly Advertising Practices

Eco-Friendly Advertising Practices refer to strategies and techniques used by companies and brands to promote their products or services in a sustainable and environmentally conscious manner. These practices aim to minimize negative impacts on the environment while still effectively reaching target audiences and achieving marketing objectives.One aspect of eco-friendly advertising is the use of sustainable materials and production processes. This may involve using recycled or biodegradable materials for packaging, print materials, and promotional items. Companies may also opt for energy-efficient methods of production that reduce carbon emissions and minimize resource consumption.Another important aspect is the responsible use and disposal of advertising materials. This can include using digital platforms and online advertising methods that have a lower environmental footprint compared to traditional print or broadcast media. Companies can also implement strategies to reduce the amount of physical advertising materials, such as distributing electronic brochures or using digital signage instead of printed banners.In addition to material choices, eco-friendly advertising practices also focus on the messaging and content of advertisements. Brands can showcase their commitment to sustainability by promoting environmentally friendly practices, such as energy conservation or waste reduction. This can create a positive brand image and resonate with consumers who prioritize sustainability when making purchasing decisions.Furthermore, eco-friendly advertising practices often encourage consumers to adopt more sustainable behaviors. Advertisements may provide information and tips on eco-friendly lifestyles or guide consumers towards environmentally friendly products or services. By promoting eco-conscious choices, companies can not only attract environmentally conscious consumers but also contribute to the overall well-being of the planet.Overall, eco-friendly advertising practices embody the principles of sustainability and responsibility. They prioritize the use of sustainable materials, energy-efficient production methods, digital platforms, and responsible messaging to minimize negative environmental impacts. By adopting these practices, companies can demonstrate their commitment to environmental stewardship while also maintaining effective marketing strategies.

Eco-Friendly Advertising

Eco-friendly advertising refers to the practice of promoting a product, service, or brand while minimizing its negative impact on the environment. It involves using sustainable and renewable resources, reducing waste, and adopting environmentally friendly practices throughout the advertising process. Eco-friendly advertising aims to raise awareness about sustainable living, climate change, and conservation by integrating green principles into marketing campaigns. This type of advertising is often used by businesses that want to align their values with environmentally conscious consumers and differentiate themselves from competitors.

Effective Frequency

Effective frequency, in the context of advertisement, refers to the optimal number of times an individual needs to be exposed to an advertising message in order to create the desired impact or influence on their purchasing behavior. It is based on the premise that repeated exposure to an advertisement is essential for the target audience to remember, recognize, and be persuaded by the message being conveyed. The effective frequency concept recognizes the limited attention span and information processing capacity of individuals. In a cluttered media environment, where consumers are exposed to numerous messages from different brands, it becomes critical for advertisers to strike a balance between repetition and overexposure. The goal is to achieve sufficient exposure without losing the audience's interest or causing advertising fatigue.

Efficiency

The term "efficiency" in the context of advertisements refers to the ability of an advertisement to achieve its intended goals and objectives in the most effective and economical way. It is a measure of how well an advertisement performs in terms of generating desired outcomes while utilizing minimum resources. Efficiency in advertising is commonly assessed through various metrics and indicators such as return on investment (ROI), cost per acquisition (CPA), click-through rate (CTR), and conversion rate. These measures help advertisers and marketers determine the effectiveness and efficiency of their campaigns and make informed decisions to optimize their advertising strategies.

Email Marketing Automation Platforms Evaluation

Email marketing automation platforms are digital tools that help businesses streamline and optimize their email marketing efforts. These platforms provide a wide range of features and functionalities that enable businesses to create, send, track, and analyze their email campaigns in an automated and efficient manner. These platforms allow businesses to automate various aspects of their email marketing campaigns, such as list segmentation, email creation and design, scheduling and sending, and performance tracking. They also offer advanced targeting and personalization options, allowing businesses to deliver highly tailored and relevant content to their subscribers. One of the key benefits of email marketing automation platforms is their ability to save time and effort for businesses. By automating repetitive and time-consuming tasks, such as list management and email scheduling, businesses can focus on other important activities, such as strategy development and content creation. Furthermore, these platforms provide businesses with valuable insights and analytics on their email campaigns. They track key metrics, such as open rates, click-through rates, and conversion rates, allowing businesses to measure the effectiveness of their campaigns and make data-driven decisions to improve their results. Email marketing automation platforms also offer integrations with other marketing tools and platforms, such as customer relationship management (CRM) systems and e-commerce platforms. This enables businesses to create seamless and integrated marketing workflows, effectively combining email marketing with other marketing channels and strategies. In summary, email marketing automation platforms are powerful tools that enable businesses to automate and optimize their email marketing efforts. They provide a wide range of features and functionalities that help businesses save time, enhance personalization, and improve the effectiveness of their email campaigns. By using these platforms, businesses can achieve better results and drive higher engagement with their subscribers.

Email Marketing Automation Platforms

Email Marketing Automation Platforms are software tools that help businesses automate and streamline their email marketing campaigns. These platforms are specifically designed for advertisement purposes and enable businesses to create, schedule, and send targeted email campaigns to their subscribers. With Email Marketing Automation Platforms, businesses can create personalized email templates and automatically send them based on specific triggers or actions taken by the recipients. These triggers can include actions such as subscribing to a newsletter, making a purchase, or abandoning a shopping cart. The main advantage of using an Email Marketing Automation Platform for advertisement is the ability to deliver highly targeted and personalized content to subscribers. These platforms allow businesses to segment their subscribers based on various criteria such as demographics, interests, past purchases, or website behavior. By targeting specific segments with relevant content, businesses can significantly increase their conversion rates and ROI. In addition to personalization, Email Marketing Automation Platforms offer a range of features to help businesses optimize their email campaigns. These features may include A/B testing, which allows businesses to test different versions of their emails to see which performs better. They may also include advanced analytics and reporting tools, which provide insights into the effectiveness of email campaigns, allowing businesses to make data-driven decisions for their advertisement strategies. Overall, Email Marketing Automation Platforms provide businesses with a powerful tool to streamline and optimize their email marketing efforts. By automating repetitive tasks and personalizing content, businesses can reach their target audience more effectively and drive better results from their advertisement campaigns.

Email Marketing Automation

Email Marketing Automation is a form of advertising that involves using software and technology to automate and streamline the process of sending targeted emails to a specific audience. It enables businesses to create and send personalized emails to their subscribers or customers, based on their interests, preferences, and behavior. With Email Marketing Automation, businesses can automate various stages of the email marketing campaign, from lead generation to nurturing leads, and from converting leads into customers to retaining and engaging existing customers. This automation helps businesses save time, effort, and resources, while also optimizing the effectiveness and efficiency of their email marketing efforts. The process begins with building an email list, which involves collecting email addresses from interested individuals or potential customers. This can be done through various methods such as website opt-in forms, social media campaigns, or offline events. Once the email list is created, businesses can use automation software to segment the list and categorize subscribers based on their demographics, interests, or buying behavior. Next, businesses can create email templates or campaigns that are tailored to the needs and preferences of each segment. These emails can be personalized with the recipient's name, specific offers, or relevant content. The automation software allows businesses to schedule the delivery of these emails based on predefined triggers or actions, such as a subscriber joining a particular segment or a customer abandoning a shopping cart. In addition to sending automated emails, Email Marketing Automation also enables businesses to track and analyze the performance of their campaigns. They can monitor metrics such as open rates, click-through rates, and conversion rates to assess the effectiveness of their email marketing efforts. This data can be used to further optimize and refine future campaigns, ensuring maximum engagement and conversions. Overall, Email Marketing Automation is a powerful tool for businesses to connect with their audience and drive customer engagement and conversions. By leveraging automation software, businesses can save time, deliver highly targeted and personalized messages, and achieve better results from their email marketing campaigns.

Email Marketing

Email marketing refers to the practice of sending promotional messages or advertisements to a group of individuals via email. It is a form of direct marketing that utilizes email as a means to deliver targeted messages to a specific audience. Email marketing campaigns typically involve sending messages to a list of subscribers who have opted in to receive promotional content. These subscribers may have voluntarily provided their email addresses, signed up for a newsletter, made a purchase, or otherwise expressed interest in the products or services offered by the sender. The goal of email marketing is to build and nurture relationships with customers, increase brand awareness, and drive sales. It allows businesses to reach a large number of people at once, delivering personalized content directly to their inbox. This enables companies to tailor their messages to the specific interests and needs of their subscribers, resulting in a higher likelihood of engagement and conversion. Email marketing can take various forms, including newsletters, product updates, event invitations, and abandoned cart reminders. By strategically segmenting their email lists and crafting compelling content, marketers can effectively target different groups within their audience and deliver highly relevant messages. One of the key advantages of email marketing is its cost-effectiveness. Compared to traditional advertising methods, such as print ads or television commercials, email marketing requires minimal investment. It eliminates the need for physical materials and distribution costs, making it a highly economical choice for businesses of all sizes. Furthermore, email marketing allows for easy tracking and analysis of campaign performance. Marketers can monitor metrics such as open rates, click-through rates, and conversion rates to assess the effectiveness of their email campaigns. This data provides valuable insights into audience preferences and behavior, enabling marketers to refine their strategies and optimize future campaigns. In conclusion, email marketing is a powerful tool for businesses to communicate with their audience, promote their products or services, and drive sales. By delivering personalized messages directly to subscribers' inboxes, it allows businesses to build relationships and engage with customers in a targeted and cost-effective manner.

Emotion In Advertising Analysis Methods

The method of emotion in advertising analysis refers to the systematic examination and evaluation of how emotions are strategically incorporated into advertisements to influence consumer behavior. It involves analyzing the various emotional appeals, triggers, and tactics used by advertisers to create a desired emotional response in viewers or potential customers. This analysis method encompasses different approaches and techniques that help in understanding the emotional aspects of advertising messages. It involves scrutinizing the use of facial expressions, body language, voice tone, music, colors, and storytelling techniques to evoke specific emotional responses, such as happiness, excitement, nostalgia, fear, or empathy.

Emotion In Advertising Analysis

Emotion in advertising refers to the strategic use of emotional appeals and stimuli in advertisements to elicit specific emotional responses from the target audience. This technique aims to create a strong emotional connection between the consumer and the brand, product, or message being promoted, ultimately influencing their attitudes, beliefs, and behaviors. By leveraging various emotions such as happiness, sadness, fear, anger, surprise, and nostalgia, advertisers seek to evoke powerful feelings and associations that can impact consumer decision-making. Emotionally appealing advertisements often resonate with consumers on a deeper level, making the brand or product more memorable and meaningful to them.

Emotion In Advertising Assessment

An emotion in advertising refers to the use of specific feelings or reactions to create a connection with the audience and influence their behavior or decision-making process. It involves the strategic incorporation of emotions, such as happiness, fear, sadness, or excitement, into the advertisement's content, design, or storytelling techniques. Emotion in advertising serves several purposes. Firstly, it helps to capture the audience's attention by appealing to their emotional side, as our emotions are powerful drivers of attention and memory. By evoking emotions, advertisements can stand out in a cluttered advertising space and leave a lasting impression on viewers. Furthermore, emotion in advertising can play a crucial role in building brand awareness and brand affinity. By associating positive emotions with a brand, advertisers aim to create a favorable perception of their product or service in the minds of consumers. If a consumer feels happy or inspired while watching an advertisement, they are more likely to associate those emotions with the brand and develop a positive attitude towards it. This can ultimately lead to increased brand loyalty and repeat purchases. Moreover, emotions in advertising can be powerful tools for driving consumer behavior. Advertisers often use emotions as a way to persuade or influence consumers to take action, such as making a purchase, subscribing to a service, or supporting a cause. For example, an advertisement that triggers fear or urgency may prompt consumers to engage in a specific behavior in order to avoid potential negative consequences. However, it is important for advertisers to strike a balance when using emotions in advertising. While arousing emotions can be effective, advertisements that rely solely on emotional manipulation without providing substantial information or delivering on promises may be seen as disingenuous or manipulative. Consumers value authenticity and transparency, so it is essential for advertisers to ensure that the emotions evoked in their

141

advertisements are genuine and aligned with the brand's values or product benefits.

Emotion In Advertising

Emotion in advertising refers to the use of psychological tactics and techniques to invoke specific feelings and reactions in consumers. It involves the strategic use of imagery, language, and storytelling to connect with the audience on an emotional level. The primary goal of incorporating emotion in advertising is to create a deep, lasting impression that drives consumers to take desired actions, such as making a purchase or developing a positive perception of a brand. Advertising professionals understand that emotions play a significant role in consumer decision-making. By targeting specific emotions, advertisers can shape the way consumers perceive and interact with a product or service. Emotionally-driven advertisements are designed to tap into the customer's desires, fears, aspirations, and values to establish a personal connection. The use of emotion in advertising can take various forms. One common approach is the use of humor to generate positive emotions. Funny advertisements often make consumers laugh, allowing them to associate that positive emotion with the brand. This can create a positive brand image and increase the likelihood of purchase or brand loyalty. Advertisers may also employ nostalgia to trigger sentimental emotions and connect with consumers' memories and past experiences. Nostalgic advertisements can evoke a sense of longing or sentimentality, which can create a strong emotional bond with the brand and enhance consumer engagement with the advertisement. Another powerful technique is the use of fear or anxiety. Advertisements that highlight potential negative consequences of not using a particular product or service can create a sense of urgency and compel consumers to take action. Fear-based advertising is often used in industries such as health and safety or insurance. Emotion in advertising can also be employed to align a brand with a specific value or belief. By associating a product or service with a particular emotional cause, advertisers seek to evoke empathy and create a sense of purpose or social responsibility while promoting their offerings. In conclusion, emotion in advertising is the deliberate use of psychological tactics to appeal to consumers' emotions. By leveraging emotions such as humor, nostalgia, fear, and values, advertisers aim to forge a genuine bond with their target audience, increasing brand recognition, loyalty, and purchase intent. The successful incorporation of emotion in advertising can make a brand stand out in a crowded marketplace and create lasting connections with consumers.

Emotional Appeal

An emotional appeal in an advertisement refers to the use of persuasive language, visuals, or storytelling techniques to elicit an emotional response from the audience. It aims to connect with people's feelings and emotions in order to influence their buying decisions or opinions about a product, service, or cause. Advertisements often use emotions such as happiness, sadness, fear, excitement, or nostalgia to create a connection with the audience and motivate them to take action. By tapping into these emotions, advertisers can strengthen the impact of their message and make it more memorable and persuasive.

Endorsement

An endorsement, in the context of Advertisement, refers to a formal declaration or approval of a product, service, or brand by a person, organization, or celebrity. It is a way of promoting and establishing credibility for the advertised item by associating it with a reputable individual or entity. Endorsements are commonly used in advertisements to build trust and persuade consumers to purchase the endorsed product. When a well-known person or organization vouches for the quality or effectiveness of a particular item, it can greatly influence consumer perceptions and purchasing decisions.

Engagement Advertising Strategies Development

Engagement advertising refers to a strategic approach used in the field of advertisement that aims to create a deeper connection and interactive experience between a brand and its target audience. This type of advertising involves designing and implementing various strategies to actively engage and captivate consumers, rather than simply delivering a message or promoting a product or service. The primary objective of engagement advertising is to foster a two-way communication between the brand and its audience, which ultimately enhances brand awareness, builds brand loyalty, and drives customer engagement and conversion. This approach recognizes that traditional advertising methods often fall short in capturing the attention and interest of consumers who are bombarded by countless messages on various platforms. One common engagement advertising strategy is interactive and immersive content. Brands utilize interactive elements such as quizzes, games, polls, and surveys to encourage consumers to actively participate and engage with the brand. By offering entertainment or educational value, brands can create a memorable experience that not only captures attention but also strengthens the brand's association in the consumer's mind. Social media platforms have also become integral to engagement advertising strategies. Brands leverage social media channels to initiate conversations, encourage user-generated content, and build a community around their brand. By creating valuable and shareable content, brands can generate organic reach and engagement, as well as enable consumers to become brand ambassadors. Influencer marketing is another key component of engagement advertising. Brands collaborate with influencers who have a significant following and influence over their target audience. By partnering with these influencers, brands can tap into their credibility and engage with their followers through authentic and relatable content, including sponsored posts, testimonials, or collaborations. Furthermore, personalized and targeted advertising plays a crucial role in engagement advertising strategies. Brands leverage data and analytics to gain insights into consumer behavior, preferences, and interests. This information enables brands to deliver tailored advertisements that resonate with individual consumers, optimizing engagement and conversion rates. In conclusion, engagement advertising is a strategic approach that goes beyond conventional advertising methods, focusing on creating interactive, meaningful, and personalized experiences for the audience. By prioritizing engagement and connection, brands can establish a deeper relationship with their target consumers, fostering loyalty and driving business growth.

Engagement Advertising Strategies

Engagement advertising strategies refer to the various techniques and approaches used by advertisers to actively involve and interact with their target audience. This form of advertising aims to create a two-way communication channel between the advertiser and the consumer, allowing for a deeper level of engagement and brand connection. The primary objective of engagement advertising strategies is to encourage consumers to actively participate and interact with the advertisement, rather than passively consuming the content. These strategies are designed to capture and maintain the attention of the audience, leading to a higher level of involvement, brand recall, and potential conversion.

Engagement Advertising

Engagement advertising refers to a marketing strategy that aims to capture and maintain the attention and interest of the target audience. It involves creating interactive and immersive experiences for consumers, encouraging them to actively participate and engage with the advertisement rather than passively viewing it.Engagement advertising relies on the principle that engaged consumers are more likely to remember and respond positively to advertisements. It seeks to establish a two-way communication between the brand and the consumer, fostering a deeper relationship and creating a sense of brand loyalty.One common form of engagement advertising is interactive ads, which allow users to interact with the ad by clicking, swiping, or tapping on different elements. These ads often include quizzes, games, or other interactive features that keep the user engaged and entertained while delivering the brand message. By actively involving the consumer, engagement advertising aims to create a memorable and impactful experience that resonates with the target audience.Another form of engagement advertising is social media campaigns, which leverage various platforms such as Facebook, Instagram, and Twitter to engage with consumers. These campaigns encourage users to like, share, or comment on the advertisements, creating a ripple effect that expands the reach of the brand message. By tapping into the social nature of these platforms, engagement advertising aims to generate buzz and word-of-mouth promotion.Engagement advertising also encompasses influencer marketing, where brands collaborate with influencers or celebrities to promote their products or services. By leveraging the influencer's established audience and credibility, engagement advertising seeks to create a personal and relatable connection with consumers. This form of advertising often includes sponsored social media posts, product reviews, or endorsements, which encourage consumers to actively engage with the brand.In conclusion, engagement advertising is a marketing strategy that prioritizes active consumer participation and interaction. By creating immersive and interactive experiences, engagement advertising aims to capture the attention and interest of the target audience, fostering a deeper relationship between the brand and the consumer.

Engagement Rate

The engagement rate in the context of advertisement refers to the measure of how actively and deeply the target audience is interacting with a particular advertising campaign or content. It is a metric that helps advertisers evaluate the success and effectiveness of their advertisements in capturing and maintaining the attention and interest of their audience. The engagement rate is calculated by dividing the total number of engagements (such as likes, comments, shares, clicks, etc.) by the total number of impressions (the number of times the ad was viewed or encountered by users). It is usually expressed as a percentage, indicating the proportion of people who interacted with the ad compared to the overall number of people who were exposed to it. A high engagement rate is generally considered desirable as it indicates that the advertisement is resonating well with the target audience, creating a meaningful connection, and generating interest and action. It implies that the ad has caught the attention of users, elicited a response or reaction from them, and encouraged them to interact further or explore the advertised offering. On the other hand, a low engagement rate suggests that the advertisement may not be effectively capturing the attention of users or stimulating their interest. It may indicate that the ad is not relevant, compelling, or appealing enough to generate a response or promote further engagement. In addition to helping advertisers assess the overall performance of their advertisements, the engagement rate can be used to compare and benchmark different campaigns, ad formats, platforms, or target audience segments. By analyzing the engagement rates of various ads, advertisers can identify which ads are more engaging and effective in driving user interaction, and optimize their advertising strategies accordingly. Overall, the engagement rate is a crucial metric in the world of advertising as it provides valuable insights into the level of audience engagement and the effectiveness of ad campaigns. By monitoring and analyzing this metric, advertisers can make informed decisions, refine their strategies, and deliver more impactful and engaging advertisements to their target audience.

Ethical Advertising Practices

Ethical Advertising Practices can be defined as the set of principles and guidelines that govern the conduct and behavior of advertisers in promoting their products or services. These practices aim to ensure that advertising is fair, honest, and transparent, and that it does not mislead, deceive, or manipulate consumers. Ethical advertising practices require that advertisers be truthful and accurate in their claims about their products or services. Advertisers should not make false or exaggerated statements that could deceive consumers or create unreasonable expectations. They should provide clear and complete information about the features, benefits, and limitations of their products or services, enabling consumers to make informed decisions. Advertisements should also be presented in a manner that is easily understandable and not misleading. Another important aspect of ethical advertising practices is respect for consumer privacy and consent. Advertisers should obtain permission before using consumers' personal information for targeted advertising. They should also ensure that their advertisements do not infringe upon consumers' rights or exploit vulnerable individuals, such as children or those with limited cognitive abilities. Furthermore, ethical advertising practices promote respect for cultural, social, and environmental values. Advertisers should avoid creating and perpetuating stereotypes or promoting discriminatory practices. They should be sensitive to cultural and social diversity and ensure that their advertisements do not offend or marginalize any particular group. Advertisers should also take steps to minimize the negative environmental impact of their advertising activities, such as reducing waste or promoting sustainable practices. In summary, ethical advertising practices encompass honesty, transparency, respect for consumer privacy, and adherence to cultural, social, and environmental values. Advertisers should strive to communicate their messages in a truthful and responsible manner, respecting the rights and well-being of consumers while also considering the broader impact of their advertising activities.

Ethical Advertising

Ethical advertising refers to the practice of conducting advertising campaigns in a manner that is respectful, honest, and fair to all parties involved, including the advertisers, consumers, and society at large. It involves adhering to moral principles and ethical standards while promoting products or services to the target audience. One of the key aspects of ethical advertising is the transparent and truthful portrayal of the advertised products or services. Advertisers should provide accurate and honest information about the features, benefits, and limitations of their offerings. They should refrain from making false or exaggerated claims that can mislead or deceive consumers. Furthermore, ethical advertising entails respecting the privacy and consent of individuals. Advertisers should ensure that they obtain the necessary permissions and approvals before using personal information for targeted advertising. They should also provide users with clear options to opt-out of personalized advertising if they so desire. In addition, ethical advertising emphasizes the importance of promoting diversity and inclusion. Advertisements should avoid any form of discrimination based on race, ethnicity, gender, religion, or any other protected characteristic. They should celebrate diversity and represent diverse groups of people in a respectful and authentic manner. Moreover, ethical advertising acknowledges the social and environmental impacts of products and services. Advertisers should strive to promote sustainable and responsible practices that minimize harm to the environment and society. They should avoid supporting or endorsing any activities or products that contribute to negative social or environmental consequences. Overall, ethical advertising is about conducting advertising campaigns with integrity, accountability, and social responsibility. It is about building trust with consumers by providing them with truthful information and respecting their rights. By adhering to ethical standards, advertisers can contribute to a healthier and more transparent advertising industry that benefits both businesses and consumers.

Event Marketing

Event marketing, in the context of advertisement, refers to a strategic marketing approach whereby a company or organization promotes its products, services, or brand through the organization or sponsorship of events. These events can range from trade shows, conferences, exhibitions, seminars, product launches, fundraisers, sporting events, festivals, or any other gathering that attracts a specific target audience. The primary objective of event marketing is to create a memorable experience for the attendees while simultaneously promoting the company's offerings. By associating their brand with a well-executed event, businesses aim to establish a positive impression, build brand awareness, foster customer loyalty, generate leads, and ultimately drive sales. Event marketing offers several advantages over other forms of traditional advertising. Firstly, it provides a unique opportunity to engage with potential customers in a more personal and interactive way. By using face-to-face interactions, demonstrations, product samples, or immersive experiences, companies can create a lasting impact and forge deeper connections with their target audience. Secondly, events allow businesses to tailor their marketing messages and product demonstrations to a specific audience who are already interested in their industry or niche. This targeted approach ensures that marketing efforts are optimized for maximum effectiveness, as attendees are more likely to be receptive and engaged with the company's offerings. Moreover, event marketing can also serve as a platform for networking and building partnerships with other industry players. By participating in industry-specific events, companies can showcase their expertise, establish credibility, and develop relationships with potential clients, partners, and suppliers. In conclusion, event marketing plays a crucial role in the advertising landscape by providing companies with a strategic avenue to promote their brand, products, or services through the organization or sponsorship of events. By creating memorable experiences, engaging with their target audience, and leveraging targeted marketing messages, businesses can drive brand awareness, foster customer loyalty, generate leads, and ultimately drive sales.

Event Sponsorship Planning Procedures

Event sponsorship planning procedures refer to the systematic process of developing a strategy and implementing activities to secure sponsorships for an event. In the context of advertisement, event sponsorship involves partnering with businesses or organizations to promote their products or services in exchange for financial support or other resources for the event. The planning procedures for event sponsorship typically include the following steps: 1. Define sponsorship objectives: The first step is to clearly define the objectives and goals of the event sponsorship. This involves determining what the event hopes to achieve through sponsorship, such as increasing brand visibility, reaching a specific target audience, or generating revenue. 2.

Identify target sponsors: Next, the event organizers identify potential sponsors who align with the event's objectives and target audience. This may involve conducting research, networking, and creating a list of potential sponsors to approach. 3. Package and pitch sponsorship opportunities: Once the target sponsors are identified, the event organizers develop sponsorship packages that outline the various opportunities available for sponsors. These packages may include details on branding opportunities, promotional activities, onsite presence, and other benefits offered to sponsors. A compelling pitch is then created to present these sponsorship packages to potential sponsors. 4. Reach out to potential sponsors: In this step, event organizers initiate contact with potential sponsors and present the sponsorship opportunities to them. This may involve sending personalized emails, making phone calls, or setting up face-to-face meetings to discuss the benefits of sponsoring the event. 5. Negotiate and finalize sponsorship agreements: Once a potential sponsor expresses interest, the negotiation process begins. The event organizers and the sponsor discuss the terms of the sponsorship agreement, including the financial contribution or resources to be provided, as well as the expected deliverables and benefits for the sponsor. Once the agreement is finalized, a contract or agreement is signed between both parties. 6. Activate and fulfill sponsorship obligations: Once the sponsorship agreements are in place, the event organizers activate the sponsorship by implementing the agreed-upon promotional activities and fulfilling any obligations outlined in the contract. This may include displaying sponsor logos, providing advertising space, conducting product demonstrations, or any other mutually agreed-upon activities. By following these event sponsorship planning procedures, event organizers can maximize the potential of securing sponsorships and effectively leverage them for advertisement purposes.

Event Sponsorship Planning

Event sponsorship planning in the context of advertisement refers to the strategic process of securing financial support, resources, and promotional opportunities from external organizations or brands for an event in exchange for advertising exposure and associated benefits. The primary objective of event sponsorship planning is to create mutually beneficial partnerships between event organizers and sponsors. Event organizers seek sponsorship opportunities to fund and enhance their events, while sponsors aim to increase brand visibility, reach target audiences, and achieve marketing objectives by associating themselves with the event and its target audience.

Event Sponsorship

Event sponsorship is a form of advertisement where a company or organization provides financial or material support to an event in exchange for promotional benefits. It involves the sponsorship of various types of events such as sports competitions, conferences, festivals, charity events, and trade shows. Sponsoring an event allows companies to reach a specific target audience and gain exposure to a large number of attendees. By associating their brand with a particular event, sponsors can enhance brand recognition and create positive brand associations. Event sponsorship can help companies build credibility and trust among consumers, as they are seen as supporters of a valued event.

Experiential Advertising Campaigns

Experiential advertising campaigns refer to a type of advertisement strategy that focuses on creating immersive and interactive experiences for consumers. Instead of relying solely on traditional advertising methods such as print or television, experiential campaigns aim to engage potential customers by involving them in unique brand experiences. These campaigns typically take the form of events, installations, or activities that allow consumers to directly interact with the brand, its product, or its message. The goal is to create a memorable and meaningful connection between the consumer and the brand, resulting in increased brand awareness, loyalty, and ultimately, sales.

Experiential Advertising

Experiential advertising, also known as engagement marketing, is a form of advertisement that aims to create a memorable and immersive experience for the target audience. It goes beyond traditional promotional methods by actively involving consumers in a hands-on, sensory-rich experience that fosters a personal connection with the brand or product being advertised. Unlike conventional advertising techniques, which rely on passive consumption of media messages, experiential advertising seeks to actively engage consumers and encourage their participation. This can be achieved through various means, such as interactive installations, live events, product demonstrations, or experiential stunts. The goal is to capture attention, evoke emotions, and leave a lasting impression on the audience. Experiential advertising leverages the power of sensory stimuli to engage multiple senses, such as sight, sound, touch, taste, and smell. By offering a multi-sensory experience, brands aim to create a deeper and more meaningful connection with consumers. For example, a perfume brand may create a pop-up store where customers can not only see and hear about their product but also engage their sense of smell by sampling different scents. One of the key advantages of experiential advertising is its ability to generate word-of-mouth buzz. When consumers have a positive and memorable experience with a brand, they are more likely to share it with others, either through social media, personal conversations, or online reviews. This organic form of promotion can significantly enhance a brand's reach and credibility. Furthermore, experiential advertising allows brands to garner valuable insights about their target audience. By observing consumer behavior and preferences during interactive experiences, marketers can gather data that can inform future marketing strategies and product development. This feedback loop enables brands to tailor their offerings to better meet consumer needs and preferences. In conclusion, experiential advertising is a dynamic and immersive form of advertisement that aims to actively engage consumers through interactive and multi-sensory experiences. By creating memorable moments and forging personal connections, brands can foster positive word-of-mouth and gain valuable insights about their target audience.

Experiential Marketing Events Execution Techniques

Experiential marketing events execution techniques refer to the strategic and tactical actions taken to plan, organize, and implement experiential marketing campaigns that aim to engage consumers on a personal level and create memorable brand experiences. These techniques involve a range of activities and considerations, such as event planning, venue selection, creative concept development, brand activations, and interactive elements that enhance consumer engagement and interaction. The goal is to immerse consumers in the brand's offerings and values, fostering emotional connections and loyalty.

Experiential Marketing Events Execution

Experiential marketing events execution, in the context of advertising, refers to the implementation and management of events or experiences that aim to create meaningful interactions between a brand or product and its target audience. These events are designed to provide a unique and memorable experience to consumers, going beyond traditional advertising methods and allowing them to actively engage with the brand. Experiential marketing events execution involves careful planning, organization, and coordination of various elements to create an immersive experience. This can include activities such as pop-up shops, product demonstrations, interactive installations, brand activations, and live performances. The goal is to create a direct and personal connection with consumers, building brand awareness, loyalty, and ultimately driving sales. This form of marketing capitalizes on the power of emotions and memorable experiences to leave a lasting impression on consumers. By creating an environment where customers can directly interact with a brand, experiential marketing events execution aims to foster positive brand associations, generate word-of-mouth, and encourage social sharing of the experience. These events often leverage social media and online platforms to amplify their reach and impact by encouraging users to share their experiences using branded hashtags or through user-generated content. The execution of experiential marketing events requires a deep understanding of the target audience and their preferences, as well as creative thinking and attention to detail. Event logistics, such as location selection, event setup, staffing, and timing, play a crucial role in the success of these experiences. Additionally, partnerships with relevant influencers or industry experts can help enhance the credibility and reach of the event. In conclusion, experiential marketing events execution in the context of advertisement involves the strategic planning and implementation of events or experiences that aim to create meaningful and immersive interactions between a brand or product and its target audience. Through the use of creative and memorable experiences, these events aim to leave a lasting impression on consumers and drive brand awareness, loyalty, and ultimately, sales.

Experiential Marketing Events

Experiential marketing events are promotional activities that aim to engage and involve consumers in a memorable and tangible way. This form of advertisement goes beyond traditional advertising methods by creating an immersive experience that allows consumers to directly interact with the brand or product. Through experiential marketing events, brands can create a unique and memorable experience for their target audience. These events often take place in public spaces, such as shopping malls, parks, or city centers, and are designed to capture the attention and interest of passersby. By providing an interactive and engaging experience, brands can create a lasting impression and a positive association with their products or services.

Experiential Marketing

Experiential marketing, in the context of advertising, refers to a distinctive approach that aims to create a memorable and engaging experience for consumers. This form of marketing transcends traditional methods by focusing on enabling individuals to personally interact with a brand, product, or service. Unlike other advertising techniques that rely heavily on one-way communication, such as television or print ads, experiential marketing encourages active participation from consumers. It seeks to immerse them in unique and captivating experiences, allowing them to see, touch, hear, taste, or smell the offering in a tangible way.

Exposure

Exposure in the context of advertisement refers to the number of people who are potentially reached by an advertising campaign or message. It measures the visibility and reach of an advertisement to a target audience. Exposure is an essential metric in advertising as it indicates the potential impact and effectiveness of an ad. It helps advertisers evaluate the success of their campaigns and make informed decisions on how to allocate their resources.

External Advertising Agencies Evaluation Criteria

An external advertising agency is a third-party organization that specializes in creating and executing marketing and advertising campaigns for businesses. These agencies work with companies to develop strategic plans, create advertisements, and provide support services to help businesses reach their target audience and meet their marketing objectives. When evaluating external advertising agencies, there are several key criteria to consider: 1. Experience and Expertise: It is important to assess the agency's experience and expertise in the advertising industry. Look for agencies that have a proven track record of successful campaigns and have worked with businesses in your industry or similar industries. Their experience indicates their understanding of the market and their ability to create effective advertisements. 2. Creativity and Innovation: A good advertising agency should be able to think creatively and come up with innovative ideas that can capture the attention of the target audience. Look for agencies that have a portfolio of unique and engaging advertisements that stand out from their competitors. 3. Strategic Planning: Effective advertising requires careful strategic planning. Evaluate the agency's ability to develop a comprehensive marketing strategy that aligns with your business goals and target audience. Look for agencies that can provide insights and recommendations on the best advertising channels, messaging, and tactics to achieve your objectives. 4. Communication and Collaboration: Communication is key when working with an external agency. Assess the agency's ability to listen to your needs, objectives, and concerns, and their willingness to collaborate with your team. Look for agencies that are responsive, proactive, and maintain open lines of communication throughout the advertising campaign. 5. Budget and Cost-Effectiveness: Consider the agency's pricing structure and whether it fits within your budget. Evaluate their ability to deliver high-quality advertising services within your financial limitations. Look for agencies that provide transparent pricing and can offer cost-effective solutions without compromising on the quality of their work. Overall, when evaluating external advertising agencies, consider their experience, creativity, strategic planning capabilities, communication skills, and cost-effectiveness to ensure that you partner with an agency that can effectively promote your business and help you achieve your marketing goals.

External Advertising Agencies Evaluation

An external advertising agency is a company or organization that provides services related to advertising on behalf of another company. These agencies specialize in creating and implementing advertising campaigns across various media platforms to promote and market their clients' products or services. External advertising agencies play a crucial role in the overall marketing strategy of a business. They are responsible for developing creative concepts, designing advertisements, selecting appropriate media outlets, and managing the execution of campaigns. These agencies have extensive expertise in understanding consumer behavior, market trends, and effective communication strategies.

External Advertising Agencies

An external advertising agency refers to a business entity that specializes in creating and implementing advertising campaigns on behalf of other companies or organizations. These agencies work independently from the client and are hired to help create, plan, and manage their advertising efforts. External advertising agencies typically offer a range of services that can support various aspects of the advertising process. This may include market research, creative development, media planning and buying, and campaign analysis. They often have a team of professionals with expertise in different areas, such as copywriting, graphic design, and digital marketing, to ensure the successful execution of campaigns across different media platforms. Companies may choose to work with external advertising agencies for several reasons. One of the main benefits is the expertise and experience they bring to the table. These agencies often have a deep understanding of market trends, consumer behavior, and effective advertising strategies. They can provide valuable insights and recommendations to help businesses develop compelling advertisements that resonate with their target audience. External agencies also offer businesses the advantage of specialized skills and resources. They often have access to industry-specific tools, software, and data analytics platforms that enable them to optimize campaigns and track their performance. This can save businesses time, effort, and resources, as they can rely on the agency's capabilities to ensure the effective delivery of their advertising messages. Working with an external advertising agency can also provide businesses with a fresh perspective. These agencies work with clients from various industries, allowing them to adopt a more objective view of the market and create innovative campaigns. They can bring new ideas and strategies to the table, helping businesses stand out from the competition and make a lasting impact on their target audience. In conclusion, external advertising agencies play a crucial role in helping businesses develop and implement successful advertising campaigns. Through their expertise, resources, and fresh perspective, they support businesses in reaching their marketing goals and effectively engaging with their target audience.

Eye Tracking

Eye tracking, in the context of advertisement, refers to the technology and method used to measure and analyze the visual behavior of individuals when exposed to various promotional materials, such as advertisements and marketing campaigns. It involves tracking and recording the movement of the eyes as they fixate, move, or scan different elements of an advertisement, providing valuable insights into what attracts and holds the viewer's attention. By using specialized equipment, such as eye-tracking cameras or sensors, researchers can accurately monitor and analyze eye movements, including fixations (when the eyes focus on a specific point) and saccades (rapid eye movements between fixations). This data enables advertisers and marketers to gain a deeper understanding of how consumers engage with their ads and make informed decisions on design, placement, and content.

Eyetracking In Advertising Research Approaches

Eyetracking in advertising research refers to the use of specialized technology to track and measure the eye movements and fixations of individuals when exposed to advertising stimuli. By employing eyetracking techniques, researchers are able to gain insights into how consumers interact with advertisements, specifically focusing on where their attention is directed and how long they spend looking at specific elements within the ad. This information can then be used to evaluate the effectiveness of various advertising strategies and techniques.

Eyetracking In Advertising Research

Eyetracking in advertising research refers to the technique of tracking and measuring eye movements and gaze patterns of individuals while they interact with advertisements. It involves the use of specialized technologies, such as eye-tracking devices and software, to collect data on where and how long individuals look at specific elements within an advertisement. The objective of utilizing eyetracking in advertising research is to gain insights into how consumers visually engage with advertisements and to understand which elements are most effective in capturing their attention. By analyzing eye movement data, researchers can determine which parts of an advertisement are most noticed, how individuals scan the advertisement, and the order in which they focus on different elements.

Eyetracking In Advertising

Eyetracking in advertising refers to the use of eye-tracking technology to measure and analyze the visual attention of individuals towards advertisements. This technology allows advertisers to gain insights into how people look at different elements within an advertisement, such as headlines, images, and calls to action. With eyetracking, advertisers can determine which parts of an advertisement attract the most attention, understand how people's gaze moves across the ad, and identify potential areas of improvement to increase effectiveness. By tracking eye movements and fixations, advertisers can gain valuable information about consumer behavior and preferences.

Fictional Advertising Characters Development Methods

Development methods for fictional advertising characters refer to the processes and approaches used to create and establish these characters for use in advertisements. These methods include various techniques and strategies aimed at crafting memorable and relatable characters that effectively communicate the desired message or promote a specific product or brand. One common method is the use of audience research and data analysis to identify the target market's preferences, interests, and needs. This information helps advertisers understand the specific characteristics and traits that would resonate with their audience. By conducting surveys, focus groups, and analyzing market trends, advertisers can gain insights into what type of fictional character would most effectively engage potential customers. Another approach is to draw inspiration from cultural and societal influences. Advertisers may create characters that reflect certain values, behaviors, or lifestyles that are relevant and appealing to the target audience. These characters can embody ideals or aspirations that consumers can relate to, making them more likely to connect with the advertised product or brand. Developing fictional characters for advertisements also involves considering the medium or platform where the character will be showcased. Characters can be tailored to suit the specific requirements of television, radio, print, or digital media, ensuring that they are optimized for maximum impact and effectiveness within the chosen medium. An essential aspect of character development is ensuring consistency and continuity. Advertisers strive to create characters with distinct personalities, traits, and visual appearances that remain consistent across different advertisements and campaigns. This consistency helps build brand recognition and fosters a sense of familiarity and trust among consumers. Lastly, humor and emotional appeal are often employed as part of character development in advertising. Characters that can evoke strong emotions or make viewers laugh are more likely to be memorable and shareable, which can lead to increased brand exposure and engagement.

Fictional Advertising Characters Development

Fictional advertising characters development refers to the process of creating and evolving fictional characters specifically designed for advertising purposes. These characters are carefully crafted to represent a brand or product and are used in various forms of marketing communications to attract and engage audiences. The development of fictional advertising characters involves several key steps. The first step is identifying the target audience and understanding their preferences, needs, and behaviors. This helps in determining the traits and characteristics that the fictional character should possess to resonate with the audience and build a connection with them. Once the target audience is defined, the next step is to create the fictional character and bring them to life. This involves defining their appearance, personality, backstory, and overall identity. The character's appearance is typically designed to reflect the brand's image and values, while their personality is crafted to match the desired brand attributes, such as reliability, innovation, or friendliness. Developing a backstory for the character helps to give them depth and make them relatable to the audience. It can include details about their past, their motivations, and their goals. This backstory is often revealed gradually through multiple advertisements or marketing campaigns, allowing the audience to develop a connection and bond with the character over time. As the character is introduced to the audience, their persona and traits are reinforced through consistent messaging and storytelling. This ensures that the audience associates the character with the brand and recognizes them as a symbol or representative of the product or service being advertised. The development of fictional advertising characters is an ongoing process. Over time, they may undergo changes and adaptations based on consumer feedback, market trends, or the brand's strategic objectives. This evolution helps to keep the characters relevant and engaging, ensuring their continued effectiveness in advertising campaigns.

Fictional Advertising Characters

Fictional advertising characters are fictional personalities created to represent a brand or product in advertisements. They are designed to capture consumers' attention, create a memorable image for the brand, and convey specific messages or values associated with the product or company. These characters often have distinct visual features, catchphrases, or personality traits that make them easily recognizable and memorable to consumers. They can range from animated animals or objects to human-like characters with exaggerated characteristics. Famous examples include the Geico Gecko, Tony the Tiger, the Pillsbury Doughboy, and the Marlboro Man.

Flash Advertising Techniques

Flash advertising techniques refer to the use of Flash technology, a multimedia software platform, in designing and creating visually engaging advertisements. With its ability to integrate various media elements, such as graphics, animations, and videos, Flash becomes a powerful tool for creating interactive and dynamic advertisements. Flash-based ads captivate the audience's attention through visually compelling and eye-catching designs. By incorporating movement, special effects, and interactive features, these ads have the potential to create a memorable and immersive experience for viewers.

Flash Advertising

Flash advertising refers to the use of Adobe Flash technology to create interactive and animated advertisements for online platforms. It allows advertisers to incorporate rich multimedia elements such as graphics, audio, and video into their advertisements, enhancing their visual appeal and engagement with the audience. Flash advertising is widely used in digital marketing campaigns, particularly on websites and ad networks. It provides advertisers with a versatile and dynamic tool to deliver their brand messages effectively and capture the attention of their target audience.

Freemium Advertising Models Implementation Steps

Freemium advertising models are an approach to advertising where the basic services or content are offered for free, while more advanced features or premium content are available for a fee. This model allows businesses to attract a larger user base by providing free services, while generating revenue from users willing to pay for enhanced features or additional content. The implementation of a freemium advertising model involves several steps. Firstly, businesses need to identify their target audience and determine which services or content they are willing to offer for free. This could be a basic version of their product or access to certain features or content. Next, they need to develop a monetization strategy for the premium offerings. This could involve offering a subscription plan, in-app purchases, or additional services that users can purchase. Once the basic and premium offerings are identified, the next step is to create a seamless user experience. It is important to design the interface in a way that encourages users to upgrade to the premium version, while still providing value to those using the free version. Businesses also need to establish metrics to track user behavior and engagement. This data can help optimize the freemium model and identify opportunities for upselling or cross-selling premium features. Furthermore, businesses should implement effective marketing and promotional strategies to attract users to the freemium offering. This may involve creating

151

enticing offers, leveraging social media channels, or partnering with influencers or other businesses to increase visibility. Lastly, it is crucial to continuously iterate and improve the freemium model based on user feedback and market trends. This involves analyzing user data, identifying pain points, and making necessary adjustments to enhance the overall user experience and drive conversions. In summary, the implementation of a freemium advertising model involves identifying the basic and premium offerings, creating a seamless user experience, establishing metrics, implementing marketing strategies, and iterating based on user feedback. This approach allows businesses to attract a larger user base while generating revenue from users willing to pay for additional features or content.

Freemium Advertising Models Implementation

A freemium advertising model is an implementation strategy where a company offers a product or service for free to a large audience, with the intention of generating revenue through advertising. It relies on the concept of providing a basic version of the product or service for free, while offering additional features or benefits at a cost. This advertising model works by attracting a wide user base through the free offering, which can include basic functionality or limited access to certain features or content. The goal is to build a large user base that advertisers can target with their ads, allowing the company to generate revenue through advertising partnerships.

Freemium Advertising Models

A freemium advertising model is a type of advertising strategy where a company offers a basic version of their product or service for free, while charging for additional premium features or functionalities. This model is most commonly used in the digital advertising space, especially in mobile apps and online platforms. In a freemium advertising model, the free version of the product or service often includes advertisements that generate revenue for the company. These advertisements can take various forms, such as banners, pop-ups, or sponsored content. The goal is to entice a large user base to use the free version, in order to maximize the reach and visibility of the advertisements. The free version of the product or service typically has limited functionality or may be ad-supported, creating an incentive for users to upgrade to the premium version. The premium version usually offers additional features, removes advertisements, or provides a more enhanced user experience. The company earns revenue from these premium upgrades or subscriptions. One of the main advantages of the freemium advertising model is its ability to attract a large number of users by offering free access to the product or service. This helps create brand awareness and build a user base, which can be monetized through advertisements. Additionally, the model allows users to test out the basic functionalities of the product or service before committing to a paid upgrade. However, the freemium advertising model also has its limitations. The success of this model heavily relies on the ability to convert free users into paying customers. To achieve this, the free version needs to offer enough value and convenience to incentivize users to upgrade. Moreover, the company must strike the right balance between the free and premium versions, ensuring that the free version is compelling enough to attract users, while the premium version offers sufficient additional value to justify the cost.

Frequency Cap Management

Frequency cap management is a crucial aspect of advertisement campaign management, which involves setting limits on the number of times an ad is displayed to a specific user or within a particular time frame. The purpose of frequency capping is to prevent ad fatigue and ensure that ads are not overly repetitive, which can lead to lower user engagement and decreased campaign performance. By implementing frequency caps, advertisers can control the exposure of their ads to ensure that they reach a wide audience without becoming intrusive or annoying. This limits the possibility of users becoming frustrated or disinterested in the advertised product or service. Advertisers can set caps based on different parameters, such as the number of impressions per user, per day, per week, or per month, depending on their advertising goals and objectives.

Frequency Cap

A frequency cap, in the context of advertisement, refers to a limit set on the number of times a particular ad can be shown to an individual user within a specific time period. It aims to prevent overexposure of a specific ad to the same user and helps to ensure a more diverse and balanced ad experience. Implementing a frequency cap is essential for advertisers to prevent ad fatigue and to maintain the effectiveness of their campaigns. It ensures that users are not bombarded with the same ad repeatedly, which can lead to annoyance and decreased interest in the promoted product or service.

Frequency Capping

Frequency capping, in the context of advertisement, refers to the practice of limiting the number of times an ad is shown to a particular user within a given time period. By implementing frequency capping, advertisers can control the exposure of their ads to ensure that users are not bombarded with the same ad repeatedly. This strategy aims to strike a balance between maximizing the reach and effectiveness of an ad campaign while also avoiding the potential annoyance and diminishing returns that excessive ad repetition may cause.

Full-Service Advertising Agency Services

A full-service advertising agency is a company that provides a comprehensive range of advertising services to clients. These agencies typically have teams of professionals with expertise in various areas of advertising, such as creative design, media planning, strategy development, market research, and campaign execution. One of the key advantages of working with a full-service advertising agency is that it offers a one-stop solution for all advertising needs. Clients can benefit from the convenience of having all their advertising activities handled by a single agency, which can save time and effort in coordinating different aspects of a campaign. This also helps ensure consistency in messaging and branding across various advertising channels. The services offered by a full-service advertising agency can vary depending on the specific needs of the client. Some common services include: Creative Services: This involves the development of visually appealing and engaging advertisements, including graphic design, copywriting, and video production. The agency's creative team works closely with the client to understand their brand identity and marketing goals, and then develops compelling ad concepts that resonate with the target audience. Media Planning and Buying: This involves strategizing and implementing advertising campaigns across various media channels, such as television, radio, print, outdoor, and digital platforms. The agency's media team conducts market research to identify the most effective media outlets for reaching the target audience and negotiates with media vendors to secure favorable ad placements and rates. Market Research: This involves gathering and analyzing data about the target market, competitors, and industry trends to inform advertising strategies. The agency's research team conducts surveys, interviews, and data analysis to gain insights that can guide the development of effective advertising campaigns. Campaign Management: This involves overseeing the execution of advertising campaigns, including monitoring performance, making adjustments as needed, and ensuring that all deliverables are met on time and within budget. The agency's account management team serves as the main point of contact for the client, coordinating the efforts of different teams within the agency to ensure seamless campaign execution. In addition to these core services, a full-service advertising agency may also offer other specialized services, such as social media management, public relations, event marketing, and website development. The goal is to provide clients with a comprehensive set of advertising solutions that can effectively reach and engage their target audience, drive brand awareness, and generate desired business outcomes.

Full-Service Advertising Agency

A full-service advertising agency is an agency that offers a comprehensive range of services to assist businesses with their advertising and marketing needs. They work closely with clients to develop and implement effective advertising campaigns that help promote and sell products or services. The main objective of a full-service advertising agency is to create and execute advertising strategies that reach the target audience and generate maximum impact. They typically have a team of professionals with expertise in various areas such as creative design, copywriting, market research, media planning, and digital marketing. One of the key tasks of a full-service advertising agency is to conduct thorough market research and analysis to understand the target audience, competition, and industry trends. This helps them develop strategic insights and identify effective advertising channels to reach the target audience. Based on the research findings, the agency creates compelling and engaging advertising content that effectively communicates the brand message. This includes designing advertisements, creating catchy slogans or taglines, and developing persuasive copy. The creative team works closely with the client to ensure that the advertisements align with the brand identity and objectives. Once the advertisements are developed, the agency then plans the media placement to ensure that they reach the target audience. This involves selecting the appropriate media channels such as television, radio, print, outdoor advertising, and digital platforms. The agency negotiates with media outlets to secure the best rates and placements for the advertisements. In addition to traditional advertising channels, full-service advertising agencies also specialize in digital marketing. They are well-versed in utilizing online platforms such as search engine marketing, social media advertising, email marketing, and content marketing to reach and engage with the target audience. Throughout the advertising campaign, the agency continuously monitors and measures the effectiveness of the advertisements. They analyze key metrics such as reach, impressions, click-through rates, and conversions to evaluate the success of the campaign and make any necessary adjustments. In conclusion, a full-service advertising agency offers a comprehensive range of services to help businesses plan, create, and execute effective advertising campaigns. They utilize their expertise in various areas to reach the target audience, generate maximum impact, and deliver measurable results for their clients.

Gamification In Advertising Strategies Planning

Gamification in advertising strategies planning refers to the incorporation of game elements and mechanics into advertising campaigns with the aim of engaging and motivating consumers to interact with brands and take desired actions. By leveraging the principles of gamification, advertisers can create immersive and interactive experiences that capture the attention and interest of their target audience. This involves the use of various game-like elements such as challenges, rewards, leaderboards, badges, and levels to incentivize and compel consumers to actively participate in brand promotions. The goal is to make the advertisement more enjoyable and memorable, fostering a positive brand perception and encouraging consumer loyalty.

Gamification In Advertising Strategies

Gamification in advertising strategies refers to the incorporation of game-like elements and mechanics into advertising campaigns with the aim of engaging and motivating the target audience. By utilizing game mechanics such as points, levels, challenges, rewards, and competition, advertisers seek to enhance user experiences and encourage active participation. When implemented effectively, gamification in advertising strategies can result in increased brand awareness, improved customer engagement, and higher conversion rates. It creates a more interactive and immersive experience for consumers, enticing them to spend more time with the brand and its messaging.

Gamification In Advertising

Gamification in advertising refers to the incorporation of game elements and mechanics into advertising campaigns to engage and motivate target audiences. It involves applying game design techniques such as points, challenges, rewards, and competition to make advertisements more interactive and enjoyable for consumers. By integrating elements of play and competition, gamification aims to capture the attention of consumers and enhance their involvement and interest in the advertising content. It provides an immersive experience that encourages users to actively participate and interact with the brand or product being promoted.

Gamification

Gamification in the context of advertisement refers to the use of game elements and mechanics to engage and motivate consumers in promotional activities. It involves incorporating elements such as challenges, rewards, competition, and achievements into advertising campaigns to captivate and incentivize target audiences. By employing gamification techniques, advertisers aim to enhance brand awareness, foster consumer loyalty, and drive customer engagement. Games and interactive experiences have the potential to capture consumers' attention and create memorable brand experiences, leading to increased brand recall and affinity.

Geo-Conquesting Advertising Tactics Implementation

Geo-conquesting advertising tactics implementation refers to the strategic use of location-based targeting to target customers of a competitor's business and deliver relevant advertising messages to them. This approach allows advertisers to reach potential customers who are in close proximity to a competitor's physical location, enticing them to consider an alternative product or service. The process involves identifying the geographical boundaries of a competitor's store or business location and setting up a digital advertising campaign to specifically target individuals within that area. By leveraging location data from mobile devices or IP addresses, advertisers can determine the physical proximity of potential customers to a competitor's business. This enables them to deliver targeted and personalized advertising messages to those individuals in real-time, effectively capturing their attention when they are near the competitor's location. Geo-conquesting can be implemented through various digital advertising channels, including display advertising on mobile apps and websites, social media platforms, and search engine marketing. Advertisers can create tailored messages and offers that highlight the unique selling points of their products or services compared to the competition. For example, a fast food chain may advertise a limited-time discount or a special promotion to individuals who are near a competitor's restaurant, enticing them to try their food instead. The effectiveness of geo-conquesting advertising tactics relies heavily on the accuracy of location data and the ability to deliver timely and relevant advertising messages. Advertisers must utilize robust geofencing technology and reliable location data providers to ensure precise targeting. It is also crucial to optimize the ad delivery process to minimize response times and increase the likelihood of engagement. By implementing geo-conquesting advertising tactics effectively, businesses can gain a competitive advantage by reaching potential customers who are actively considering a purchase in their specific industry or niche.

Geo-Conquesting Advertising Tactics

Geo-conquesting advertising tactics refer to a targeted marketing strategy that involves delivering personalized advertisements to consumers based on their physical location, with the specific aim of diverting them from competitors or capturing a competitive market share. With the advancements in mobile technology and the widespread use of smartphones, geo-conquesting has become a popular advertising method for businesses looking to capitalize on the growing trend of location-based marketing. By utilizing GPS and geofencing technologies, advertisers can specifically target consumers based on their proximity to certain locations, such as competitors' stores or high-traffic areas.

Geo-Conquesting Advertising

Geo-Conquesting Advertising is a targeted digital advertising strategy that utilizes location-based targeting to reach potential customers when they are near or within the vicinity of a competitor's physical location. By leveraging geofencing technology, advertisers can define a virtual boundary around their competitors' physical stores, offices, or other relevant locations. When a user enters this predefined geographic area, they become eligible to receive targeted advertisements from the advertiser, usually displayed on their mobile devices. This form of advertising aims to capture the attention of consumers who are already in a buying mindset by delivering personalized and relevant messages related to their proximity to a competitor. It allows advertisers to highlight their own offerings, promotions, or unique selling points to potentially divert customers away from their competitors to their own business. Geo-conquesting advertising typically employs various targeting parameters such as demographic data, consumer behavior, and interests to refine the audience receiving the advertisements. This enables advertisers to tailor their messaging to specific customer segments and increase the chances of engagement and conversion. Once a user enters the designated geographic area, ad impressions can be delivered through various channels, including display ads, in-app ads, social media ads, or push notifications. These advertisements can feature compelling copy, visuals, or even exclusive incentives to entice potential customers to choose the advertiser's business over their competitor's. Effectiveness of geo-conquesting advertising can be measured through metrics such as click-through rates, conversions, and footfall tracking. By analyzing the performance of these targeted campaigns, advertisers can gauge the impact of their messaging and optimize their strategies to maximize engagement and ultimately drive business growth. In conclusion, geo-conquesting advertising is a location-based targeting technique that allows advertisers to reach audiences near their competitors' physical locations. By strategically delivering personalized advertisements to these potential customers, advertisers aim to influence their purchase decisions and gain a competitive edge in the market.

Geo-Fencing Advertising Strategies

Geo-fencing advertising strategies refer to the use of location-based technology to target and deliver personalized advertisements to consumers within a specific geographic area. This technique allows advertisers to reach their target audience in a more precise and efficient manner by narrowing the scope of their advertising campaigns to a particular region or location. Geo-fencing advertising works by creating a virtual boundary or "fence" around a specific area, such as a store, event venue, or neighborhood. This fence is established using GPS, Wi-Fi, cellular data, or RFID technology. When a user enters or exits this designated area, they trigger a response from the advertiser's mobile app or website. This response can include sending push notifications, displaying relevant ads, or providing special offers or discounts.

Geo-Fencing Advertising

Geo-fencing advertising is an innovative marketing strategy that utilizes location-based technology to deliver targeted advertisements to specific geographic areas. It involves setting virtual boundaries, known as geofences, around predefined locations such as stores, events, or neighborhoods. When a user enters or exits a geofenced area, their mobile device triggers a location signal that enables businesses to send relevant advertisements directly to their device. This allows companies to reach consumers at the right time and place, increasing the effectiveness of their marketing campaigns. Geo-fencing also provides valuable insights into user behavior and preferences, allowing advertisers to refine their messaging and personalize their offers.

Geographic Segmentation

Geographic segmentation is a marketing strategy that focuses on dividing a target market into specific geographic areas based on various factors such as location, climate, population density, and cultural characteristics. By doing so, advertisers can tailor their advertisements to suit the needs and preferences of consumers in different geographic locations. This strategy recognizes that consumer behavior and preferences can vary significantly depending on where individuals reside. Different geographic regions can have distinct cultural, economic, and social dynamics that influence consumer buying decisions. For example, a product that appeals to consumers in one area may not be as popular or relevant in another. Therefore, geographic segmentation helps advertisers overcome these differences by tailoring their advertisements to specific regions and demographic groups within those areas.

Geotargeting

Geotargeting is a strategic marketing technique that aims to deliver relevant advertisements to a specific audience based on their geographical location. It utilizes data about a user's location, such as their IP address or GPS coordinates, to determine which ads will be displayed to them. Advertisers leverage geotargeting to ensure that their marketing messages reach the right people in the right place and at the right time. By tailoring their advertisements to local audiences, businesses can increase the chances of connecting with potential customers who are more likely to be interested in their products or services.

Global Advertising

Global advertising refers to the practice of promoting products, services, or brands on a worldwide scale. It involves creating and delivering persuasive messages through various communication channels to reach a diverse audience across different countries and cultures. The concept of global advertising emerged with the globalization of markets, advancements in technology, and the increasing interconnectedness of people around the world. It has become an essential marketing strategy for businesses seeking to expand their reach beyond national boundaries and tap into international markets. Global advertising campaigns require careful planning and customization to effectively convey messages that resonate with target audiences in different countries. Advertisers need to consider cultural nuances, language barriers, and local preferences to ensure that their messages are relevant, understandable, and persuasive. One of the key challenges in global advertising is striking the right balance between standardization and localization. Standardization involves developing a consistent brand image and message that can be used across multiple markets, while localization involves adapting the advertising content to suit the specific needs and preferences of individual markets. To achieve successful global advertising, advertisers often collaborate with advertising agencies or consultants with local expertise who can provide insights into target markets. They also leverage various media channels and platforms, such as television, print, digital, and social media, to effectively deliver their messages to a worldwide audience. In addition to reaching a wider audience, global advertising offers several advantages. It enables economies of scale by allowing businesses to leverage their advertising investments across multiple markets. It also helps in building a consistent brand image and recognition, which can enhance brand equity and customer loyalty. However, global advertising is not without its challenges. Apart from cultural and language barriers, advertisers also face legal and regulatory considerations in different countries. They need to comply with local laws and regulations regarding advertising content, product claims, and promotion techniques. In conclusion, global advertising is a strategic approach to advertising that aims to reach a diverse audience in different countries through the effective delivery of persuasive messages. It requires careful planning, customization, and consideration of cultural nuances and local preferences. By striking the right balance between standardization and localization, businesses can leverage global advertising to expand their market reach, build brand equity, and achieve international success.

Google Ads

Google Ads is an online advertising platform developed by Google, which allows advertisers to display their advertisements on various Google platforms, including the search engine results page and websites within the Google Display Network. It is a pay-per-click (PPC) advertising model, where advertisers bid on specific keywords or target audience demographics to have their ads displayed to relevant users. Google Ads offers a variety of ad formats, including text ads, display ads, video ads, and app promotion ads, allowing advertisers to reach their target audience through different mediums. Advertisers can create and manage their campaigns through the Google Ads dashboard, where they can monitor their ad performance, adjust their bids, and control their ad spend.

Google Display Network Optimization Techniques

Google Display Network Optimization Techniques refer to the strategies and practices used to enhance the performance and effectiveness of advertising campaigns on the Google Display Network (GDN). The GDN is a collection of websites, apps, and other digital platforms where businesses can display their ads to reach a wider audience. Effective GDN optimization techniques involve several key principles. Firstly, audience targeting plays a crucial role in increasing ad relevance and engagement. By analyzing the demographics, interests, and behaviors of the target audience, advertisers can tailor their ads to be more appealing and deliver them to the right users at the right time. This can be achieved through various targeting options provided by Google, such as affinity audiences, custom intent audiences, and remarketing. Secondly, optimizing ad creatives is essential for capturing users' attention and driving clicks or conversions. Advertisers should design visually appealing and compelling display ads that effectively communicate their value proposition and call-to-action. It's important to experiment with different ad formats, sizes, colors, and messaging to find the most engaging combination. Additionally, utilizing responsive display ads can dynamically adjust the size, appearance, and format of the ads to match the requirements of different websites and platforms within the GDN. Furthermore, strategic ad placement is key to maximizing exposure and performance. Advertisers can choose to display their ads on specific websites, placements, or topics that are relevant to their target audience or industry. By honing in on placements that have high traffic or align with the desired audience's interests, ads are more likely to receive clicks and conversions. Utilizing placement exclusions is also recommended to avoid displaying ads on websites that are irrelevant or low-performing. Lastly, continuous monitoring and optimization are necessary to ensure campaign success. By analyzing the performance metrics provided by Google Ads, advertisers can gain insights into the effectiveness of their ads, placements, and targeting strategies. Adjustments can be made to optimize bidding strategies, budgets, ad rotations, or targeting parameters to achieve better results and return on investment.

Google Display Network Optimization

Google Display Network Optimization refers to the process of fine-tuning and improving advertisements that are displayed on websites within the Google Display Network. The Google Display Network is a vast collection of partner websites and mobile apps where advertisers can showcase their ads to a wide audience. With optimization, advertisers aim to enhance the performance and effectiveness of their display campaigns. The core objective of optimization is to maximize the return on investment (ROI) by achieving better ad visibility, attracting more relevant clicks, increasing conversions, and ultimately driving more revenue. This process involves employing various strategies and tactics to enhance the targeting, placement, ad format, and overall campaign structure. One of the essential aspects of Google Display Network Optimization is audience targeting. Advertisers have the ability to specify audience demographics, interests, and behaviors to ensure their ads are displayed in front of the right people. They can also utilize remarketing, which allows them to target users who have previously engaged with their website or shown interest in their products or services. Additionally, placement targeting plays a crucial role in optimization. Advertisers can select specific websites, mobile apps, or even individual pages within these platforms to display their ads. By hand-picking relevant and high-quality placements, advertisers can increase the chances of their ads being shown to an engaged audience, which can lead to improved performance. Ad formats also need to be optimized to grab users' attention and deliver a compelling message. The Google Display Network supports various ad formats, including text ads, image ads, video ads, and responsive ads. Advertisers should experiment with different formats to identify what resonates best with their target audience and drives the desired actions. Furthermore, continuous monitoring and analysis are integral to optimization. Advertisers should regularly review campaign performance metrics, such as click-through rate (CTR), conversion rate, and cost per conversion. By identifying underperforming ads or placements, advertisers can make data-driven decisions to optimize their campaigns and allocate resources more effectively. In conclusion, Google Display Network Optimization involves refining and improving advertisements displayed on partner websites and mobile apps. Advertisers utilize audience targeting, placement targeting, ad format optimization, and continuous monitoring to boost ad performance and achieve better ROI.

Google Display Network

The Google Display Network (GDN) is an advertising network owned and operated by Google. It allows advertisers to display their advertisements across a wide variety of websites, video platforms, and mobile apps that are part of the Google Network. The GDN uses a combination of automatic and manual targeting techniques to ensure that ads reach the right users at the right time. Advertisers can target their advertisements based on factors such as demographics, interests, specific websites or apps, keywords, and more. One of the key benefits of using the GDN is its extensive reach. With over 2 million websites and reaching over 90% of internet users worldwide, the GDN provides advertisers with a vast audience to target their advertisements to. Another advantage of the GDN is its ability to provide visual and engaging advertisements. Advertisers can use a variety of ad formats on the GDN, including text ads, image ads, video ads, and interactive ads. This allows advertisers to create visually appealing and interactive advertisements that can capture users' attention and increase engagement. The GDN also offers various targeting options to help advertisers reach their desired audience. Advertisers can use demographic targeting to reach users based on factors such as age, gender, and location. They can also use contextual targeting to display ads on websites or apps that are relevant to their target audience. Additionally, advertisers can use remarketing to target users who have previously interacted with their website or app. In conclusion, the Google Display Network is an extensive advertising network that allows advertisers to display their advertisements across various websites, video platforms, and mobile apps. With its wide reach, visual ad formats, and advanced targeting options, the GDN is a powerful tool for advertisers looking to reach their target audience and increase engagement.

Green Advertising Initiatives

Green advertising initiatives refer to strategies and campaigns implemented by businesses to

158

promote environmentally-friendly products, services, and practices. These initiatives aim to raise awareness about sustainability issues and encourage consumers to choose eco-friendly options. In today's world, where environmental concerns are becoming increasingly important, green advertising initiatives play a vital role in shaping consumer behavior and promoting sustainable practices. By incorporating eco-friendly messages and portraying their products or services as environmentally responsible, businesses seek to differentiate themselves from their competitors and attract a growing segment of environmentally conscious consumers.

Green Advertising

Green advertising refers to the practice of promoting products or services in a way that emphasizes their environmentally friendly attributes or positions the brand as an advocate for sustainability. It involves using various advertising strategies and messaging techniques to educate and persuade consumers to make environmentally conscious choices. Green advertising aims to address growing concerns about the impact of human activities on the environment and encourage individuals to adopt more sustainable behaviors. It often highlights a brand's commitment to reducing its carbon footprint, conserving resources, or supporting eco-friendly practices. One common approach in green advertising is to focus on the product itself and its environmentally friendly features. Advertisements may highlight energy efficiency, use of recycled materials, or biodegradability to appeal to environmentally conscious consumers. This strategy aims to associate the brand with positive environmental values and differentiate it from less sustainable competitors. Another strategy in green advertising involves promoting corporate social responsibility or sustainability initiatives undertaken by the brand. Advertisements may showcase the company's efforts to reduce waste, support renewable energy sources, or engage in conservation projects. By highlighting these initiatives, green advertising seeks to build trust and loyalty among consumers who prioritize sustainable practices. Green advertising campaigns often rely on persuasive messaging techniques to encourage consumers to choose environmentally friendly options. These techniques may include emotional appeals, such as evoking concerns about the future of the planet or the well-being of future generations. Advertisements may also use social norms and peer pressure to influence behavior by emphasizing the growing popularity of sustainable choices. Overall, green advertising aims to leverage consumer awareness and concern for the environment to drive demand for environmentally friendly products and encourage sustainable behaviors. By promoting the benefits of sustainable choices and associating the brand with positive environmental values, green advertising seeks to create a positive image for the brand while contributing to the larger goal of preserving the environment.

Greenwashing In Advertising Awareness Methods

Greenwashing in advertising refers to the deceptive practice of making misleading or exaggerated claims about the environmental benefits or sustainability of a product, service, or company in order to attract environmentally conscious consumers. This form of advertising aims to create a positive image of the brand as environmentally friendly, socially responsible, or sustainable, while often lacking substantial evidence or genuine commitment to these values. The term "greenwashing" is derived from the word "whitewashing," which means to cover up or gloss over flaws or wrongdoing. Similarly, greenwashing involves the use of clever marketing strategies, messaging, and visual cues to give the impression of environmental friendliness or sustainability without actually making substantial or meaningful changes in the product or company's practices.

Greenwashing In Advertising Awareness

Greenwashing in advertising refers to the deceptive practice of promoting a product or service as environmentally friendly or sustainable, when in reality it does not meet the required standards or fails to have a significant positive impact on the environment. This misleading advertising technique aims to mislead consumers by creating a false perception of the company's environmental commitment. Companies engage in greenwashing in order to appeal to a growing consumer demand for environmentally responsible products and services. However, instead of implementing substantial changes to their operations or products, they simply use misleading language, symbols, or images to give the impression that they are environmentally conscious.

Greenwashing In Advertising

Greenwashing in advertising refers to the deceptive marketing practices used by companies to portray themselves as environmentally friendly or sustainable when in reality, their products or operations are detrimental to the environment. It is a form of misleading advertising where companies exploit the growing consumer demand for eco-friendly products and services. Companies engage in greenwashing to manipulate consumers' perception and create an illusion of being environmentally conscious. They use various strategies to convey a false sense of sustainability, such as using images of nature, green colors, or eco-friendly buzzwords in their advertisements.

Guerilla Marketing

Guerilla marketing, in the context of advertisement, refers to unconventional, low-cost marketing strategies that involve using creative and innovative tactics to grab the attention of the target audience. Unlike traditional marketing approaches, guerilla marketing relies on ingenuity and resourcefulness rather than a large budget. This form of marketing aims to create a memorable and impactful experience for consumers, often through unexpected means. It requires thinking outside the box and finding unique ways to interact with potential customers, often in unconventional locations or situations. By breaking the mold and challenging traditional advertising norms, guerilla marketing seeks to attract attention and generate buzz.

Guerrilla Advertising Campaigns

Guerrilla advertising campaigns refer to unconventional marketing strategies implemented to capture the attention of a target audience in unexpected and non-traditional ways. This form of advertising relies on creating a buzz and generating word-of-mouth through unique and memorable tactics. The primary goal of guerrilla advertising is to break away from the clutter of traditional advertising methods and stand out in a crowded marketplace. It often involves high levels of creativity and imagination to create an impact while leveraging limited resources.

Guerrilla Advertising

Guerrilla advertising refers to unconventional marketing strategies and tactics that aim to create a buzz and generate attention for a product or service. It is a form of guerrilla marketing, which seeks to engage with consumers through unconventional means, often in unexpected places and in innovative ways. Unlike traditional advertising methods, guerrilla advertising is characterized by its low-cost nature and high creativity. It typically relies on the element of surprise and aims to disrupt the usual flow of day-to-day life to capture the target audience's attention. It often involves using unconventional mediums and locations, such as street art, viral videos, flash mobs, and interactive installations. One key aspect of guerrilla advertising is its ability to create a memorable and shareable experience for consumers. By deploying out-of-the-box ideas and leveraging unexpected environments, guerrilla campaigns can leave a lasting impression on their audience. They often tap into emotions, humor, or shock value to trigger a response and make the brand or product more memorable. Another advantage of guerrilla advertising is its potential for reaching a wide audience through word-of-mouth and social media. When executed successfully, guerrilla campaigns can generate significant buzz and online engagement, amplifying their impact far beyond their initial implementation. This organic spread of the campaign helps to maximize its effect without the need for substantial financial investment. However, guerrilla advertising also carries certain risks. Due to its unconventional nature, there is always the potential for backlash, particularly if the campaign is perceived as intrusive or offensive. It is crucial for brands to carefully consider their target audience, cultural sensitivities, and ethical implications when planning and executing guerrilla advertising strategies. In summary, guerrilla advertising is a creative and disruptive form of marketing that aims to engage audiences in unconventional ways. With its potential for generating buzz and creating memorable experiences, it offers brands an opportunity to stand out in a saturated advertising landscape. However, careful planning and consideration of the potential risks are necessary to ensure the success and effectiveness of guerrilla campaigns.

Guerrilla Marketing

Guerrilla Marketing is a creative and unconventional advertising strategy that aims to create a memorable and engaging experience for the target audience. It involves using low-cost or unconventional methods to promote a product, service, or brand, often relying on creativity and innovation rather than a large marketing budget. This marketing approach is characterized by its ability to surprise and captivate consumers, making it difficult to ignore or forget. It often takes advantage of unexpected locations, situations, or events to grab attention, relying on word-of-mouth and viral marketing to spread the message.

Impression

An impression in the context of advertisements refers to the number of times an ad is displayed or viewed by users online. It is a metric used to measure the reach and visibility of an advertisement campaign. When an ad is served on a website or mobile app, it is considered as an impression. Impressions can be recorded whether the user actively engages with the ad or not. Each time the ad is loaded or shown on a user's screen, it counts as an impression.

In-App Advertising Platforms

In-App Advertising Platforms are digital tools or software programs that facilitate the creation, management, and delivery of advertisements within mobile applications. These platforms provide advertisers with the means to effectively reach and engage their target audience through a variety of ad formats and targeting options. Through In-App Advertising Platforms, advertisers can connect with app publishers and developers to display their ads to users while they are using specific mobile apps. The platforms typically offer a range of ad formats, including display ads, video ads, native ads, and interactive ads, allowing advertisers to choose the most suitable format for their campaign objectives and target audience. The platforms also provide advanced targeting capabilities, enabling advertisers to reach their desired audience based on various criteria such as demographic data, user behavior, location, and interests. This allows for more precise targeting and helps advertisers maximize the impact of their ads by displaying them to users who are more likely to be interested in their products or services. In addition to ad creation and targeting, In-App Advertising Platforms also offer features for ad management and optimization. Advertisers can monitor the performance of their ads in real-time, track key metrics such as impressions, clicks, and conversions, and make adjustments to their campaigns as needed to improve results. The platforms may provide tools for A/B testing, allowing advertisers to test different ad creatives or targeting parameters to identify the most effective approach. In-App Advertising Platforms play a crucial role in the mobile advertising ecosystem, as they serve as intermediaries between advertisers and app publishers, facilitating the monetization of mobile apps through ad revenue. They provide a streamlined and efficient way for advertisers to reach their target audience within mobile apps, while also enabling app publishers to generate revenue by displaying relevant and engaging ads to their users. Overall, In-App Advertising Platforms offer a comprehensive solution for creating, managing, and delivering advertisements within mobile applications. They empower advertisers to effectively engage with their target audience, improve campaign performance, and achieve their advertisement objectives.

In-App Advertising

In-App Advertising refers to the delivery of advertisements within a mobile application. It involves the placement of promotional content, usually in the form of banners, videos, or interstitials, that is seamlessly integrated into the app's user interface. Unlike traditional forms of advertising that occur outside of the app, such as TV commercials or display ads on websites, in-app advertising takes advantage of the captive audience and high engagement levels of app users. It allows advertisers to reach their target audience directly within the app, where users are already highly engaged and focused on the content.

In-Banner Video Ads Creation

In-Banner Video Ads Creation refers to the process of designing and developing video advertisements that are displayed within a web banner on a website. These ads are typically created using HTML5 technology, allowing for interactive and engaging content. The goal of In-Banner Video Ads Creation is to capture the attention of website visitors and deliver a compelling message through the use of video content. These ads can be displayed on various websites and are commonly seen on news websites, blogs, and entertainment platforms.

161

In-Banner Video Ads

In-Banner Video Ads are a form of online advertising that involves the display of video content within a banner ad unit on a webpage. These video ads autoplay or play upon user interaction, providing an engaging and interactive experience for viewers. In-Banner Video Ads are designed to capture the attention of users as they browse the internet. The video content can vary in length, ranging from a few seconds to several minutes, depending on the advertising campaign and platform. These ads are typically placed on websites that have high traffic and attract a specific target audience.

In-Game Advertising Strategies

In-game advertising strategies refer to the various techniques and methods used by advertisers to promote their products or services within video games. This form of advertising involves integrating branded content or ads directly into the gameplay or virtual environment of a video game, aiming to engage and influence players while they are actively engaged in the game. One common in-game advertising strategy is product placement, where real-life products or brands are seamlessly integrated into the virtual world of a video game. This can include placing branded items within the game environment, such as billboards, posters, or virtual storefronts, or incorporating actual products as usable items or power-ups within the gameplay. Product placement allows advertisers to reach a captive audience of gamers who are already invested in the game and may be more receptive to the brand message. Another popular in-game advertising strategy is immersive advertising, which involves creating an interactive experience that blends seamlessly with the gameplay. This can include creating in-game events or challenges that are sponsored by a brand, where players are encouraged to complete tasks or objectives to earn rewards or in-game currency. By associating their brand with positive gaming experiences, advertisers aim to establish a deeper emotional connection with players and increase brand recall and preference. Dynamic in-game advertising is another effective strategy, which involves delivering real-time ads that can be updated or changed based on factors such as player demographics or location. This allows advertisers to target specific audiences within the game environment and deliver relevant ads that are tailored to each player's interests or preferences. Dynamic ads can also be used to promote time-sensitive offers or limited-time events, creating a sense of urgency and driving immediate actions from players. In conclusion, in-game advertising strategies encompass a range of techniques aimed at promoting brands and products within video games. By integrating advertisements directly into gameplay or the virtual environment, advertisers can engage players and deliver targeted messages that resonate with their target audience. These strategies aim to leverage the immersive nature of video games and the high levels of player engagement to create memorable brand experiences and drive measurable results for advertisers.

In-Game Advertising

In-Game Advertising refers to the placement of advertisements within video games to promote products or services to players. It involves integrating branded content or messaging directly into the gameplay or environment of a game to engage the user and create a unique advertising experience. In-Game Advertising takes advantage of the immersive nature of video games and the large audience they attract to deliver targeted marketing messages. These advertisements can range from simple billboard placements within the game environment to more elaborate and interactive forms such as product placements, video ads, or even virtual brand sponsorships. The primary goal of In-Game Advertising is to reach a highly engaged and captive audience. Given the interactive nature of video games, players are deeply involved in the gameplay experience, making them more receptive to the advertising messages seamlessly integrated into the game. This form of advertising capitalizes on the attention and focus of players, ensuring that the brand message is delivered effectively. Furthermore, In-Game Advertising allows advertisers to target specific demographics, interests, or regions based on the characteristics of the game and its player base. By leveraging player data and analytics, advertisers can optimize their campaigns to reach the most relevant and receptive audience. This level of targeting makes In-Game Advertising an attractive option for brands looking to connect with specific consumer segments. However, it is crucial for game developers and advertisers to strike a balance between incorporating advertisements seamlessly into the game and preserving the overall gaming experience. Intrusiveness or poorly executed advertising can negatively impact the player's enjoyment and potentially lead to a negative perception of the brand. In conclusion, In-Game Advertising offers a unique and engaging way for brands to reach a highly engaged audience within the gaming environment. It provides opportunities for immersive and interactive advertising experiences while allowing for precise targeting based on gaming demographics and player behavior. By carefully integrating advertisements into video games, brands can effectively connect with their target audience and drive brand awareness and engagement.

In-Market Audience Targeting Techniques Assessment

In-Market Audience Targeting Techniques Assessment is a process in advertising where marketers evaluate and analyze the behavior, interests, and purchasing intent of potential customers to effectively target ads and campaigns towards individuals who are likely to make a purchase in the near future. By identifying and understanding the specific audience segments that are actively researching and contemplating a purchase, marketers can tailor their advertisements to be highly relevant and persuasive, increasing the chances of converting these potential customers into actual buyers.

In-Market Audience Targeting Techniques

In-market audience targeting techniques in the context of advertising refer to the strategies and methods used by advertisers to reach and engage with specific groups of consumers who are actively researching or intending to make a purchase in a particular product or service category.The primary objective of in-market audience targeting is to deliver relevant advertisements to users who have shown some level of interest or intent in buying a product or service. By focusing ad campaigns on in-market audiences, advertisers can increase the likelihood of reaching potential customers who are farther along in the purchase journey and more likely to convert.

In-Market Audience Targeting

In-Market Audience Targeting is a strategic approach used in online advertising to reach potential customers who are actively researching and considering making a purchase in a specific product or service category. By analyzing user behavior and online activities, advertisers can identify individuals who have shown a strong intent or interest in a particular offering, allowing them to tailor their ads and messaging to better resonate with these potential customers. This targeting method relies on data gathered from user search queries, website visits, and interactions within websites and apps. Advertisers leverage this data to identify patterns and trends in user behavior that indicate an individual's intent to make a purchase. For example, if a user frequently searches for and visits websites related to travel destinations and vacation packages, they may be categorized as an in-market audience for travel services. Once an in-market audience has been identified, advertisers can create tailored ad campaigns aimed at capturing their attention and driving them towards making a purchase. These campaigns may include personalized ad copy, relevant offers or discounts, and targeted landing pages that align with the customer's specific interests and needs. One of the key benefits of in-market audience targeting is its ability to connect advertisers with customers who are more likely to convert, resulting in higher ROI and increased sales. By focusing their advertising efforts on individuals who have demonstrated a strong intent to purchase, advertisers can optimize their marketing budgets and ensure that their messages are being delivered to the most relevant and receptive audience. In-market audience targeting can be particularly effective for businesses operating in highly competitive industries or niche markets, where reaching the right customers at the right time is crucial for success. By delivering ads to individuals who are actively in the market for a specific product or service, advertisers can increase their chances of driving conversions and gaining a competitive edge.

In-Store Advertising

In-Store Advertising refers to the promotional activities carried out within a physical retail store to engage and influence customers' purchasing decisions. Such advertising tactics aim to increase brand awareness, drive sales, and improve the overall shopping experience for consumers.

Influencer Marketing

Influencer marketing is a type of advertisement strategy that involves partnering with influential individuals, commonly known as influencers, to promote a brand or product to a targeted audience. These influencers have established credibility and a loyal following within a specific niche or industry, making them influential figures in the eyes of their followers and potential customers. The main goal of influencer marketing is to leverage the influencers' authority, expertise, and strong online presence to create a positive association and increase brand awareness and visibility. This type of advertising relies on the influencers' ability to connect with their followers on a personal level and influence their purchase decisions.

Influencer Partnerships In Advertising Management

Influencer partnerships in advertising management refer to collaborations between brands and individuals who have a strong social media presence and influence over their followers. These partnerships are aimed at promoting a brand or its products to a target audience through sponsored content, endorsements, or product placements on the influencer's social media platforms.Such partnerships are a strategic way for brands to tap into the influencer's credibility and reach, as they typically have a dedicated and engaged following. Influencers could be celebrities, industry experts, bloggers, or social media personalities who have achieved a significant following on platforms like Instagram, YouTube, TikTok, or Twitter.

Influencer Partnerships In Advertising

Influencer Partnerships in Advertising refer to collaborations between brands and social media influencers to promote a product or service. Influencers are individuals who have a strong online presence and a large following on platforms like Instagram, YouTube, and TikTok. They have the ability to influence the purchasing decisions of their followers through their content and recommendations. When brands collaborate with influencers, they leverage the influencer's credibility and reach to create content that showcases their product or service in a positive light. This can be done through sponsored posts, product reviews, brand endorsements, or influencer-hosted events or giveaways.

Infomercial

An infomercial is an advertisement that is typically longer in duration than a standard television commercial, ranging from 15 minutes to an hour or more. It is designed to inform and persuade viewers about a specific product or service, often in a persuasive and demonstrative manner. Infomercials are commonly aired during off-peak hours on television channels and are sometimes referred to as "paid programming" or "direct response television" (DRTV). They utilize various strategies to capture the attention and interest of viewers, with the ultimate goal of driving direct sales or generating leads. Unlike traditional commercials, infomercials provide more in-depth information about the featured product or service. They often include testimonials from satisfied customers, expert endorsements, and detailed explanations of the benefits and features of the product. Infomercials frequently employ the use of visual aids, demonstrations, and customer success stories to build credibility and increase viewer engagement. The structure of an infomercial typically follows a specific formula. It typically begins with a captivating introduction that hooks viewers' attention and highlights a common problem or need that the product or service can address. The infomercial then proceeds to present the features and benefits of the product or service, emphasizing how it can provide a solution to the viewer's problem. Throughout the infomercial, various persuasive techniques are used to compel viewers to take action. These may include limited-time offers, exclusive discounts, bonus items, and testimonials from individuals who have experienced positive results from using the product or service. Call-to-action prompts are also included, urging viewers to make a purchase or contact the company directly through a toll-free number or website. Infomercials have been successful in promoting a wide range of products and services, including fitness equipment, kitchen appliances, beauty products, and self-help programs, among others. They offer an extended platform for companies to showcase their offerings and create a sense of urgency and desire in potential customers. In conclusion, an infomercial is a long-form advertisement designed to inform and persuade viewers about a particular product or service. By utilizing demonstrations, testimonials, and persuasive techniques, infomercials aim to capture viewer attention, convey product benefits, and drive direct sales or generate leads.

Innovative Advertising Campaigns Creation Steps

An innovative advertising campaign is a strategic and creative approach to promoting a product, service, or brand that utilizes unconventional methods, unconventional mediums, or unique ideas to captivate and engage the target audience. It aims to disrupt the traditional advertising practices and stand out in a crowded marketplace by delivering an impactful message that resonates with consumers. Creating an innovative advertising campaign involves several steps to ensure its success: 1. Understanding the Target Market: The first step is to conduct thorough research and gain a deep understanding of the target market. This includes demographics, psychographics, interests, and behaviors of the intended audience. By knowing their preferences and needs, advertisers can tailor their campaign to resonate with the target audience. 2. Defining Clear Objectives: It is crucial to set clear objectives for the advertising campaign. These objectives could be increasing brand awareness, boosting sales, changing consumer perceptions, or launching a new product. Clear objectives help guide the creative process and measure the success of the campaign. 3. Developing Creative Concepts: Once the objectives are defined, the creative team can brainstorm and develop innovative concepts that align with the brand's message and appeal to the target audience. This involves thinking outside the box and exploring unconventional ideas that can grab attention and leave a lasting impression. 4. Choosing the Right Mediums: An innovative advertising campaign may utilize a variety of mediums to reach the target audience. This could include traditional media, such as television and print, as well as digital platforms like social media, online videos, or mobile apps. The selection of mediums should be based on the target audience's media consumption habits and preferences. 5. Executing and Monitoring the Campaign: Once the creative concepts and mediums are finalized, the campaign is executed across chosen channels. During this phase, it is important to monitor the campaign's performance and make necessary adjustments to optimize its effectiveness. This includes tracking key metrics, analyzing consumer feedback, and staying updated on industry trends. An innovative advertising campaign can differentiate a brand from its competitors and create a memorable impact on consumers. By following these steps, advertisers can develop unique and engaging campaigns that capture attention and drive results.

Innovative Advertising Campaigns Creation

An innovative advertising campaign refers to the development and execution of a unique and creative strategy aimed at promoting a product, service, or brand. It involves the use of unconventional and imaginative approaches to capture the attention of the target audience and create a lasting impact. Such campaigns typically rely on innovative ideas, concepts, and techniques to stand out in a crowded advertising landscape. They often break through traditional advertising norms and boundaries, challenging established practices to generate buzz, intrigue, and engagement among consumers.

Innovative Advertising Campaigns

Innovative advertising campaigns are creative and unique strategies used by companies to promote their products or services. These campaigns are designed to capture the attention of the target audience and differentiate the brand from competitors in a crowded marketplace. Unlike traditional advertising campaigns, which may rely on conventional approaches such as print media, television, or radio advertisements, innovative campaigns strive to think outside the box and utilize unconventional methods to convey the brand's message. These campaigns often incorporate elements of surprise, humor, interactivity, or technology to engage and captivate consumers.

Integrated Marketing Communications (IMC)

Integrated Marketing Communications (IMC) is a strategic approach to advertising and promotions that coordinates and aligns various marketing communication channels and tactics to deliver a consistent and compelling message to target audiences. IMC involves the integration of different advertising tools, such as advertising, public relations, sales promotion, direct marketing, and personal selling, in order to create a unified and synergistic marketing communication strategy. The goal of IMC is to ensure that all marketing communication efforts are working together harmoniously to maximize the impact and effectiveness of a company's advertising message. By integrating various communication tools and channels, IMC allows marketers to reach their target audience through multiple touchpoints and reinforce their message consistently throughout the customer journey. IMC starts with a deep understanding of the target audience and their preferences, behaviors, and needs. This knowledge allows marketers to develop a comprehensive communication strategy that addresses the target audience's concerns and motivates them to take action. This strategy is then implemented across different communication channels, ensuring that the message is tailored to each channel's specific requirements and capabilities. IMC also involves the development and management of a consistent brand image and identity across all communication channels and touchpoints. By using consistent visual elements, slogans, and messaging, a company can strengthen its brand recognition and build long-term customer loyalty. In addition to coordination and consistency, IMC emphasizes the importance of measurement and evaluation. By tracking and analyzing the performance of each communication channel and tactic, marketers can identify what works and what doesn't, and make informed decisions to optimize their advertising efforts. In conclusion, Integrated Marketing Communications (IMC) is a strategic approach to advertising that involves the integration and coordination of various marketing communication channels and tactics to deliver a consistent and compelling message to target audiences. By aligning all marketing communication efforts and ensuring consistency and measurement, IMC allows marketers to maximize the impact and effectiveness of their advertising message.

Interactive Advertising Campaigns

Interactive advertising campaigns refer to promotional strategies that involve two-way communication and engagement between the advertiser and the target audience. Unlike traditional advertising methods, which mainly rely on one-way communication, interactive campaigns aim to actively involve consumers and encourage their active participation. This type of advertising utilizes various digital media platforms and technologies to create interactive experiences that captivate the audience and encourage them to take specific actions. Some common examples of interactive advertising campaigns include interactive videos, interactive social media posts, gamified quizzes or contests, and augmented reality experiences.

Interactive Advertising

Interactive advertising refers to a form of advertising that engages the viewers in a two-way communication, enabling them to actively participate and have a direct impact on the advertisement. It allows for a dynamic and personalized user experience by encouraging interaction through various digital platforms and devices. This type of advertising leverages technology and interactivity to capture the attention and interest of the target audience. By providing a platform for users to engage with the advertisement, it aims to create a deeper connection and enhance brand recall. Interactive advertising can take various forms, including interactive videos, quizzes, games, polls, surveys, and augmented reality experiences. One of the primary benefits of interactive advertising is its ability to generate higher levels of audience engagement and participation. By enabling users to actively interact with the advertisement, it creates a sense of involvement and empowers them to shape their own experiences. This level of engagement often leads to increased brand awareness, message retention, and ultimately higher conversion rates. Additionally, interactive advertising allows for data collection and real-time feedback, providing valuable insights into consumer preferences, behaviors, and interests. Marketers can use this data to refine their advertising strategies, target their audience more effectively, and deliver more personalized and relevant content. This data-driven approach enables advertisers to optimize their campaigns and achieve better ROI. Furthermore, interactive advertising is often more memorable and impactful than traditional static advertising. By incorporating elements of gamification, storytelling, and immersive experiences, it captivates the viewers' attention and creates a lasting impression. The interactive nature of these advertisements also encourages social sharing and viral marketing, amplifying their reach and impact. In conclusion, interactive advertising is a dynamic and engaging form of advertising that allows for direct user interaction and participation. It leverages technology, data, and interactivity to create a personalized and memorable user experience. By facilitating two-way communication, interactive advertising drives higher engagement, audience involvement, and brand recall, ultimately leading to improved campaign outcomes and business results.

Interactive Video Ads Development Tools

Interactive video ads development tools refer to the software or platforms that enable advertisers or marketers to create, customize, and deploy interactive video advertisements. These tools provide a range of features and functionalities that enhance the engagement and interactivity of video advertisements, helping businesses effectively communicate their messages and capture the attention of their target audience. Interactive video ads development tools typically offer a user-friendly interface, allowing advertisers to easily design and edit their video ads. They provide a variety of templates, themes, and animations that can be customized to match the brand's visual identity. These tools often include drag-and-drop functionality, making it simple to add interactive elements such as clickable hotspots, forms, quizzes, or product showcases within the video. These development tools may incorporate advanced targeting and segmentation capabilities, enabling advertisers to deliver personalized and relevant video ads to specific audience segments. In addition, they often provide analytics and tracking features, allowing advertisers to measure the performance of their video ads and gain valuable insights into viewer behavior and engagement. By utilizing interactive video ads development tools, advertisers can create immersive and captivating experiences for their viewers. Interactive elements can be used to encourage viewer participation, such as interactive polls, games, or surveys within the video. This level of interactivity increases viewer engagement and brand awareness, ultimately leading to higher conversion rates and improved return on investment (ROI) for advertisers. Furthermore, these development tools often support compatibility with various digital advertising platforms and social media channels. This allows advertisers to easily distribute their interactive video ads across multiple channels, ensuring maximum reach and visibility for their campaigns. In summary, interactive video ads development tools empower advertisers to create engaging and interactive video advertisements that captivate their audience. By leveraging these tools, advertisers can enhance their brand messaging, increase viewer engagement, and drive better results from their video advertising campaigns.

Interactive Video Ads Development

Interactive video ads development refers to the process of creating and designing video advertisements that encourage viewer engagement and participation. Unlike traditional video ads that are purely passive, interactive video ads aim to involve the audience by allowing them to interact with the content in various ways. These ads often include interactive elements such as clickable buttons, overlays, hotspots, or quizzes that prompt viewers to take specific actions while watching the video. By integrating interactivity into the ad experience, advertisers can enhance brand engagement, optimize user experience, and increase conversion rates.

Interactive Video Ads

Interactive Video Ads are a type of online advertising that utilizes video content in order to engage and interact with the viewer. These ads are designed to capture the viewer's attention and encourage them to actively participate and engage with the ad's content. Unlike traditional video ads that are passive and one-way, interactive video ads provide a dynamic and immersive experience for the viewer. They often incorporate interactive elements such as clickable hotspots, quizzes, games, or other call-to-actions that allow the viewer to actively engage with the ad's content.

Interstitial Ad

Interstitial Ad An interstitial ad is a type of advertisement that appears in between content or as a pop-up while a user is engaged in an online activity. It is designed to capture the user's attention by displaying a full-screen ad that covers the entire screen or a significant portion of it for a designated period of time. Interstitial ads are commonly used in mobile apps, websites, and games to monetize content and generate revenue. They are often displayed between pages or levels, interrupting the user's flow and requiring them to interact with the ad before proceeding. Interstitial ads can be displayed as static images, videos, or interactive rich media formats. These ads typically offer advertisers a higher engagement rate compared to other ad formats, as they have the ability to captivate the user's attention due to their full-screen nature. This increased engagement can lead to higher click-through rates and conversions for advertisers, making interstitial ads an effective marketing tool. In terms of user experience, interstitial ads can be perceived as disruptive or intrusive, especially if they appear too frequently or hinder the user's ability to access desired content. However, they can also be seen as an opportunity for advertisers to deliver compelling messages and promotions to a captive audience. Advertisers often use various targeting and customization options to ensure that interstitial ads are shown to relevant audiences. This helps increase the likelihood of the ad being well-received and positively impacting the user's overall experience.

Interstitial Ads

Interstitial ads are a type of advertisement that appears between two content pages or screens, interrupting the user's flow to deliver promotional messages or content. These ads are typically displayed on websites, mobile apps, or gaming platforms. The purpose of interstitial ads is to capture the user's attention and generate higher engagement by displaying immersive and visually appealing content. They usually cover the entire screen, providing an interactive and eye-catching experience. Interstitial ads are designed to create a moment of interaction with the user, presenting them with an opportunity to engage with the promoted product or service. They can include various types of content, such as images, videos, animations, or interactive elements. These ads often include a call-to-action (CTA) button, encouraging users to take a specific action, such as downloading an app, signing up for a newsletter, making a purchase, or exploring more about the advertised product or service. The CTA is usually prominently displayed for easy visibility and enables instant interaction. Due to their interruptive nature, interstitial ads have the potential to capture the user's attention and generate higher conversion rates compared to other types of advertisements. However, they can also be considered intrusive, as they disrupt the user's browsing or app experience. Therefore, it is important for advertisers to strike a balance between delivering compelling content and respecting the user's experience. Additionally, interstitial ads can be targeted based on various factors, such as user demographics, browsing behavior, or previous interactions with the advertiser's website or app. This targeting helps deliver more relevant and personalized ads, increasing the chances of capturing the user's interest and achieving the desired marketing objectives.

Interstitial Video Ads Creation

Interstitial Video Ads are a type of advertisement that appear in between two content pages or during a break in a video stream. These ads provide marketers with a way to engage with their target audience by displaying a short video clip. Interstitial Video Ads are typically displayed full-screen and can be a few seconds or several minutes in duration. They are designed to capture the attention of the viewer and deliver a compelling message or call to action. Unlike traditional video ads, which play at the beginning or during a video, Interstitial Video Ads interrupt the user's experience and demand their full attention.

Interstitial Video Ads Planning Approaches

Interstitial video ads planning approaches refer to the different strategies and techniques used by advertisers to effectively incorporate interstitial video ads into their campaigns. Interstital video ads are full-screen advertisements that appear in between different stages of content consumption, such as during the transition between levels in a mobile game or while loading a webpage. These ads often provide a highly immersive and engaging experience for viewers as they take up the entire screen, encouraging higher levels of user attention. There are several key approaches to consider when planning interstitial video ads: 1. Placement targeting: This approach involves strategically placing interstitial video ads at specific points during the user's journey. Advertisers leverage data on user behavior and engagement patterns to determine the most opportune moments for displaying these ads. For example, an advertiser may choose to show an interstitial video ad after a user completes a specific action within an app or right before a user accesses premium content. 2. Contextual targeting: With this approach, interstitial video ads are targeted to align with the surrounding content and user interests. Advertisers analyze the context of the content being consumed or the demographics and preferences of the user to ensure relevance and increase the chances of capturing the viewer's attention. For instance, a sports brand may display an interstitial video ad featuring a new line of sneakers during a live streaming sports event. 3. Frequency capping: Advertisers need to strike a balance between capturing user attention and avoiding ad fatigue. Frequency capping involves setting limits on how often interstitial video ads are shown to individual users within a given time period. By controlling the frequency of these ads, advertisers can prevent annoyance and improve overall campaign effectiveness. 4. Creative design and length: The design and length of interstitial video ads play a crucial role in their success. Advertisers should create visually captivating and compelling ads that grab viewers' attention within the first few seconds. Additionally, keeping the ad duration short and concise is important to minimize user disruption and ensure a positive viewing experience. In conclusion, interstitial video ads planning approaches encompass various strategies such as placement targeting, contextual targeting, frequency capping, and creative design considerations. By implementing these approaches effectively, advertisers can enhance the impact and effectiveness of their interstitial video ad campaigns.

Interstitial Video Ads Planning

Interstitial Video Ads

An interstitial video ad is a type of advertisement that appears between two content pages or during a transition within a video. Unlike other types of video ads that are embedded within the content itself, interstitial video ads are displayed in full-screen format and cover the entire screen, temporarily interrupting the user's viewing experience. These ads are typically designed to be visually engaging and attention-grabbing, using motion, sound, and interactive elements to capture the viewer's interest. They can last anywhere from a few seconds to several minutes, depending on the specific ad campaign.

Keyword Advertising Research

Keyword advertising research refers to the process of conducting an in-depth analysis and exploration of keywords that are relevant to an advertisement campaign. This research helps identify the most effective keywords to use in online advertising to reach the target audience and maximize the impact of the advertisement. Keyword advertising research involves examining the search terms and phrases that potential customers are using when looking for products or services similar to what the advertiser is offering. By understanding these keywords, advertisers can create ads that are more likely to appear in relevant search results, increasing the chances of capturing the attention of potential customers.

Keyword Advertising

Keyword advertising refers to a type of online advertising where ads are displayed based on the keywords or phrases entered by users in search engines or other online platforms. It involves bidding on specific keywords or phrases in order to have ads appear when users search for those terms. When a user enters a keyword or phrase into a search engine, the search engine algorithm scans its database to find relevant websites or content that match the user's query. Along with the organic search results, search engines also display paid advertisements that are related to the user's search terms. These paid ads are typically displayed at the top or side of the search engine results page (SERP), above or alongside the organic results. Keyword advertising works on a pay-per-click (PPC) model, where advertisers bid on keywords and pay a certain amount each time their ad is clicked. The bidding process determines the placement and visibility of ads on the SERP. Advertisers compete for top positions on the page, as higher placement generally leads to more clicks and visibility. Advertisers select keywords that are relevant to their products or services and have the potential to attract their target audience. The selection of keywords is crucial as it determines the success of a keyword advertising campaign. It is important to choose keywords that have high search volumes and low competition to maximize visibility and minimize costs. Keyword advertising offers several benefits for advertisers. It allows them to reach a highly targeted audience, as ads are displayed to users who are actively searching for specific products or services. It also provides instant visibility, as ads are displayed immediately after the keyword is entered. Additionally, keyword advertising provides measurable results, as advertisers can track the performance of their ads and optimize their campaigns based on data and insights.

Keyword Research For Advertising Effectiveness

Keyword research for advertising effectiveness is the process of identifying and selecting the most relevant and impactful keywords to use in advertisements, with the aim of reaching and engaging target audiences effectively. Keywords play a crucial role in advertising as they are the words or phrases that potential customers use when searching for products, services, or information related to a business. By conducting keyword research, advertisers can gain insights into the language and terminology their target audience uses, and can align their advertising efforts accordingly.

Keyword Research For Advertising

Keyword research for advertising refers to the process of identifying and selecting relevant keywords that potential customers may use when searching for products or services online. This research is crucial for advertising campaigns as it helps to optimize the targeting and effectiveness of online ads. The goal of keyword research in advertising is to understand the language and terms that customers use when searching for products, as well as to identify popular and relevant keywords that can be incorporated into ad campaigns. By selecting appropriate keywords, advertisers can increase the visibility and reach of their ads, reaching potential customers who are actively looking for what they have to offer.

Landing Page Optimization For Ads Tools Evaluation

Landing Page Optimization for Ads Tools Evaluation refers to the process of analyzing and testing the effectiveness of different tools used in online advertising campaigns to optimize landing pages. It involves evaluating various tools and techniques to determine which ones are most effective in improving the performance of landing pages and increasing conversions. The purpose of landing page optimization is to improve the user experience and maximize the return on investment (ROI) from advertising campaigns. By evaluating different tools, marketers can identify areas of improvement and make data-driven decisions to enhance their landing pages. This process involves testing different elements such as headlines, images, calls to action, forms, and layout to determine which combination results in the highest conversion rates.

Landing Page Optimization For Ads Tools

Landing Page Optimization for Ads Tools refers to the process of improving the effectiveness and efficiency of landing pages used in advertisements. It involves making strategic changes to landing pages in order to increase conversions and achieve marketing goals. Landing pages are the web pages that users land on after clicking on an advertisement. They are specifically designed to convert visitors into customers by encouraging them to take a desired action, such as making a purchase or filling out a form. However, not all landing pages are effective in achieving these goals. Many factors can hinder their performance, such as poor design, confusing layout, or lack of persuasive content. Landing Page Optimization for Ads Tools encompasses a range of techniques and strategies aimed at addressing these issues and optimizing the performance of landing pages. It involves analyzing data and user behavior to identify areas for improvement and implementing changes that will lead to better conversion rates. The first step in Landing Page Optimization is conducting a thorough analysis of the current landing page. This involves collecting and analyzing data on user behavior, such as bounce rate, time on page, and conversion rate. It also entails reviewing the design and content of the landing page to identify any potential areas for improvement. Based on the analysis, changes can then be made to the landing page to optimize its performance. This may include improving the design and layout, enhancing the call-to-action, making the page more user-friendly, or optimizing the content to better align with user needs and expectations. Further optimization can be achieved through A/B testing, where different versions of the landing page are created and tested against each other to determine which one performs better. This allows marketers to make data-driven decisions and continuously improve the effectiveness of their landing pages. In conclusion, Landing Page Optimization for Ads Tools is an essential aspect of advertisement campaigns. By optimizing landing pages, marketers can improve conversion rates, generate more leads, and ultimately achieve their marketing objectives.

Landing Page Optimization For Ads

Landing Page Optimization for Ads refers to the process of improving the performance of a landing page that is specifically designed for advertising purposes. It involves implementing strategies and techniques to enhance the effectiveness of the landing page in relation to the ads it is associated with. The primary goal of landing page optimization for ads is to maximize the conversion rate, which is the percentage of visitors who take the desired action on the landing page after clicking on the ad. This desired action could be making a purchase, filling out a form, subscribing to a newsletter, or any other predetermined goal. There are various aspects that can be optimized on a landing page to achieve better results. Firstly, the visual design and layout of the landing page should be appealing and visually stimulating to grab the attention of visitors. A clean and organized design with relevant visuals can significantly impact the user experience. Secondly, the content on the landing page must be concise and compelling. It should clearly communicate the value proposition, benefits, and key messages related to the advertised product or service. Attention-grabbing headlines, concise copy, and a strong call to action can all contribute to improve conversion rates. Furthermore, the landing page should be optimized for mobile devices. With the prevalence of smartphones and tablets, ensuring a seamless mobile experience is crucial for capturing and retaining the attention of mobile users. Responsive design, fast loading times, and easy navigation are all essential factors for mobile optimization. Additionally, the landing page should align with the ad that directs users to it. The messaging, visuals, and overall experience should be consistent with the ad to avoid confusion and maintain a seamless user journey. A consistent and cohesive experience helps build trust and credibility with visitors. In conclusion, landing page optimization for ads involves strategically improving the design, content, mobile experience, and alignment of a landing page to maximize its conversion rate. By continuously testing and optimizing various elements of the landing page, advertisers can enhance their ad campaigns and achieve better results.

Landing Page

Landing Page Definition A landing page is a web page specifically designed to capture the attention of visitors and prompt them to take a desired action, such as making a purchase, signing up for a newsletter, or filling out a contact form. It is a crucial component of any online advertising campaign, as it serves as the entry point for potential customers and helps convert them into leads or customers. The purpose of a landing page is to provide a focused and persuasive message that convinces visitors to take the desired action.

Lead Generation Advertising Tactics

Lead generation advertising tactics refer to the strategies and methods used by advertisers to attract and capture the interest of potential customers, with the goal of collecting their contact information and nurturing them towards becoming paying customers. These tactics involve various advertisement techniques and channels, such as search engine marketing (SEM), social media advertising, display ads, email marketing, and content marketing. Advertisers employ compelling visuals, persuasive copywriting, and targeted messaging to encourage individuals to take action, such as filling out a form, subscribing to a newsletter, or requesting more information. The primary objective of lead generation advertising is to build a pool of qualified leads, individuals who have shown a genuine interest in a company's product or service. By obtaining their contact details, advertisers can initiate ongoing communication, providing valuable content and offers to nurture the leads over time, eventually converting them into paying customers. Lead generation advertising tactics often involve using landing pages - dedicated webpages created specifically to capture information from visitors. Advertisers design these pages to be concise, visually appealing, and focused on a single call-to-action (CTA). The copywriting on landing pages is carefully crafted to clearly communicate the value proposition and benefits of the offer, enticing visitors to provide their contact details in exchange. Another popular lead generation tactic is the use of lead magnets. These are valuable resources, such as e-books, whitepapers, or exclusive content, offered to prospects in exchange for their contact information. By providing high-quality and relevant resources, advertisers can incentivize individuals to share their details and establish themselves as thought leaders in their industry. Lead generation advertising tactics also rely on targeting the right audience. Advertisers use various targeting parameters, such as demographics, geolocation, interests, and behavioral data, to reach individuals who are most likely to be interested in their offering. This helps to maximize the effectiveness and efficiency of the advertising campaigns, ensuring that the ad dollars are spent on reaching the right prospects. In summary, lead generation advertising tactics encompass a range of strategies and techniques used by advertisers to attract potential customers, capture their contact information, and nurture them towards becoming paying customers. These tactics involve various advertisement channels, compelling visuals, persuasive copywriting, and targeted messaging to engage and convert leads successfully.

Lead Generation Advertising

Lead generation advertising is a marketing strategy designed to attract and capture potential customers, known as leads, by utilizing various advertising channels and tactics. The primary goal of lead generation advertising is to generate interest in a product or service and gather contact information from interested individuals. Lead generation advertising can be implemented through online and offline methods. Online methods include search engine marketing, social media advertising, display advertising, and email marketing, while offline methods include print advertisements, direct mail, and telemarketing. The specific channels and tactics used depend on the target audience and budget constraints of the advertiser. One of the fundamental components of lead generation advertising is a compelling offer or incentive that encourages individuals to provide their contact information. This offer can take the form of a discount, free trial, educational content, or any other value proposition that resonates with the target audience. By providing an attractive offer, advertisers can overcome potential objections and capture leads more effectively. Lead generation advertising also typically involves the use of landing pages. A landing page is a web page specifically designed with the sole purpose of capturing lead information. It contains a form where individuals can enter their contact details in exchange for the offer. The landing page should be concise, visually appealing, and optimized for conversion to encourage visitors to complete the form. Once the leads are captured, they can be further nurtured through various marketing strategies such as email marketing, content marketing, and retargeting. The goal is to build a relationship with the leads and guide them through the sales funnel until they become customers. In summary, lead generation advertising aims to attract and capture potential customers by utilizing various advertising channels and tactics. It involves the creation of compelling offers, the use of landing pages to capture lead information, and the subsequent nurturing of leads through targeted marketing strategies. By implementing effective lead generation advertising strategies, businesses can increase their customer base and drive revenue growth.

Lead Generation

Lead generation, in the context of advertisement, refers to the process of attracting and capturing potential customers or leads for a product, service, or business. It involves various strategies and tactics employed by advertisers to gather information about individuals who have expressed interest in their offerings. The primary goal of lead generation is to build a database of potential customers who can be nurtured and converted into paying customers. By generating leads, advertisers can directly target individuals who have shown some level of interest, increasing the chances of converting them into sales.

Lead Nurturing In Advertising Strategies Implementation

Lead nurturing in advertising strategies implementation refers to the process of cultivating and nurturing potential customers or leads to build relationships and encourage them to progress through the sales funnel. It involves delivering personalized content and interacting with leads at various stages of their buying journey to increase engagement and conversion rates. The goal of lead nurturing is to establish trust and credibility with leads, providing them with valuable information and resources that address their specific needs and concerns. By consistently delivering relevant content and staying in touch with leads, advertisers can build strong relationships, establish brand loyalty, and drive repeat business.

Lead Nurturing In Advertising Strategies

Lead Nurturing In Advertising

Lead nurturing in advertising refers to the process of building and maintaining relationships with potential customers throughout their buying journey in order to convert them into loyal, paying customers. This process involves providing relevant and valuable information to prospects at each stage of the sales funnel, guiding them towards making a purchase decision. The goal of lead nurturing is to educate and engage potential customers, address their concerns, and ultimately, drive them to take a desired action.

Local Advertising Campaigns

Local advertising campaigns refer to the marketing efforts that focus on promoting products or services to a specific geographical area or a local community. These campaigns are designed to reach and engage with the target audience within a limited geographic radius, typically within the same city or region. Local advertising campaigns utilize various channels and mediums, both online and offline, to effectively communicate with the local audience. Traditional methods such as newspaper ads, radio spots, billboards, and direct mail are often used to increase visibility and generate awareness within the local community. These offline channels allow businesses to directly target potential customers who live or work in the vicinity. With the rise of digital technologies, local advertising campaigns have also embraced online platforms to reach a wider audience and leverage the benefits of targeted marketing. Online advertisements through search engines, social media, and display networks enable businesses to specifically target users based on their location and demographics. This allows for more precise targeting and reduces wastage of resources on audiences outside the local area. One of the key advantages of local advertising campaigns is the ability to build strong relationships with the local community. By emphasizing the local aspect of the business, these campaigns create a sense of familiarity and trust among potential customers. Local businesses can utilize their knowledge of the area and community to position themselves as trusted experts within the local market. Local advertising campaigns also provide businesses with the opportunity to personalize their messaging and promotions. By understanding the needs and preferences of the local audience, businesses can tailor their advertisements to resonate with the target customers. This personal touch can result in higher engagement and better response rates compared to generic, non-localized advertising. In conclusion, local advertising campaigns focus on promoting products or services to a specific local market. By utilizing a combination of traditional and digital channels, businesses can effectively reach and engage with the local audience. These campaigns help build relationships, personalize messaging, and ultimately drive business growth within the local community.

Local Advertising

Local advertising refers to the promotional activities conducted by businesses or individuals within a specific geographical area. It is a marketing strategy that aims to target potential customers who reside or work in close proximity to the business location. The main objective of local advertising is to increase brand awareness, attract local customers, and drive sales within the targeted area. Local advertising can take various forms, including print ads in local newspapers or magazines, billboards in high-traffic areas, radio or television commercials aired in a specific region, direct mail campaigns to local households, and online advertisements targeted to users in a specific location. In recent years, digital advertising platforms have become increasingly popular for local advertising, as they offer cost-effective and highly targeted options.

Local Business Advertising Planning Strategies

Local business advertising planning strategies refer to the methods and tactics utilized by businesses to promote their products or services to a specifically targeted local audience. These strategies are designed to effectively reach and engage potential customers within a specific geographic area, typically within a specific city or region. The goal of local business advertising planning strategies is to increase brand awareness, attract new customers, and ultimately drive sales within the local market. To achieve these objectives, businesses analyze the local market and tailor their advertising efforts accordingly.

Local Business Advertising Planning

Local business advertising planning refers to the process of developing a strategic approach to promoting a business to its target audience within a specific geographic area. This planning typically involves defining advertising objectives, identifying target demographics, selecting appropriate advertising channels, creating compelling ad content, and setting a budget and timeline for implementation. The first step in local business advertising planning is to establish clear objectives. These objectives can vary depending on the specific needs and goals of the business, such as increasing brand awareness, driving foot traffic to a physical location, generating leads, or boosting sales. The objectives should be specific, measurable, achievable, relevant, and time-bound (SMART), providing a framework for the planning process. Next, it is essential to identify the target demographics for the business. This involves conducting market research and analyzing data to determine the characteristics, preferences, and behaviors of the target audience. By understanding the target demographics, businesses can tailor their advertising strategies to effectively reach and engage potential customers. Once the objectives and target demographics are established, the next step is to select the most appropriate advertising channels. These channels can include various traditional and digital platforms, such as print media, radio, television, outdoor signage, search engine advertising, social media, email marketing, and local directories. The selection of channels should be based on the target audience's media consumption habits, budget constraints, and advertising objectives. Creating compelling ad content is crucial for successful local business advertising. The content should be persuasive, informative, and engaging to capture the attention and interest of the target audience. It should highlight the unique selling points of the business, convey a strong value proposition, and include a clear call-to-action that encourages the audience to take the desired action, such as visiting the business, making a purchase, or contacting for more information. Finally, local business advertising planning involves setting a budget and timeline for implementation. The budget should take into account the costs associated with advertising channels, ad creation, and any additional marketing resources required. The timeline should outline specific milestones and deadlines to ensure timely execution of the advertising plan.

Local Business Advertising

Local business advertising refers to the marketing efforts made by small businesses to promote their products or services within a specific geographic location. It involves utilizing various advertising strategies and channels to reach and engage with the target audience in a local area. Local business advertising plays a vital role in helping small businesses increase brand awareness, attract new customers, and drive sales. By focusing on the local community, these businesses can establish a strong presence and build relationships with their target market.

Location-Based Advertising

Location-Based Advertising refers to a marketing strategy that involves delivering advertisements to individuals based on their geographical location. It utilizes the GPS capabilities of mobile devices to target consumers who are in close proximity to a specific business or location. The goal of location-based advertising is to deliver relevant ads to potential customers at the right time and place, increasing the chances of influencing their purchasing decisions. This form of advertising has gained popularity with the widespread adoption of smartphones and other mobile devices that have location tracking capabilities. By leveraging the real-time data provided by these devices, advertisers are able to target users based on their current location, allowing them to deliver more personalized and contextually relevant advertisements.

Location-Based Mobile Ads Implementation Methods

Location-based mobile ads implementation methods refer to the process of delivering targeted advertisements to users based on their geographical location. These methods rely on the use of mobile devices, such as smartphones or tablets, which have built-in GPS capabilities that allow advertisers to determine the location of the device. There are several methods that can be used to implement location-based mobile ads. One method is through the use of geofencing, which involves defining virtual boundaries or perimeters around specific geographical areas. When a user enters or exits these boundaries, they can be targeted with relevant ads. Geofencing can be especially effective for businesses with physical locations, as it allows them to target potential customers who are in close proximity to their stores.

Location-Based Mobile Ads Implementation

Location-Based Mobile Ads Implementation refers to the process of designing and executing targeted advertising campaigns on mobile devices based on the user's geographical location. Location-based mobile advertising leverages the GPS and Wi-Fi capabilities of mobile devices to deliver ads that are specifically tailored to the user's current location. This form of advertising provides marketers with the opportunity to reach consumers at the right place and time, increasing the chances of engagement and conversion. Implementing location-based mobile ads involves several steps. Firstly, marketers define the target audience and set specific parameters related to location, such as radius or specific geographic boundaries. These parameters help

174

ensure that the ads are displayed to users who are most likely to be interested in the products or services being advertised. Once the target audience and location parameters are defined, marketers can proceed to create compelling ad content. This includes designing visually appealing graphics or videos, as well as crafting compelling ad copy that resonates with the intended audience. The content should be concise, relevant, and persuasive to capture the attention of mobile users. The next step in implementation is selecting the appropriate mobile ad platform or network. There are a variety of platforms available, each offering different features and targeting capabilities. Marketers evaluate these platforms based on factors such as reach, targeting options, ad formats, and pricing models to determine the best fit for their campaign objectives. After selecting the platform, marketers set up their location-based mobile ad campaigns by configuring the targeting parameters, budget, and duration. This involves specifying the location targeting options, such as targeting specific cities or regions, setting bid prices, and determining the campaign duration. Once the campaign is live, marketers closely monitor its performance and make necessary adjustments to optimize results. They track metrics such as impressions, clicks, conversions, and return on investment (ROI) to gauge the effectiveness of the ad campaign. This data helps in identifying areas for improvement and refining the targeting strategy for future campaigns. In conclusion, location-based mobile ads implementation is the process of designing and executing targeted advertising campaigns on mobile devices that leverage the user's geographical location. By delivering relevant ads to users based on their current location, marketers can enhance engagement and conversion rates, leading to more effective and efficient advertising campaigns.

Location-Based Mobile Ads

Location-based mobile ads are a type of advertisement that is targeted to a specific geographic location, using the GPS capabilities of mobile devices. These ads are designed to reach consumers who are in close proximity to a particular business or location, in order to increase the likelihood of engagement and conversion. By leveraging the GPS data from mobile devices, location-based mobile ads are able to deliver personalized and relevant content to consumers based on their real-time location. This allows businesses to reach potential customers who are physically nearby and may be more likely to visit their store or make a purchase.

Market Development Advertising Strategies

Market development advertising strategies refer to the various approaches and techniques used by companies to expand their existing market and reach new customers through targeted and effective advertising campaigns. These strategies aim to increase brand awareness, attract new customers, and ultimately drive sales and revenue growth. There are several key components that define market development advertising strategies. Firstly, companies must identify new market segments or customer groups that have a potential need or interest in their products or services. This involves thorough market research and analysis to understand the demographics, behaviors, and preferences of these target audiences. Once the target market is identified, companies can then develop advertising messages and campaigns that effectively communicate the value and benefits of their products or services to these new customer segments. These messages should highlight the unique selling points and competitive advantages of the company, creating a compelling reason for customers to choose them over competitors. Market development advertising strategies often utilize a mix of different advertising mediums and channels to reach the target audience. This may include traditional channels such as television, radio, print media, and outdoor advertising, as well as digital channels such as online display ads, social media marketing, email campaigns, and search engine optimization. Effective market development advertising strategies also involve careful planning and execution. Companies need to determine the appropriate budget allocation for advertising activities, set clear objectives and goals, and regularly monitor and evaluate the effectiveness of their campaigns. This allows companies to make necessary adjustments and improvements to ensure maximum impact and return on investment. In summary, market development advertising strategies are essential for companies looking to expand their market reach and attract new customers. By identifying new target audiences, developing compelling advertising messages, utilizing various advertising channels, and evaluating campaign effectiveness, companies can effectively promote their products or services, increase brand awareness, and ultimately drive business growth. """"

Market Development Advertising

Market development advertising refers to the strategic process of identifying and targeting new markets for a product or service through various advertising techniques. It involves expanding the reach and influence of a brand by appealing to a different set of customers or geographical areas. Market development advertising aims to increase the customer base and revenue streams by tapping into untapped markets or creating new demand for existing products or services. This strategy is particularly beneficial for businesses looking to sustain growth or expand their operations.

Market Research

Market research, in the context of advertisement, refers to the systematic gathering, analyzing, and interpreting of information about a specific target market or audience. The main purpose of market research in advertising is to gain valuable insights and understanding of consumer behavior, preferences, and needs, in order to develop more effective advertising strategies. Market research involves collecting both qualitative and quantitative data through various research techniques such as surveys, interviews, focus groups, and observation. The collected data is then analyzed to identify patterns, trends, and correlations that can inform advertising decisions and help shape the overall marketing strategy. By conducting market research, advertisers are able to identify their target audience and understand their demographics, interests, lifestyles, and purchasing behaviors. This enables them to create advertisements that are more relevant and appealing to their target market, increasing the chances of capturing their attention and influencing their purchasing decisions. Market research also helps advertisers evaluate the effectiveness of their current advertising campaigns and identify areas for improvement. Through this process, they can assess the impact of their advertisements, measure brand awareness and recognition, and gauge customer satisfaction and loyalty. This feedback is crucial in guiding the development of future advertising efforts and optimizing the allocation of advertising budgets. In addition, market research enables advertisers to stay updated with industry trends, competitive landscape, and technological advancements. By keeping a pulse on the market, advertisers can identify emerging opportunities or potential threats that may impact their advertising strategies. This proactive approach allows them to adapt and adjust their advertising efforts to stay ahead of the competition and maintain a strong position in the market. In conclusion, market research is an essential component of advertising that helps advertisers gain valuable insights into their target market, improve the effectiveness of their advertisements, evaluate campaign performance, and stay informed about industry dynamics. By leveraging market research findings, advertisers can develop more targeted and impactful advertising strategies that resonate with their audience and drive business growth.

Market Segmentation

Market segmentation refers to the process of dividing a broad target market into smaller, more specific groups based on common characteristics such as demographic, geographic, psychographic, and behavioral factors. The goal of market segmentation is to better understand and reach the needs and preferences of different customer segments, in order to develop more tailored and effective advertising strategies. Demographic segmentation involves categorizing consumers based on demographic factors such as age, gender, income, education level, occupation, and marital status. This type of segmentation allows advertisers to target specific age groups or genders that are most likely to be interested in their products or services. For example, a company selling baby products may focus their advertisements on young parents or expectant mothers, who are more likely to be interested in their offerings. Geographic segmentation involves dividing the market based on geographical factors such as location, climate, or cultural differences. This type of segmentation can be useful for businesses with specific regional or cultural preferences. For example, a tourism agency may target their advertisements towards individuals living in a certain city or region, promoting vacation packages that align with the local climate and culture. Psychographic segmentation involves classifying consumers based on their lifestyle, personality traits, interests, or values. This type of segmentation allows advertisers to tap into the emotional and psychological aspects of their target audience, by creating ads that resonate with their values or aspirations. For instance, a company selling luxury products may target affluent individuals who value status and exclusivity in their lifestyle choices. Behavioral segmentation involves dividing consumers based on their purchasing behaviors or patterns. This type of segmentation allows advertisers to target individuals who have previously demonstrated an interest or loyalty to a certain product or

176

brand. For example, an online retailer may send personalized advertisements to customers who have recently made a purchase, offering them related or complementary items.

Marketing Automation Platforms Selection Criteria

A marketing automation platform is a software tool that allows companies to automate repetitive marketing tasks, streamline workflows, and measure the effectiveness of their marketing campaigns. It provides a centralized system for managing and executing various marketing activities, such as email marketing, social media marketing, lead generation, customer segmentation, and campaign tracking. When selecting a marketing automation platform, there are several criteria to consider. Firstly, the platform should have a user-friendly interface that allows marketers to easily navigate and manage their campaigns. It should provide intuitive drag-and-drop functionality and customizable templates for creating email campaigns, landing pages, and forms. Secondly, the platform should offer advanced segmentation capabilities. This means that it should allow marketers to divide their audience based on various criteria, such as demographics, behavior, or purchase history. This enables marketers to personalize their messaging and target specific segments with relevant content, improving the effectiveness of their campaigns. Thirdly, the platform should provide robust tracking and reporting features. It should be able to accurately track and measure key performance metrics, such as email open rates, click-through rates, conversion rates, and revenue generated. This allows marketers to analyze the success of their campaigns and make data-driven decisions to optimize their marketing strategies. Furthermore, the platform should integrate seamlessly with other marketing tools and systems, such as customer relationship management (CRM) software and social media platforms. This ensures that data can be easily shared between systems, enabling marketers to have a unified view of their marketing efforts and streamline their workflows. In addition, the platform should provide automation capabilities beyond just email marketing. It should support multi-channel marketing automation, allowing marketers to automate tasks such as social media posting, lead scoring, and campaign scheduling. This saves time and resources for marketers, allowing them to focus on strategic activities.

Marketing Automation Platforms Selection

A Marketing Automation Platform is a software technology that enables businesses to automate their marketing efforts across multiple channels, such as email, social media, and websites. It allows companies to streamline their marketing processes, increase efficiency, and personalize their communication with customers. These platforms are designed to assist businesses in managing and automating various marketing tasks, such as lead generation, lead nurturing, email marketing, social media management, and campaign tracking. They provide a centralized hub for businesses to manage their marketing campaigns and gain insights into the effectiveness of their efforts.

Marketing Automation Platforms

Marketing Automation Platforms are software tools that enable businesses to automate, streamline, and manage their marketing activities, processes, and campaigns. These platforms provide a centralized system where marketers can efficiently execute and monitor their various marketing tasks, such as email campaigns, social media marketing, lead generation, customer segmentation, and behavior tracking. Marketing Automation Platforms offer a wide array of features and functionalities that allow marketers to automate repetitive and time-consuming tasks, effectively saving time and effort. These platforms typically include features such as: 1. Email Marketing Automation: This feature enables marketers to automate email campaigns, including sending personalized emails, setting up triggered responses based on customer actions, and managing email lists and subscriptions. 2. Lead Management and Tracking: Marketing Automation Platforms allow businesses to capture and track lead information, analyze lead behavior, and nurture leads throughout the sales funnel. Marketers can easily segment leads based on various criteria and send targeted messages to specific groups of leads. 3. Social Media Marketing: These platforms often provide tools for managing and scheduling social media posts, tracking social media interactions, and analyzing social media performance. Marketers can save time by scheduling posts in advance and monitoring their social media presence from a centralized platform. 4. Campaign Management: Marketing Automation Platforms offer features for planning, executing, and monitoring marketing campaigns across various channels. Marketers can create and manage campaigns, track campaign performance and ROI, and make data-driven decisions to optimize their marketing efforts. 5. Analytics and Reporting: These platforms provide robust analytics and reporting capabilities to track and measure the success of marketing activities. Marketers can gain valuable insights into campaign performance, customer behavior, conversion rates, and more, enabling them to make data-driven decisions and optimize future marketing strategies. In conclusion, Marketing Automation Platforms play a crucial role in enabling businesses to automate and optimize their marketing efforts. By leveraging the features and functionalities offered by these platforms, marketers can efficiently manage and execute their marketing activities, generate and nurture leads, and drive better results in their marketing campaigns.

Media Buying Strategies Assessment Approaches

Media buying is the process of purchasing advertising space or time from various media outlets such as TV, radio, print, and digital platforms. It involves strategically selecting the most suitable media channels to reach the target audience effectively. To maximize the impact and success of media buying, advertisers employ different assessment approaches or strategies. One common assessment approach in media buying is the reach and frequency strategy. In this approach, advertisers aim to maximize the reach, which refers to the number of unique individuals exposed to the advertisement. They also focus on frequency, which pertains to the number of times the target audience is exposed to the ad. By carefully managing the balance between reach and frequency, advertisers can ensure that their message reaches a wide audience while also reinforcing it with repeated exposure.

Media Buying Strategies Assessment

Media buying strategies refer to the various tactics and approaches used by advertisers to purchase advertising space or time on different media platforms. These strategies are designed to help advertisers reach their target audience effectively and efficiently, while also maximizing the return on investment for their ad campaigns. There are several key factors that advertisers consider when developing media buying strategies. These include target audience demographics, media consumption behaviors, budget allocation, and campaign objectives. By carefully analyzing these factors, advertisers can make informed decisions about where and when to place their ads to achieve the desired results. One common media buying strategy is to use demographic data and audience insights to identify the most relevant media channels for reaching the target audience. For example, if the target audience is primarily young adults interested in sports, advertisers may choose to place ads on popular sports websites or during televised sporting events. Budget allocation is another important aspect of media buying strategies. Advertisers must determine how much of their advertising budget to allocate to different media channels. This decision is often based on factors such as the reach and cost of each channel, as well as the desired frequency of ad placements. Advertisers may choose to allocate a larger portion of their budget to media channels that offer a greater reach or a lower cost per impression. Campaign objectives also play a crucial role in media buying strategies. Advertisers must align their media buying decisions with the overall goals of their ad campaigns. For example, if the objective is to increase brand awareness, advertisers may choose to focus on media channels that offer high visibility and broad reach. On the other hand, if the objective is to generate sales leads, advertisers may prioritize media channels that have a proven track record of driving conversions. In conclusion, media buying strategies are carefully planned approaches that advertisers use to purchase advertising space or time on different media platforms. These strategies take into account factors such as target audience demographics, media consumption behaviors, budget allocation, and campaign objectives, to ensure that ad campaigns reach the right audience at the right time, and generate the desired results.

Media Buying Strategies

Media buying refers to the process of purchasing advertising space or time in various media outlets, such as television, radio, print, or digital platforms. It is a strategic approach used by advertisers and marketing professionals to reach a target audience, increase brand visibility, and promote products or services. The primary objective of media buying is to effectively allocate an advertising budget to maximize the return on investment (ROI). This involves careful research, analysis, and negotiation to identify the most suitable media channels that align with the campaign objectives and target market demographics. By selecting the right media outlets, advertisers can ensure that their messages reach the desired audience at the right time, in the most cost-effective manner. When developing media buying strategies, advertisers consider factors such as target audience profile, media consumption habits, and campaign goals. They utilize various metrics and data, such as ratings, circulation, reach, and frequency, to assess the potential reach and impact of different media options. This helps in making informed decisions about where to allocate the advertising budget for maximum exposure and engagement. Effective media buying also involves identifying the most suitable media placements within the selected outlets. Advertisers can choose between different formats, time slots, or sections based on their target audience behavior and preferences. This ensures that the advertisements are positioned in the right context and have a higher likelihood of capturing the attention of the intended audience. Furthermore, media buying strategies often involve negotiation and purchasing of advertising space at competitive rates. Media buyers leverage their relationships with media representatives to secure advantageous deals and optimize the budget. They strive to obtain the best possible rates, discounts, or added value in terms of bonus airtime or space. In summary, media buying strategies are essential for advertisers to effectively promote their products or services through various media outlets. By conducting thorough research, analysis, and negotiation, advertisers can make informed decisions on how to allocate their advertising budgets and achieve optimal results in terms of audience reach, engagement, and return on investment.

Media Buying

Media buying is the strategic process of purchasing advertising space or time on various media platforms to promote a product, service, or brand. It involves negotiating and securing media placements to reach the intended target audience effectively. In today's digital era, media buying has expanded beyond traditional channels such as television, radio, and print to include online platforms like websites, social media, and mobile apps. The aim is to maximize the visibility and impact of the advertisements while optimizing the allocated budget.

Media Kit

A media kit is a comprehensive promotional tool that provides potential advertisers with information about a media company's audience, reach, and advertising options. It serves as a resource for advertisers to understand the available advertising opportunities, rates, and packages offered by the media company. The main purpose of a media kit is to persuade advertisers to invest in advertising with the media company by showcasing the benefits and value of their advertising platforms. A well-designed media kit should be visually appealing, easy to navigate, and contain all the necessary information that an advertiser may need to make an informed decision. The content of a media kit usually includes: - Overview of the media company: This section provides an overview of the media company, including its history, mission, values, and target audience. It highlights the media company's unique selling propositions, such as its reach, credibility, and audience engagement. - Audience demographics: This section presents detailed information about the media company's audience, including their age, gender, location, interests, and buying behavior. It helps advertisers understand the market segment they will be reaching through advertising with the media company. - Advertising options: This section outlines the various advertising options available to advertisers, such as print ads, digital ads, sponsored content, and event sponsorships. It describes the different formats, sizes, and placements for each advertising option and provides examples or case studies to demonstrate their effectiveness. - Advertising rates and packages: This section includes the pricing structure for advertising with the media company, including rates for different ad sizes, durations, and placements. It also presents any special packages or discounts available to advertisers, such as bulk discounts or bundled advertising options. - Testimonials and success stories: This section features testimonials or success stories from previous advertisers who have had positive results from advertising with the media company. It helps build trust and credibility by showing potential advertisers that others have had successful experiences with the company's advertising platforms. - Contact information: This section provides the contact details of the media company's advertising team, including phone numbers, email addresses, and social media handles. It allows potential advertisers to easily get in touch with the company for further inquiries or to initiate an advertising partnership. In conclusion, a media kit is a comprehensive promotional tool that provides potential advertisers with all the necessary information they need to make an informed decision about advertising with a media company. It showcases the media company's audience, reach, and advertising options while highlighting its unique selling propositions and previous success stories.

Media Planning

Media Planning is a strategic process that involves the selection and coordination of various media platforms to deliver the marketing message of a brand or product to the target audience effectively. It focuses on identifying the most suitable media channels and allocating resources to maximize the reach and impact of advertising campaigns. In the realm of advertisement, media planning plays a crucial role in ensuring that the right message is conveyed to the right audience at the right time. It begins with a thorough understanding of the target market and their media consumption habits. This includes analyzing their demographics, interests, behaviors, and preferences. Once the target audience is identified, media planners conduct research to assess the available media options that would provide the greatest reach and engagement. These options can span across traditional channels such as television, radio, print, and outdoor advertising, as well as digital platforms like social media, search engines, websites, and mobile apps. The media planning process involves evaluating different factors such as the media's reach, frequency, cost, and impact. Planners consider factors like the media's relevancy to the target audience, its ability to generate awareness and interest, and its feasibility within the allocated budget. They also take into account the timing and duration of the campaign, ensuring that the advertising message is delivered consistently and timely. Once the media options are assessed, planners develop a detailed media plan that outlines the recommended media channels, the budget allocation for each channel, and the expected performance metrics. This plan serves as a roadmap for the entire advertising campaign. Throughout the campaign, media planners closely monitor and optimize the advertising efforts. They track the performance of each media channel, measure the campaign's effectiveness, and make necessary adjustments to achieve the desired objectives. They also evaluate the return on investment (ROI) to assess the success of the media plan. Overall, media planning is a crucial component of advertising that aims to optimize the reach and impact of advertising campaigns by strategically selecting and coordinating various media platforms. It is a dynamic and iterative process that requires continuous evaluation and optimization to ensure the desired outcomes.

Media Reach

Media reach is a term used in the field of advertising to refer to the total number of people or audience members that are exposed to a particular advertisement or marketing campaign. In simple terms, media reach measures the overall coverage and exposure of an advertisement across various channels and platforms. It provides insights into the potential audience size that can be reached by a specific advertisement, helping advertisers to evaluate the effectiveness and potential impact of their campaigns.

Mobile Advertising Apps Evaluation Criteria

Mobile advertising apps evaluation criteria refer to the standards and factors used to assess the effectiveness, efficiency, and suitability of mobile advertising applications. These criteria help advertisers and marketers to determine which mobile advertising apps are most suitable for their specific advertising goals and objectives. When evaluating mobile advertising apps, several criteria can be considered: 1. Targeting capabilities: This criterion assesses the app's ability to reach the desired audience accurately. It includes features like demographic targeting, location-based targeting, and contextual targeting. Effective targeting ensures that the ads are seen by the right users, increasing the chances of conversions and minimizing wasted impressions. 2. Ad format variety: This criterion examines the range of ad formats supported by the app. The app should offer diverse ad formats such as banners, interstitials, videos, and native ads, allowing advertisers to choose the formats that best align with their campaign goals and creative content. 3. User experience: User experience plays a vital role in the success of mobile advertising campaigns. Evaluating apps based on user experience criteria involves assessing factors like ad placement, frequency capping, ad intrusiveness, and integration with the overall app interface. Ads should not disrupt the user experience or negatively affect app usage. 4. Performance tracking and analytics: This criterion focuses on the app's ability to provide comprehensive performance tracking and analytics. It includes features like impression tracking, click-through rates (CTR), conversion tracking, and attribution modeling. The app should provide detailed insights and data that enable advertisers to monitor, optimize, and measure the effectiveness of their campaigns. 5. Audience reach: Evaluating an app's audience reach involves considering factors such as total user base, active user base, and geographical coverage. The app should have a significant and relevant user base, ensuring that the ads reach a wide audience and have the potential to generate conversions. 6. Cost-effectiveness: This criterion examines the overall cost-effectiveness of using the mobile advertising app. It involves considering factors like ad pricing models (e.g., CPC, CPM, CPI), return on investment (ROI), and the app's pricing structure. The app should provide a good balance between cost and performance, offering competitive pricing and favorable ROI for advertisers. By evaluating mobile advertising apps based on these criteria, advertisers can make informed decisions and choose the most suitable app that aligns with their advertising goals, effectively reaching their target audience, enhancing user experience, and maximizing campaign success.

Mobile Advertising Apps Evaluation

Mobile advertising apps can be defined as software applications that are designed specifically for mobile devices to display advertisements to users. These apps are created with the purpose of delivering targeted and relevant advertising content to users while they are using their mobile devices, such as smartphones or tablets. These apps typically utilize various advertising techniques and strategies to capture the attention of users and promote products or services. They may display banner ads, interstitial ads, video ads, or native ads within the app interface. The advertisements can be delivered in different formats, sizes, and positions depending on the design and functionality of the app. The primary goal of mobile advertising apps is to generate revenue through advertising. Developers or publishers of these apps may partner with advertising networks or platforms to serve ads within their apps. They earn money through various monetization models, such as pay-per-click (PPC), cost-per-impression (CPM), or cost-per-install (CPI). These models allow advertisers to pay only when users interact with or view their ads, ensuring that advertisers are getting value for their advertising spend. Mobile advertising apps also offer benefits to both advertisers and users. For advertisers, these apps provide a platform to reach a large and diverse audience, increase brand visibility, and drive user engagement. They can target their ads based on user demographics, location, behavior, or interests, which allows for more effective advertising campaigns. Users, on the other hand, benefit from these apps by receiving personalized and relevant ads that match their preferences and needs. This can enhance their overall mobile experience and make advertising more informative and engaging. In conclusion, mobile advertising apps are software applications designed for mobile devices to display targeted and relevant advertisements. These apps serve as a platform for advertisers to reach a wide audience and generate revenue, while also providing users with personalized and engaging ads. They utilize various advertising techniques and monetization models to deliver effective and impactful advertising campaigns.

Mobile Advertising Apps

A mobile advertising app is a software application specifically designed and developed to promote products, services, or brands on mobile devices such as smartphones and tablets. These apps are used by advertisers to reach and engage with their target audience, driving awareness, generating leads, and ultimately increasing sales. Mobile advertising apps utilize various strategies and techniques to deliver targeted and personalized advertisements to mobile users. These apps often leverage user data, such as location, demographics, and browsing behavior, to deliver relevant and context-specific ads. Through advanced targeting capabilities, advertisers can ensure their ads are shown to users who are most likely to be interested in their offerings.

Mobile Advertising

Mobile advertising refers to the practice of promoting products or services through mobile devices such as smartphones and tablets. It involves delivering targeted advertisements to users on their mobile devices, often within apps or mobile websites. Mobile advertising has become increasingly popular in recent years due to the widespread use of smartphones and the ability to reach a large and diverse audience. It offers advertisers the opportunity to connect with consumers on a more personal and intimate level, as mobile devices are often considered highly personal and are carried with individuals throughout the day. There are various types of mobile advertising formats, including display ads, native ads, video ads, and interstitial ads. Display ads are the most common form of mobile advertising and are usually banners or images that appear within a mobile app or website. Native ads are designed to match the format and style of the app or website and blend in with the user experience. Video ads are short video clips that play before, during, or after video content. Interstitial ads are full-screen ads that appear between content, such as when transitioning from one web page to another within an app. One of the key benefits of mobile advertising is its ability to target specific audiences based on factors such as demographics, location, and user behavior. Advertisers can leverage the wealth of data available on mobile devices to deliver more relevant and personalized ads. This not only enhances the user experience but also increases the likelihood of engagement and conversion. Mobile advertising also offers a range of measurement and tracking capabilities, allowing advertisers to analyze the effectiveness of their campaigns and make data-driven decisions. They can track metrics such as impressions, clicks, conversions, and return on investment (ROI). This helps advertisers optimize their campaigns and allocate resources to the most successful channels and strategies.

Mobile App Advertising Platforms

A mobile app advertising platform is a technology-based platform that allows advertisers to promote their mobile applications to relevant users through various advertising formats on mobile devices. These platforms provide a centralized system for managing, optimizing, and measuring the performance of mobile app advertising campaigns. Mobile app advertising platforms offer a range of targeting options that enable advertisers to reach specific segments of the mobile app user base. These targeting options may include demographic targeting (such as age, gender, and location), behavioral targeting (based on user interests and past behaviors), and contextual targeting (based on the content and context of the app in which the ad is shown). Through mobile app advertising platforms, advertisers can choose from different ad formats such as interstitial ads, banners, native ads, and video ads to deliver their marketing messages to app users. These ad formats are designed to capture the attention of users and encourage them to engage with the advertised app. Mobile app advertising platforms also provide tools and features for optimizing and measuring the performance of ad campaigns. Advertisers can use these tools to set campaign goals, define key performance indicators (KPIs), and track the performance of their ads in real-time. They can also conduct A/B testing to compare different ad creatives, targeting options, and bidding strategies to identify the most effective approach for their campaigns. In addition, mobile app advertising platforms often offer access to a large network of mobile apps, allowing advertisers to reach a wide audience across multiple apps and publishers. They provide ad inventory management systems that allocate ad placements based on factors such as ad relevance, bidding price, and user experience. Overall, mobile app advertising platforms empower advertisers to connect with their target audience through mobile apps and drive app installs, user engagement, and conversions. By leveraging the targeting, ad format options, optimization tools, and network reach provided by these platforms, advertisers can maximize the impact and effectiveness of their mobile app advertising campaigns.

Mobile App Advertising

Mobile app advertising refers to the practice of promoting and marketing mobile applications to a targeted audience through various digital advertising channels such as mobile websites, social media platforms, search engines, and mobile apps themselves. This form of advertising aims to increase app visibility, drive app downloads, and generate app engagement by leveraging the widespread use of smartphones and tablets. It allows app developers, publishers, and marketers to reach potential users on their mobile devices and effectively communicate the value and benefits of their apps.

Multichannel Advertising Campaigns Execution

Multichannel advertising campaigns execution refers to the process of implementing and managing a comprehensive advertising strategy across multiple channels in order to reach a wide and diverse target audience. It involves the coordination and integration of various marketing and advertising techniques across offline and online channels to create a cohesive and impactful campaign. In a multichannel advertising campaign, different channels such as television, radio, print media, digital platforms, social media, and outdoor advertising are utilized to deliver the brand message and promote products or services. The aim is to maximize the brand's visibility and engagement by targeting consumers through multiple touchpoints. The execution of a multichannel advertising campaign involves several key steps. Firstly, a thorough understanding of the target audience is necessary to identify the most effective channels to reach them. This may involve conducting market research, analyzing customer data, and studying consumer behavior patterns. Once the target audience and channels are identified, the next step is to develop a cohesive message and creative assets that are tailored to each channel. This requires adapting the message to suit the unique characteristics and requirements of each medium, while ensuring brand consistency and alignment. After the development stage, the campaign is implemented across the selected channels. This involves negotiating and purchasing media space in the case of traditional channels, and setting up digital advertising campaigns in the case of online channels. Throughout the execution process, continuous monitoring and tracking of campaign performance is necessary to make adjustments and optimize results. Multichannel advertising campaigns offer several advantages. By leveraging multiple channels, they provide greater reach and exposure, enabling brands to connect with their target audience in different contexts and platforms. They also facilitate increased customer engagement and interaction, as consumers are reached through their preferred channels and can interact with the brand through various media. Furthermore, multichannel campaigns allow for greater flexibility and adaptability. By diversifying the advertising mix, brands can respond to changing market conditions and consumer preferences more effectively. They can also leverage the strengths of each channel to enhance overall campaign effectiveness. In conclusion, multichannel advertising campaign execution is the strategic and coordinated implementation of an advertising strategy across various channels in order to maximize reach, engagement, and campaign effectiveness. It involves understanding the target audience, developing tailored messages and assets, and executing campaigns through a mix of offline and online channels. By taking a multichannel approach, brands can enhance their visibility, engagement, and overall marketing impact.

Multichannel Advertising Campaigns

Multichannel advertising campaigns refer to strategic marketing efforts that utilize multiple channels or platforms to promote a product, service, or brand to a target audience. This type of advertising campaign aims to reach consumers through various channels simultaneously or sequentially, in order to optimize visibility and engagement. The key aspect of multichannel advertising campaigns is their ability to combine the strengths of different channels to create a cohesive and impactful marketing strategy. These campaigns often include a mix of traditional advertising channels such as television, radio, print media, and outdoor advertising, as well as digital channels such as social media, websites, email marketing, search engine advertising, and mobile applications. By leveraging multiple channels, companies can increase the reach and frequency of their brand messages, ensuring that they target potential customers through different touchpoints and at various stages of the consumer journey. Multichannel advertising campaigns enable businesses to connect with their audience in different ways, considering their preferences and behavioral patterns. Moreover, multichannel advertising campaigns allow for better segmentation and targeting. Businesses can tailor their messaging and creative assets to suit the specific characteristics and preferences of different channels or platforms. For example, they can create visually appealing videos for social media platforms, while focusing on concise and impactful copy for email marketing campaigns. Another advantage of multichannel advertising campaigns is the ability to track and measure performance across different channels. Businesses can gather data and insights on how each channel contributes to overall campaign success, as well as make optimizations and reallocate resources based on performance metrics. In conclusion, multichannel advertising campaigns integrate multiple channels and platforms to maximize brand exposure, engage consumers, and drive desired actions. By utilizing a mix of traditional and digital channels, businesses can create a comprehensive marketing strategy that reaches their target audience through various touchpoints, tailors messaging, and measures performance effectively.

Native Advertising Platforms Assessment Criteria

Native advertising platforms assessment criteria refer to the guidelines, parameters, or standards used to evaluate and measure the effectiveness, relevance, and impact of native advertising platforms. These criteria assist advertisers, marketers, and publishers in determining the suitability and success of using specific native advertising platforms to promote their products or services. One of the critical assessment criteria for native advertising platforms is the seamless integration of the advertisement with the surrounding content. This means that the ad should blend in naturally with the user experience and not disrupt or interrupt the browsing or reading flow. Native ads should not be intrusive, overly promotional, or deceive users into clicking on them. Instead, they should appear as a part of the platform's native content, offering value, information, or entertainment to the users. Another essential aspect to consider is the relevancy and contextual alignment of the native ads with the platform and its audience. The ads should be tailored to match the platform's content, tone, and style, ensuring that they resonate with the target audience. By aligning the ad messaging and format with the user's interests and preferences, native advertising platforms can enhance engagement and conversion rates. Transparency and disclosure are also crucial assessment criteria for native advertising platforms. The platforms must clearly distinguish native ads from organic content, preventing confusion or misleading users. They should provide disclosure labels or markers that explicitly indicate the presence of sponsored or promoted content, ensuring transparency and trust. Additionally, assessing the performance analytics and measurement capabilities of native advertising platforms is essential. Advertisers and marketers need access to comprehensive data and insights regarding ad impressions, clicks, conversions, and other relevant metrics. The platform should offer robust tracking and reporting tools that enable campaign optimization, measurement of return on investment (ROI), and assessment of the ad's effectiveness. Furthermore, native advertising platforms should support various ad formats, sizes, and placements to meet advertisers' diverse needs. They should provide flexibility in terms of visual elements, multimedia content, and interactive features to deliver engaging and impactful ads to the audience. In conclusion, native advertising platforms assessment criteria include evaluating the seamless integration, relevancy, transparency, performance analytics, and ad format flexibility. By considering these criteria, advertisers can make informed decisions about choosing the most suitable native advertising platforms to effectively reach and engage their target audience. Native advertising platforms assessment criteria refer to the guidelines, parameters, or standards used to evaluate and measure the effectiveness, relevance, and impact of native advertising platforms. These criteria assist advertisers, marketers, and publishers in determining the suitability and success of using specific native advertising platforms to promote their products or services.

Native Advertising Platforms Assessment

Native advertising platforms refer to online advertising solutions that seamlessly integrate ads with the surrounding content on a website or app, making them appear as natural and native elements rather than distinct advertisements. This form of advertising seeks to provide a non-disruptive and cohesive user experience by blending promotional messages with editorial or user-generated content. Native ads are designed to match the look, feel, and tone of the platform on which they are displayed, making them more engaging and less likely to be ignored or blocked by users. These platforms offer advertisers the ability to reach their target audience in a non-intrusive manner, resulting in higher brand visibility, increased user engagement, and ultimately driving conversions.

Native Advertising Platforms

Native advertising platforms refer to online advertising platforms that enable advertisers to create and distribute advertising content that seamlessly blends in with the surrounding editorial content of websites and digital platforms. Unlike traditional display ads that are clearly marked as advertisements, native ads are designed to mimic the look and feel of the editorial content on the platform. These platforms provide advertisers with a means to reach their target audience in a non-disruptive manner by integrating their advertising content into the native user experience. By matching the style and format of the surrounding content, native ads can appear more organic and less intrusive, increasing the likelihood of user engagement and interaction.

Native Advertising

Native advertising is a form of advertisement that seamlessly blends in with the content of the platform it is displayed on, thus appearing as a natural and non-disruptive part of the user

184

experience. It is designed to look and feel like the editorial or organic content of the platform, in order to engage the audience in a more authentic way.Native advertisements are often created to mimic the style, format, and tone of the surrounding content, making them less intrusive and more likely to be noticed and engaged with by the users. These ads can appear in various forms, such as articles, videos, images, sponsored posts, or even social media updates.

Native Video Advertising Creation

Native Video Advertising Creation refers to the process of producing and developing video content that seamlessly integrates with the surrounding platform or environment in which it is displayed, in order to provide a non-disruptive and more engaging advertising experience. Native video advertising aims to blend in with the format, style, and context of the platform, allowing it to appear as part of the organic content rather than a separate advertising element. By adopting a native approach, the video advertisement is more likely to capture the attention of the audience and generate a higher level of interest and engagement.

Native Video Advertising

Native video advertising refers to a type of advertisement that seamlessly blends into the user's online experience, appearing as a natural part of the content. This form of advertising aims to create a non-disruptive and engaging experience for the viewer by providing relevant and valuable video content within the context of the platform or website they are using. Unlike traditional video ads that often interrupt and disrupt the user's experience, native video advertising is carefully integrated into the surrounding content, making it less intrusive and more likely to be viewed and engaged with by the audience. These ads are designed to match the look, feel, and tone of the platform on which they appear, ensuring that they blend in harmoniously and provide a seamless user experience.

Niche Advertising Markets Analysis Methods

Niche advertising markets analysis refers to the process of evaluating and understanding specific advertising markets that cater to narrow or specialized audience segments. It involves identifying the unique needs, preferences, and characteristics of these niche markets in order to develop effective advertising strategies and campaigns. There are several methods that can be used to analyze niche advertising markets. These methods provide valuable insights into the target audience and help advertisers make informed decisions regarding their advertising efforts. Here are some commonly used methods: 1. Market research: Conducting thorough market research is essential to understanding niche advertising markets. This involves gathering and analyzing data about the target audience, their demographics, interests, and purchasing behavior. Market research can be done through surveys, interviews, focus groups, and data analysis. 2. Competitor analysis: Analyzing competitors in the niche market provides insights into their advertising strategies and tactics. This involves researching their target audience, messaging, channels used, and campaign effectiveness. By understanding the competition, advertisers can identify gaps and opportunities to differentiate their own campaigns. 3. Segmentation analysis: Segmenting the niche market based on various criteria such as demographics, psychographics, and behavior allows advertisers to better understand the distinct subgroups within the target audience. This analysis helps in tailoring advertising messages and campaigns to specific segments, maximizing relevance and effectiveness. 4. Trend analysis: Examining industry trends, consumer behavior patterns, and market dynamics is crucial for niche advertising markets. This analysis helps advertisers stay updated with the latest trends and adapt their strategies accordingly. It also enables them to identify emerging opportunities or potential threats to their advertising efforts. 5. Data analytics: Leveraging data analytics tools and techniques can provide valuable insights into the performance and impact of advertising campaigns. By analyzing metrics such as reach, engagement, conversions, and return on investment, advertisers can measure the effectiveness of their efforts and optimize their strategies accordingly. In conclusion, niche advertising markets analysis involves evaluating specific markets that cater to narrow audience segments. By utilizing various methods such as market research, competitor analysis, segmentation analysis, trend analysis, and data analytics, advertisers can gain a deeper understanding of their target audience and develop effective advertising strategies.

Niche Advertising Markets Analysis

A niche advertising market analysis refers to the process of evaluating and analyzing specific, specialized markets or target audiences for the purpose of creating strategic advertising campaigns. It involves examining the characteristics, preferences, behavior, and needs of a specific niche audience to develop highly targeted marketing messages and reach the desired customer segment effectively. By conducting a niche advertising market analysis, businesses gain insights into the unique qualities and interests of their target audience, allowing them to create advertisements that speak directly to their needs and desires. This analysis helps marketers identify the most effective advertising channels, messages, and creative approaches to engage and convert their niche audience.

Niche Advertising Markets

Niche advertising markets refer to specific segments or subsets of the overall advertising industry that cater to a particular target audience or specialized product/service. These markets are characterized by their narrow focus and specific appeal, often seeking to reach a smaller, more defined demographic or consumer group. Niche advertising can be seen as a form of targeted marketing, where advertisers aim to reach a specific audience with their messages and promotions.

Niche Advertising Targeting

Niche advertising targeting refers to the strategy of focusing ad campaigns on specific and well-defined segments of the market, known as niches. These niches represent groups of consumers who share similar characteristics, interests, behaviors, or needs. The objective of niche advertising targeting is to tailor marketing messages and deliver them to the most relevant audience, increasing the effectiveness and efficiency of advertising efforts. By identifying and understanding the unique traits and preferences of niche segments, advertisers can develop highly customized and targeted campaigns. This approach allows them to reach consumers who are more likely to be interested in their products or services, maximizing the potential for engagement and conversion. Niche advertising targeting helps advertisers break through the clutter of mass advertising and connect with consumers on a more personal level.

Niche Advertising

Niche advertising refers to the practice of targeting a specific, specialized audience or market segment with tailored advertising messages and campaigns. This approach focuses on reaching a small, well-defined group of individuals who share common interests, needs, or characteristics. The goal of niche advertising is to directly engage and connect with a specific audience to effectively convey relevant messages and encourage desired actions. By understanding the unique preferences, behaviors, and motivations of the target niche, advertisers can craft highly targeted and personalized campaigns that resonate with this particular group.

Niche Marketing

Niche marketing is a focused advertising strategy that targets a specific segment of the market. It involves identifying a narrow, specialized subset of consumers with distinct needs, preferences, and interests, and tailoring marketing efforts to appeal directly to this group. This approach aims to position a product or service as uniquely suited to meet the needs of a particular niche audience, effectively connecting with them on a personal and relatable level. By understanding the specific characteristics and behaviors of the target niche, marketers can develop highly targeted and customized promotional campaigns. These campaigns are designed to resonate with the niche audience by addressing their specific pain points, desires, or aspirations. Niche marketing allows companies to differentiate themselves from competitors by offering a unique value proposition that strictly caters to the needs of the niche market. Niche marketing relies on thorough market research to identify viable niche segments and understand their distinct characteristics. This research helps marketers gain insights into the niche audience's demographics, psychographics, buying behavior, and consumption patterns. By collecting and analyzing this data, businesses can refine their marketing strategies and create campaigns that effectively communicate the benefits and advantages of their products or services to the niche market. Implementing a successful niche marketing strategy requires clear

186

positioning and messaging that speaks directly to the desires and pain points of the targeted niche. Marketers work to craft compelling and persuasive marketing materials that resonate with the niche audience and demonstrate the unique value their product or service offers. This may involve developing specialized content, using niche-specific language or imagery, and leveraging niche-specific channels or platforms to reach the intended audience effectively. In conclusion, niche marketing is an advertising approach that focuses on catering to the specific needs and interests of a narrow segment of consumers. By tailoring marketing efforts to resonate with this niche audience, businesses can differentiate themselves from competitors and establish a strong connection with their target market. Through thorough research and targeted messaging, niche marketing enables companies to position their products or services as the ideal solution for the specific needs of a particular niche market.

Online Advertising Network Selection

In the context of online advertising, network selection refers to the process of choosing the most suitable advertising network to run digital ad campaigns. An advertising network is a platform that connects advertisers with publishers, allowing advertisers to display their ads on various websites or mobile apps. The goal of network selection is to identify the network that aligns with the advertiser's objectives, targets the desired audience, and offers the best return on investment (ROI) for the advertising campaign. When selecting an advertising network, advertisers evaluate several factors. Target audience reach and relevance are crucial considerations, as the network should have a substantial user base that matches the advertiser's target demographic. Additionally, the network's ability to reach users across multiple platforms, such as desktop, mobile, or in-app, is advantageous for reaching a wider audience. Another critical factor is the network's ad inventory. Advertisers look for networks that offer a wide range of ad formats and placements, including banners, videos, native ads, and social media placements. The availability of different ad sizes and positions allows advertisers to create diverse and engaging campaigns to maximize ad visibility and user engagement. The network's targeting options also play a significant role in network selection. Advertisers seek networks that provide sophisticated targeting capabilities, such as demographic targeting, geographic targeting, behavioral targeting, or interest-based targeting. These options enable advertisers to narrow down the audience and deliver ads to users who are more likely to be interested in their products or services. The pricing model is another consideration during network selection. Advertisers assess the cost-effectiveness of the network's pricing model, which can include cost per click (CPC), cost per mille (CPM), or cost per action (CPA). The network's pricing should align with the advertiser's budget and campaign objectives. Furthermore, advertisers evaluate the network's performance tracking and reporting capabilities. Robust analytics and reporting tools allow advertisers to monitor the performance of their campaigns in real-time, enabling them to optimize their strategies and make data-driven decisions. In conclusion, network selection for online advertising involves choosing an appropriate advertising network by considering factors such as target audience reach, ad inventory, targeting options, pricing models, and performance tracking capabilities. By carefully evaluating these factors, advertisers can make informed decisions and maximize the effectiveness of their digital advertising campaigns.

Online Advertising Network

An online advertising network is a platform that connects advertisers with publishers to facilitate the buying and selling of digital advertising space. It acts as a marketplace, allowing advertisers to display their ads on various websites and apps, and enabling publishers to monetize their online content by hosting these ads. Advertisers use online advertising networks to reach their target audience more effectively. These networks have access to large inventories of ad spaces across a wide range of websites and apps, giving advertisers the opportunity to reach a diverse and extensive audience. By using targeting and tracking technologies, online advertising networks can help advertisers serve their ads to specific demographics, interests, and behavior segments, increasing the effectiveness of their campaigns. Publishers benefit from online advertising networks by generating revenue through the display of ads on their websites or apps. These networks provide a streamlined process for managing and optimizing advertisements, making it easier for publishers to monetize their digital properties. They handle tasks such as ad serving, tracking, and payment processing, relieving publishers of the burden of managing individual advertising relationships. Online advertising networks employ various ad formats, including text ads, display banners, video ads, and native ads. They offer different pricing models, such as cost per click (CPC), cost per thousand impressions (CPM), and cost per action (CPA), giving advertisers flexibility in how they pay for their campaigns. These networks also provide performance metrics and analytics to track the effectiveness and ROI of advertising campaigns. In summary, an online advertising network is a digital marketplace that connects advertisers and publishers, allowing them to buy and sell advertising space. It enables advertisers to reach their target audience more efficiently while providing publishers with a streamlined process for monetizing their digital properties. With various ad formats, pricing models, and performance tracking capabilities, online advertising networks play a crucial role in the digital advertising ecosystem.

Online Advertising

Online advertising refers to the promotional activities carried out on the internet to reach and engage with potential customers. It involves the use of various online platforms, websites, and social media platforms to display advertisements and promote products or services. Online advertising can take many different forms, including display ads, search engine advertising, social media advertising, email marketing, and video advertising. Display ads are graphical ads that are displayed on websites and can be in the form of banners, pop-ups, or interstitial ads. Search engine advertising involves placing ads on search engine results pages, usually in the form of text ads that are relevant to the user's search query. Social media advertising, on the other hand, utilizes social media platforms like Facebook, Instagram, and Twitter to target specific audiences based on their interests, demographics, and behavior. These ads can appear in users' newsfeeds, in the sidebar, or as sponsored posts. Email marketing involves sending promotional messages and advertisements directly to a person's email inbox, usually through a newsletter or a targeted email campaign. Video advertising has become increasingly popular, with platforms like YouTube and TikTok offering opportunities for businesses to run video ads before or during content playback. These ads can range from short video clips to longer, more engaging advertisements. Online advertising offers several benefits to businesses. It allows for precise targeting, ensuring that advertisements are displayed to the right audience, increasing the chances of conversion. It also offers flexibility in terms of budget, as businesses can allocate their ad spend according to their needs and goals. Online advertising also provides real-time analytics and tracking, allowing businesses to measure the effectiveness of their campaigns and make necessary adjustments. In conclusion, online advertising encompasses a range of promotional activities carried out on the internet. It leverages various online platforms to display advertisements and reach potential customers. With its targeting capabilities and flexibility, online advertising has become an essential tool for businesses to promote their products and services in the digital era.

Online Video Advertising Strategies Planning

Online video advertising strategies planning refers to the process of developing a comprehensive plan to effectively promote products or services through video content that is distributed online. This involves identifying target audiences, determining objectives, creating compelling video content, and selecting appropriate platforms for distribution. The first step in online video advertising strategies planning is to identify the target audience. This involves gathering data and insights about the demographics, interests, and online behavior of the intended audience. This information helps in tailoring the video content and choosing the most relevant platforms for reaching the target audience. Once the target audience is identified, the next step is to determine the objectives of the video advertising campaign. These objectives can vary depending on the specific needs of the business or brand. Some common objectives include increasing brand awareness, driving website traffic, generating leads, and boosting sales. After setting the objectives, the next step is to create compelling video content. The videos should be visually engaging, informative, and resonate with the target audience. The content should clearly communicate the message and value proposition of the product or service being advertised. Selecting the appropriate platforms for video distribution is another crucial aspect of online video advertising strategies planning. There are various platforms available for video distribution, such as YouTube, social media platforms (e.g., Facebook, Instagram), and video ad networks. The choice of platforms should be based on factors like target audience demographics, preferred media consumption habits, and ad budget. In addition to platform selection, video ad targeting is an important consideration. This involves determining the specific criteria for displaying the video ads, such as location, age, gender, and interests. By targeting the ads to a specific audience, the chances of reaching the right viewers and achieving campaign objectives are increased. Measurement and analysis of the campaign performance are also essential in online video advertising strategies planning. This involves tracking key metrics such as views, impressions, click-through rates, and conversions. By analyzing the data, insights can be gained into the effectiveness of the campaign and adjustments can be made accordingly. In conclusion, online video advertising strategies planning involves identifying the target audience, setting objectives, creating compelling video content, selecting appropriate platforms, targeting the ads, and measuring campaign performance. By carefully planning and executing these strategies, businesses and brands can effectively promote their products or services through online video advertising.

Online Video Advertising Strategies

Online video advertising strategies refer to the various approaches used by advertisers to promote their products, services, or brand through video content on digital platforms. These strategies are designed to maximize the reach, engagement, and conversion of the target audience, ultimately driving business objectives and increasing brand awareness. The first strategy is creating captivating and high-quality video content that resonates with the target audience. This includes careful planning, scriptwriting, and production of videos that effectively communicate the brand's message and value proposition. The content should be engaging, informative, and visually appealing to capture the attention of viewers and encourage them to take the desired action. Another important video advertising strategy is audience targeting. Advertisers utilize data-driven insights to identify and understand their target audience's demographic, interests, and online behavior. This allows them to deliver customized video ads to the right viewers at the right time, increasing the chances of engagement and conversion. By targeting specific audience segments, advertisers can optimize their ad spend and make their campaigns more cost-effective. Furthermore, video advertising strategies often involve optimizing the video content for different platforms and devices. Advertisers adapt their videos to fit the specific requirements and formats of various digital platforms, such as social media, websites, and mobile apps. This ensures that the videos are displayed correctly and provide an optimal viewing experience regardless of the device or screen size. Lastly, video advertising strategies also focus on measuring and analyzing campaign performance. Advertisers track key performance indicators (KPIs), such as views, clicks, engagement rate, and conversion rate, to evaluate the effectiveness of their video ads. This data-driven approach allows advertisers to identify strengths and weaknesses in their campaigns and make data-backed optimizations to improve results. Overall, online video advertising strategies combine creative content creation, audience targeting, platform optimization, and data analysis to maximize the success of video advertising campaigns. By utilizing these strategies, advertisers can effectively reach and engage their target audience, drive brand awareness, and achieve their marketing goals in the digital landscape.

Online Video Advertising

Online video advertising refers to the use of videos to promote a product, service, or brand through digital platforms on the internet. It involves the dissemination of targeted video content with the goal of capturing the attention and interest of online users, ultimately leading to desired actions such as product purchases, website visits, or brand awareness. In recent years, online video advertising has gained significant popularity due to the widespread availability of high-speed internet connections and the growing consumption of video content on various online platforms. This form of advertising offers unique advantages compared to traditional forms of advertising, such as television commercials or print ads. One of the key benefits of online video advertising is its ability to engage users with rich and interactive content. Videos have the power to convey a message more effectively and emotionally than static images or text-based ads. By utilizing visual and auditory elements, advertisers can create compelling storytelling experiences that resonate with viewers on a deeper level. Additionally, online video advertising allows for precise targeting and personalization. With advanced targeting capabilities, advertisers can reach specific audiences based on demographics, interests, and online behavior. This level of precision ensures that the message reaches the right people at the right time, maximizing the chances of conversion and minimizing wasted ad spend. Another advantage of online video advertising is its measurability. Advertisers can track various metrics, such as view counts, engagement rates, click-through rates, and conversions, to evaluate the effectiveness of their campaigns. These insights enable advertisers to optimize their strategies in real-time, making data-driven decisions to improve campaign performance. Furthermore, online video advertising offers flexibility and versatility. Advertisers can choose from different video ad formats, including pre-roll ads, mid-roll ads, and post-roll ads, depending on their goals and target audience. They can also leverage various platforms, such as social media platforms, video-sharing platforms, or websites, to reach a wide range of users and increase brand exposure. In summary, online video advertising is a dynamic and impactful marketing strategy that leverages the power of videos to capture the attention and interest of online users. With its ability to engage, target, measure, and adapt, online video advertising has become an essential tool for businesses to promote their products or services effectively in the digital age.

Out-Of-Home Advertising

Out-of-home advertising, also known as outdoor advertising, refers to any type of advertising that reaches consumers while they are outside of their homes. It encompasses various forms of advertisements that target people when they are on the go, including billboards, transit ads, street furniture ads, digital signage, and more. Out-of-home advertising is designed to capture the attention of consumers in public spaces and expose them to brand messages. It operates in high-traffic areas such as streets, highways, airports, bus stops, and shopping centers, aiming to reach a wide audience and generate brand awareness.

Out-Of-Home (OOH) Media Planning Approaches

Out-of-Home (OOH) Media Planning Approaches refer to the strategies and techniques used by advertisers and media planners to effectively utilize outdoor advertising channels to reach and engage with their target audience. OOH media includes various forms of advertising that are displayed outside of the consumer's home, such as billboards, transit ads, street furniture, and digital screens. There are several approaches that advertisers can take when planning their OOH media campaigns: The Location-Based Approach: This approach involves selecting the most relevant and high-traffic locations for placing OOH advertisements. Media planners research and analyze data on consumer behavior, demographics, and traffic patterns to identify prime locations for maximum reach and impact. By strategically placing ads in areas where the target audience is likely to be present, advertisers can effectively capture their attention and generate brand awareness. The Contextual Approach: In this approach, media planners consider the contextual relevance of the OOH advertisement to the surrounding environment. They aim to align the message and creative content of the ad with the specific location or event where it will be displayed. For example, a sunscreen brand may choose to advertise on billboards near beaches or outdoor festivals to leverage the contextual relevance and target consumers who are more likely to be interested in their product. The Creative Approach: This approach focuses on crafting visually appealing and engaging OOH advertisements that can capture attention and leave a lasting impression on viewers. Media planners collaborate with creative teams to develop innovative and impactful ad concepts that stand out in the outdoor advertising landscape. By utilizing creative elements such as vivid imagery, bold typography, and interactive features, advertisers can effectively communicate their brand message and drive consumer engagement. The Cross-Channel Approach: This approach leverages the synergy between OOH media and other advertising channels to create a cohesive and integrated marketing campaign. Media planners coordinate OOH ads with digital, print, and broadcast media channels to reinforce brand messaging and increase campaign reach. For example, OOH ads can be synchronized with social media campaigns or QR codes can be incorporated into billboards to drive online interactions and track campaign effectiveness. Overall, these approaches to OOH media planning help advertisers optimize their outdoor advertising efforts by strategically selecting locations, considering contextual relevance, utilizing creative elements, and integrating with other advertising channels. By adopting these approaches, advertisers can effectively deliver their brand message, engage their target audience, and achieve their marketing objectives.

Out-Of-Home (OOH) Media Planning

Out-of-Home (OOH) media planning is a strategic process of determining the most effective ways to communicate with a target audience through billboards, transit advertising, street furniture, and other forms of outdoor advertising. OOH media planning involves analyzing various factors such as the target demographic, location, traffic patterns, and competitive landscape to create a plan that maximizes brand exposure and drives desired consumer actions. This form of advertising is particularly useful in reaching audiences when they are out of their homes and in the public space, where they are more likely to engage with the message.

Out-Of-Home (OOH) Media

Out-of-Home (OOH) media refers to any type of advertising that reaches consumers while they are outside of their homes. This form of media typically includes billboards, transit ads, street furniture ads, and digital screens located in public spaces. OOH media is highly effective in capturing consumers' attention as they are often exposed to these advertisements when they are out and about, engaging in various activities such as commuting, shopping, or socializing. These advertisements are strategically placed in high-traffic areas to maximize their reach and impact.

Outdoor Advertising Planning

Outdoor advertising planning refers to the process of strategically creating, organizing, and executing advertising campaigns in outdoor spaces to effectively reach a target audience. This type of advertising is often displayed in public areas such as roads, highways, bus stops, airports, shopping centers, and other crowded places where people gather. The main goal of outdoor advertising planning is to capture the attention of potential consumers and create brand awareness. This is achieved by strategically selecting the most suitable locations for displaying advertisements, considering factors such as high traffic volumes, target demographics, and consumer behavior patterns.

Outdoor Advertising

Outdoor advertising refers to the placement of promotional messages and signage in outdoor locations with the aim of reaching a large audience. It is a form of advertising that is executed in an outdoor environment and includes a variety of mediums such as billboards, posters, transit advertising, and street furniture advertising. This type of advertising is designed to capture the attention of people who are out and about, whether they are walking, driving, or using public transportation. It typically makes use of large, eye-catching visuals and concise messages to quickly communicate a brand's message or promote a specific product or service.

PPA Advertising Campaigns

PPA stands for Pay Per Action. PPA advertising campaigns refer to a specialized form of online advertising where advertisers only pay when a specific action is completed by the user. This action may include making a purchase, filling out a form, downloading a file, or signing up for a newsletter, among others. In PPA advertising, the advertiser pays for a desired action instead of simply paying for ad impressions or clicks. This ensures that the advertiser only pays for results that directly contribute to their marketing goals. It also helps in maximizing the return on investment (ROI) by minimizing the risk of paying for ineffective ads.

PPC Bidding Optimization Techniques

PPC bidding optimization techniques refer to the strategies and tactics used to improve the performance and efficiency of pay-per-click (PPC) advertising campaigns. PPC advertising involves placing ads on search engine results pages (SERPs) and other websites, and advertisers pay a fee each time their ad is clicked. Bidding optimization techniques aim to maximize the return on investment (ROI) by increasing click-through rates (CTR), improving conversion rates, and reducing the cost per click (CPC). There are several PPC bidding optimization techniques that advertisers can implement to achieve better results. Firstly, keyword research and selection are crucial for effective bidding. By identifying relevant and high-performing keywords, advertisers can target their ads to the right audience and increase the likelihood of conversions. Monitoring and analyzing keyword performance metrics, such as search volume, competition, and cost, can help advertisers make informed bidding decisions. Secondly, ad copy optimization plays a vital role in PPC bidding optimization. Well-crafted and compelling ad copy can attract more clicks and increase CTR. Advertisers should continuously

191

test different variations of ad copy and headlines to identify which combination produces the best results. A/B testing is commonly used to compare the performance of different ad elements and make data-driven decisions for bidding optimization. Landing page optimization is another important technique in PPC bidding optimization. When users click on an ad, they are directed to a landing page where they can complete the desired action, such as making a purchase or filling out a form. Optimizing landing pages involves ensuring relevancy between the ad and the landing page, improving load speed, enhancing user experience, and implementing persuasive elements to encourage conversions. By optimizing landing pages, advertisers can increase conversion rates and improve the overall effectiveness of their PPC campaigns. Furthermore, bid management tools and automation can significantly streamline the bidding optimization process. These tools use algorithms and machine learning to analyze historical performance data and adjust bids in real-time. By automatically adjusting bids based on factors such as time of day, device, location, and audience segmentation, bid management tools can maximize ROI and reduce manual bid management efforts. In conclusion, PPC bidding optimization techniques are essential for advertisers to improve the performance and efficiency of their PPC campaigns. Through keyword research, ad copy optimization, landing page optimization, and bid management tools, advertisers can increase CTR, improve conversion rates, and reduce CPC, ultimately maximizing their ROI.

PPC Bidding Optimization

PPC bidding optimization refers to the process of maximizing the effectiveness and efficiency of pay-per-click (PPC) advertising campaigns by analyzing and adjusting bidding strategies. PPC advertising is a model where advertisers pay a fee each time their ad is clicked, and bidding optimization focuses on getting the most value out of each click by optimizing the bid amount. The goal of PPC bidding optimization is to achieve the highest return on investment (ROI) from advertising spend. This is accomplished by finding the right balance between bid amounts, ad positions, and click-through rates (CTRs) to maximize the number of clicks and conversions generated within a given budget. To optimize PPC bidding, advertisers need to continuously monitor and analyze various performance metrics, such as the average cost per click (CPC), conversion rate, and cost per acquisition (CPA). By tracking and analyzing these metrics, advertisers can identify underperforming keywords, ad groups, or campaigns and make data-driven adjustments to improve overall campaign performance. There are several techniques and strategies that can be employed for PPC bidding optimization. One common approach is to segment campaigns and ad groups based on performance and adjust bids accordingly. For example, high-performing keywords or ad groups may warrant higher bids to maintain their top positions, while underperforming ones may require lower bids or even removal from the campaign. Another key aspect of PPC bidding optimization is keyword research and selection. By identifying relevant keywords with high search volume and low competition, advertisers can increase their chances of generating clicks and conversions at a lower cost. Additionally, negative keyword analysis helps in filtering out irrelevant search queries that may trigger ads, thus reducing wasteful ad spend. Bid adjustments based on factors such as device, location, time of day, and audience can also contribute to PPC bidding optimization. For example, if certain keywords or ad groups perform better on mobile devices, advertisers can increase bids for mobile users to capture more clicks and conversions from that segment. Lastly, monitoring and adjusting bidding strategies based on competition is also crucial for PPC bidding optimization. Analyzing competitor bid data and market trends can help advertisers make informed decisions regarding their bidding strategies, such as when to increase bids to maintain a competitive edge or when to scale back to avoid overpaying for clicks. Overall, PPC bidding optimization is a continuous and iterative process that requires ongoing monitoring, analysis, and adjustments to maximize the effectiveness and efficiency of PPC advertising campaigns. By optimizing bidding strategies, advertisers can improve their ROI, generate more qualified traffic, and ultimately achieve their advertising goals.

PPL Advertising Campaigns

PPL Advertising Campaigns refer to Pay-Per-Lead advertising campaigns in the context of advertisement. This type of campaign involves advertisers paying for leads or potential customers instead of paying for clicks or impressions. In PPL Advertising Campaigns, advertisers only pay for leads that meet specific criteria or actions defined by the advertisers themselves. These criteria can include actions such as signing up for a newsletter, filling out a contact form, requesting a quote, or making a purchase. The advertisers set the criteria based on their specific marketing goals and objectives.

PPS Advertising Campaigns

A PPS advertising campaign, also known as pay-per-sale advertising campaign, is a type of advertisement strategy where advertisers only pay when a sale or transaction occurs as a result of the campaign. This approach ensures that advertisers only pay for the desired outcome rather than for the number of viewers or clicks on their ads. PPS advertising campaigns work on the principle of a commission-based model, where the advertiser and publisher enter into an agreement that the publisher will be compensated for each sale generated through their advertising efforts. This compensation is typically in the form of a percentage of the sale made, which is agreed upon before the campaign starts.

PPV Ads Creation Steps

A PPV (Pay-Per-View) ad refers to a form of advertising where advertisers pay a fee each time their ad is viewed by a user. These ads are commonly used in online marketing campaigns to promote products or services and generate potential customers. The process of creating PPV ads involves several key steps. These steps help ensure that the ad effectively reaches the target audience and maximizes the advertiser's return on investment. 1. Define Advertising Objectives: The first step in creating a PPV ad is to clearly define the advertising objectives. This involves understanding the desired outcome of the ad campaign, whether it is to increase brand awareness, generate leads, or drive sales. 2. Identify Target Audience: Once the objectives are defined, the next step is to identify the target audience. This includes defining the demographics, interests, and preferences of the potential customers who are most likely to respond to the ad. 3. Research Keywords: Keyword research is an important step in creating effective PPV ads. This involves identifying the keywords and phrases that are relevant to the product or service being promoted and have high search volumes. 4. Create Compelling Ad Copy: The ad copy is the text that appears in the ad. It should be concise, persuasive, and tailored to resonate with the target audience. The copy should highlight the unique selling points of the product or service and include a clear call-to-action. 5. Design Engaging Visuals: In addition to the ad copy, visuals play a crucial role in attracting the audience's attention. The visuals should be eye-catching, relevant to the ad content, and aligned with the brand's identity. 6. Set Ad Budget: Setting a budget is essential to ensure that the ad campaign stays within the allocated financial resources. The budget should be determined based on the advertising objectives and the expected reach and frequency of the ads. 7. Choose Ad Platform: There are various platforms available for running PPV ads, such as social media platforms, search engines, and specialized ad networks. The choice of platform depends on the target audience's online behavior and the ad campaign's objectives. 8. Optimize for Performance: Once the ad is live, continuous monitoring and optimization are necessary to improve its performance. This involves analyzing key performance indicators, such as click-through rates and conversion rates, and making adjustments to improve the ad's effectiveness. By following these steps, advertisers can create PPV ads that effectively reach their target audience and drive the desired outcomes. The process requires careful planning, research, and ongoing optimization to ensure the best possible return on investment for the advertiser.

PPV Ads Creation

A PPV (Pay Per View) ad refers to a type of online advertising model where advertisers pay a certain fee each time their ad is viewed by users. This model is commonly used in video advertising, where ads are displayed to users before, during, or after a video content. In a PPV ad model, advertisers are charged based on the number of ad views or impressions rather than clicks or conversions. This means that advertisers pay for each view their ad receives, regardless of whether the user takes any further action, such as clicking on the ad or making a purchase. The fee for each view is typically predetermined or negotiated between the advertiser and the advertising platform.

PPV Advertising Campaigns

A PPV (pay-per-view) advertising campaign refers to a marketing strategy where advertisers pay for each view or interaction their ad receives. This type of campaign involves delivering ads to a targeted audience through various digital channels, such as websites, search engines, social media platforms, or mobile applications. In a PPV advertising campaign, advertisers often collaborate with publishers or ad networks to distribute their ads to a specific group of viewers who are likely to be interested in their products or services. The main objective is to generate brand awareness, drive targeted traffic to the advertiser's website, and ultimately, convert viewers into customers.

Paid Search Advertising Strategies

Paid search advertising strategies are a set of tactics used by businesses to create and run effective online advertisements that appear on search engine results pages. These strategies involve targeting specific keywords and creating ads that are relevant to users' search queries. When users enter a search query that matches the chosen keywords, the ads are displayed at the top or bottom of the search results, labeled as sponsored or paid results. The primary goal of paid search advertising is to increase website traffic, attract potential customers, and generate leads or sales. It allows businesses to reach a targeted audience who are actively searching for products or services related to their industry. By bidding on keywords, businesses can secure ad placements and only pay when their ads are clicked, which is known as pay-per-click (PPC) advertising.

Paid Search Advertising

Paid Search Advertising refers to a type of online advertising where advertisers pay to display their ads on search engine result pages (SERPs). It involves the creation of advertisements that are shown to users who search for specific keywords or phrases on search engines like Google, Bing, or Yahoo. Paid search advertising operates on a pay-per-click (PPC) model, meaning advertisers only pay when a user actually clicks on their ad. The ads are typically displayed at the top or bottom of the search engine results page, labeled as "sponsored" or "ad." These ads are targeted to specific keywords and are designed to be relevant to the search query. Paid search advertising allows advertisers to reach a highly targeted audience who are actively searching for products, services, or information related to their business. By bidding on specific keywords, advertisers can increase the likelihood that their ads will be shown when users search for those keywords. The success of paid search advertising relies on thorough keyword research, understanding the target audience, and creating compelling ad copy that encourages users to click. Advertisers can also set a budget for their campaigns, controlling how much they are willing to spend on clicks and how long the ads will be displayed. One of the key benefits of paid search advertising is the ability to track and measure performance. Advertisers can analyze data such as click-through rates, conversion rates, and return on investment to assess the effectiveness of their campaigns. This data allows advertisers to make informed decisions, optimize their ads, and improve their overall advertising strategy. In summary, paid search advertising is a form of online advertising where advertisers pay to display ads on search engine result pages. It offers a targeted approach to reach potential customers who are actively searching for relevant information, products, or services. By utilizing strategic keyword bidding and compelling ad copy, advertisers can increase their visibility and drive traffic to their websites.

Pay-Per-Action (PPA) Advertising

Pay-Per-Action (PPA) advertising is a performance-based marketing model in the field of online advertising. It involves advertisers paying only when a specified action is completed by a user, such as making a purchase, submitting a form, or downloading an app. PPA advertising is also known as cost-per-action (CPA) advertising or performance-based advertising. With PPA advertising, advertisers have better control over their advertising expenses as they are only charged when a desired action is achieved. This makes it a cost-effective and efficient form of advertising. It shifts the risk from the advertiser to the publisher or ad network, as they are responsible for delivering the desired actions.

Pay-Per-Call Advertising Campaigns Management

Pay-per-call advertising campaigns management refers to the process of organizing,

194

overseeing, and optimizing advertising campaigns that are based on a pay-per-call model. In this model, advertisers only pay when a potential customer makes a phone call to the advertised phone number. The management of pay-per-call advertising campaigns involves various activities aimed at maximizing the effectiveness and efficiency of these campaigns. This includes identifying target audiences, selecting appropriate advertising channels, creating compelling ad copy, and allocating budgets effectively.

Pay-Per-Call Advertising Campaigns

Pay-Per-Call Advertising Campaigns are a form of advertising where advertisers pay for calls generated by their advertisements. Instead of paying for clicks or impressions, advertisers are charged based on the number of calls received. This type of campaign is commonly used for businesses that rely heavily on phone calls for sales and leads. Pay-Per-Call campaigns typically involve the use of unique phone numbers that are assigned to specific advertisements. When a potential customer sees the advertisement and decides to make a call, they dial the designated phone number provided in the ad. This number is often different from the business's main contact number and can be tracked to measure the success of the campaign. Unlike traditional advertising methods, Pay-Per-Call campaigns provide a more direct and measurable way of gauging customer interest. Advertisers are only charged when a phone call is made, ensuring that they are paying for tangible leads rather than just online interactions. This type of advertising can be especially effective for industries such as home services, legal services, automotive, and healthcare, where customers are more likely to call for inquiries or appointments. When implementing a Pay-Per-Call campaign, advertisers have the ability to set specific criteria for the calls they want to receive. This includes factors such as geographical location, call duration, and time of day. By targeting specific demographics, advertisers can ensure that they are reaching their desired audience and maximizing their return on investment. Overall, Pay-Per-Call Advertising Campaigns offer a cost-effective and results-driven approach to advertising. They provide a way for businesses to directly connect with potential customers and track the success of their campaigns in real-time. With the increasing use of mobile phones and the preference for phone calls over other forms of communication, Pay-Per-Call campaigns are becoming an increasingly popular and effective advertising strategy.

Pay-Per-Call Advertising

Pay-Per-Call Advertising is a form of marketing where advertisers pay for inbound phone calls received as a result of their advertisements. This type of advertising provides a direct and measurable way for businesses to generate leads and engage with potential customers. With Pay-Per-Call Advertising, an advertiser creates and places advertisements across various channels such as online search engines, websites, social media platforms, or offline media like television and radio. These advertisements contain a call-to-action that prompts viewers or readers to make a phone call to a specific phone number provided by the advertiser. When a consumer sees the ad and decides to call the advertised phone number, the call is tracked and recorded by a specialized Pay-Per-Call platform. This platform assigns a unique tracking number to each advertisement to accurately measure the effectiveness of the campaign. The call is then transferred to the advertiser's phone through call forwarding or a call center, allowing them to directly interact with the potential customer. The unique aspect of Pay-Per-Call Advertising is that advertisers only pay when a call is made and connected to their phone. In other words, they pay for the leads generated through phone calls instead of paying for ad impressions or clicks. This pay-per-call model provides a higher level of accountability and return on investment as advertisers only pay for tangible results - real customer interactions. This form of advertising is particularly beneficial for businesses that rely on phone calls to generate sales or conversions, such as service-based industries like plumbers, lawyers, insurance agents, or travel agencies. It allows advertisers to directly connect with potential customers who are already interested and ready to engage, leading to higher conversion rates and increased revenue. In conclusion, Pay-Per-Call Advertising is a targeted marketing strategy that enables businesses to connect with potential customers through phone calls. By paying for inbound calls, advertisers have more control over their advertising budget and can measure the effectiveness of their campaigns in real-time.

Pay-Per-Click (PPC) Bidding

195

Pay-Per-Click (PPC) bidding is a method used in online advertising to determine how much an advertiser is willing to pay for each click on their advertisement. It is a form of auction-based pricing, where advertisers bid on specific keywords or phrases that are relevant to their target audience. In PPC bidding, advertisers set a maximum bid amount that they are willing to pay for each click. This bid is usually based on the perceived value of a click, which is determined by factors such as the competitiveness of the keyword, the quality of the advertisement, and the potential return on investment. The advertiser with the highest bid for a particular keyword or phrase will typically have their advertisement displayed at the top of the search results or on relevant websites. Once an advertisement is displayed, the advertiser is only charged when someone clicks on their ad. Hence the term "pay-per-click." The amount that the advertiser is charged per click is typically based on a formula that takes into account the bids of other advertisers, the quality of the advertisement, and the relevance of the ad to the user's search query or browsing history. PPC bidding allows advertisers to have more control over their advertising budget and to target specific keywords or phrases that are relevant to their products or services. It also allows advertisers to track and measure the effectiveness of their campaigns, as they can see how many clicks each ad receives and how much they are paying for each click. However, it is important for advertisers to carefully manage their PPC campaigns to ensure that they are getting a good return on their investment. Advertisers should regularly analyze the performance of their ads, adjust their bidding strategies, and optimize their advertisements to improve their click-through rates and conversion rates.

Pay-Per-Click (PPC)

Pay-Per-Click (PPC) is an advertising model in which advertisers pay a fee each time their ad is clicked on. It is a way of buying visits to a website rather than earning those visits organically. In a PPC campaign, advertisers bid on specific keywords or phrases relevant to their target audience. When a user enters a search query containing those keywords, the search engine displays the advertiser's ad. These ads typically appear at the top or bottom of search engine results pages (SERPs), or on websites that are part of the display network.

Pay-Per-Lead (PPL) Advertising

Pay-per-lead (PPL) advertising is a type of online marketing strategy where advertisers pay for each qualified lead generated through their ads. Unlike pay-per-click (PPC) advertising, where advertisers pay for each click on their ads, PPL advertising focuses on actual leads that are potential customers for the advertiser. In PPL advertising, the advertiser sets specific criteria for what constitutes a qualified lead. This could be a user filling out a contact form, subscribing to a newsletter, or requesting more information about a product or service. When a user meets these criteria and becomes a lead, the advertiser is charged a predetermined amount for that lead.

Pay-Per-Sale (PPS) Advertising

Pay-Per-Sale (PPS) advertising, also known as cost-per-sale (CPS) advertising, is a pricing model used in the digital advertising industry. It is a performance-based marketing strategy where advertisers only pay for advertising when a sale is made. In the PPS model, advertisers collaborate with publishers or affiliate marketers to promote their products or services. The publishers place advertisements on their websites or other digital platforms, and they are only compensated when a sale is generated through their efforts.

Pay-Per-View (PPV) Ads

Pay-Per-View (PPV) Ads are a form of online advertising that allows advertisers to present their content to a targeted audience on a pay-per-view basis. In this advertising model, advertisers pay a predetermined fee each time their ad is viewed by a user. PPV ads are typically displayed within websites, mobile apps, or video content platforms. With PPV ads, the advertiser only pays when their ad is actually viewed, providing a more cost-effective approach compared to other advertising models such as pay-per-click (PPC) or cost-per-mille (CPM). This means that advertisers have a higher level of control over their advertising budget as they only incur costs when their ads are seen by potential customers.

Pay-Per-View (PPV) Advertising

Pay-Per-View (PPV) advertising refers to a marketing strategy where advertisers pay a fee each time their advertisement is viewed by a user. It is a form of digital advertising that allows brands to reach a targeted audience and measure the success of their campaigns based on the number of views or impressions received. In the context of online advertising, PPV advertising works on a cost-per-view (CPV) model, where advertisers only pay for actual views of their ads. This is in contrast to traditional advertising models like cost-per-click (CPC) or cost-per-impression (CPM), where advertisers pay for clicks or impressions regardless of whether the user engages with the ad or not. PPV advertising typically operates through advertising networks or platforms that offer access to a large inventory of websites or apps where ads can be displayed. Advertisers can choose their target audience based on demographics, interests, or browsing behavior and bid for ad placements on relevant websites or apps. When a user visits a website or uses an app that participates in the PPV advertising network, an ad is displayed either as a pop-up, pre-roll video, or banner. The advertiser is charged only when the ad is fully loaded and displayed on the user's screen. PPV advertising offers several advantages for advertisers. Firstly, it ensures that advertisers only pay for actual views, making it a cost-effective advertising method. Secondly, it provides precise targeting options, allowing advertisers to reach their intended audience with relevant messages. Thirdly, PPV advertising allows for real-time tracking and analytics, enabling advertisers to measure the success of their campaigns and make adjustments as needed. On the other hand, PPV advertising may also face some challenges. Users, particularly those who are not interested in the ad, may quickly close the pop-up or skip the video, resulting in fewer views. Additionally, ad blockers or other software may prevent ads from being displayed, reducing the potential reach of the campaign. In conclusion, PPV advertising is a digital marketing strategy where advertisers pay a fee for each view of their ads. It offers cost-effective targeting options and real-time tracking for advertisers, while also facing challenges in capturing user attention and dealing with ad blockers.

Performance-Based Ads Analysis Metrics

Performance-based ads analysis metrics refer to the specific factors and measurements used to evaluate the effectiveness and success of advertisements, particularly those that are tied to specific performance goals or outcomes. These metrics are used to determine how well an ad campaign or individual ad is performing in terms of achieving its intended objectives, such as driving conversions, increasing brand awareness, or generating leads. By analyzing these metrics, advertisers and marketers can assess the overall performance of their ads and make data-driven decisions to optimize their advertising strategies.

Performance-Based Ads Analysis

Performance-based ads, also known as pay-per-performance ads or performance marketing, are a type of advertising where an advertiser pays only when a specific action is completed by the user. This action can include making a purchase, filling out a form, downloading an app, or any other desired conversion. The main objective of performance-based ads is to generate measurable results and a positive return on investment for the advertiser. Unlike traditional advertising methods where advertisers pay for impressions or clicks, performance-based ads focus on actual outcomes or conversions that directly impact the advertiser's bottom line.

Performance-Based Ads

Performance-Based Ads are a type of advertisement where advertisers only pay when specific actions or outcomes are achieved. This form of advertising focuses on measurable results, such as clicks, conversions, or sales, rather than simply displaying the ad to a large audience. Unlike traditional advertising models, where an advertiser pays for ad placement regardless of its effectiveness, performance-based ads allow advertisers to only pay when their desired goals are met. This could include actions such as a user clicking on the ad, signing up for a newsletter, making a purchase, or completing any other predefined action that the advertiser deems valuable.

Performance-Based Advertising Metrics

Performance-based advertising metrics refer to the set of measurements and analytics used to evaluate the effectiveness and success of advertising campaigns. These metrics provide advertisers and marketers with valuable insights and data regarding the performance of their ad campaigns, allowing them to make data-driven decisions and optimize their advertising strategies. These metrics are based on specific performance indicators or goals that are set by the advertiser and can vary depending on the specific objectives of the campaign. Some common performance-based advertising metrics include impressions, click-through rate (CTR), conversion rate, return on investment (ROI), and cost per acquisition (CPA).

Performance-Based Advertising

Performance-based advertising is a type of advertising model where advertisers pay only when certain predefined actions or goals are achieved. Unlike traditional forms of advertising where advertisers pay a fixed fee for ad placement, performance-based advertising focuses on the actual outcome or performance of the ad campaign. In performance-based advertising, advertisers typically define certain actions or goals that they want to be achieved, such as clicks, conversions, sales, or leads. These actions or goals are commonly referred to as key performance indicators (KPIs). Advertisers only pay when these KPIs are met or achieved, which makes the model more cost-effective and measurable compared to other forms of advertising.

Personalized Advertising Strategies

Personalized advertising strategies refer to the use of targeting and customization techniques in advertising campaigns to deliver highly relevant and tailored content to individual consumers. The goal of personalized advertising is to increase the effectiveness of marketing efforts by presenting advertisements that resonate with the specific interests, preferences, and needs of each consumer. By collecting and analyzing data on consumer behavior, demographics, and characteristics, advertisers can create targeted messages that are more likely to capture attention and drive action.

Personalized Advertising

Personalized advertising refers to the practice of tailoring advertisements to individual users based on their interests, preferences, and behaviors. It involves using various data points, including demographic information, browsing history, purchase history, and social media activity, to create targeted ads that are more likely to resonate with the intended audience. This type of advertising is made possible by the vast amount of data that is collected and analyzed by advertisers and marketing platforms. By leveraging this data, advertisers can create highly customized campaigns that deliver the right message to the right person at the right time.

Personalized Video Advertising Strategies Development

Personalized video advertising strategies development refers to the process of creating and implementing targeted promotional campaigns through the use of personalized videos. In this context, personalized videos refer to video content that is tailored to the specific interests, preferences, and characteristics of individual viewers. The development of personalized video advertising strategies involves several key steps. First, advertisers must gather data and insights about their target audience. This can include demographic information, browsing behavior, purchasing history, and social media activity, among other sources of information. By analyzing this data, advertisers can gain a deep understanding of their audience and identify specific segments or individuals to target with personalized videos. Next, advertisers must craft the video content itself. This involves creating videos that are relevant, engaging, and compelling to the target audience. The content should resonate with the viewers on a personal level and address their specific needs, desires, or pain points. Once the video content is created, advertisers must determine the most effective distribution channels and platforms for reaching their intended audience. This can include social media platforms, video sharing websites, email marketing campaigns, or targeted advertising networks. Advertisers must also consider factors such as optimal timing, frequency, and placement of the personalized videos to maximize their impact. During the campaign, advertisers should continuously monitor and measure the performance and effectiveness of their personalized video advertising strategies. This can involve tracking metrics such as views, click-through rates, conversions, and customer feedback. By analyzing these metrics, advertisers can identify what is working well and make adjustments or optimizations as needed to ensure the success of the campaign. In summary, personalized video advertising strategies development involves the targeted creation and distribution of video content that is tailored to the specific interests and characteristics of individual viewers. By leveraging data and insights about the target audience, advertisers can create personalized videos that resonate with viewers on a personal level, and effectively reach and engage their intended audience.

Personalized Video Advertising Strategies

Personalized video advertising strategies refer to the specific approach and tactics employed by advertisers to tailor video ads to individual viewers or target audiences. This involves using data and technology to analyze user preferences, demographics, and behaviors, and then creating and delivering personalized video content that resonates with each viewer on a one-to-one basis. These strategies aim to maximize the effectiveness of video advertisements by making them more relevant, engaging, and impactful for the intended audience. By delivering personalized messages and content, advertisers can increase the chances of capturing people's attention, generating interest, and driving desired actions such as clicks, conversions, or brand awareness.

Personalized Video Advertising

Personalized video advertising refers to the practice of creating and delivering customized video content to individual viewers based on their interests, preferences, and demographics. It involves tailoring the video message and its presentation to engage and resonate with each viewer on a personal level. In traditional advertising, the same video ad is typically shown to a large audience without considering their individual characteristics or preferences. However, personalized video advertising takes advantage of the vast amount of data available on each viewer to create a more targeted and relevant advertising experience. By analyzing data such as browsing history, purchase behavior, and social media activity, advertisers can gain insights into a viewer's interests, needs, and preferences. They can then use this information to deliver video ads that are more likely to capture the viewer's attention and drive engagement. Personalized video ads can be customized in several ways. Firstly, the content of the video can be tailored to align with the viewer's interests. For example, if a viewer has previously shown an interest in fitness products, they may be shown a video ad promoting a new line of workout gear. In addition to content, the presentation of the video can also be personalized. This can include aspects such as language, location, and the viewer's name or other personal details. For instance, a viewer located in New York City may see a video ad with local landmarks in the background, creating a sense of familiarity and relevance. The goal of personalized video advertising is to create a more engaging and impactful advertising experience for viewers. By delivering ads that are tailored to each viewer's individual interests and preferences, advertisers can increase the likelihood of capturing their attention, driving brand awareness, and ultimately, influencing their purchasing decisions.

Podcast Advertising Networks Evaluation Criteria

A podcast advertising network is a platform that connects podcasters with advertisers, facilitating the monetization of podcasts through the placement of ads. When evaluating podcast advertising networks, several criteria can be considered to ensure the effectiveness and success of advertising campaigns. One important criterion is the network's reach and audience demographics. Advertisers typically look for networks that have a wide reach and can target specific demographics that align with their target market. The size and characteristics of a network's audience can greatly impact the reach and effectiveness of an advertising campaign.

Podcast Advertising Networks Evaluation

Podcast advertising networks are platforms that facilitate the buying and selling of advertisement space within podcasts. These networks work by connecting advertisers with podcasters, allowing them to reach their target audience through the medium of recorded audio content. Podcasts have become increasingly popular in recent years, with millions of listeners tuning in to various shows on a regular basis. This has created a unique opportunity for advertisers to reach their target audience in a more personalized and engaging way. Podcast advertising networks play a crucial role in this process by providing a centralized platform for advertisers to find podcasts that align with their brand and target market. One of the key benefits of using podcast advertising networks is the ability to reach a highly engaged audience. Unlike traditional radio or television advertising, podcast listeners are often more invested in the content they are consuming. This means that they are more likely to pay attention to and retain the information delivered through podcast advertisements. Podcast advertising networks also offer advertisers the opportunity to target their ads to specific demographics or niches. This level of targeting is possible through data analysis and audience profiling. Advertisers can select podcasts that align with their target market's interests, ensuring that their message reaches the right people at the right time. Furthermore, podcast advertising networks provide advertisers with valuable analytics and reporting tools. This allows them to track the performance of their ads, measure the reach and engagement of their campaigns, and make data-driven decisions to optimize their advertising strategies. In conclusion, podcast advertising networks are instrumental in connecting advertisers with podcasters, allowing them to reach a highly engaged audience through targeted and data-driven advertising campaigns. These networks provide a centralized platform for advertisers to find the right podcasts and utilize valuable analytics tools to measure and optimize the performance of their advertisements.

Podcast Advertising Networks

A podcast advertising network refers to a service or platform that connects podcasters with advertisers, facilitating the buying and selling of advertising space within podcasts. These networks act as intermediaries between podcast creators and brands looking to reach podcast listeners with their marketing messages. Podcast advertising networks typically offer various ways for advertisers to engage with podcast audiences. They might provide options such as host-read ads, pre-roll or mid-roll placements, sponsorships, or branded content. The networks also assist podcasters in optimizing their advertising revenue by matching them with relevant brands and managing the implementation and tracking of ad placements.

Podcast Advertising

Podcast advertising refers to the practice of promoting products, services, or brands through audio content on podcasts. It involves the insertion of advertisements into podcast episodes, typically delivered by the podcast hosts or by voice actors. These advertisements are integrated into the podcast's content, creating a seamless and engaging experience for the listeners. Podcast advertising offers a unique combination of audience engagement and targeting capabilities. As podcasts have gained popularity, so has the potential for brands to reach a diverse and dedicated audience. Podcast listeners tend to be highly engaged and loyal, often tuning in for extended periods of time. This presents a valuable opportunity for advertisers to capture the attention of listeners who are more likely to be receptive to their messages.

Podcast Sponsorship Programs

Podcast Sponsorship Programs refer to the advertising initiatives in the form of sponsorships within podcasts. These programs involve a partnership between the podcast creators and a company or brand, where the brand financially supports the podcast in exchange for advertising opportunities and exposure to the podcast's audience. The primary goal of podcast sponsorship programs is to promote a brand, product, or service to a highly engaged and targeted audience. As podcasts have gained significant popularity over the years, they have become an attractive medium for advertisers looking to reach a niche demographic. In a podcast sponsorship program, the advertiser typically pays a fee to the podcast creator or network for the opportunity to have their brand mentioned or featured in the podcast's episodes. This can take various forms, including pre-roll, mid-roll, or post-roll advertisements. Pre-roll advertisements are placed at the beginning of an episode, providing the advertiser with prime visibility. Mid-roll advertisements are inserted during the middle of an episode, while post-roll advertisements appear at the end. These placements vary depending on the specific agreement between the advertiser and the podcast creator. The sponsorship can also include additional promotional opportunities, such as host-read advertisements, where the podcast host personally endorses the brand. These endorsements are often highly valued by advertisers due to the trust and rapport the hosts have built with their audience. Podcast sponsorship programs offer several benefits for advertisers. Firstly, they provide access to a loyal and engaged audience who actively tunes in to listen to specific content. This targeted nature of podcast audiences allows advertisers to reach consumers who are genuinely interested in their products or services. Additionally, podcast sponsorships allow for a longer and more intimate form of advertising. Unlike traditional commercials, podcast advertisements are seamlessly integrated into the content, making them less disruptive and more likely to be listened to by the audience. Furthermore, podcast advertising has been found to be highly effective in creating brand awareness and driving purchase intent. Studies have shown that podcast listeners are more receptive to advertising messages and are more likely to consider purchasing from brands they hear about on podcasts. In conclusion, podcast sponsorship programs serve as a valuable advertisement avenue for brands and companies. By partnering with podcast creators, advertisers can leverage the podcast's engaged audience to effectively promote their products or services. These programs provide unique advertising opportunities that are highly targeted, seamlessly integrated, and capable of driving brand awareness and purchase intent among podcast listeners.

Podcast Sponsorship

Podcast sponsorship in the context of advertisement refers to a partnership between a company or brand and a podcast, where the company provides financial support in exchange for the podcast promoting its products or services. This type of advertising allows businesses to reach a targeted audience of listeners who are interested in specific topics or industries. Podcast sponsorship can take various forms, such as pre-roll, mid-roll, or post-roll advertisements. Pre-roll ads are played at the beginning of an episode, mid-roll ads are inserted during the episode, and post-roll ads are played at the end. These ads typically include a brief message from the sponsor, which may promote their products, services, or brand image.

Point-Of-Purchase (POP) Advertising

Point-of-Purchase (POP) Advertising refers to a marketing technique where advertisements are strategically placed at the point of purchase or point of sale, typically at retail locations. The purpose of POP advertising is to attract customers' attention, increase brand visibility, and ultimately drive sales at the point of purchase. This type of advertising is designed to influence consumers' purchasing decisions by providing information or incentives to make a specific purchase. POP advertisements are usually displayed near the checkout counter or in high-traffic areas of a retail store, such as aisle end caps or product displays.

Political Advertising Campaigns

Political advertising campaigns refer to strategic efforts made by political candidates, parties, or interest groups to influence public perceptions and sway voter opinions in order to gain support and win elections. These campaigns typically involve the creation and dissemination of advertisements across various media channels to convey political messages and promote desired political outcomes. Political advertisements are designed to reach a wide audience and employ various persuasive techniques to shape public sentiment, mobilize voters, and shape the narrative surrounding particular political issues or individuals. These campaigns often leverage emotional appeals, graphic visuals, catchy slogans, and compelling storytelling to make their messages resonate with the target audience. In the modern era, political advertising campaigns have expanded beyond traditional mediums such as television, radio, and print to encompass digital platforms and social media. Online advertisements, email marketing, social media posts, and influencer endorsements have become key components of political campaigns, allowing for wider reach, targeted messaging, and real-time engagement with voters and potential supporters. Political advertising campaigns typically include both positive and negative messaging. Positive advertisements highlight a candidate's accomplishments, policy proposals, or positive attributes, seeking to create a favorable image. Negative advertisements, on the other hand, aim to discredit opponents, question their credibility, or highlight potential weaknesses or controversial stances. These contrasting approaches are intended to influence public perception and shape voter attitudes. Regulations governing political advertising campaigns vary across jurisdictions, with laws dictating the disclosure of funding sources, spending limits, and the accuracy of claims made in advertisements. Some countries, for instance, require disclaimers identifying who funded the advertisement to improve transparency and inform viewers of potential biases. Violations of these regulations can carry legal

201

consequences, underscoring the importance of adhering to the legal framework governing political campaign ads.

Political Advertising

Political advertising refers to the promotional efforts made by political parties, candidates, or interest groups to influence public opinion and garner support for their political agendas. It is a form of communication aimed at persuading voters to vote for a particular candidate or party, or to support a specific political issue or ideology. Political advertising can take various forms, such as television and radio commercials, print advertisements, online banners, social media posts, and direct mail campaigns. These advertisements typically highlight the strengths and achievements of a candidate or party while disparaging their opponents, often through the use of persuasive language, emotional appeals, and sometimes misleading or exaggerated claims. One of the main goals of political advertising is to shape public perception and create a favorable image for a candidate or party. This is often achieved by emphasizing their achievements, leadership qualities, and policy proposals, with the aim of instilling confidence and trust in the minds of voters. Political advertisements also play a crucial role in building name recognition and increasing awareness among the electorate, particularly in highly competitive races or for lesser-known candidates. Moreover, political advertising serves as a platform for candidates and parties to communicate their policy positions, address current issues, and rally support for their initiatives. They use these advertisements to convey their stance on various topics, such as the economy, healthcare, education, national security, and social issues, in order to attract voters who resonate with those positions. While political advertising is a common practice during election campaigns, it is not without controversy. Critics argue that political advertisements often prioritize style over substance, relying on emotional appeals and soundbites rather than providing voters with detailed policy information. Moreover, some critics believe that political advertising contributes to the overall polarization and negative tone of political discourse, as candidates and parties seek to cast their opponents in a negative light. In conclusion, political advertising plays a significant role in the political landscape, serving as a means for candidates and parties to promote themselves, shape public opinion, and rally support. It can be a powerful tool for engaging and persuading voters, but it also raises questions about the ethics and impact of marketing tactics in the realm of politics.

Political Campaign Advertising Planning Strategies

Political campaign advertising planning strategies refer to the methods and approaches used to effectively create and execute advertising campaigns for political candidates or parties. These strategies are designed to reach and influence target audiences, convey key messages, and ultimately persuade voters to support a particular candidate or party. One important aspect of advertising planning strategies is identifying and defining the target audience. This involves conducting research and analysis to understand the demographics, interests, and concerns of the electorate. By knowing the characteristics of the target audience, campaigns can tailor their messages and media placement to resonate with potential voters. Another key element of planning strategies is message development. Political campaigns need to define their platform and position on various issues. They must craft compelling messages that differentiate them from their opponents and resonate with voters. These messages should be concise, clear, and memorable, aiming to evoke an emotional response or tap into the values and beliefs of the target audience. Once the messages are established, campaigns must determine the most effective channels and mediums to reach their target audience. This includes traditional media such as television, radio, newspapers, and direct mail, as well as digital platforms like social media, websites, and online ads. Strategic media planning ensures that ads are placed in locations and formats that maximize exposure and impact. In addition to media placement, timing is crucial in campaign advertising planning strategies. Campaigns need to determine the optimal timing for releasing ads to maximize their influence. This may involve launching ads during specific events, key moments in the campaign calendar, or in response to competing ads or news cycles. Measuring and evaluating the effectiveness of advertising is another critical aspect of planning strategies. Campaigns utilize metrics such as reach, frequency, and response rates to assess the impact of their ads. This helps them make data-driven decisions on adjustments or refinements to their advertising approach, ensuring that resources are allocated efficiently. In summary, political campaign advertising planning strategies involve identifying the target audience, developing compelling messages, selecting appropriate media channels, timing ad releases strategically, and evaluating the effectiveness of ads. By employing effective planning strategies, political campaigns can increase their chances of persuading voters and achieving their electoral objectives.

Political Campaign Advertising Planning

Political campaign advertising planning refers to the strategic process of developing and implementing advertising campaigns to support a political candidate or cause. It involves careful consideration of the target audience, message, media channels, and budget to effectively reach and persuade voters. The planning stage of political campaign advertising is crucial in order to create a well-rounded and impactful campaign. It begins with research and analysis to identify the target audience and understand their demographics, interests, and concerns. This information helps in crafting a message that resonates with the intended audience and addresses their needs and aspirations. Once the target audience is defined, the next step is to develop a compelling message. This message should be concise, focused, and memorable. It should highlight the candidate's strengths, achievements, and policy positions, while also effectively countering any opposition or criticism. The goal is to present a consistent and positive image of the candidate or cause throughout the campaign. After establishing the message, the planning process moves on to determining the most effective media channels to deliver the campaign's message. This may include television commercials, radio ads, print advertisements, direct mail, online advertising, or a combination of these formats. The choice of media channels depends on factors such as the target audience's media consumption habits, budget constraints, and the reach and impact of each medium. The budgeting phase of campaign advertising planning is essential to ensure the efficient allocation of resources. It involves estimating the costs associated with developing and airing advertisements, as well as any additional expenses such as production, research, and tracking. Setting a realistic budget helps prevent overspending and ensures that the campaign can reach as many voters as possible within the allocated resources. Overall, political campaign advertising planning aims to create a strategic and impactful advertising campaign that effectively communicates the candidate's message to the target audience. It involves thorough research, careful message development, thoughtful media selection, and efficient budget allocation. By leveraging these elements, campaigns can increase their visibility, influence voter opinions, and ultimately drive support for the candidate or cause.

Political Campaign Advertising

Political Campaign Advertising refers to the use of advertising tactics and strategies to promote a political candidate or party and persuade voters to support their campaign. It is a form of communication that aims to influence public opinion and shape voter behavior. Political campaign ads can take various forms, including television and radio commercials, print ads in newspapers and magazines, online advertisements, direct mail, and even billboards. These ads typically highlight the candidate's qualifications, policy positions, achievements, and vision for the future. They may also attack opponents, criticize their policies, or question their suitability for office.

Poster Advertising Campaigns Execution Steps

Poster advertising campaigns execution steps refer to the systematic process of designing, creating, and implementing a series of posters with the aim of promoting a product, service, event, or brand. These steps ensure that the campaign is effective, visually appealing, and reaches the target audience.The first step in executing a poster advertising campaign is defining the campaign objective. This involves determining what the campaign aims to achieve, whether it is to increase brand awareness, drive sales, or promote an event. Once the objective is established, the next step is to identify the target audience. Understanding who the posters are intended to reach is crucial for crafting effective messages and visuals.After defining the objective and target audience, the campaign message and visuals need to be developed. This step involves brainstorming, conceptualizing, and creating a compelling message that aligns with the campaign's objective. The visuals, including images, graphics, and typography, should be chosen carefully to attract attention and effectively convey the message.Once the message and visuals are finalized, the design process begins. This involves creating the layout, selecting the color scheme, and arranging the elements on the poster. The design should be visually appealing, easy to read, and consistent with the brand's visual identity.After the design is completed, it is time to produce the posters. This may involve printing the posters in various sizes or formats, depending on where they will be displayed. Quality printing is essential to ensure clear, vibrant, and durable posters that can effectively communicate the message.Once the posters are produced, distribution and display come into play. The posters need to be strategically placed in locations where the target audience is likely to see them. This may include billboards, bus stops, community centers, or other high-traffic areas. Effective distribution and display maximize the campaign's reach and visibility.Finally, it is crucial to monitor and evaluate the campaign's performance. This involves tracking metrics such as reach, engagement, and conversion rates to assess the campaign's effectiveness. Monitoring allows for adjustments and optimization throughout the campaign period to improve results.In conclusion, executing a poster advertising campaign involves defining the objective, identifying the target audience, developing the message and visuals, designing the posters, producing them, distributing and displaying them strategically, and monitoring and evaluating the campaign's performance.

Poster Advertising Campaigns

Poster advertising campaigns are a form of advertisement that utilizes posters to promote a product, service, event, or brand. Posters are typically large printed sheets that display a visually appealing layout with concise and persuasive messages that aim to grab the attention of the audience and convey the desired marketing message. These campaigns are designed to create awareness, generate interest, and ultimately persuade the target audience to take a desired action, such as making a purchase, attending an event, or supporting a cause. Posters are effective in reaching a wide audience as they can be strategically placed in various locations, such as public spaces, shopping centers, bus stops, and train stations, ensuring maximum visibility. The key objective of a poster advertising campaign is to effectively communicate the marketing message in a visually engaging and memorable way. The design elements of the poster, such as colors, typography, images, and layout, play a crucial role in capturing attention and conveying the intended message. The use of bold graphics, captivating visuals, and catchy taglines or slogans are common strategies employed in poster advertising campaigns. Furthermore, poster advertising campaigns often incorporate creative concepts and storytelling techniques to create an emotional connection with the audience. By appealing to their emotions, advertisers aim to leave a lasting impact and encourage a positive response. For example, a poster promoting a charity organization may showcase images of people in need, evoking empathy and inspiring viewers to donate or get involved. The success of a poster advertising campaign relies on several factors, including the target audience, the message being conveyed, and the effectiveness of the design. These campaigns must be carefully planned, taking into consideration the demographics, preferences, and behaviors of the intended audience. Additionally, the poster should clearly communicate the key benefits or unique selling points of the product, service, or event being promoted. In conclusion, poster advertising campaigns are a powerful tool for marketers to reach and engage a wide audience. By utilizing visually appealing designs, concise messages, and strategic placement, these campaigns aim to capture attention, generate interest, and drive desired actions. Effective poster advertising campaigns have the ability to leave a lasting impression and create a positive association between the audience and the advertised brand or idea.

Poster Advertising

Poster advertising refers to the use of posters as a visual medium for promoting a product, service, or event. It is a form of advertisement that involves creating and displaying posters in strategic locations to attract the attention of potential customers or audience. The primary purpose of poster advertising is to communicate a message quickly and effectively to a large audience. Posters typically feature eye-catching visuals, bold typography, and concise copy to capture attention and convey key information. They are designed to be visually appealing and visually impactful to make a lasting impression on viewers. Poster advertising can be used in various contexts, including commercial advertising, political campaigns, social awareness campaigns, and event promotions. It is commonly seen on billboards, walls, notice boards, and other public spaces where it can reach a wide range of people. Posters can also be distributed directly to specific target audiences or displayed in indoor spaces like shopping malls or exhibition halls. One of the advantages of poster advertising is its cost-effectiveness. Compared to other forms of advertising like television or radio commercials, posters are relatively inexpensive to produce and distribute. They can be printed in large quantities at a lower cost, allowing businesses or organizations to reach a broader audience without breaking the bank. Another benefit of poster advertising is its reach and visibility. By strategically placing posters in high-traffic areas or locations where the target audience is likely to be present, advertisers can maximize the exposure of their message. Posters have the potential to reach a large number of people, even those who may not actively seek out advertising messages. However, poster advertising also has its limitations. Posters rely heavily on visual elements, which means they may not be accessible to individuals with visual impairments. Additionally, posters have limited space for conveying information, so advertisers must carefully choose concise and impactful messages to capture viewers' attention and interest. Furthermore, there is no guarantee that all individuals who see the poster will respond to the message or take the desired action. In conclusion, poster advertising is a visual form of advertisement that uses posters to communicate messages to a large audience. It is a cost-effective and visually impactful way to promote products, services, events, or causes. By strategically placing posters in high-traffic areas, businesses and organizations can maximize the reach and visibility of their message. However, it is essential to consider the limitations of poster advertising, such as its reliance on visual elements and limited space for conveying information.

Pre-Roll Ads Creation

Pre-Roll Ads Creation refers to the process of developing and producing promotional video advertisements that are displayed to viewers before the main video content. These ads are commonly used in digital advertising campaigns and are primarily seen on online video platforms, such as YouTube and social media sites. The creation of pre-roll ads involves several steps and considerations. The first step is brainstorming and developing a creative concept that aligns with the brand's marketing objectives. This includes identifying the target audience, understanding their preferences, and crafting a message that resonates with them. Once the concept is finalized, the next step is scriptwriting. The script should be concise, engaging, and deliver the key message effectively within a short time frame, usually between 15 to 30 seconds. It should grab the viewer's attention immediately and encourage them to take action or develop interest in the product or service being promoted. After the script is written, the pre-roll ad goes into the production phase. This involves hiring actors or voice-over artists, recording the audio, and shooting or animating the visuals. The production should reflect the brand's identity and maintain a high level of professionalism to enhance the ad's effectiveness. Once the production is completed, the ad goes into the editing phase. This involves trimming unnecessary footage, adding special effects or graphics, and optimizing the ad for various platforms and screen sizes. Additionally, music or sound effects may be added to enhance the overall appeal and create a cohesive experience for the viewer. Finally, the pre-roll ad is ready for distribution. It can be uploaded directly to platforms like YouTube or shared with ad networks for wider reach. Advertisers can also target specific demographics or interests to ensure the ad is shown to the most relevant viewers, increasing the likelihood of engagement and conversion. In conclusion, pre-roll ads creation encompasses the process of developing video advertisements that are displayed before main video content. It involves conceptualizing, scriptwriting, production, editing, and distribution to effectively engage viewers and achieve marketing objectives.

Pre-Roll Ads

Pre-roll ads are a type of online advertisement that appear before the selected content is played, such as video or audio. These ads have become increasingly popular due to the rise of digital platforms and online streaming services. Pre-roll ads are typically short in duration, usually ranging from a few seconds to a minute. They are designed to capture the viewer's attention and deliver a targeted message or promotion. These ads are usually skippable after a certain period, such as five seconds, allowing the viewer to proceed to the content if they are not interested. Non-skippable pre-roll ads, on the other hand, do not provide an option to skip and force the viewer to watch the entire ad.

Product Placement In Film Strategies Development

Product placement in film refers to the practice of incorporating branded products or services into movies as a form of advertising. It is a strategic marketing technique used by companies to promote their offerings by associating them with popular films, characters, or celebrities. The placement of these products can be explicit or subtle, ranging from displaying logos and brand names prominently to featuring products as integral parts of the storyline. The development of product placement strategies in films involves careful planning and coordination between advertisers, filmmakers, and production companies. Advertisers identify suitable movies that align with their target audience and brand image. They analyze the film's genre, storyline, and audience demographics to ensure compatibility with their product. The chosen movies may vary from big-budget blockbusters to independent films, depending on the desired reach and target market. Once the films are selected, advertisers negotiate contracts and agreements with the production companies. This involves determining the placement's duration, positioning, and prominence within the movie. Advertisers may also provide financial support to the film production in exchange for exclusive or extensive product placement opportunities. The agreements define the rights and obligations of both parties, ensuring the appropriate representation of the brands on screen. During the filmmaking process, cooperation between advertisers and the production team is essential. Advertisers may work closely with set decorators, prop masters, or costume designers to ensure proper integration of the products into the movie's visual elements. This collaboration also ensures that the placement does not disrupt the coherence of the film or feel forced to the audience. Product placement in film offers several advantages to advertisers. Firstly, it allows for a strategic placement of products in a highly engaging and immersive environment. Films often evoke strong emotional responses from viewers, increasing the chances of brand recall and recognition. Additionally, product placement enables advertisers to reach a wide and diverse audience, including those who may actively avoid traditional advertising formats. Overall, product placement in film is a powerful advertising tool that leverages the popularity and influence of movies to promote brands and products. When executed effectively, it seamlessly integrates branded offerings into the cinematic experience, providing mutual benefits to advertisers, filmmakers, and viewers alike.

Product Placement In Film Strategies

Product placement in film refers to the practice of featuring branded products or services in movies or television shows for promotional purposes. It involves the strategic integration of products into the narrative of a film, aiming to create brand awareness, enhance brand image, and influence consumer behavior. This form of advertising blends seamlessly with the storyline, immersing the audience in a world where the featured products become part of the characters' lives. The main objective of product placement is to expose the audience to branded products or services in an organic and non-intrusive way. By associating products with popular movies or TV shows, advertisers hope to tap into the emotional connection viewers develop with the characters and their stories. This connection can subconsciously influence consumer behavior and create a desire to own or use the featured products.

Product Placement In Film

Product Placement in film refers to the strategic placement of branded products, services, or logos within the content of a film or television program, with the intent of promoting and advertising those products to the audience. It is a form of subliminal advertising that aims to influence consumer behavior by integrating products seamlessly into the narrative or visual elements of a film. Product Placement has become a common practice in the film industry, as it allows companies to gain exposure and generate brand awareness in a non-intrusive manner. By featuring their products within popular films or television shows, advertisers can reach a wide audience and tap into the emotional connection that viewers have with the characters and storylines.

Product Placement

Product placement refers to the marketing strategy in which products or brands are incorporated into media content such as movies, television shows, music videos, or video games to promote or advertise them. It involves the intentional integration of products within the storyline or visual elements of the content, aiming to create a subtle and immersive advertising experience for the audience. This form of advertising is a direct result of the increasing commercialization of media and the need for brands to find new and creative ways to reach their target consumers. Unlike traditional advertisement formats where products are showcased explicitly through commercials or commercials, product placement seeks to integrate brands more seamlessly into the content, blurring the line between advertising and entertainment. By strategically placing products within popular media, advertisers can effectively reach a wide and diverse audience, leveraging the popularity and influence of the content and its associated characters or celebrities. Product placement is especially prevalent in the entertainment industry, with movies and television shows often featuring prominent placements of specific products or brands that are relevant to the storyline or the character's image. While product placement can be an effective advertising strategy, it poses challenges in terms of maintaining transparency and the potential for ethical concerns. It is important for viewers to be aware that the integration of products within the content is a deliberate marketing technique and not an organic part of the story. Various regulations and guidelines exist to ensure transparency in product placement, such as requiring the disclosure of placements during the credits or through on-screen notifications. Moreover, the success of product placement relies heavily on the audience's acceptance and receptiveness to the integration of brands within the content. If done poorly or in an intrusive manner, it can disrupt the viewing experience and evoke negative responses from viewers, potentially affecting the brand's image. Therefore, careful and strategic planning is crucial to ensure that the integration of products aligns seamlessly with the story and enhances the overall viewer experience without overshadowing it.

Programmatic Ad Buying Platforms Assessment

Programmatic ad buying platforms, in the context of advertising, refer to tech-driven online platforms that automate the process of buying and selling digital ad inventory. These platforms use algorithms and data science to streamline the buying and selling of advertisements in real-time auctions. With programmatic ad buying platforms, advertisers can define their targeting criteria, such as demographics, interests, and browsing behavior. The platforms then use this information to find the most relevant ad inventory available across multiple websites and apps. The entire process is automated, allowing advertisers to reach their desired audience at scale.

Programmatic Ad Buying Platforms

A programmatic ad buying platform refers to a technology-powered tool or system used in the advertising industry to automate and optimize the process of purchasing digital advertising space. These platforms enable advertisers and agencies to buy ad inventory across multiple websites, apps, and other digital platforms in a more efficient and targeted manner. The main purpose of programmatic ad buying platforms is to streamline the purchasing process by removing the need for manual negotiations and direct communication between buyers and sellers. Instead, these platforms use data-driven algorithms and real-time bidding to match the right ad to the right audience at the right time.

Programmatic Ad Buying

Programmatic ad buying is the automated process of buying and selling digital advertising space. It involves the use of technology and algorithms to target specific audiences, optimize ad placements, and effectively manage advertising campaigns across multiple platforms. In programmatic ad buying, advertisers can purchase ad inventory in real-time through an auction-based system. This allows advertisers to reach their intended audience with precision, as the process takes into account various data points such as demographics, browsing behavior, and interests. This data-driven approach eliminates the need for manual negotiations and allows for more efficient and cost-effective ad buying.

Programmatic Advertising

Programmatic advertising refers to the use of automated technology and algorithms to buy and sell advertising space in real-time. It utilizes software and data to target specific audiences and deliver relevant advertisements, rather than relying on manual processes. Traditional advertising methods typically involve negotiation between advertisers and publishers, where ad space is bought and sold based on predetermined rates. This process can be time-consuming and inefficient, often resulting in less effective targeting and potentially lower return on investment for advertisers. Programmatic advertising streamlines this process by leveraging data and technology to make real-time decisions about which ad space to buy and at what price. It allows advertisers to reach their target audience more effectively by using advanced targeting options such as demographic information, browsing behavior, and location data.Programmatic advertising is made possible through the use of demand-side platforms (DSPs) and supply-side platforms (SSPs). DSPs enable advertisers to set their targeting criteria and bid on ad impressions across multiple publishers. SSPs, on the other hand, enable publishers to make their ad inventory available to multiple buyers through automated auctions.Programmatic advertising offers several advantages over traditional advertising methods, including improved targeting accuracy, increased efficiency, and real-time ad optimization. With programmatic advertising, advertisers can reach their target audience at the right time and in the right context, which can result in higher conversion rates and better overall campaign performance.Overall, programmatic advertising revolutionizes the way advertising is bought and sold, providing advertisers with greater control and efficiency, and publishers with increased monetization opportunities. It continues to evolve and innovate, with advancements in machine learning and artificial intelligence further enhancing its capabilities and effectiveness.

Programmatic Display Advertising Platforms

A programmatic display advertising platform is a technology solution that allows advertisers to buy ad inventory across a variety of websites and apps automatically, using algorithms and real-time bidding. These platforms use data and targeting capabilities to help advertisers reach their desired audience and optimize their campaigns for maximum impact. The main goal of programmatic display advertising platforms is to make the process of buying and managing digital advertising more efficient and effective. Instead of manually negotiating and buying ad placements on individual websites, advertisers can use these platforms to streamline the process and reach a larger and more targeted audience.

Programmatic Display Advertising

Programmatic display advertising refers to the automated buying and selling of ad space on websites through the use of artificial intelligence (AI) and real-time bidding (RTB) technologies. It allows advertisers to target specific audiences and deliver ads in a more efficient and precise manner. Programmatic display advertising works by using data-driven algorithms to identify potential customers based on their online behavior, demographics, and interests. Advertisers can define their target audience by selecting various targeting options such as age, gender, location, and interests. These algorithms then analyze the available ad inventory in real-time and determine the best placement for the ad based on factors like relevance, bid price, and available budget.

Programmatic Video Advertising Platforms

Programmatic video advertising platforms are technological tools that facilitate the buying and selling of video ad space in an automated and data-driven manner. These platforms utilize algorithms and machine learning to optimize ad placements and target specific audience segments. Programmatic video advertising platforms offer a wide range of features and capabilities to advertisers and publishers. Advertisers can access a vast inventory of video ad slots across various websites, apps, and streaming platforms, allowing them to reach a large and diverse audience. These platforms enable precise targeting based on demographic, geographic, and behavioral data, ensuring that ads are displayed to the most relevant viewers. These platforms also provide advanced analytics and reporting tools that give advertisers insights into the performance of their video ads. Advertisers can track metrics such as impressions, clicks, viewability, conversions, and engagement, allowing them to optimize their campaigns in real-time. Additionally, programmatic video advertising platforms often offer integration with third-party measurement and verification tools to ensure transparency and accuracy in ad measurement. For publishers, programmatic video advertising platforms offer a streamlined process for managing and monetizing video ad inventory. These platforms enable publishers to set their pricing and ad placement rules, providing them with control over their monetization strategy. Publishers can also leverage the platform's optimization algorithms to maximize their revenue by filling empty ad slots with the most valuable ads. In summary, programmatic video advertising platforms revolutionize the way video ads are bought and sold. By leveraging automation, data, and analytics, these platforms enable advertisers to reach the right audience at the right time while providing publishers with efficient monetization solutions.

Programmatic Video Advertising

Programmatic Video Advertising refers to the process of buying and selling video ad space in an automated and data-driven manner. It involves the use of algorithms and software to target specific audiences and deliver personalized video advertisements across various digital platforms. The programmatic approach to video advertising offers advertisers more control and efficiency in reaching their target audience. It allows them to define their campaign objectives, target specific demographics, and allocate their budget more effectively. This is achieved through the use of real-time data and artificial intelligence, which help advertisers identify and engage with the right audience at the right time. One key advantage of programmatic video advertising is its ability to deliver ads in a non-disruptive way. By leveraging user data and behavioral insights, advertisers can serve video ads that are relevant and tailored to the viewer's interests and preferences. This reduces the chances of ad fatigue and improves the overall user experience. Another benefit of programmatic video advertising is its flexibility and scalability. Advertisers can easily adjust their campaigns in real-time, based on the performance and audience response. They can optimize their targeting, creative elements, and placements to ensure maximum reach and engagement. Additionally, programmatic video advertising provides detailed analytics and reporting that give advertisers valuable insights into the effectiveness of their campaigns. They can track key metrics such as impressions, click-through rates, and conversions, and use this data to continuously refine and optimize their ad strategies. In conclusion, programmatic video advertising revolutionizes the traditional ad-buying process by using automation, data, and AI to deliver highly targeted and personalized video ads. It offers advertisers greater control, efficiency, and scalability in reaching their target audience. By delivering non-disruptive ads that are relevant to viewers, programmatic video advertising enhances the user experience and maximizes campaign effectiveness.

Promotional Advertising

Promotional advertising refers to a marketing strategy that aims to attract and encourage customers to purchase a particular product or service through various communication channels. This form of advertisement typically highlights the benefits, features, and unique selling points of the product or service, with the ultimate goal of driving sales and increasing brand awareness. Promotional advertising can take many forms, including television commercials, radio spots, print advertisements, online banners, social media posts, and email campaigns. The key characteristic of this type of advertising is its explicit focus on generating immediate action from consumers, such as making a purchase or signing up for a service.

Public Relations (PR)

Public Relations (PR) in the context of advertisement refers to the strategic communication process aimed at building and maintaining a positive image and reputation for a company or brand. It involves managing the spread of information between an organization and its target audience, with the ultimate goal of influencing public perception and behavior in a favorable way. PR professionals employ various tactics and techniques to effectively convey key messages and shape public opinion. They work closely with media outlets, such as newspapers, magazines, television, and online platforms, to secure coverage and generate positive publicity. This can be achieved through press releases, interviews, feature stories, and other forms of media exposure. Additionally, PR professionals also engage in reputation management, which involves monitoring and responding to public opinions and concerns on platforms such as social media. By proactively addressing issues and maintaining an open line of communication, they strive to protect and enhance the reputation of the brand or company. Moreover, PR campaigns often include event planning and execution. This may involve organizing product launches, press conferences, sponsorship opportunities, or charity initiatives. Through these events, PR professionals aim to create meaningful connections with the target audience and generate positive brand associations. Furthermore, PR plays a crucial role in crisis communication. In the event of a negative incident or controversy, PR professionals are responsible for managing the organization's response and mitigating damage to its reputation. By providing timely and transparent communication, they strive to rebuild trust and maintain stakeholders' confidence. In summary, Public Relations (PR) in the context of advertisement is a strategic communication process that aims to build and maintain a positive image and reputation for a company or brand. It involves managing the spread of information, engaging with media outlets, conducting reputation management, organizing events, and addressing crisis situations. By effectively utilizing these PR tactics, organizations can enhance their brand image, shape public opinion, and ultimately achieve their marketing and advertising goals.

Public Service Advertising Initiatives

Public Service Advertising Initiatives refer to advertisements and campaigns created with the intention of promoting public welfare, societal change, or raising awareness about important issues. Unlike conventional advertisements which aim to promote products or services, public service advertising initiatives are focused on providing information, education, and encouraging positive behavioral changes among the general public. These initiatives are typically sponsored by government agencies, non-profit organizations, corporations, or media outlets, with the goal of addressing a wide range of social, environmental, and health concerns. The primary objective is to create public awareness and encourage individuals to take action or adopt behaviors that contribute to the betterment of society as a whole.

Public Service Advertising

Public Service Advertising, also known as PSA, is a form of advertisement that aims to promote public welfare and educate the general public about important social issues. Unlike commercial advertising that promotes products or services for the benefit of a particular business or organization, public service advertising focuses on benefiting society as a whole. PSAs are typically created by government agencies, non-profit organizations, or foundations and are aired or published through various media channels such as television, radio, print, outdoor billboards, and online platforms. They are designed to grab the attention of the target audience and convey a specific message or call to action related to a social cause. One of the main purposes of public service advertising is to raise awareness about critical issues that affect communities and individuals. These issues can include health and safety concerns, environmental protection, poverty alleviation, human rights, anti-drug campaigns, road safety, and much more. By bringing attention to these topics, PSAs aim to inspire positive behavioral changes and promote social responsibility. Public service advertisements often employ emotionally appealing storytelling techniques to engage the audience and evoke empathy or a sense of urgency. They may feature real-life scenarios, testimonials, or thought-provoking visual elements to create a lasting impact on viewers or listeners. The messaging in PSAs is usually straightforward, aiming to inform, motivate, or educate individuals about a particular issue. Furthermore, public service advertising plays a crucial role in mobilizing support and resources for non-profit organizations and charities. By promoting their mission, values, and activities, PSAs seek to encourage the public to donate money, volunteer their time, or get involved in community initiatives. They aim to inspire empathy, compassion, and a sense of social responsibility in order to foster a more compassionate and caring society. In conclusion, public service advertising is an important tool for promoting social causes, raising awareness, and motivating positive change. Through creatively crafted messages, PSAs strive to make a lasting impact on individuals, communities, and society as a whole. By leveraging the power of media and targeting specific audiences, public service advertising holds the potential to make a significant difference in addressing important societal issues.

Public Service Announcements (PSAs) Planning

Public Service Announcements (PSAs) are short advertisements or messages that are meant to inform, educate, or raise awareness about important social issues, causes, or public health and safety concerns. These announcements are typically broadcasted on various media platforms, including television, radio, print, and online channels, with the aim of reaching a wide audience. The main purpose of PSAs is to promote and encourage positive social change by delivering important messages that can benefit individuals, communities, or society as a whole. They are usually created and disseminated by governmental agencies, non-profit organizations, or other entities that have a vested interest in addressing specific social concerns or issues. PSAs are known for their concise and impactful nature, often using persuasive techniques to capture audience attention and provoke a response. They may employ a variety of creative elements, such as storytelling, visual imagery, emotional appeals, or celebrity endorsements, to effectively communicate the intended message. The content of PSAs can range from addressing public health concerns (e.g., anti-smoking campaigns, promoting vaccination), raising awareness about

210

social issues (e.g., fighting discrimination, combating climate change), encouraging community engagement (e.g., volunteering, voting), or promoting safety practices (e.g., seatbelt usage, fire prevention). PSAs are meant to inform and educate the public, aiming to create awareness about specific topics and encourage individuals to take action or adopt certain behaviors that promote social well-being. They serve as reminders and catalysts for change, motivating individuals to make informed decisions or participate in activities that can contribute to the betterment of society. By utilizing various media channels and reaching a broad audience, PSAs have the potential to influence public opinion, challenge established norms, and drive collective action towards a common goal. In conclusion, PSAs play a crucial role in raising awareness, educating the public, and promoting positive social change. Through their impactful messages and creative delivery, they serve as powerful tools for addressing social concerns, inspiring action, and fostering a more informed and engaged society.

Public Service Announcements (PSAs)

A Public Service Announcement (PSA) is a short, informative advertisement created by a non-profit organization or government agency with the aim of promoting public welfare or raising awareness about important social issues. Unlike commercial advertisements that aim to sell products or promote a particular brand, PSAs focus on imparting information or delivering important messages to the public. They are typically broadcasted on television, radio, or other media platforms, and are often created with the intention of benefiting society as a whole.

Radio Ad Production Management Techniques

Radio ad production management techniques refer to the strategies and processes used to effectively plan, organize, and execute the production of radio advertisements. These techniques are essential for ensuring that radio ads are created and delivered successfully, reaching the intended target audience and achieving the desired marketing objectives. One key technique in radio ad production management is the development of a comprehensive production plan. This involves identifying the objectives of the radio ad campaign, conducting research on the target audience, and determining the key message and tone of the advertisement. The production plan outlines the timeline, budget, and resources required for the project, helping to ensure that all aspects of the production process are properly coordinated and executed. Effective communication and collaboration are critical in radio ad production management. This involves working closely with the creative team, including writers, voiceover artists, and sound engineers, to develop and refine the concept and script for the radio ad. Clear and regular communication with stakeholders, such as the client or advertising agency, is also important to ensure that expectations are managed and feedback is incorporated throughout the production process. Utilizing appropriate project management tools and techniques is another essential aspect of radio ad production management. This includes creating a production schedule, assigning tasks and responsibilities, and monitoring progress to ensure that deadlines are met. Regular meetings, both with the internal production team and any external stakeholders, can help to track progress, address any issues, and make necessary adjustments to the production plan. Quality control and attention to detail are also paramount in radio ad production management. This involves reviewing and revising the script and storyboard, overseeing the recording and editing process to ensure high-quality audio, and conducting thorough checks for any errors or omissions. Adherence to industry regulations and standards, such as ensuring compliance with broadcasting guidelines and legal requirements, is also essential. In conclusion, radio ad production management techniques encompass a range of strategies and processes aimed at effectively planning, organizing, and executing radio advertisements. By utilizing comprehensive production plans, fostering clear communication and collaboration, employing project management tools, and maintaining a focus on quality control, radio ad production can be successfully managed, resulting in impactful and engaging advertisements that effectively reach the target audience.

Radio Ad Production Management

Radio ad production management refers to the process of overseeing the creation, planning, and execution of radio advertisements. This involves managing various aspects of the production, such as scriptwriting, voice talent selection, sound design, and post-production editing. The role of radio ad production management begins with the initial concept development. This includes collaborating with clients or advertising agencies to understand their goals, target audience, and desired messaging. The production manager works closely with the creative team to come up with a compelling script that effectively communicates the intended message and captures the listener's attention. Once the script is finalized, the production manager coordinates the selection of voice talent. This involves finding the right voice to match the brand image and target audience. The manager may work with professional voice actors or utilize in-house resources, depending on the budget and requirements of the project. In addition to voice talent, the production manager oversees the sound design elements of the radio ad. This includes selecting appropriate music, sound effects, and creating a cohesive audio experience that enhances the message. The manager ensures that the sound design aligns with the desired emotions and atmosphere of the advertisement. After the voice recording and sound design are complete, the production manager takes on the role of post-production editing. This involves fine-tuning the audio, ensuring smooth transitions, removing any background noise, and optimizing the overall quality of the advertisement. The manager ensures that the final edited version meets the client's specifications and aligns with industry standards. Throughout the production process, the radio ad production manager collaborates with various stakeholders, including clients, creative teams, voice talent, sound engineers, and post-production editors. They effectively communicate and coordinate all aspects of the production to ensure a seamless and successful radio ad campaign.

Radio Ad Production

A radio ad production refers to the process of creating and producing an advertisement specifically designed to be played on the radio. Radio ads are audio-based and utilize sound and voiceovers to convey a message or promote a product or service. The production of a radio ad involves several essential steps. The first step is concept development, where the advertising team brainstorm ideas and concepts for the ad. They consider the target audience, the desired message, and the overall goal of the advertisement. Once a concept is agreed upon, the scriptwriting process begins. The script is the written content of the radio ad and serves as the blueprint for the production. It includes dialogue, sound effects, and any music or jingles that will be incorporated. The script is carefully crafted to capture the audience's attention and effectively communicate the intended message within a specified timeframe. After the script is finalized, the next step is voiceover casting. The advertising team selects professional voice actors or announcers whose voices align with the tone and style of the ad. A voiceover session is then scheduled, during which the actors record their lines in a professional studio. The recorded lines are then edited and mixed to ensure clarity and smooth transitions. In addition to the voiceover, sound effects and music play a vital role in radio ad production. The sound effects, such as doorbell rings or car engine revving, help create a dynamic and engaging soundscape. Background music or jingles are chosen to enhance the ad's mood and make it memorable. Once all the elements are recorded and mixed, the final step is post-production editing. This involves fine-tuning the audio, removing any unwanted background noise, adjusting levels, and making sure the ad meets the required technical specifications for radio broadcasting. The finished radio ad is then ready for distribution to radio stations or other platforms for airing. Overall, radio ad production is a multi-step process that involves concept development, scriptwriting, voiceover casting, sound design, and post-production editing. It requires creativity, attention to detail, and careful planning to create an effective and compelling radio advertisement that effectively reaches and resonates with the target audience.

Radio Advertising

Radio advertising refers to the practice of promoting products or services through radio broadcasts. It is a form of mass communication that utilizes audio content to convey commercial messages to a wide audience. Radio advertisements typically consist of recorded or live spoken messages that are played on radio stations at designated times. These advertisements aim to capture the attention of listeners and persuade them to take action, such as making a purchase or visiting a website.

Radio Spots Production

Radio spots production refers to the process of creating audio advertisements that are specifically designed to be aired on radio stations. These advertisements are typically short, ranging from 15 to 60 seconds in length, and aim to promote a product, service, or brand to a targeted audience.During the radio spots production process, various elements are combined to create an impactful and engaging advertisement. This includes scriptwriting, voiceover recording, sound effects, and music selection. The goal is to capture the attention of listeners and deliver a persuasive message that encourages them to take action, such as making a purchase or visiting a website.

Radio Spots

Radio spots refer to short advertisements that are broadcasted on radio stations. These ads are typically around 15 to 60 seconds in length and are used to promote products, services, or events to a wide audience. Radio spots are a popular form of advertising due to the extensive reach of radio stations and the ability to target specific demographics. They are an effective way to communicate messages to consumers while they are engaged in other activities, such as driving, working, or relaxing at home.

Real-Time Advertising Bidding Strategies Development

Real-Time Advertising Bidding Strategies Development refers to the process of creating and implementing effective strategies for participating in real-time bidding (RTB) auctions in online advertising. RTB auctions occur in milliseconds, allowing advertisers to bid for and win impressions on digital platforms in real-time. Developing effective bidding strategies involves several key considerations. Firstly, advertisers must analyze and understand the data available to them regarding target audiences, demographics, and website content. This analysis helps determine the value of each impression and the likelihood of its conversion. Advertisers can then allocate their budget accordingly and bid strategically based on their key performance indicators (KPIs).

Real-Time Advertising Bidding Strategies

Real-time advertising bidding strategies refer to the techniques that advertisers use to optimize their bids in real-time auctions in order to maximize their chances of winning an ad placement and achieving their desired advertising goals. These strategies involve the use of advanced algorithms and data analysis to evaluate various factors such as user demographics, website content, ad placement location, and bidding prices in real-time. By considering these factors, advertisers can make informed decisions about how much to bid for each ad placement opportunity. One commonly used bidding strategy is known as maximum bid, where advertisers set a predetermined maximum bid limit for each impression. In this strategy, the advertiser sets the maximum amount they are willing to pay for an ad placement, and the real-time bidding system automatically adjusts the actual bid based on the competition from other advertisers. This allows advertisers to remain competitive in the auction while staying within their budget constraints. Another popular bidding strategy is known as dynamic bidding. This strategy involves adjusting the bidding amount based on real-time data about the user and their behavior. For example, if the user has shown a high level of interest in the advertised product or service, the advertiser might choose to increase their bid in order to increase the chances of winning the ad placement. On the other hand, if the user is not likely to convert or engage with the ad, the advertiser might reduce their bid or opt-out of the auction altogether. Furthermore, advertisers can also utilize goal-based bidding strategies, where the bidding amount is optimized based on the desired outcome of the campaign. For instance, if the advertiser's goal is to maximize the number of clicks or conversions, they might prioritize bidding higher for placements that have historically generated more clicks or conversions. Overall, real-time advertising bidding strategies play a crucial role in optimizing ad placements and maximizing the return on investment for advertisers. By taking into account various factors and utilizing advanced algorithms, advertisers can make intelligent bidding decisions that help them achieve their advertising goals effectively and efficiently in the dynamic and competitive landscape of digital advertising.

Real-Time Advertising Bidding

Real-Time Advertising Bidding refers to the process in the field of digital advertising where advertisers participate in a real-time auction to bid for ad impressions. Advertisers typically use programmatic advertising platforms or ad exchanges to participate in these auctions and bid on various ad slots across websites, mobile apps, or other digital platforms. In real-time advertising bidding, a publisher or website owner puts their ad inventory up for auction, often using an ad server or supply-side platform (SSP). Advertisers then submit their bids through a demand-side platform (DSP), specifying the maximum price they are willing to pay for each impression. The highest bidder wins the auction, and their ad is served to the user. This type of advertising is known for its efficiency and targeting capabilities. It allows advertisers to reach their desired audience in real-time based on a variety of factors such as demographics, browsing behavior, location, and interests. By bidding on individual impressions, advertisers can optimize their campaigns and ensure that they only pay for ad placements that are likely to generate the desired results. Real-time advertising bidding has revolutionized the advertising industry by making the buying and selling of ad inventory more efficient and transparent. It has also enabled the rise of programmatic advertising, which automates the process of buying and selling ad space. This has significantly streamlined the workflow for advertisers and publishers, allowing them to reach larger audiences and maximize their return on investment.

Rebranding Campaigns Execution Steps

A rebranding campaign is a strategic marketing initiative undertaken by a business or organization to change the perception, image, or branding of their product, service, or overall brand identity. It involves a series of planned steps and actions to execute the rebranding goals effectively and achieve the desired outcome. Execution steps for rebranding campaigns typically include the following: 1. Research and Analysis: Conduct thorough market research, competitor analysis, and customer insights to understand the current brand perception and identify areas for improvement. This step helps in positioning the rebranding effort strategically. 2. Define Objectives and Target Audience: Clearly define the objectives and goals of the rebranding campaign. Identify the target audience and segment them based on demographics, psychographics, or other relevant factors. This step helps in establishing a clear direction for the campaign. 3. Develop Rebranding Strategy: Create a comprehensive rebranding strategy that outlines the key messages, unique selling propositions, visual identity, and overall brand positioning. This strategy should align with the defined objectives and target audience. 4. Design Visual Elements: Develop new visual elements such as logos, color schemes, typography, and overall brand imagery that reflect the desired brand persona and resonate with the target audience. These elements should convey the message and essence of the rebranding campaign. 5. Communicate the Rebrand: Implement consistent and integrated marketing communications across various channels to communicate the rebranding message to the target audience. This may involve advertising, public relations, social media, website updates, and other promotional activities. 6. Train and Engage Internal Stakeholders: Conduct training sessions or workshops to educate and involve internal stakeholders, including employees, in the rebranding process. This step ensures everyone understands and supports the new brand identity. 7. Launch and Monitor: Execute the rebranding campaign and closely monitor its impact. Measure key performance indicators (KPIs), track customer feedback, and make adjustments as needed. Regularly evaluate the success of the rebranding efforts and make any necessary improvements.

Rebranding Campaigns Execution

A rebranding campaign execution refers to the implementation of strategies and tactics designed to promote and establish a new brand image or identity for a company, product, or service. It involves a series of advertising and marketing activities aimed at reintroducing the brand to the target audience and creating awareness and acceptance of the revamped brand identity. The execution of a rebranding campaign typically involves several key steps. First, a brand audit is conducted to assess the current brand image and identify the reasons and objectives for the rebranding effort. This includes evaluating the competition, target audience, and market trends. Next, a comprehensive brand strategy is developed, which outlines the goals, messaging, and positioning of the new brand. This strategy serves as a roadmap for the execution of the campaign and guides the creation of various marketing materials. The next step is the creative development, where the new brand identity is translated into visual elements such as logos, colors, typography, and other brand assets. The new brand identity should align with the brand strategy and reflect the desired image and positioning of the company or product. Once the creative elements are finalized, they are integrated into various marketing channels and touchpoints. This may include advertising campaigns, social media profiles, website redesign, packaging, signage, and other marketing collateral. Consistency across these channels is crucial to ensure that the new brand message is effectively communicated to the target audience. Throughout the execution of the rebranding campaign, monitoring and evaluation should take place to measure the effectiveness and impact of the new brand image. Feedback from customers, market research, and other metrics can provide insights into the success of the rebranding effort and inform any necessary adjustments or refinements. In conclusion, a rebranding campaign execution involves the implementation of strategies and tactics to promote and establish a new brand image. It encompasses various steps such as brand audit, strategy development, creative development, integration into marketing channels, and monitoring and evaluation.

Rebranding Campaigns

Rebranding campaigns in the context of advertisement refer to the strategic efforts taken by a company or organization to change or alter its brand image, identity, or perception among its target audience and the market as a whole. It involves a comprehensive and deliberate process of repositioning the brand, modifying its visual elements, refining its messaging, and adjusting its overall market positioning. The primary objective of a rebranding campaign is to create a new and improved image for the brand, which resonates better with its target audience, differentiates itself from competitors, and aligns with the company's current and future goals and values. A successful rebranding campaign can enhance brand visibility, attract new customers, re-engage existing customers, drive sales, and ultimately contribute to the overall growth and success of the business.

Rebranding

Rebranding in the context of advertising refers to the process of changing the image, identity, or perception of a product, service, or organization. It involves creating a new brand identity and communication strategy to position the entity in a different light in the minds of consumers. Rebranding typically occurs when a company wants to reposition itself in the market, target a new audience, or recover from a negative reputation. It aims to rejuvenate the brand, attract new customers, and increase market share. Rebranding can involve various elements, such as a new name, logo, tagline, packaging, and advertising campaign.

Remarketing Ad Campaigns Management Techniques

Remarketing ad campaign management techniques refer to the strategies and methods used to effectively create, implement, and optimize ad campaigns that target individuals who have previously interacted with a company's website, products, or services. This form of online advertising aims to reconnect with potential customers who have shown interest but have not yet made a purchase or conversion. The first step in managing a remarketing ad campaign is determining the target audience. This involves analyzing website data, such as user behavior, demographics, and interests, to identify potential customers who are most likely to convert. Once the target audience is defined, ads can be customized to appeal to their specific needs and preferences. Next, the ad content and design need to be carefully crafted to capture the attention of the target audience. The messaging should be compelling and relevant, highlighting the unique selling points of the product or service. Visual elements, such as images or videos, can also be used to make the ads more engaging and memorable. The placement of the ads is crucial for their success. Remarketing ad campaigns typically utilize display advertising networks, social media platforms, and search engine advertising to reach the target audience across various online channels. The ads should be strategically placed where potential customers are likely to see them, such as on popular websites, relevant blogs, or social media feeds. Tracking and analyzing the performance of the ad campaigns is essential for optimizing their effectiveness. This involves monitoring key metrics, such as click-through rates, conversion rates, and return on investment. Based on the data collected, adjustments can be made to the campaign settings, targeting options, or ad content to improve results and maximize ROI. In conclusion, remarketing ad campaign management techniques involve analyzing target audience data, creating compelling ad content, strategically placing ads, and continuously monitoring performance to effectively reach and convert potential customers who have previously shown interest in a company's offerings.

Remarketing Ad Campaigns Management

Remarketing Ad Campaigns Management is a process of strategically planning and executing online advertising campaigns targeted towards individuals who have previously interacted with a business or its website. This technique involves displaying tailored advertisements to these individuals in order to re-engage them and encourage them to take additional actions. Remarketing ad campaigns are effective because they allow businesses to reach out to an audience that has already shown some level of interest or engagement. By targeting individuals who have previously visited a website, viewed specific products, or performed certain actions, businesses can create personalized advertisements that resonate with their interests and needs. Effective management of remarketing ad campaigns requires careful planning and execution. It begins with defining the target audience and deciding on the criteria for inclusion in the remarketing list. This could include individuals who have abandoned their shopping carts, visited specific pages, or completed certain conversion goals. Once the target audience is defined, the next step is to create compelling and relevant ads that will capture their attention. These ads should be designed to remind the audience of their previous interaction with the business and provide a clear call-to-action to encourage them to take further action. In addition to creating compelling ads, proper management of remarketing ad campaigns involves monitoring and optimizing their performance. This includes tracking key metrics such as click-through rates, conversion rates, and return on investment. By analyzing this data, businesses can make informed decisions about adjusting their campaign strategies to improve results.

Remarketing Ad Campaigns

Remarketing ad campaigns, also known as retargeting ad campaigns, are a type of online advertising strategy that focuses on targeting individuals who have previously interacted with a business or visited their website. This form of advertising involves displaying personalized ads to these individuals as they browse other websites or use mobile apps, with the goal of bringing them back to the company's website and encouraging them to complete a desired action, such as making a purchase or filling out a form. The concept behind remarketing ad campaigns is based on the idea that individuals who have already shown interest in a company or its offerings are more likely to convert into customers compared to those who have never engaged with the business before. By targeting these individuals with relevant and compelling ads, remarketing campaigns aim to increase brand awareness, drive website traffic, and ultimately boost sales or conversions.

Remarketing Advertising Strategies

Remarketing advertising strategies refer to the techniques used by marketers to target and reach out to a specific audience who have previously shown interest in a product or service. It involves displaying targeted advertisements to these potential customers as a way of reminding them about the brand and encouraging them to make a purchase or take a desired action. One of the key elements of remarketing advertising strategies is the use of cookies or tracking pixels. When a user visits a website or interacts with an online ad, a cookie is placed on their browser, allowing marketers to track their behavior and interests. This information is then used to tailor personalized ads that are relevant to the user's previous online activities. Remarketing allows marketers to stay engaged with potential customers who have already shown some level of interest in their brand. By reaching out to these individuals with targeted ads, marketers can increase the chances of conversion as they are already familiar with the brand and its offerings. There are various types of remarketing strategies that marketers can employ. One common approach is site remarketing, which involves showing ads to users who have previously visited a specific website or webpage. Another strategy is search remarketing, where ads are displayed to users who have conducted specific keyword searches related to the brand or product. Another effective method is social media remarketing, which involves targeting users who have engaged with a brand's social media content or visited their social media profile. This enables marketers to display relevant ads on platforms like Facebook, Instagram, or LinkedIn. Dynamic remarketing is another powerful strategy where ads are personalized based on the specific products or services that a user has shown interest in. For example, if a user visits a clothing store website and views a particular item, dynamic remarketing can display ads for that specific item to remind the user and encourage them to make a purchase. In conclusion, remarketing advertising strategies involve targeting and reaching out to a specific audience who have previously shown interest in a product or service. By utilizing cookies and tracking pixels, marketers can display personalized ads to remind and persuade potential customers to take action. The various types of remarketing strategies offer marketers an effective way to engage with their audience and increase the chances of conversion.

Remarketing Advertising

Remarketing advertising refers to a marketing strategy that involves targeting individuals who have previously interacted with a brand or visited its website. It aims to re-engage these potential customers and encourage them to take the desired action, such as making a purchase or signing up for a newsletter. This form of advertising relies on the use of cookies or pixel tracking to track the online behavior of users. When a user visits a website or performs a specific action, such as adding an item to their shopping cart, a cookie is placed on their browser. This cookie then allows the brand to display targeted ads to the user as they browse other websites across the internet. These ads are often personalized and tailored based on the user's previous interactions with the brand. The main goal of remarketing advertising is to increase brand awareness and conversion rates. By targeting individuals who have already expressed interest in a brand, remarketing allows companies to stay top of mind and remind potential customers of their offerings. By showing relevant ads to these users, brands can provide a more personalized experience and increase the likelihood of conversion. Remarketing can take various forms, such as display ads, social media ads, or email campaigns. Display ads are the most common form of remarketing and are typically displayed on websites that are part of the ad network. Social media platforms also offer remarketing options, allowing brands to target users who have interacted with their social media profiles or visited their website. Email remarketing involves sending targeted emails to individuals who have abandoned their shopping carts or shown interest in specific products. In summary, remarketing advertising is a strategy that targets individuals who have already engaged with a brand. By displaying personalized ads to these users as they browse the internet, companies aim to re-engage potential customers and increase brand awareness and conversion rates. It is an effective way to stay top of mind and encourage individuals to take the desired action.

Remarketing

Remarketing is a strategic advertising technique where targeted online ads are displayed to users who have previously interacted with a website, product, or service. It aims to reconnect with potential customers who may have shown interest but did not make a purchase or conversion during their initial visit. By utilizing cookies and other tracking mechanisms, remarketing allows businesses to deliver tailored ads to individuals as they browse other websites or use online platforms. These ads can be displayed through various channels, such as search engines, social media platforms, or websites within an ad network.

Responsive Ads Design

Responsive Ads Design refers to the practice of creating digital advertisements that automatically adapt and adjust to different screen sizes and devices, providing an optimal viewing experience for users. In today's highly mobile and multi-device world, where people access the internet through smartphones, tablets, laptops, and desktop computers, it is crucial for advertisers to ensure that their ads are easily readable and visually appealing across various devices and screen sizes. Responsive Ads Design involves using a combination of flexible layouts, images, and media queries to achieve this goal.

Responsive Ads

Responsive ads are advertisements that are designed to adapt and adjust their layout, size, and format to fit different screen sizes and devices. They are created using responsive design principles, which allow the ads to automatically adjust their appearance based on the device and screen resolution of the user. Responsive ads are important in today's digital advertising landscape because they enable advertisers to reach and engage with their audience across different devices, including desktop computers, laptops, smartphones, and tablets. By using responsive ads, advertisers can ensure that their message is effectively delivered to users, regardless of the device they are using to access the internet.

Retail Advertising Displays Planning Approaches

Retail advertising displays planning approaches refer to the strategies and methods used by retailers to design and implement displays that effectively promote their products and enhance customer engagement. These approaches involve careful consideration of various factors such as target audience, product positioning, store layout, and marketing objectives, to create visually appealing and impactful displays that drive sales and increase brand awareness. One common approach is the use of thematic displays, where retailers create displays based on a specific theme or concept. Thematic displays help to create a cohesive and immersive shopping experience for customers, as they can relate to the story or idea behind the display. For example, a retailer selling outdoor camping gear may create a display that resembles a camping scene, complete with tents, campfire, and camping equipment. This approach not only captures the attention of potential customers but also helps to convey the benefits and features of the products in a more memorable way.

Retail Advertising Displays Planning

Retail advertising displays planning refers to the process of strategically organizing and designing promotional materials and advertisements in a retail setting to effectively communicate a brand's message, entice customers, and drive sales. This planning process involves carefully considering various elements, such as the layout of the retail space, target audience, product positioning, and competitive landscape, to create visually appealing, informative, and persuasive advertising displays that grab the attention of shoppers and encourage them to make a purchase. Retail advertising displays can come in various forms, including window displays, in-store signage, shelf talkers, floor graphics, end-cap displays, and point-of-sale materials. Each of these display types serves a specific purpose within the overall marketing strategy, with the aim of increasing brand awareness, generating interest, promoting products or services, and ultimately influencing consumer behavior. The planning process begins with identifying the key marketing objectives and understanding the target audience. This information helps in determining the appropriate messaging, tone, and design aesthetics that will resonate with the intended customers. Factors such as seasonality, product launches, and promotional campaigns also need to be taken into account to ensure the advertising displays are timely and relevant. Once the objectives and target audience are established, the layout of the retail space must be considered. This involves analyzing the store's floor plan, traffic flow, and focal points to determine the most optimal locations for the advertising displays. Retailers often employ visual merchandisers or professional designers to create visually compelling and cohesive displays that enhance the overall shopping experience. The design and content of the advertising displays are equally important. The use of eye-catching graphics, compelling headlines, and concise yet informative messaging helps to communicate the brand's value proposition and differentiate it from competitors. Effective use of colors, fonts, and layout ensures that the displays are visually appealing and easy to understand, even from a distance. Regular evaluation and monitoring of the effectiveness of the advertising displays are important to determine their impact on sales and brand perception. This can involve analyzing sales data, customer feedback, and conducting surveys to gauge the success of specific campaigns and make necessary adjustments for future planning.

Retail Advertising Displays

Retail advertising displays refer to visual marketing materials that are strategically placed in retail stores to promote products or brands. These displays are designed to grab the attention of customers and effectively convey key messages about the advertised products. Retail advertising displays can come in various forms, including posters, banners, shelf talkers, aisle signs, floor graphics, and digital screens. The aim is to create an attractive and engaging visual presentation that encourages customers to make a purchase. These displays are often placed in high-traffic areas of the store, such as near the entrance, checkout counters, or in prominent locations throughout the store to maximize their impact.

Rich Media Advertising Campaigns

Rich media advertising campaigns refer to a type of advertising strategy that utilizes engaging and interactive multimedia elements to deliver promotional messages to target audiences.

These campaigns aim to capture the attention and interest of consumers by incorporating various elements such as videos, animations, audio, and interactive features. The use of rich media in advertising allows for a more dynamic and immersive experience for consumers. Unlike traditional static banner ads, rich media ads offer a higher level of interactivity and engagement, enabling consumers to interact with the ad content in real-time. This interactivity can range from simple actions such as hovering over an element to reveal additional information, to more complex interactions like playing games or completing forms within the ad itself.

Rich Media Advertising Formats Assessment Criteria

Rich media advertising formats refer to the various types of interactive and multimedia advertisements that are designed to engage and captivate viewers. These formats go beyond traditional static banner ads and incorporate elements such as animation, video, audio, and interactive features. One of the key criteria for assessing rich media advertising formats is interactivity. These formats enable users to interact with the ad by clicking, hovering, or performing other actions. This interactivity enhances user engagement and allows for a more personalized and immersive advertising experience. Another important criterion is visual appeal. Rich media formats are designed to be visually striking and attention-grabbing, utilizing vibrant colors, eye-catching graphics, and dynamic elements. The visual appeal of these formats helps to capture the viewer's attention and encourage them to interact with the ad. The ability to deliver a clear message is also a crucial criterion for rich media advertising formats. These formats allow for more creative storytelling and messaging compared to traditional static ads. They provide advertisers with the opportunity to convey their brand message in a more compelling and memorable way, using engaging visuals, audio, and interactive elements to effectively communicate their product or service. Another aspect to consider is the compatibility of rich media advertising formats across different devices and platforms. With the increasing use of mobile devices, it is essential for these formats to be seamlessly displayed and fully functional on various screen sizes and operating systems. This ensures that the ad reaches a wider audience and maximizes its impact. Furthermore, the performance and tracking capabilities of rich media formats are important assessment criteria. Advertisers need to be able to track and measure the effectiveness of their campaigns, including metrics such as click-through rates, engagement rates, and conversions. Rich media formats should provide robust tracking and analytics tools to enable advertisers to optimize their campaigns and make data-driven decisions. In conclusion, rich media advertising formats are interactive and multimedia-based advertisements that aim to engage and captivate viewers. Interactivity, visual appeal, clear messaging, compatibility, and performance tracking are key criteria for assessing these formats. By meeting these criteria, rich media advertising formats can effectively communicate brand messages, maximize audience reach, and drive desired actions. Rich media advertising formats refer to interactive and multimedia ads designed to engage viewers. Assessment criteria include interactivity, visual appeal, message clarity, compatibility, and performance tracking.

Rich Media Advertising Formats Assessment

Rich media advertising formats refer to a diverse range of advertising formats that incorporate advanced digital features, interactive elements, and multimedia content to engage viewers and drive higher levels of user interaction. These formats go beyond traditional static banner ads or text-based advertisements and utilize various technologies to deliver a more immersive and interactive advertising experience. Rich media advertisements often include elements such as videos, audio, animations, interactive games, and clickable elements that allow users to engage with the ad content. This dynamic and visually appealing format aims to capture the attention of the target audience and increase the chances of successful conversions and engagement. Unlike traditional ads, rich media formats take advantage of advanced technologies and capabilities provided by modern web browsers and digital platforms. They are designed to overcome the limitations of static ads and leverage the capabilities of modern devices and internet connectivity. Rich media ads can be displayed on websites, mobile applications, social media platforms, and other digital channels. They can appear in various sizes and formats, such as expandable banners, interstitial ads, video ads, or interactive overlays. These formats are usually delivered using HTML5, which has become the de-facto standard for multimedia content on the web due to its cross-platform compatibility and rich media capabilities. The main advantages of rich media advertising formats are their ability to captivate and engage users, resulting in higher brand awareness, increased click-through rates, and improved conversion rates. Interactive elements encourage users to spend more time interacting with the ad, leading to a more positive and memorable experience. Additionally, rich media ads allow for more targeted and personalized campaigns, as they can adapt to the user's preferences, behavior, and context. Data-driven optimization techniques can be applied to collect and analyze user interactions, enabling advertisers to refine and improve their messaging and creative content. In conclusion, rich media advertising formats encompass a wide range of interactive and visually engaging ad formats that aim to captivate and engage users. These formats leverage advanced digital technologies to deliver a more immersive and interactive advertising experience. By incorporating multimedia content, interactive elements, and data-driven optimization, rich media ads can generate higher levels of user engagement, increase brand awareness, and improve conversion rates.

Rich Media Advertising Formats

Rich Media Advertising Formats refer to dynamic and highly interactive digital advertisements that utilize various media elements such as graphics, audio, video, and animations to engage and captivate target audiences. These formats go beyond traditional static banner ads, offering more immersive and visually appealing experiences for users.Rich media ads are designed to break through the clutter of online advertising and grab users' attention. They can be seamlessly integrated into websites, social media platforms, mobile apps, and other digital channels, ensuring maximum visibility and reach.

Rich Media Advertising

Rich media advertising is a type of advertisement that utilizes interactive and dynamic elements, such as video, audio, animations, and other engaging features, to enhance the ad's impact and capture the audience's attention. Unlike traditional static ads, rich media ads provide a more immersive and captivating experience for viewers. Rich media advertisements are designed to provide a higher level of engagement and interactivity compared to their static counterparts. They can include various multimedia elements, such as videos, audio clips, animations, interactive games, surveys, and more, allowing users to actively participate and interact with the ad content. This interactivity not only grabs the attention of the audience but also encourages them to spend more time engaging with the ad, increasing the chances of delivering the intended message effectively. One of the key advantages of rich media advertising is its ability to offer a more personalized and targeted experience to users. By leveraging user data and preferences, advertisers can tailor the content and presentation of rich media ads to specific individuals or target segments. This personalization helps in creating a more relevant and impactful ad experience, leading to higher engagement and conversion rates. Furthermore, rich media ads provide additional space for advertisers to convey their message effectively. With the inclusion of multimedia elements, advertisers can communicate complex ideas or showcase products and services in a more comprehensive and visually appealing manner. This not only makes the ad more memorable but also helps in building brand awareness and driving desired actions from the audience. Rich media advertising also allows for better tracking and measurement of ad performance. Advertisers can gather detailed data about user interactions, such as clicks, video views, time spent, and conversions, providing valuable insights into the effectiveness of the ad campaign. This data-driven approach enables advertisers to optimize their ad strategies and make informed decisions to improve future campaign performance.

Search Advertising

Search advertising refers to a form of online advertising that aims to promote products or services by displaying relevant ads within the search engine results page (SERP). It involves creating and bidding on keywords that are relevant to the target audience's search queries. In search advertising, advertisers bid on specific keywords or phrases that are commonly used by users when searching for products or services on search engines like Google or Bing. When a user enters a keyword or phrase into the search engine, the search engine algorithm determines which ads to display based on factors such as bid amount, ad relevancy, and ad quality.

Search Engine Advertising (SEA)

Search Engine Advertising (SEA) refers to a form of online advertising where advertisements are displayed on search engine results pages (SERPs) in response to a user's search query. The goal of SEA is to generate website traffic and increase brand visibility by targeting relevant keywords that users are searching for. SEA allows advertisers to bid on specific keywords that are relevant to their business or industry. When a user searches for those keywords, the search engine displays the advertiser's advertisement in a prominent position on the SERP, typically above or alongside the organic search results. Advertisers pay the search engine a fee each time a user clicks on their advertisement, hence the term "pay-per-click" advertising. One of the main advantages of SEA is its ability to deliver highly targeted advertising. Advertisers can choose when and where their advertisements are displayed, based on factors such as location, language, and device. This level of targeting ensures that advertisements are shown to users who are more likely to be interested in the products or services being offered. Furthermore, SEA provides measurable results and allows advertisers to track the performance of their campaigns. Advertisers can access data such as the number of clicks, impressions, click-through rates (CTRs), and conversion rates. This data can be used to optimize campaigns, make informed decisions, and improve the return on investment (ROI) of advertising efforts. In conclusion, Search Engine Advertising (SEA) is a powerful tool for businesses that want to increase their online visibility and drive targeted traffic to their websites. By bidding on relevant keywords and displaying advertisements on search engine results pages, advertisers can connect with potential customers at the moment they are actively searching for products or services. The ability to target specific audiences and track campaign performance makes SEA an effective and efficient form of online advertising.

Search Engine Advertising Tactics

Search Engine Advertising Tactics refers to the strategies and techniques used by businesses and marketers to promote their products or services through paid advertisements on search engine platforms. These tactics are aimed at improving the visibility, relevance, and effectiveness of the advertisements, ultimately driving targeted traffic to the advertiser's website. One common tactic used in search engine advertising is keyword targeting. This involves selecting relevant keywords or phrases that are frequently searched by users and incorporating them into the ad's content. By targeting these keywords, advertisers can ensure that their ads are displayed to users who are actively searching for related products or services, increasing the likelihood of attracting potential customers. Another important tactic is ad copy optimization. Advertisers must create compelling and persuasive ad copy that effectively captures the attention of users and entices them to click on the ad. The copy should be concise and succinct, highlighting the unique selling points of the product or service in a convincing manner. Bidding strategies are also crucial in search engine advertising. Advertisers bid on specific keywords or phrases, and their ad placement is determined based on their bid amount and ad quality. Effective bidding strategies involve finding the right balance between bid amount and expected return on investment, ensuring that the ads are displayed prominently without overspending on the advertising budget. Furthermore, ad targeting is a tactic used to reach a specific audience. Platforms offer various targeting options, such as demographic targeting, location targeting, and interest targeting, allowing advertisers to deliver their ads to a relevant and interested audience segment. By narrowing down the target audience, advertisers can maximize the relevance and impact of their ads, improving the overall advertising performance. Additionally, ad testing is a vital tactic to optimize the effectiveness of search engine advertising. Advertisers often test different variations of ad copy, imagery, and calls-to-action to identify the most successful combinations. Through rigorous testing and analysis, advertisers can refine their ads to maximize click-through rates and conversions, ultimately driving better results.

Search Engine Marketing (SEM) Tools Selection

Search Engine Marketing (SEM) Tools Selection refers to the process of choosing and using tools and technologies to effectively manage and optimize online advertising campaigns on search engines. SEM tools help advertisers analyze and improve the performance of their advertisements, allocate budgets, and target specific keywords and audiences to achieve their marketing goals. The selection of SEM tools is crucial for advertisers as it directly impacts the success of their advertising campaigns. These tools assist in various aspects of SEM, such as keyword research, ad creation, bid management, performance tracking, and reporting. By utilizing these tools, advertisers can make informed decisions, optimize their campaigns, and maximize their return on investment (ROI).

221

Search Engine Marketing (SEM) Tools

Search Engine Marketing (SEM) Tools are online tools and software platforms designed to help advertisers create, manage, and optimize their advertising campaigns on search engines. These tools provide various features and functionalities that enable advertisers to effectively target their desired audience, increase their visibility in search engine results pages (SERPs), drive traffic to their websites, and ultimately increase their sales and conversions. SEM tools allow advertisers to perform keyword research and analysis, helping them identify the most relevant and high-performing keywords to include in their ad campaigns. By understanding which keywords are frequently searched by their target audience, advertisers can create compelling ads that are more likely to appear in relevant search results. Additionally, SEM tools provide insights into the competition for specific keywords, allowing advertisers to make informed decisions on bidding strategies and budget allocation. Furthermore, SEM tools enable advertisers to set up and manage their paid search campaigns efficiently. These tools provide a user-friendly interface where advertisers can organize their campaigns, ad groups, and keywords, as well as create and edit their ad copies. SEM tools also offer features for automated ad optimization, such as ad scheduling, budget management, and performance tracking. By utilizing these features, advertisers can ensure that their campaigns are running effectively and generating the desired results. In addition to campaign management, SEM tools provide powerful analytics and reporting capabilities. Advertisers can access comprehensive data on their campaign performance, including impressions, clicks, click-through rates (CTRs), conversions, and return on investment (ROI). By analyzing these metrics, advertisers can identify trends, adjust their strategies, and optimize their campaigns for better performance. SEM tools may also offer advanced features, such as conversion tracking and attribution modeling, which provide deeper insights into the customer journey and the impact of different advertising touchpoints. In summary, Search Engine Marketing (SEM) Tools are essential resources for advertisers to maximize the effectiveness of their online advertising campaigns. These tools empower advertisers to research and select the most relevant keywords, efficiently manage their campaigns, and analyze their performance. By leveraging SEM tools, advertisers can optimize their advertising efforts, reach their target audience, and drive valuable traffic to their websites.

Self-Service Advertising Platform Selection

A self-service advertising platform refers to a digital platform that allows advertisers to create, manage, and optimize their advertising campaigns without the need for assistance from third-party vendors or agencies. It offers a user-friendly interface, giving advertisers control and flexibility in their advertising efforts. This advertising platform streamlines the entire process, from campaign creation to performance tracking and analysis. Advertisers can easily set up their campaigns by selecting target audiences, defining budgets, and choosing ad formats. They can also customize their creatives and messaging to match their branding and marketing objectives. One of the key advantages of a self-service advertising platform is its self-serve nature. Advertisers have the freedom to create and manage campaigns on their own, eliminating the need for constant back-and-forth communication with an agency or account manager. This enables quick decision-making and efficient execution of advertising strategies. Additionally, self-service advertising platforms offer robust targeting options. Advertisers can choose specific demographics, interests, locations, or behavior segments to ensure their ads reach the most relevant audience. Ad platforms often provide valuable insights and data analytics, empowering advertisers to make data-driven decisions and refine their targeting strategies over time. Furthermore, self-service platforms usually support multiple advertising channels, including search engines, social media platforms, mobile apps, and websites. This allows advertisers to reach their target audience across different platforms and devices with a cohesive and integrated advertising strategy. Overall, a self-service advertising platform empowers advertisers to take full control of their advertising campaigns, offering a user-friendly interface, comprehensive targeting options, and valuable analytics. By utilizing such a platform, advertisers can increase their efficiency, optimize their budget allocation, and maximize the impact of their advertising efforts.

Self-Service Advertising Platform

A self-service advertising platform is a digital platform that allows advertisers to create, manage, and optimize their advertising campaigns in a self-service manner, without the need for direct interaction or assistance from the platform operator. The platform provides advertisers with a user-friendly interface and a range of tools and features that enable them to easily set up and customize their campaigns. This includes selecting their target audience, defining their advertising objectives, choosing ad formats and placements, setting their budget and bid strategy, and monitoring the performance of their campaigns. By offering a self-service model, the platform empowers advertisers to have greater control and flexibility over their advertising efforts. They can quickly launch and pause campaigns, make changes to their targeting and creative assets, and access real-time reporting and analytics to evaluate the effectiveness of their campaigns. This self-service approach allows advertisers to iterate and optimize their campaigns in real-time, maximizing their return on investment. Moreover, a self-service advertising platform often provides advertisers with access to a wide range of advertising inventory across multiple channels and platforms. This may include display advertising on websites, mobile advertising in apps, video advertising on streaming platforms, and more. Advertisers can choose the specific channels and platforms that align with their target audience and advertising goals, ensuring maximum reach and impact. In addition to the flexibility and control it offers, a self-service advertising platform is often accompanied by robust targeting capabilities. Advertisers can leverage various targeting options such as demographic targeting, geographic targeting, behavioral targeting, and interest-based targeting to reach the most relevant audience for their products or services. In summary, a self-service advertising platform is a digital tool that empowers advertisers to create, manage, and optimize their advertising campaigns with minimal assistance. It offers a user-friendly interface, a range of features, and access to diverse advertising inventory, allowing advertisers to have control, flexibility, and precise targeting in their advertising efforts.

Shopper Marketing Research

Shopper Marketing Research refers to the systematic collection and analysis of data regarding consumer behavior, purchasing habits, and decision-making processes in order to develop effective advertising strategies and campaigns targeted at shoppers. It aims to evaluate and understand how shoppers interact with products and brands during the shopping process, with the ultimate goal of influencing their purchase decisions. Shopper Marketing Research provides insights into various aspects of a consumer's shopping journey, including their motivations, preferences, and behaviors. It involves gathering data from multiple sources such as surveys, interviews, observation, and market analysis to gain a comprehensive understanding of the target audience's shopping habits and preferences. This data is then analyzed to identify trends, patterns, and opportunities for marketing and advertising efforts. The key focus of Shopper Marketing Research is to understand the shopper's mindset and decision-making process while making purchase decisions. This includes analyzing factors such as product placement, packaging, pricing, promotions, and overall shopping experience. By understanding these factors, marketers can develop targeted and persuasive advertising strategies that appeal to shoppers at various stages of the shopping journey, from awareness to consideration and ultimately purchase. Shopper Marketing Research plays a crucial role in the development of effective advertising campaigns. It helps marketers identify and understand their target audience, their needs, and their purchase motivations. By gaining insights into shoppers' preferences and behaviors, marketers can tailor their advertisements to resonate with the target audience, increasing the likelihood of converting them from potential shoppers to actual customers. In conclusion, Shopper Marketing Research is a vital component of advertisement strategy development. It involves the systematic collection and analysis of data to understand consumer behavior and decision-making processes. By gaining insights into shoppers' habits and preferences, marketers can develop effective advertising campaigns that resonate with the target audience and influence their purchase decisions.

Shopper Marketing

Shopper marketing, in the context of advertisement, refers to the strategic activities and tactics employed by brands and retailers to influence consumers' purchasing decisions at the point of sale. It encompasses a range of marketing techniques that aim to engage shoppers, build brand awareness, and drive conversions within the retail environment. The primary goal of shopper marketing is to understand and leverage consumer behavior, preferences, and shopping patterns in order to effectively promote products or services and drive sales. It involves developing targeted marketing campaigns that resonate with shoppers and prompt them to

223

make purchase decisions in favor of a particular brand or product.

Social Advertising Campaigns

Social advertising campaigns are a form of advertising that specifically target and engage with consumers through social media platforms. These campaigns aim to create brand awareness, promote products or services, and ultimately drive customer engagement and sales. Social advertising campaigns leverage the immense reach and popularity of social media platforms such as Facebook, Instagram, Twitter, and LinkedIn to reach a wide and targeted audience. These campaigns are designed to take advantage of the high levels of user activity and engagement on these platforms, allowing brands to interact directly with their customers and build a strong online presence.

Social Advertising

Social advertising refers to the practice of promoting products, services, or brands through various social media platforms and online communities. It involves utilizing the features and tools present on these platforms to reach and engage with a target audience effectively. With the rise of social media platforms such as Facebook, Instagram, Twitter, and LinkedIn, social advertising has become an integral part of many companies' marketing strategies. The main objective of social advertising is to generate brand awareness, increase website traffic, drive conversions, and foster customer loyalty.

Social Media Advertising Budgets Analysis Methods

Social media advertising budgets analysis methods refer to the techniques and strategies used to assess and evaluate the allocation of financial resources for advertising campaigns on social media platforms. These methods involve analyzing and examining the effectiveness, efficiency, and return on investment (ROI) of social media advertising efforts. The purpose of this analysis is to optimize and maximize the impact and outcomes of advertising campaigns, ensuring that budget allocations are appropriately allocated and utilized to achieve desired results.

Social Media Advertising Budgets Analysis

Social media advertising budgets analysis refers to the process of evaluating and determining the amount of money allocated towards advertising campaigns on social media platforms. This analysis involves examining various factors such as target audience, campaign objectives, and expected return on investment to determine an appropriate budget for social media advertising. During the analysis, marketers assess the specific needs and goals of the advertising campaign. This includes identifying the target audience and understanding their behavior and preferences on social media platforms. By understanding the target audience, marketers can allocate appropriate resources to reach and engage with them effectively. Another important aspect of social media advertising budgets analysis is considering the campaign objectives. Different types of advertising campaigns may have varying objectives such as brand awareness, lead generation, or sales conversion. The budget allocated to each campaign will be determined by the specific objectives and the expected outcomes. The analysis also involves evaluating the potential return on investment (ROI) for the advertising campaigns. Marketers have to estimate the expected revenue generated from the campaign and compare it to the allocated budget. This helps in determining the effectiveness and profitability of the advertising efforts on social media platforms. Additionally, social media advertising budgets analysis also takes into consideration the costs associated with various advertising formats and strategies on social media platforms. Different platforms offer different advertising options such as sponsored posts, display ads, or influencer collaborations. Marketers have to evaluate the costs and benefits of each option to make informed decisions about budget allocation. In conclusion, social media advertising budgets analysis is a crucial process in the overall advertising strategy. It involves assessing the target audience, campaign objectives, expected ROI, and costs associated with different advertising options. By conducting a thorough analysis, marketers can allocate budgets effectively, ensuring the maximum impact of social media advertising campaigns.

Social Media Advertising Budgets

Social media advertising budgets refer to the amount of money that a business or organization sets aside specifically for advertising on social media platforms. These platforms can include popular networks such as Facebook, Instagram, Twitter, LinkedIn, and Snapchat, among others. Advertising on social media has become increasingly important for businesses and organizations as they try to reach their target audience in a more targeted and effective way. Social media advertising allows businesses to create and customize ads that are displayed to users based on their demographics, interests, and online behavior. This targeting capability makes social media advertising a valuable tool for reaching a specific audience and generating results.

Social Media Advertising

Social media advertising refers to the practice of promoting products, services, or brands using social media platforms as a medium. It involves creating and sharing content on social media channels to reach a target audience and increase brand visibility and engagement. Social media platforms such as Facebook, Instagram, Twitter, LinkedIn, and Snapchat have millions, if not billions, of active users. These platforms provide businesses with the opportunity to connect with their target audience on a more personal level and make use of various advertising formats to capture their attention. One of the key advantages of social media advertising is its ability to reach a highly targeted audience. Social media platforms collect vast amounts of data on their users, including their demographics, interests, and behaviors. This data allows advertisers to create highly specific audience segments and deliver personalized ads to those who are most likely to be interested in their products or services. Social media advertising offers a wide range of ad formats to cater to different marketing objectives. These formats include image ads, video ads, carousel ads, sponsored content, and influencer partnerships. Each format offers its own unique benefits and can be tailored to suit the brand's message and goals. Another key advantage of social media advertising is its cost-effectiveness. Compared to traditional advertising methods, social media advertising often requires a lower budget while offering the potential for greater reach and results. Advertisers have the option to set their budget and bidding strategies to control their ad spend and maximize their return on investment. In addition to promoting products and services, social media advertising can also be used to build brand awareness, foster customer loyalty, and drive website traffic. It allows businesses to engage with their audience through comments, likes, and shares, creating a sense of community and establishing a strong brand presence. In conclusion, social media advertising is a powerful tool for businesses to reach and engage with their target audience on various social media platforms. It offers highly targeted audience segmentation, a wide range of ad formats, cost-effectiveness, and the ability to achieve various marketing objectives. By leveraging the benefits of social media advertising, businesses can increase brand visibility, generate leads, and drive conversions.

Sponsored Content

Sponsored content refers to a form of advertising where a brand pays to have its promotional material placed within an online platform or media channel, typically in a way that appears to be organic or natural content. The purpose of sponsored content is to create brand awareness, generate leads, and drive customer engagement. Unlike traditional advertisements that are clearly labeled as such, sponsored content is designed to blend in with the surrounding content and provide value to the target audience. It often takes the form of articles, videos, social media posts, or other types of content that align with the platform's regular content. By integrating promotional material into the user's browsing experience, sponsored content aims to capture their attention and generate interest in the brand or product being advertised.

Sponsored Search Advertising Strategies

Sponsored search advertising strategies refer to the techniques and approaches used by advertisers to promote their products, services, or brands through paid search engine results. As the name suggests, sponsored search ads are advertisements that appear at the top or bottom of search engine result pages (SERPs) when users search for specific keywords or phrases. One commonly used strategy in sponsored search advertising is keyword targeting. Advertisers identify relevant keywords that are frequently searched by their target audience and bid on those keywords. When a user searches for one of these keywords, the advertiser's sponsored ad appears at the top or bottom of the SERP, increasing its visibility and the chances of attracting potential customers. Another strategy is ad copy optimization. Advertisers focus on creating compelling and concise ad copy that effectively communicates their value proposition to the audience. The ad copy should be relevant to the keywords being targeted and provide a clear call-to-action, encouraging users to click on the ad and visit the advertiser's website. Furthermore, sponsored search ads can be geographically targeted. Advertisers can choose to display their ads only to users in specific locations, maximizing the relevance of their ads and optimizing their advertising budget. Additionally, advertisers can use various ad extensions to enhance the visibility and effectiveness of their sponsored search ads. Ad extensions allow advertisers to provide additional information, such as phone numbers, addresses, or product links, directly in their ads, increasing the chances of user engagement and click-through rates. Monitoring and analysis are crucial parts of sponsored search advertising strategies. Advertisers should regularly monitor the performance of their ads, including click-through rates, conversion rates, and return on investment. Based on the data obtained, advertisers can make adjustments to their keyword targeting, ad copy, or bid amounts to optimize their campaigns and achieve better results. In conclusion, sponsored search advertising strategies involve the careful selection of keywords, optimization of ad copy, geographic targeting, and the use of ad extensions to attract and engage users. Continuous monitoring and analysis of campaign performance help advertisers refine their strategies and maximize the effectiveness of their sponsored search ads.

Sponsored Search Advertising

Sponsored search advertising is a form of online advertising where advertisers pay to have their ads appear at the top or side of search engine results pages (SERPs) when users search for specific keywords or phrases. These ads are typically labeled as "sponsored" or "ad" to clearly indicate that they are paid advertisements. With sponsored search advertising, advertisers bid on keywords or phrases that are relevant to their products or services. When a user enters a search query that includes those keywords, the search engine's algorithm determines which ads are displayed based on a combination of factors such as bid amount, ad relevance, and ad quality score. When an advertiser's ad is clicked by a user, they are directed to the advertiser's website or landing page, and the advertiser is charged a fee for that click. This fee, known as cost-per-click (CPC), is determined through an auction system where advertisers compete for ad placements by bidding on keywords. Sponsored search advertising offers several advantages for advertisers. First, it allows businesses to reach a highly targeted audience who are actively searching for their products or services, increasing the likelihood of conversions. Second, the pay-per-click model ensures that advertisers only pay when users click on their ads, providing a level of cost control and measurable return on investment. Third, online advertising platforms often provide tools and analytics to track and optimize ad performance, allowing advertisers to refine their campaigns and improve results over time. However, there are also challenges associated with sponsored search advertising. Competition for popular keywords can drive up bid prices, making it more expensive for advertisers to secure top ad placements. Advertisers must also carefully manage their campaigns to ensure they are targeting the right keywords, optimizing ad copy, and monitoring performance to maximize their return on investment. In summary, sponsored search advertising is a way for advertisers to promote their products or services by bidding on keywords and having their ads displayed prominently in search engine results. It offers targeted reach, cost control, and measurable results, but requires careful management and optimization to be effective.

Sponsored Social Posts Management Techniques

Sponsored social posts management techniques refer to the strategies and practices employed to effectively manage and optimize sponsored posts on social media platforms for advertisement purposes. These techniques involve various tasks and activities such as planning, creation, scheduling, monitoring, analyzing, and optimizing sponsored social media posts to maximize their reach, engagement, and conversion rates. One key aspect of sponsored social posts management is planning. It involves understanding the target audience, defining campaign objectives, and determining the most suitable social media platforms and ad formats to achieve those objectives. This includes selecting the right mix of sponsored content, whether it be images, videos, carousels, or stories, to convey the intended message to the target audience effectively. The creation of sponsored social posts is another critical element. It entails developing compelling and visually appealing content that aligns with the brand's image, values,

226

and messaging. This may involve collaborating with graphic designers, copywriters, and video editors to produce high-quality and engaging content. Ensuring that the sponsored posts are optimized for mobile devices and adhere to the platform's guidelines is also crucial. Scheduling allows advertisers to determine the best times and frequencies to publish their sponsored social posts. This involves considering factors such as the target audience's online behaviors, peak usage times, and competitor activities. By scheduling posts strategically, advertisers can ensure maximum exposure and engagement by reaching their audience when they are most active on social media. Monitoring the performance of sponsored social posts is essential for effective management. This includes tracking key metrics such as impressions, clicks, engagement rates, and conversions. Analyzing these metrics helps advertisers evaluate the effectiveness of their campaigns and make data-driven decisions to optimize future sponsored posts. Monitoring also involves keeping an eye on user comments, messages, and mentions, allowing for timely responses and engagement. Optimization is an iterative process that involves making continuous improvements based on the insights gained from monitoring and analysis. By testing different ad variations, targeting options, and messaging strategies, advertisers can learn what works best for their target audience and refine their approach to maximize results. Overall, sponsored social posts management techniques play a vital role in maximizing the impact and effectiveness of advertising campaigns on social media platforms. By employing these strategies, advertisers can optimize their sponsored content, reach their target audience, and achieve their marketing objectives.

Sponsored Social Posts Management

Sponsored Social Posts Management refers to the process of effectively managing and optimizing sponsored posts on social media platforms for advertising purposes. Social media has become a powerful tool for businesses to reach and engage with their target audience. Sponsored posts, also known as promoted or boosted posts, are a form of paid advertising on social media platforms where businesses pay to have their content displayed to a wider audience. This can help increase brand visibility, generate leads, and drive website traffic. The management of sponsored social posts involves various activities, including planning, creation, scheduling, monitoring, and analyzing the performance of these posts. This process ensures that businesses are able to maximize the impact and return on investment of their sponsored content. First, planning plays a crucial role in sponsored social posts management. It involves identifying the objectives, target audience, and key messages for the campaign. Understanding the goals and audience helps businesses determine which social media platforms to use and the type of content that will resonate with their audience. Next, the creation of sponsored posts involves designing visually appealing and engaging content that aligns with the brand's image and objectives. This can include catchy headlines, compelling visuals, and clear calls to action. The content should be tailored to suit the specific platform and audience, ensuring maximum impact and relevance. Scheduling is another important aspect of sponsored social posts management. It involves determining the optimal timing for posting the sponsored content to reach the target audience when they are most active and likely to engage. The scheduling may also involve A/B testing to identify the most effective posting times for different audience segments. Monitoring the performance of sponsored social posts is essential to ensure that the campaign is on track and achieving the desired results. This involves tracking metrics such as reach, engagement, click-through rates, and conversions. By closely monitoring the performance, businesses can identify any areas for improvement and make data-driven decisions to optimize future sponsored posts. In conclusion, sponsored social posts management is a vital component of successful social media advertising. It involves the strategic planning, creation, scheduling, monitoring, and analysis of sponsored posts to maximize their impact and effectiveness. By efficiently managing and optimizing sponsored social posts, businesses can reach a wider audience, increase brand awareness, and drive desired actions from their target audience.

Sponsored Social Posts

Sponsored social posts refer to advertisements that appear on social media platforms and are identified as paid content. These posts are created and published by brands, influencers, or businesses to promote their products or services to a wider audience. Unlike organic social posts, which are shared by users without any monetary incentive, sponsored social posts are backed by a financial investment. The primary goal of these posts is to increase brand awareness, attract potential customers, and drive conversion rates.

Storytelling In Advertising Strategies Development

Storytelling in advertising strategies development refers to the use of narrative elements and techniques to communicate a brand message or promote a product or service in a compelling and engaging manner. It involves the creation of a story or narrative structure that captures the attention of the target audience, evokes emotions, and connects with them on a deeper level. Storytelling in advertising is a powerful tool that allows marketers to go beyond simple factual information and forge a stronger bond with consumers. By weaving a narrative around a brand or product, advertisers can create a more memorable and impactful experience for their audience. Instead of bombarding consumers with a series of features and benefits, storytelling enables advertisers to frame their message in a relevant and relatable context.

Storytelling In Advertising Strategies

Storytelling in advertising strategies is the practice of using narrative techniques to communicate a brand message or persuade an audience to take a desired action. It involves crafting a compelling story that resonates with the target audience, evokes an emotional response, and captures their attention. The use of storytelling in advertising has become increasingly popular as it allows brands to create a deeper connection with consumers. Rather than simply presenting facts and features, storytelling engages the audience on a more personal and relatable level.

Storytelling In Advertising Techniques

Storytelling in advertising is a technique used to engage and captivate the target audience by presenting a narrative that resonates with their emotions and values. It involves crafting a compelling story within an advertisement to create a connection with the viewers, leaving a lasting impact on their minds. The primary objective of storytelling in advertising is to convey a brand's message in a memorable and relatable way. By using storytelling techniques, advertisers can grab the attention of consumers and make them emotionally invested in the advertisement. This emotional connection allows brands to establish a deeper relationship with their consumers, ultimately influencing their buying decisions.

Storytelling In Advertising

Storytelling in advertising refers to the strategic use of narrative elements and storytelling techniques to convey a brand's message, connect with the audience, and create an emotional impact. It involves crafting a compelling story that captures the audience's attention, engages their emotions, and motivates them to take action. Storytelling in advertising aims to evoke emotions, build trust, and establish a deeper connection between the brand and the consumer. By presenting a narrative that is relatable, inspiring, or entertaining, advertisers can effectively communicate the values, benefits, and unique selling propositions of a product or service.

Super Bowl Advertisements Planning Approaches

Super Bowl advertisements planning approaches refer to the strategies and methods used by companies and brands to create and execute effective and engaging advertisements during the Super Bowl, which is one of the most-watched television events in the United States. The first planning approach is the creative concept development. This involves brainstorming and ideation sessions to come up with unique and memorable ideas for the advertisement. The focus is on creating a concept that stands out from the competition and resonates with the target audience. The creative team may consider humor, emotion, storytelling, or a combination of these elements to capture viewers' attention and leave a lasting impression. The second planning approach is the production and execution. Once the creative concept is finalized, the production process begins. This includes casting actors, hiring a production crew, selecting filming locations, and creating visual and audio elements for the advertisement. The objective is to bring the concept to life and ensure that the final product aligns with the company's brand identity and messaging. The third planning approach is the media planning and buying. Super Bowl advertisements require careful consideration of when and where the ad will be aired during the game. Media planners analyze data and audience demographics to determine the optimal placement for maximum reach and impact. The buying process involves negotiating with broadcasters to secure ad spots and managing the budget effectively. The fourth planning approach is the pre- and post-advertisement activities. Pre-advertisement activities involve creating buzz and anticipation through teaser campaigns, social media promotions, and public relations efforts. Post-advertisement activities include monitoring and analyzing the advertisement's performance, engaging with viewers' feedback on social media, and leveraging the advertisement's success to enhance the brand's overall marketing strategy.

Super Bowl Advertisements Planning

Super Bowl advertisements planning refers to the process of strategizing and organizing the creation and placement of advertisements during the Super Bowl, which is the annual championship game of the National Football League (NFL) in the United States. Super Bowl ads are known for their high-profile campaigns, creativity, and enormous reach to a wide audience. The planning phase of Super Bowl advertisements involves several key steps. Firstly, advertisers need to thoroughly understand their target audience and their preferences. This includes collecting and analyzing demographic data, psychographic information, and consumer behavior trends. By gaining insight into their target audience, advertisers can tailor their advertisements to maximize their impact and resonate with viewers. Once the target audience is identified, the next step in the planning process is determining the advertisement's creative concept. Advertisers brainstorm catchy and memorable ideas, considering factors such as humor, emotions, storytelling, and celebrity endorsements. The creative concept should align with the brand's image, values, and marketing objectives. After finalizing the creative concept, the advertisers move on to the production phase. This involves scriptwriting, storyboarding, casting actors or celebrities, and filming or animating the advertisement. Super Bowl ads often have high production values, as companies strive to create visually stunning and attention-grabbing content that will stand out among the multitude of ads showcased during the game. Simultaneously, advertisers need to plan the media placement of their advertisements. This typically involves negotiating with network broadcasters to secure airtime during the Super Bowl broadcast. As the Super Bowl is one of the most-watched television events in the United States, the cost of airtime can be extremely high. Advertisers must allocate their budgets wisely while ensuring their ads reach the right viewers at the right moments. In addition to the broadcast placement, advertisers nowadays also plan for digital and social media placement. Super Bowl ads generate buzz and discussions online, and advertisers leverage that by releasing teasers and snippets of their ads on various digital platforms. They may also launch social media campaigns, encouraging viewers to engage with their brand before, during, and after the game. In conclusion, Super Bowl advertisements planning encompasses the strategic process of identifying the target audience, developing creative concepts, producing captivating ads, and strategically placing them during the Super Bowl. It requires careful consideration of the brand's objectives, audience preferences, and budget allocation in order to maximize the impact and effectiveness of the advertisements.

Super Bowl Advertisements

Super Bowl advertisements refer to the commercials that are aired during the Super Bowl, which is the annual championship game of the National Football League (NFL). These advertisements are considered to be some of the most prestigious and expensive marketing opportunities for brands. Super Bowl advertisements are known for their high production values, creative concepts, and star-studded casts. Companies invest heavily in creating unique and memorable commercials that stand out during this highly competitive event, which attracts millions of viewers. The cost of airing these commercials during the Super Bowl is exceptionally high, making it a highly sought-after platform for companies to promote their products or services.

Targeted Email Advertising Campaigns Management

Targeted email advertising campaigns management refers to the process of planning, executing, and monitoring email marketing campaigns that are specifically designed to reach and engage a defined target audience. This form of advertising involves sending promotional messages or newsletters directly to individuals who have expressed interest in a particular product, service, or topic.Effective management of targeted email advertising campaigns requires a strategic approach that focuses on maximizing reach and engagement while minimizing spam complaints and unsubscribes. It involves several key steps, including audience segmentation, message customization, campaign scheduling, and performance tracking.

Targeted Email Advertising Campaigns

Targeted email advertising campaigns refer to the strategic use of personalized emails to reach a specific audience with relevant and tailored advertising messages. This form of advertisement allows marketers to directly communicate with individuals who have expressed interest in their products or services, or who fit specific demographic or behavioral criteria. By utilizing targeted email campaigns, advertisers can optimize their outreach efforts by delivering content to recipients who are more likely to engage and convert. These campaigns typically begin by building an email list of potential customers who have opted in to receive communications from the advertiser. This can be done through various means such as website sign-ups, subscription forms, or lead generation efforts. Once the email list is established, marketers can segment their audience based on various factors such as demographics, interests, purchase history, or browsing behavior. This segmentation allows for the creation of highly personalized and relevant email content that resonates with the recipient. By tailoring the messaging to specific segments, marketers can increase the chances of recipients opening the emails, engaging with the content, and taking desired actions such as making a purchase or signing up for a service. To ensure maximum effectiveness, targeted email advertising campaigns often employ automation and optimization techniques. Automation tools can be used to send personalized emails at scale, allowing marketers to efficiently reach a large number of recipients while still maintaining a personalized touch. Optimization techniques such as A/B testing can be applied to test different email formats, subject lines, or calls to action, and determine which variations yield the best results. Furthermore, targeted email advertising campaigns can also benefit from metrics and analytics to measure their success. By tracking open rates, click-through rates, conversion rates, and other key performance indicators, marketers can assess the effectiveness of their campaigns and make data-driven decisions for future improvements. In conclusion, targeted email advertising campaigns involve the use of personalized emails to deliver tailored advertising messages to specific segments of an audience. By utilizing segmentation, automation, and optimization techniques, marketers can increase the likelihood of engagement and conversion, ultimately driving business success.

Targeted Email Advertising

body { font-family: Arial, sans-serif; line-height: 1.5; padding: 10px; } Targeted Email Advertising is a form of online advertising that involves sending promotional messages or advertisements directly to a specific group of individuals through email. It is a highly effective marketing strategy that allows businesses to reach their target audience with personalized content. In targeted email advertising, marketers analyze various data points such as demographics, purchasing behavior, interests, and browsing history to identify and segment their target audience. By understanding their audience's preferences and characteristics, marketers can tailor their promotional messages to resonate with recipients, increasing the chances of conversion.

Teaser Advertising Campaigns

Teaser advertising campaigns are strategic marketing initiatives that use mysterious or provocative tactics to create anticipation and curiosity among consumers. These campaigns are designed to generate buzz and build suspense around an upcoming product, service, or event, without revealing specific details or information. The objective of a teaser advertising campaign is to capture the attention of the target audience and provoke their curiosity, leading them to seek further information about the product or event being promoted. This approach aims to create a sense of excitement and anticipation, sparking interest and generating buzz even before the actual launch or release. Teaser campaigns often rely on visual imagery, cryptic slogans, or ambiguous messages to pique the audience's curiosity. They may utilize print media, social media, television, or outdoor advertising platforms to reach a wide range of consumers. By withholding important details or keeping the audience guessing, teaser campaigns aim to create a sense of mystery and intrigue around the upcoming offering. These campaigns are particularly effective in industries where competition is fierce, or where products or events may not have immediate mass appeal. Teaser advertising can create a sense of exclusivity and build anticipation, making consumers feel like they are part of an exclusive group that is privy to

230

insider information. Moreover, teaser campaigns can also be used to gauge consumer interest and potential demand for a product or event before investing significant resources in production or development. By measuring the level of consumer engagement, marketers can make informed decisions about the viability and potential success of the offering. In conclusion, teaser advertising campaigns are a unique form of marketing that leverages curiosity and anticipation to create buzz around an upcoming product, service, or event. By withholding specific information and using provocative tactics, these campaigns aim to generate excitement and build anticipation among consumers, ultimately driving interest and demand for the offering.

Teaser Advertising

Teaser advertising is a promotional strategy used in advertising to create curiosity and generate buzz around a product or service without revealing all the details. It is primarily aimed at capturing the attention of the target audience and piquing their interest to generate anticipation and excitement before the full reveal of the product or service. This advertising technique involves teasing the audience with intriguing and cryptic messages or visual elements that provoke curiosity and leave them wanting to know more. The purpose of teaser advertising is to build anticipation, create a sense of mystery, and entice individuals to seek additional information or engage further with the brand or product.

Telemarketing Campaigns Management Techniques

Telemarketing campaigns management techniques refer to the strategies and methods used to effectively plan, execute, and monitor telemarketing campaigns in the context of advertisement. These techniques involve various activities such as target audience identification, script development, call center training, lead generation, and performance tracking. By employing telemarketing campaigns management techniques, organizations can optimize their resources and maximize the impact of their advertising efforts. The first step in managing telemarketing campaigns is to define the target audience. This involves segmenting the market based on demographics, psychographics, and other important factors to identify potential customers who are most likely to be interested in the product or service being advertised. Once the target audience is identified, the next step is to develop a script that effectively communicates the product or service benefits and addresses potential objections. The script should be concise, persuasive, and tailor-made to resonate with the specific audience segment. Training call center agents is another crucial aspect of telemarketing campaigns management. Agents should be equipped with product knowledge, effective communication skills, objection handling techniques, and sales closing strategies. Ongoing training and coaching sessions can help improve agent performance and ensure consistent messaging during customer interactions. Lead generation is a key objective of telemarketing campaigns. Techniques such as cold calling, warm calling, and lead nurturing can be utilized to generate qualified leads. Cold calling involves reaching out to potential customers who are not familiar with the product or service, while warm calling targets individuals who have shown some level of interest or engagement. Lead nurturing involves maintaining regular contact with potential customers to build relationships and increase the likelihood of conversion. Monitoring and evaluating the performance of telemarketing campaigns is essential for continuous improvement. Metrics such as call-to-sale conversion rates, average call duration, and customer feedback can provide valuable insights into the effectiveness of the campaign. By analyzing these metrics, organizations can identify areas of improvement, make data-driven decisions, and fine-tune their strategies for better results.

Telemarketing Campaigns Management

Telemarketing Campaigns Management refers to the strategic planning, coordination, and implementation of advertising initiatives conducted over the telephone with the goal of promoting products or services to potential customers. These campaigns involve a structured and systematic approach to engaging prospects through phone calls, with the aim of generating leads, making sales, and building brand awareness. The process of managing telemarketing campaigns requires careful consideration of various factors. Firstly, it involves identifying the target audience and segmenting them based on demographics, purchasing behavior, and other relevant characteristics. This helps in crafting personalized and tailored messages that resonate with the potential customers, maximizing the effectiveness of the campaign. Next, the management of telemarketing campaigns involves creating and refining scripts that guide the

231

conversation between agents and prospects. These scripts outline key selling points, address potential objections, and provide clear instructions for the agent to follow. By having a well-designed script, the campaign can ensure consistent messaging and improve the chances of success. Furthermore, telemarketing campaigns management entails training and supervising call center agents who will be executing the campaigns. Agents need to be equipped with product knowledge, sales techniques, and effective communication skills to effectively engage prospects and convert them into customers. Regular monitoring and coaching sessions help in improving agent performance and achieving campaign objectives. Monitoring and analyzing campaign performance is another crucial aspect of telemarketing campaign management. This involves tracking key metrics such as call duration, conversion rates, and customer feedback. By analyzing this data, managers can identify areas of improvement, refine campaign strategies, and make data-driven decisions to optimize performance. In conclusion, telemarketing campaigns management encompasses the entire process of planning, executing, and evaluating advertising initiatives conducted over the telephone. It involves audience segmentation, script development, agent training, and performance monitoring. By efficiently managing these campaigns, organizations can leverage the power of telemarketing to reach potential customers, drive sales, and enhance brand visibility.

Telemarketing Campaigns

Telemarketing campaigns refer to targeted marketing efforts that involve promoting products or services by making phone calls to potential customers. This form of advertisement aims to generate sales or leads by directly reaching out to individuals or businesses via telephone. In a telemarketing campaign, marketers use a list of phone numbers to contact potential customers who may have shown interest in their products or services or fit a specific demographic profile. The campaign's objective is to persuade and convince these individuals to make a purchase, subscribe to a service, or take any other desired action. Telemarketing campaigns typically involve scripts or guidelines that telecallers follow to communicate specific information about products or services. These scripts are designed to engage the prospects and highlight the benefits or features of the offering, while addressing any concerns or questions they may have. Telemarketing campaigns can adopt different approaches, such as inbound or outbound calls. In outbound telemarketing, the marketer initiates the calls to potential customers. It allows marketers to proactively reach out to a large number of potential customers and have direct conversations with them, increasing the chances of conversions. In contrast, inbound telemarketing involves setting up a dedicated phone line or call center where interested customers can call in to inquire about products or services. This approach is often used when companies run advertisements or promotions that encourage potential customers to reach out to them. Telemarketing campaigns can be effective in reaching a wide audience and creating personalized interactions. However, they also face challenges like the growing prevalence of caller identification systems and the negative perception associated with unsolicited sales calls. To overcome these challenges, telemarketing campaigns need to adopt ethical practices, comply with relevant regulations, and prioritize providing value and addressing customer needs. In summary, telemarketing campaigns involve making targeted phone calls to potential customers with the aim of promoting products or services. They rely on scripts, personalized communication, and persuasive techniques to engage prospects and drive sales or leads.

Television Advertising

Television advertising refers to the promotion of products, services, or ideas through broadcasted commercials on television networks or channels. This type of advertisement involves creating and airing video messages that aim to attract the attention and interest of a television audience. Television advertising is a highly popular and widely used marketing strategy due to the extensive reach and influence of television as a mass medium. It allows businesses to communicate their brand messages to a large and diverse audience, including individuals of different demographics, interests, and geographic locations. The impact of television advertising is significant as it has the ability to create brand awareness, shape consumer perceptions, and ultimately drive sales or action.

Text Message Advertising Campaigns

Text message advertising campaigns refer to promotional strategies that involve the use of text messages, also known as SMS (short message service), to communicate with and market to target audiences. This form of advertising leverages the widespread use of mobile phones and the effectiveness of text messaging as a direct and immediate communication channel. Text message advertising campaigns typically involve sending targeted and personalized promotional messages to individuals who have opted in to receive such communications. These campaigns can be used by businesses across various industries to reach and engage with their customer base, raise brand awareness, promote products or services, drive sales, and enhance customer loyalty. One of the key advantages of text message advertising campaigns is their high open and response rates. Unlike other forms of digital advertising, text messages are typically opened and read within minutes of being received, making them highly effective in delivering time-sensitive offers or information. Furthermore, text messages have a higher likelihood of being read compared to emails or social media posts, as they are often considered more personal and urgent. Text message advertising campaigns can employ a variety of tactics and strategies to engage with recipients. These can include offering exclusive discounts or promotions, providing valuable content or information, conducting surveys or polls, sending reminders or notifications, and encouraging customer feedback or reviews. By utilizing these techniques, businesses can not only increase customer engagement and conversions but also gather valuable insights and feedback to enhance their marketing efforts. However, it is essential for businesses to adhere to best practices and regulations when conducting text message advertising campaigns. This includes obtaining proper consent from recipients, providing clear opt-out options, ensuring message relevance and frequency, and respecting privacy laws. By following these guidelines, businesses can maintain a positive brand image, foster trust with their audience, and avoid potential legal and reputational consequences.

Text Message Advertising Campaigns Execution Steps

Text message advertising campaigns involve using SMS (short message service) to promote a product, service, or brand to a target audience. These campaigns are executed through a series of steps that ensure the effective delivery of messages and the desired impact on recipients. Here are the key steps involved in executing a text message advertising campaign: 1. Define campaign objectives: The first step is to clearly define the objectives of the campaign. This includes determining the target audience, desired outcomes, and key metrics for success. 2. Build a subscriber list: To ensure the campaign reaches the intended audience, it is crucial to build a subscriber list. This can be done through opt-in methods such as online sign-up forms, keyword-based opt-ins, or by integrating with existing customer databases. 3. Craft compelling messages: The messages should be concise, attention-grabbing, and relevant to the target audience. It is important to focus on the benefits or unique selling points of the product or service being advertised. 4. Personalization and segmentation: Tailoring the messages to specific segments of the subscriber list can greatly improve their impact. Personalization can be done by using recipients' names or other relevant information in the messages, while segmentation involves grouping subscribers based on demographics, interests, or behaviors. 5. Determine frequency and timing: It is crucial to determine the appropriate frequency and timing for sending out the messages. Bombarding recipients with too many messages or sending them at inconvenient times can lead to annoyance and opt-outs. 6. Compliance with regulations: Text message advertising is subject to regulations such as opt-in requirements and guidelines for message content. It is important to ensure compliance with these regulations to avoid legal issues or damage to the brand's reputation. 7. Test and optimize: Before fully launching the campaign, it is important to conduct tests to verify the effectiveness of the messages and the delivery system. Any issues or areas of improvement should be identified and addressed to optimize the overall campaign performance. 8. Monitor and analyze results: During the campaign, it is important to closely monitor the results and analyze key metrics such as open rates, click-through rates, conversions, and customer feedback. This data provides insights into the campaign's performance and helps make informed decisions for future campaigns or adjustments.

Text Message Advertising Campaigns Execution

A text message advertising campaign execution refers to the implementation and management of an advertising campaign that leverages text messages as a medium to deliver promotional content to a target audience. In this type of campaign, businesses use mobile phone numbers collected from customers or through opt-in processes to send promotional messages directly to their audience's phones. The goal is to create awareness, drive engagement, and ultimately, generate leads or conversions. The execution of a text message advertising campaign involves several key steps. First, businesses need to define their objectives and identify their target audience. This includes determining the demographics, interests, and behaviors of the intended recipients to ensure the messages are relevant and impactful. Next, businesses need to identify the right platform or service provider to send and manage their text message campaigns. These platforms often provide tools for managing contact lists, designing and sending messages, and tracking campaign performance. Once the platform is selected, businesses can start building their contact list. This can be done by collecting mobile phone numbers through various channels such as online forms, in-store sign-ups, or promotions. It is critical to ensure compliance with applicable regulations and obtain proper consent from recipients before sending any messages. With a contact list in place, businesses can create compelling and concise messages to be delivered via text. These messages should be designed to capture attention and provide value to the recipients. This could include limited-time offers, exclusive discounts, or personalized recommendations. After designing the messages, it is important to schedule and send them at appropriate times to maximize open rates and response rates. This might involve considering factors such as the time zone, day of the week, or specific events or holidays. Throughout the campaign, it is crucial to monitor and analyze the performance of the text message advertising campaign. This includes tracking metrics such as open rates, click-through rates, conversions, and overall engagement. These insights can be used to measure the effectiveness of the campaign and make any necessary adjustments to optimize results. In conclusion, the execution of a text message advertising campaign involves strategically planning, designing, and sending text messages to a target audience to promote products, services, or events. It requires careful consideration of the audience, platform, message content, timing, and performance metrics to achieve the desired outcomes.

Text Message Advertising Campaigns

Text message advertising campaigns refer to marketing strategies that involve sending promotional messages directly to targeted customers through text messages. This form of advertising allows businesses to reach their audience effectively and efficiently by utilizing mobile devices as a platform for communication.By leveraging the popularity and ubiquity of mobile phones, text message advertising campaigns aim to engage customers, generate leads, and increase sales. These campaigns typically involve the following key elements:1. Targeted Audience: Before launching a text message advertising campaign, businesses must identify and segment their target audience. This includes analyzing demographics, purchase behavior, and preferences to ensure that the messages reach the right individuals.2. Opt-in or Permission-based Approach: Text message advertising campaigns should abide by legal regulations, such as obtaining customer consent before sending promotional messages. This opt-in approach ensures that recipients are willing to receive marketing communications, enhancing the campaign's effectiveness.3. Timely and Relevant Messages: Successful text message advertising campaigns deliver messages that are timely and relevant to the recipients. They may include limited-time offers, personalized discounts, or updates on new products or services. This helps to capture the attention of customers and encourages them to take immediate action.4. Call-to-Action: Text message advertising campaigns often include a clear call-to-action that prompts customers to engage further. This may involve clicking on a link to visit a website, replying to the message with a specific keyword, or redeeming a coupon. A well-designed call-to-action increases the likelihood of conversion and measures the campaign's success.5. Tracking and Analytics: To evaluate the effectiveness of text message advertising campaigns, businesses utilize tracking tools and analytics. This allows them to monitor key metrics such as open rates, click-through rates, conversion rates, and customer engagement. By analyzing these metrics, businesses can optimize their campaigns for better results.In conclusion, text message advertising campaigns are a targeted and direct approach to reach customers through mobile devices. When executed strategically, they can effectively promote products or services, engage customers, and generate desired outcomes.

Text Message Advertising

Text message advertising refers to the practice of promoting products, services, or brands through SMS (Short Message Service) or text messages. It is a form of mobile marketing that utilizes the ubiquity and convenience of text messaging to reach and engage with a wide audience. Text message advertising works by sending targeted, personalized, and permission-based promotional messages to mobile phone users. These messages can include offers, discounts, updates, announcements, or any other marketing content that aims to generate awareness, interest, and conversions. One of the key advantages of text message advertising is its high engagement rate. Unlike other forms of advertising, text messages have an open rate of nearly 98%, with most people checking their messages within a few minutes of receiving them. This ensures that the campaign's message is delivered and read by a large portion of the target audience. Moreover, text message advertising allows for quick and direct communication with potential customers. Marketers can use SMS to send time-sensitive offers, reminders, or personalized recommendations based on previous purchases or customer preferences. This helps create a sense of urgency and drives immediate action from recipients. Text message advertising also enables hyper-targeting and segmentation. Marketers can collect and analyze customer data, including demographics, location, and purchase history, to create highly targeted campaigns. By segmenting the audience and tailoring the content to their specific needs and interests, marketers can significantly improve the effectiveness and efficiency of their advertising efforts. Furthermore, text message advertising offers measurable results. Marketers can track and analyze various metrics, such as click-through rates, conversion rates, and ROI, to assess the success of their campaigns and make data-driven decisions for future optimizations. In conclusion, text message advertising is a powerful marketing technique that leverages SMS to promote products, services, or brands. It allows for direct and personalized communication with a large audience, boasts high engagement rates, facilitates hyper-targeting, and provides measurable results. By implementing effective text message advertising strategies, businesses can effectively reach and engage with their target audience, ultimately driving conversions and boosting their bottom line.

Trade Advertising Approaches

Trade advertising approaches refer to the different strategies and tactics used by companies to promote their products or services to other businesses within their industry. This type of advertising is specifically targeted at B2B (business-to-business) relationships and aims to increase brand visibility, attract potential clients or partners, and ultimately drive sales. One common approach to trade advertising is through trade publications. Companies often place advertisements in industry-specific magazines, journals, or newspapers that are widely read by professionals in their field. These publications provide a platform for businesses to showcase their products, highlight their expertise, and generate interest among potential customers. By advertising in trade publications, companies can effectively reach their target audience and establish credibility within the industry. Another approach to trade advertising is participation in trade shows or industry events. Companies set up booths or exhibits to showcase their products or services and engage with potential customers, partners, or suppliers face-to-face. Trade shows provide an opportunity for businesses to demonstrate their offerings, build brand awareness, generate leads, and establish valuable business connections. This approach allows companies to interact directly with their target audience and create meaningful relationships that can lead to future business opportunities. Additionally, trade advertising can also involve direct mail campaigns. Companies may send promotional materials such as brochures, catalogs, or samples to other businesses in their industry. This approach allows for a more personalized and targeted communication strategy, as companies can tailor their messages to specific companies or individuals based on their needs or preferences. Direct mail campaigns can be highly effective in grabbing the attention of potential clients and generating response or inquiries. Furthermore, digital marketing has become an increasingly popular trade advertising approach. Companies utilize various online channels, such as websites, social media platforms, search engines, or email marketing, to reach their target audience. Through digital advertising, businesses can create engaging and interactive content, target specific demographics or industries, track performance metrics, and optimize their campaigns in real-time. This approach enables companies to leverage the power of technology and connectivity to expand their reach and engage with potential customers on a global scale.

Trade Advertising

Trade advertising refers to a type of promotional communication aimed at influencing the behavior of individuals or organizations within a specific industry or market. It is a strategic marketing approach used by businesses to communicate to targeted audiences such as retailers, wholesalers, distributors, and other trade professionals. The main purpose of trade advertising is to create awareness, generate interest, and promote products or services among members of the business community. Unlike consumer advertising, which focuses on attracting end-users, trade advertising is designed to reach professionals who have a direct impact on the purchase and distribution of goods or services.

Trade Show Sponsorships Planning Approaches

Trade show sponsorships planning approaches refer to the strategies and methods used by businesses to determine how to participate as sponsors in trade shows. A trade show sponsorship involves providing financial support or resources in exchange for brand exposure and promotional opportunities at the event. There are various approaches that businesses can take when planning trade show sponsorships. One approach is to identify specific trade shows that align with the company's target market and industry. The company may choose to sponsor trade shows that attract a large number of attendees or focus on niche trade shows that cater to a specific audience. This approach allows businesses to reach their desired customer base and make a meaningful impact on their target market.

Trade Show Sponsorships Planning

Trade show sponsorships refer to the practice of businesses providing financial support or resources to events or exhibitions in exchange for advertising and promotional opportunities. These opportunities may include the placement of company logos and branding materials throughout the event, the inclusion of sponsored content in event materials and promotional materials, and the ability to engage directly with event attendees through networking and marketing activities. Trade show sponsorships are a popular advertising strategy for businesses seeking to enhance their brand visibility and reach a targeted audience. By sponsoring a trade show, businesses can align themselves with a specific industry or market segment, positioning their brand as an authority or leader within that space. This helps to build trust and credibility among potential customers and can lead to increased sales and market share.

Trade Show Sponsorships

Trade show sponsorships refer to the financial or non-financial support provided by a company to a trade show or exhibition in exchange for advertising opportunities and brand exposure. This form of sponsorship allows businesses to promote their products or services to a targeted audience of industry professionals and potential customers. Typically, trade show sponsorships involve companies making a financial contribution to the event organizer in return for various promotional benefits. These benefits may include having the company's logo displayed prominently on event materials such as banners, signage, and promotional materials. In some cases, sponsors may also have the opportunity to display their products or services at a dedicated booth or exhibit area within the trade show floor, providing them with the chance to engage directly with attendees and generate leads.

Transit Advertising Planning

Transit advertising planning refers to the strategic process of developing and implementing advertising campaigns on various modes of public transportation. It involves creating a comprehensive strategy to deliver a brand's message to a wide and diverse audience using transit vehicles, stations, and other transit-related platforms. During the transit advertising planning process, marketers consider various factors to ensure the success of their campaigns. This includes analyzing the target audience demographics, understanding the geographical reach of transit systems, and evaluating the potential reach and frequency of exposure. By effectively planning transit advertising campaigns, brands can leverage the inherent visibility and reach of public transportation to maximize brand awareness and engagement.

Transit Advertising

Transit advertising refers to the use of advertising displays on various modes of public transportation such as buses, trains, trams, and taxis. It is an effective and efficient way for advertisers to reach a wide audience, as these vehicles are constantly moving and traveling to different areas within a city or region. Transit advertising offers numerous benefits for advertisers looking to promote their products or services. Firstly, it has a high level of visibility, as these advertising displays are easily noticeable by both pedestrians and drivers on the road. This allows for increased brand exposure and recognition. Additionally, transit advertising can target specific locations or demographics, ensuring that the advertisements reach the desired audience. There are several types of transit advertising formats that are commonly used. One popular format is exterior bus advertising, where advertisements are placed on the sides or back of buses. This allows for maximum visibility as buses travel throughout the city. Interior bus advertising is another format, where advertisements are placed inside the bus, such as above the seats or on the ceiling. This allows for a captive audience, as passengers are often seated and have more time to engage with the advertisements. Trains and trams also offer opportunities for transit advertising. Similar to buses, advertisements can be placed on the exterior or interior of these vehicles. Train and tram stations can also be utilized for advertising, with posters or digital screens displaying advertisements to commuters waiting for their train or tram. Lastly, taxis are another popular mode of transportation for transit advertising. Advertisements can be placed on the exterior of taxis, allowing for high visibility as they navigate through city streets. Additionally, the interior of taxis can be utilized for advertising, with advertisements placed on seat backs or on screens for passengers to view during their journey. In conclusion, transit advertising is an effective form of advertisement that utilizes public transportation vehicles and stations to reach a wide audience. With various formats available, advertisers have the flexibility to choose the most suitable option for their needs. The high visibility and ability to target specific locations or demographics make transit advertising a valuable marketing tool.

Transmedia Storytelling Implementation Methods

Transmedia storytelling implementation methods refer to the various strategies and techniques used in advertising to create a cohesive narrative experience across multiple media platforms. It involves the dissemination of a brand or product's story and message through different channels such as television, print, social media, websites, and more. The goal is to engage and immerse the audience in the brand's story, allowing for a deeper and more interactive experience. There are several methods commonly used in transmedia storytelling implementation in the context of advertising: 1. Multiplatform Campaigns: This method involves utilizing various media platforms to tell different aspects of the brand's story. For example, a TV commercial may introduce the main characters and concept, while a social media campaign may provide additional background information and interactive content. 2. Story Extensions: Brands can extend their story beyond traditional advertising formats by creating additional content such as web series, graphic novels, interactive games, or mobile apps. These extensions add depth to the brand's narrative and allow the audience to explore the story in different ways. 3. User-Generated Content: Encouraging the audience to actively participate in the brand's story through user-generated content is another effective method. Brands can launch contests, ask for opinions or ideas, and feature user-generated content in their campaigns. This not only increases audience engagement but also creates a sense of community around the brand. 4. Dynamic Storytelling: This method involves adapting and evolving the brand's story based on audience feedback and interactions. Brands can create personalized experiences for each individual by using data analytics and targeting specific messages to different audience segments. 5. Cross-promotion: Collaborating with other brands or influencers in related industries can help expand the reach of the brand's story. By aligning with like-minded partners, brands can leverage the existing fan base of these collaborators and cross-promote their content. Overall, transmedia storytelling implementation methods in advertising aim to create a cohesive and immersive narrative experience for the audience. By utilizing multiple media platforms, extending the story beyond traditional formats, encouraging audience participation, and dynamically adapting the narrative, brands can effectively engage and connect with their target consumers.

Transmedia Storytelling Implementation

Transmedia storytelling implementation in the context of advertisement refers to the strategic use of various media platforms and channels to create a cohesive narrative and engage target audiences through a multi-dimensional experience. Unlike traditional advertising approaches that rely on a single medium, transmedia storytelling leverages the power of multiple platforms such as television, radio, print, social media, websites, podcasts, and mobile apps, among others, to expand the brand story and enhance audience engagement.

Transmedia Storytelling

Transmedia storytelling refers to the practice of telling a cohesive story across multiple media platforms in order to engage and immerse the audience in a brand or product. Through the use of various mediums such as television, film, social media, websites, and mobile applications, transmedia storytelling aims to create a unified and interactive narrative that captivates the consumers and enhances their overall brand experience.

Triggered Emails Creation

Triggered emails creation refers to the process of designing and sending automated emails to targeted recipients based on specific actions or events. These emails are meticulously crafted to engage and convert potential customers by delivering relevant and timely content. Advertisement is an essential component of any marketing strategy, and triggered emails play a crucial role in captivating the audience's attention and driving them towards the desired action. These emails are triggered by predefined triggers, such as a user signing up for a newsletter, abandoning a shopping cart, or completing a purchase. They are highly personalized and tailor-made to each individual's behavior and interests.

Triggered Emails

Triggered Emails can be defined as a highly targeted form of advertisement that is automatically sent to a specific individual or group of individuals based on their actions, behaviors, or preferences. These emails are triggered by specific events or triggers, such as a user signing up for a newsletter, making a purchase, or abandoning a shopping cart. Triggered emails are designed to deliver relevant and timely information to recipients, increasing the likelihood of engagement and conversion. They are an effective way for advertisers to deliver personalized content, driving customer engagement, retention, and ultimately, generating higher revenue.

UGC Advertising Campaigns

UGC Advertising Campaigns, also known as User-Generated Content Advertising Campaigns, refer to marketing strategies that leverage content created and shared by consumers. In this type of campaign, brands encourage their audience to create and share content related to their products or services, which is then used for promotional purposes. UGC Advertising Campaigns have gained popularity in recent years due to the rise of social media and the increasing influence of online communities. These campaigns are a way for brands to tap into the creativity and authenticity of their customers, allowing them to become the voice and face of the brand.

User Engagement Metrics Tracking

User Engagement Metrics Tracking refers to the process of analyzing and measuring the level of interaction and involvement of users with online advertisements. It involves monitoring various metrics and data points to gain insights into user behavior and assess the effectiveness of ad campaigns in capturing and retaining user attention. The primary goal of user engagement metrics tracking is to evaluate how well an advertisement connects with the target audience and encourages them to take desired actions. By measuring and analyzing user engagement, advertisers can make informed decisions and optimize their campaigns for better performance and results.

User Engagement Metrics

User engagement metrics refer to the measures used to assess the level of interaction and involvement of users with an advertisement. These metrics provide insight into how well an advertisement captures the attention and interest of its target audience, as well as the effectiveness in driving desired actions or responses. There are various user engagement metrics used in the context of advertising, including click-through rate (CTR), bounce rate, conversion rate, average session duration, and social media engagement. CTR represents the percentage of users who click on an advertisement out of the total number of users who view it. A higher CTR indicates a higher level of user interest and engagement with the advertisement. Bounce rate measures the percentage of users who leave the website or advertisement without taking any further action after viewing only a single page. A lower bounce rate indicates a higher level of user engagement and interest. Conversion rate measures the percentage of users who complete a desired action, such as making a purchase or filling out a form, out of the total number of users who interacted with the advertisement. A higher conversion rate signifies a higher level of user engagement and effectiveness in driving desired responses. Average session duration refers to the average amount of time users spend on a website or advertisement. A longer average session duration suggests higher user engagement and interest. Social media engagement metrics include likes, comments, shares, and followers. These metrics are used to evaluate the level of user interaction and involvement with the advertisement on social media platforms. A higher number of likes, comments, shares, and followers indicate a higher level of user engagement and interest in the advertisement. Overall, user engagement metrics are crucial in analyzing the effectiveness of advertisements and understanding the level of user interest and involvement. By monitoring these metrics, advertisers can make data-driven decisions to optimize their campaigns and improve user engagement.

User-Generated Content (UGC) Advertising

User-Generated Content (UGC) advertising refers to the practice of incorporating content created by ordinary consumers into advertising campaigns. This content can take various forms, such as reviews, testimonials, photos, videos, or social media posts. UGC advertising leverages consumers' opinions, experiences, and creativity to promote products or services. UGC advertising offers several benefits for advertisers. Firstly, it helps in building trust and credibility among the audience. Consumers tend to trust content created by other consumers more than branded advertising messages. By featuring real people expressing their genuine thoughts and experiences, UGC ads establish a sense of authenticity and transparency. Secondly, UGC advertising encourages engagement and participation from consumers. When people see their own content being used in advertisements, it creates a sense of validation and pride. This motivates them to further engage with the brand, by creating and sharing more UGC. The active involvement of consumers in the advertising process also helps in fostering a sense of community and loyalty. Moreover, UGC advertising provides a cost-effective solution for brands. Instead of creating all the content themselves, brands can tap into the immense pool of UGC available online. This not only saves production costs but also ensures a continuous stream of fresh and diverse content. Additionally, UGC advertising enables brands to reach a wider audience through social sharing, as UGC is often shared among friends and family. However, UGC advertising also comes with certain challenges. Advertisers need to carefully curate and moderate the UGC to ensure its alignment with the brand values and messaging. They must also obtain consent from the creators of the UGC and ensure compliance with legal regulations. Furthermore, brands need to actively monitor and respond to user-generated content to maintain a positive brand image and address any negative feedback or criticism. In conclusion, UGC advertising harnesses the power of consumer-generated content to create impactful and engaging advertisements. By incorporating authentic and relatable content, brands can connect with their target audience on a deeper level, foster trust and loyalty, and amplify their reach.

VR Advertising Strategies

VR advertising strategies are marketing tactics used to promote products or services through virtual reality (VR) technology. VR refers to an immersive computer-generated experience that simulates a real-world environment, allowing individuals to interact with and explore a virtual setting. Unlike traditional forms of advertising, VR advertising allows brands to engage with consumers on a more sensory level. It creates an immersive experience that can capture the attention of users, leading to increased brand awareness, engagement, and conversions.

Video Advertising Metrics Analysis Methods

Video advertising metrics analysis methods are tools and strategies used to measure the performance and effectiveness of video advertisements. These methods provide valuable insights into various metrics such as engagement, reach, conversion, and overall impact of the advertisements. One commonly used method is click-through rate (CTR), which measures the percentage of viewers who click on an advertisement to visit the advertiser's website or landing page. This metric indicates how compelling the video ad is and how effectively it drives viewers to take action. Another important metric is completion rate, which measures the percentage of viewers who watch the entire video ad. A high completion rate indicates that the video content is engaging and holds the audience's attention until the end. On the other hand, a low completion rate may suggest that the ad is not interesting or relevant enough to the target audience. Viewability is another key metric that evaluates the visibility of video ads. It measures the percentage of an ad that is visible to the viewer. Viewability is important because if an ad is not fully visible on the screen, it is less likely to have a significant impact on the viewer. View-through rate (VTR) is another metric that measures the percentage of viewers who watch an ad, either partially or in full, and then subsequently take a desired action, such as visiting the advertiser's website or making a purchase. This metric helps advertisers understand the conversion effectiveness of their video ads. Engagement metrics, such as likes, shares, and comments, also provide insights into the level of audience involvement and interest in a video ad. Higher engagement metrics indicate that the ad resonates well with the audience and generates a positive response. These methods are crucial for advertisers to evaluate the success of their video ad campaigns and make data-driven decisions for optimization. By analyzing these metrics, advertisers can identify areas of improvement, refine their targeting strategies, and ultimately maximize the return on investment for their video advertising efforts.

Video Advertising Metrics Analysis

Video advertising metrics analysis refers to the process of evaluating and measuring the performance of video advertisements based on specific key performance indicators (KPIs). During video advertising campaigns, various metrics are used to assess the effectiveness and efficiency of the ads. These metrics provide insights into how the ads are performing, enabling advertisers to make data-driven decisions to optimize their campaigns. Video advertising metrics analysis involves the collection, interpretation, and reporting of these metrics to evaluate the overall success of the ad campaign.

Video Advertising Metrics

Video advertising metrics are quantitative measurements used to evaluate the performance and effectiveness of video advertisements in reaching the intended audience and achieving marketing objectives. These metrics provide valuable insights into the impact of video ad campaigns and assist advertisers in making informed decisions to optimize their video advertising strategies. One of the fundamental metrics in video advertising is the view count, which measures the number of times a video ad has been viewed. It provides an indicator of the reach and exposure of the advertisement. Advertisers can analyze view counts to monitor the popularity of their video ads and compare them against industry benchmarks or previous campaigns.

Video Advertising Networks Selection

A video advertising network, in the context of advertisement, refers to a platform or system that facilitates the distribution and monetization of video advertisements across multiple websites and digital media channels. These networks serve as intermediaries between advertisers and publishers, helping them connect and reach their target audience. Video advertising networks work by aggregating a large inventory of video ad placements from various publishers and websites. Advertisers can then purchase ad space within this network, allowing their video ads to be displayed on multiple platforms simultaneously. This enables advertisers to increase their ad reach and target specific demographics more effectively.

Video Advertising Networks

Video advertising networks are platforms that connect advertisers with publishers, facilitating the distribution and monetization of video ads across a wide range of websites and digital media channels. These networks act as intermediaries, providing a centralized marketplace for advertisers to reach their target audience and for publishers to generate revenue from their video content. Through video advertising networks, advertisers can create, manage, and optimize their video ad campaigns, reaching a larger audience than they could on individual websites. These networks typically offer a variety of targeting options, allowing advertisers to select specific demographics, interests, or behavior to ensure their ads are shown to the most relevant viewers. This targeted approach helps advertisers achieve higher engagement rates and increases the likelihood of conversions. Publishers, on the other hand, benefit from video advertising networks by monetizing their video content through ad placements. By participating in these networks, publishers can earn revenue based on the number of video ad views or clicks generated from their websites. These networks provide publishers with access to a broader pool of advertisers and often offer tools and resources to optimize ad placements, ensuring they blend seamlessly with the overall user experience. Video advertising networks utilize various ad formats, including pre-roll, mid-roll, and post-roll ads that appear before, during, or after video content. Additionally, some networks offer display ad formats that can be inserted within the video player or alongside the video content. These networks also enable advertisers to track the performance of their video ads, providing data on metrics such as views, clicks, and conversions, allowing them to refine their campaigns and maximize their return on investment. In summary, video advertising networks play a crucial role in the digital advertising ecosystem by connecting advertisers with publishers, allowing for the efficient distribution and monetization of video ads. By leveraging these networks, advertisers can reach their target audience, while publishers can generate revenue from their video content, ultimately creating a mutually beneficial arrangement within the advertising industry.

Video Advertising

Video advertising refers to the use of videos to promote a product, service, or brand through advertisements. It involves creating and distributing video content across various platforms, such as television, websites, social media, and apps, with the goal of reaching and engaging a specific target audience. Video advertisements are often brief and concise, typically lasting anywhere from a few seconds to a few minutes. They can be in the form of commercials that air during television programs or pre-roll ads that precede online videos. These ads may also appear on websites and social media feeds, including popular platforms like YouTube, Facebook, and Instagram. The main objective of video advertising is to capture viewers' attention and deliver a compelling message that persuades them to take desired actions. These actions can include purchasing a product, subscribing to a service, visiting a website, or sharing the video with others. To achieve this, video ads employ various techniques, such as storytelling, humor, emotion, or showcasing product features and benefits. Video advertising offers several advantages over other types of advertising formats. Firstly, videos are highly engaging and can communicate messages more effectively than text or images alone. Their visual and auditory elements can evoke emotions and create a memorable experience for viewers. Additionally, video ads can be more persuasive due to their ability to demonstrate products or services in action. Another advantage of video advertising is its wide reach. Videos can be shared and distributed across multiple platforms, allowing advertisers to reach a larger audience and increase brand exposure. Furthermore, video ads have the potential to go viral, generating organic reach and increasing brand awareness exponentially. Moreover, video advertising provides opportunities for precise targeting and measurement. Advertisers can use demographic, geographic, and interest-based data to deliver their video ads to specific audience segments, ensuring that they are shown to the most relevant viewers. Additionally, advertisers can track key metrics, such as video views, click-through rates, and conversions, to analyze the effectiveness of their campaigns and make data-driven optimizations. In conclusion, video advertising is a powerful marketing strategy that leverages the visual and auditory impact of videos to engage and persuade viewers. It offers unique advantages, including high engagement, wide reach, and precise targeting, making it an essential tool for advertisers to connect with their target audience and achieve their marketing objectives.

Viral Advertising Campaigns

Viral advertising campaigns, often referred to as viral marketing, are strategized marketing techniques employed by advertisers to create brand awareness, increase product visibility, and ultimately achieve a significant reach among the target audience. This form of marketing relies on the rapid spread of viral content across various online platforms, such as social media, email, blogs, and websites. Viral advertising campaigns aim to capture the attention of users and encourage them to share the content with their own network of contacts, hence exponentially increasing the campaign's reach. The content shared can take the form of videos, images, memes, articles, or interactive games, but it needs to possess certain characteristics that make it highly shareable and engage users emotionally or intellectually.

Viral Advertising

V iral advertising is a marketing technique that aims to create a buzz or generate interest in a product, brand, or service through the rapid spread of information from person to person. This form of advertising relies heavily on social media platforms, online communities, and word-of-mouth to reach a larger audience. Unlike traditional advertising methods, viral advertising focuses on creating content that is engaging, shareable, and resonates with consumers.

Viral Marketing

Viral marketing refers to a marketing strategy that aims to create a buzz and generate extensive brand awareness by leveraging the power of social media platforms, word- of-mouth, and other online channels. It involves the creation and promotion of highly shareable content that spreads rapidly across various online platforms, reaching a vast audience in a short span of time. In this approach, companies or advertisers aim to engage users and encourage them to share the content with their social networks, ultimately leading to an organic and exponential increase in brand visibility and audience reach. The success of viral marketing largely depends on the ability to evoke strong emotions or provide unique value to the audience, motivating them to share the content voluntarily. Unlike traditional advertising methods that rely on a direct message to promote a product or service, viral marketing aims to create an indirect influence and establish a more personal connection with the target audience. Viral marketing campaigns often utilize compelling storytelling, humor, provocative content, or controversial topics to capture the attention of viewers and encourage them to share the content with their friends, family, and followers on social media platforms. By tapping into the power of social networks, viral marketing enables companies to extend their reach far beyond their initial target audience, maximizing the impact of their marketing efforts. One of the key advantages of viral marketing is its potential for cost-effectiveness. By relying on user-generated sharing, viral marketing campaigns can reach a wide audience without requiring substantial financial investments in traditional advertising channels. However, creating content that has the potential to go viral and resonate with the target audience requires meticulous planning, creativity, and strategic execution.

Virtual Reality (VR) Ads Creation Steps

Virtual Reality (VR) Ads Creation Steps: Virtual Reality (VR) Ads refer to the process of creating advertisements that utilize virtual reality technology to immerse the viewer in a simulated environment. These ads are designed to engage the audience on a deeper level by providing a more interactive and immersive experience. Here are the steps involved in creating VR ads: 1. Identify the Target Audience: Begin by defining the target audience for the VR ad. Understand their demographics, preferences, and interests to ensure that the ad resonates with them. 2. Define the Objective: Determine the goal of the VR ad. Whether it is to raise brand awareness, increase sales, or drive customer engagement, clearly define the objective to guide the creative process. 3. Develop a Concept: Brainstorm and develop a concept that aligns with the objective and resonates with the target audience. Consider how virtual reality can enhance the message and deliver a memorable experience. 4. Plan the Storyboard: Create a detailed storyboard that outlines the sequence of events in the VR ad. This will serve as a visual guide for the production team and ensure a cohesive and engaging experience. 5. Choose the VR Platform: Select the appropriate VR platform or device for the ad. Consider factors such as compatibility, reach, and the desired level of immersion. 6. Create the Virtual Environment: Design and create the virtual environment that will immerse the viewer. Pay attention to detail and incorporate interactive elements to enhance the user experience. 7. Capture and Edit Footage: Use specialized cameras or software to capture and record the VR experience. Edit the footage to enhance visual quality and ensure a seamless and polished final product. 8. Incorporate Branding Elements: Integrate branding elements into the VR ad, such as logos, taglines, or product placements. Ensure that these elements are seamlessly incorporated into the virtual environment. 9. Test and Optimize: Test the VR ad on different VR devices and platforms to ensure compatibility and quality. Collect feedback from testers and make necessary optimizations to improve the overall experience. 10. Launch and Promote: Once the VR ad is finalized, launch it on the selected platforms and promote it through various channels. Monitor its performance and make adjustments if necessary to maximize its impact.

Virtual Reality (VR) Ads Creation

242

Virtual Reality (VR) Ads Creation refers to the process of developing and producing advertisements that are specifically designed to be experienced through virtual reality technology. Virtual reality is a computer-generated simulation that immerses a user in a three-dimensional environment, typically through the use of a headset. VR ads creation takes advantage of this immersive technology to create compelling and interactive advertising experiences.

Virtual Reality (VR) Ads

Virtual Reality (VR) Ads refer to advertisements that are designed specifically for virtual reality platforms and experiences. VR ads utilize the immersive and interactive nature of virtual reality technology to deliver engaging and memorable brand messages to users. These ads are created using virtual reality software and tools, allowing advertisers to develop unique and compelling experiences that transport users to virtual environments related to their products or services. VR ads can be experienced through VR headsets, which provide a fully immersive and 3D visual experience. The main objective of VR ads is to captivate users and create a strong emotional connection with the brand. By immersing users in virtual environments that are directly related to the advertised product or service, VR ads have the potential to leave a lasting impact on consumers. They enable a deep level of brand engagement and can trigger a sense of presence and empathy that traditional advertising formats often lack. VR ads can take various forms, including interactive 360-degree videos, virtual showrooms, gamified experiences, and product demonstrations. They provide users with a first-hand experience of the advertised product or service, allowing them to explore and interact with it in a virtual space. This interactivity enhances user engagement and boosts brand recall and recognition. Furthermore, VR ads have the advantage of being able to target specific audience segments, offering personalized and tailored experiences based on users' preferences and interests. This targeted approach ensures that the right message reaches the right audience, increasing the chances of converting users into customers. Overall, VR ads revolutionize the advertising industry by providing an innovative and immersive way to connect with consumers. By leveraging virtual reality technology, advertisers can create memorable experiences that not only showcase their products or services but also leave a lasting impression on users' minds.

Virtual Reality (VR) Advertising

Virtual Reality (VR) Advertising refers to the use of virtual reality technology to deliver advertising content and messages to consumers. It involves creating immersive virtual experiences that allow users to interact with brands and products in a virtual environment. VR advertising leverages the power of virtual reality technology to capture the attention and engage the senses of consumers in a way that traditional advertising methods cannot. It creates a unique and memorable experience that can leave a lasting impression on consumers. VR advertising can take various forms, such as interactive virtual reality commercials, branded virtual reality games, and virtual reality product placements. It allows advertisers to create virtual worlds and scenarios that align with their brand values and communicate their messaging effectively. One of the key advantages of VR advertising is its ability to create a sense of presence and immersion. By putting users in a virtual environment, advertisers can transport them to new places, allow them to experience products in a realistic way, and evoke emotions that can influence their purchasing decisions. Moreover, VR advertising offers a high level of interactivity, enabling users to actively engage with the advertising content. Users can navigate and explore the virtual environment, interact with virtual objects, and even customize their experiences. This level of interaction enhances user engagement and helps build a stronger connection between the brand and the consumer. VR advertising also provides advertisers with valuable data and insights. Through the use of analytics and tracking technologies, advertisers can gather data on user behavior, preferences, and responses. This data can be used to optimize and personalize future advertising campaigns, making them more relevant and effective. In conclusion, VR advertising is a cutting-edge form of advertising that harnesses the capabilities of virtual reality technology to create immersive and interactive brand experiences. It offers unique opportunities for advertisers to engage and captivate consumers in a way that traditional advertising methods cannot.

Web Banner Ads Creation

Web banner ads creation refers to the process of designing and developing graphical advertisements that are displayed on websites. These ads are typically composed of images, text, and other visual elements, and are designed to capture the attention of website visitors and entice them to engage with the advertised content or take a specific action. In the context of online advertising, web banner ads play a crucial role in promoting products, services, or events. They are commonly placed in strategic locations on websites, such as the top of the page, sidebar, or within the content itself. These ads may vary in size, shape, and layout, depending on the requirements of advertisers and the specifications set by the website or ad network where they are displayed. The main goal of web banner ads is to grab the attention of visitors and encourage them to interact with the ad. This could include clicking on the ad to visit the advertiser's website, making a purchase, signing up for a newsletter, or completing any other desired action. To achieve this, banner ads typically incorporate compelling visuals, persuasive copy, and clear call-to-action buttons or links. Web banner ads can be created using a wide range of tools and technologies. Design software such as Adobe Photoshop or Illustrator are commonly used to create the visual elements of the ad, including images, backgrounds, and logos. HTML and CSS are then used to code the ad and ensure it displays correctly on various devices and browsers. When creating banner ads, it is important to consider factors such as the target audience, the message being conveyed, and the overall aesthetic of the website where the ad will be displayed. The ad should be visually appealing, easy to read, and able to capture the viewer's attention within a short span of time. Animations, such as slideshows or transitions, can also be used to enhance the ad and make it more engaging. In conclusion, web banner ads creation involves the design and development of graphical advertisements that are displayed on websites. These ads are intended to attract the attention of website visitors and prompt them to take a specific action, such as clicking on the ad or making a purchase.

Web Banner Ads

Web Banner Ads are a form of online advertising where advertisements are displayed as graphical images on web pages. These ads are typically rectangular or square in shape and are placed strategically within the content of a website, either above, below, or alongside the main content. Banner ads are designed to attract the attention of website visitors and encourage them to click on the ad, which then redirects them to the advertiser's website or landing page. They are commonly used to promote products, services, events, and other offerings.

Webinar Advertising Strategies Planning

Webinar Advertising Strategies Planning refers to the process of devising and implementing effective promotional activities through webinars to raise awareness about a product, service, or brand and drive desired outcomes, such as lead generation, customer acquisition, or sales. Webinars have gained popularity as a cost-effective and convenient advertising tool, allowing businesses to reach a wide audience in a virtual setting. The planning phase involves several key steps to ensure that the webinar advertising campaign is successful. Firstly, it is crucial to define the objectives of the campaign. This includes determining the specific goals that the advertising efforts aim to achieve, such as increasing brand awareness, generating qualified leads, or driving conversions. Having clear objectives helps in developing a focused and targeted strategy to maximize the impact of the webinar advertisements. Next, thorough research on the target audience is necessary. Understanding the demographics, interests, and preferences of the target market enables businesses to tailor their webinar content and messaging to resonate with the intended audience. This research also helps in selecting the most appropriate platforms and channels to promote the webinars, ensuring maximum visibility and engagement. Once the target audience is identified, crafting compelling and informative webinar content becomes crucial. The content should be relevant to the target audience's needs and interests and provide valuable insights or solutions. Planning the structure and flow of the webinar, including the use of visual aids, interactive elements, and storytelling techniques, can enhance the overall effectiveness of the advertising campaign. After creating the webinar content, businesses need to consider the timing and frequency of promoting their webinars. Choosing the appropriate dates and times that align with the target audience's availability and preferences can increase attendance rates. Furthermore, promoting the webinars through various channels, such as social media, email marketing, and website banners, helps in reaching a wider audience and attracting potential participants. To ensure the success of webinar advertising strategies, it is crucial to monitor and evaluate the campaign's performance.

Tracking key metrics, such as webinar registrations, attendance rates, participant engagement, and conversions, provides insights into the effectiveness of the advertising efforts. These insights can be used to optimize and refine future webinar advertising campaigns, driving continuous improvement and better results. In conclusion, webinar advertising strategies planning involves defining objectives, conducting audience research, creating compelling content, selecting appropriate platforms, and timing the promotions effectively. Monitoring and evaluating the campaign's performance play a crucial role in refining and optimizing future webinar advertising efforts. By implementing a well-planned webinar advertising strategy, businesses can effectively promote their products, services, or brands to a targeted audience and drive desired outcomes.

Webinar Advertising Strategies

A webinar advertising strategy is a marketing approach that involves promoting and driving attendance to a webinar, which is an online seminar or presentation. Through various advertising tactics and channels, businesses aim to reach and attract a specific target audience to participate in the webinar. The primary goal of a webinar advertising strategy is to generate awareness, create interest, and ultimately convert attendees into customers or clients. This is typically achieved by providing valuable content, showcasing industry expertise, and presenting the benefits of a particular product or service.

Webinar Advertising

A webinar advertisement refers to a promotional activity that uses web-based platforms to showcase and promote a specific product, service, or event through interactive online presentations, lectures, or workshops. It aims to engage and educate a targeted audience in real-time, offering valuable insights and solutions while promoting a brand, generating leads, or driving conversions. Webinar advertising leverages the power of technology to overcome geographical boundaries, enabling businesses to reach a global audience without the need for physical presence. By utilizing audio, video, and interactive features, webinars create an immersive experience that allows participants to actively participate, ask questions, and provide feedback in real-time. This level of interactivity cultivates a sense of community, fosters trust, and enhances the overall user experience. One of the primary advantages of webinar advertising is its ability to deliver highly targeted content to a specific audience. Companies often use webinars to showcase their expertise, educate their target market, and establish themselves as thought leaders in their respective industries. By offering valuable information and addressing pain points, webinars can attract individuals who are genuinely interested in a particular topic or are seeking solutions to their challenges. This targeted approach ensures that the content resonates with the audience, increasing the chances of generating qualified leads and potential customers. Webinars also provide businesses with a platform to demonstrate the features and benefits of their products or services. Through live demos, case studies, or testimonials, companies can showcase their offerings in action, helping participants visualize how their solutions can address their specific needs. By showcasing real-world examples and success stories, webinars create a compelling narrative that builds credibility and trust, ultimately boosting the likelihood of converting prospects into customers. Additionally, webinar advertising allows companies to gather valuable data and insights about their audience. By tracking participant engagement, such as attendance, participation levels, and questions asked, businesses can gain deeper insights into their target market's preferences, pain points, and interests. This data can inform future marketing strategies, product development, and customer relationship management, enabling businesses to tailor their offerings to better serve their audience.

Word Of Mouth Marketing

Word of mouth marketing, also known as WOMM, is a form of advertising that relies on the natural conversations and recommendations made by individuals about a product or service. It is a powerful tool for businesses as it leverages the influence of satisfied customers and their personal experiences to build brand awareness and credibility. In WOMM, positive word of mouth is generated organically through customer satisfaction, outstanding product quality, exceptional customer service, or unique and memorable brand experiences. These satisfied customers become brand advocates who willingly share their positive experiences with friends, family, colleagues, and online communities. Their recommendations carry more weight and credibility compared to traditional advertising methods, as they are seen as unbiased and genuine. Word of mouth marketing can take different forms, both offline and online. Offline WOMM involves face-to-face conversations, recommendations between individuals, and physical interactions with the product or service. This could include conversations at social gatherings, recommendations to acquaintances, or product demonstrations in stores. Online WOMM, on the other hand, takes place on various digital platforms such as social media, review websites, forums, and online communities. It encompasses online discussions, customer reviews, social media shares, and influencers sharing their positive experiences with their followers. The benefits of word of mouth marketing are numerous. It helps businesses generate buzz and create a positive brand image. It can lead to increased brand awareness, customer acquisition, and loyalty. Word of mouth marketing is also cost-effective, as it relies on satisfied customers rather than costly advertising campaigns. Additionally, it has a viral nature, as positive conversations and recommendations can spread quickly and reach a wide audience. However, it is essential for businesses to actively monitor and manage word of mouth marketing campaigns. While positive word of mouth can be highly beneficial, negative word of mouth or customer dissatisfaction can spread just as quickly and harm a brand's reputation. Therefore, businesses should strive to deliver exceptional customer experiences, promptly address customer concerns, and encourage positive reviews and recommendations.

Word-Of-Mouth Advertising Campaigns Management

Word-of-Mouth Advertising Campaigns Management refers to the strategic planning, implementation, and control of marketing efforts aimed at leveraging and harnessing the power of word-of-mouth recommendations and referrals from satisfied customers or brand advocates. This type of advertising campaign focuses on stimulating and facilitating positive conversations and recommendations about a particular product, service, or brand. The goal is to encourage individuals to share their positive experiences with others, thereby expanding the reach and impact of the brand's messaging through organic and trusted channels.

Word-Of-Mouth Advertising Campaigns

Word-of-mouth advertising campaigns refer to marketing strategies that rely on the spoken recommendations of satisfied customers to promote a product, brand, or service. This form of advertising harnesses the power of personal recommendations and relies on existing customers to spread positive word about a product to their friends, family, and acquaintances. Unlike traditional advertising methods such as television commercials or print advertisements, word-of-mouth campaigns focus on generating organic, unpaid promotion through customer testimonials and referrals. In these campaigns, satisfied customers serve as brand advocates, sharing their positive experiences and opinions about a product with others in their social network.

Word-Of-Mouth Advertising Tactics

Word-of-mouth advertising tactics refer to strategies implemented by companies or individuals to encourage positive word-of-mouth recommendations and discussions about their products or services. It is a form of unpaid promotion where satisfied customers voluntarily spread the word about a brand, influencing the perceptions and purchase decisions of potential customers. One popular word-of-mouth advertising tactic is the use of brand ambassadors or influencers. These individuals are typically well-known, trusted, and influential within a specific community or industry. By leveraging their credibility and reach, companies can persuade them to promote their products or services through personal recommendations, testimonials, or sponsored content. This helps to generate positive discussions and increase brand awareness among the influencer's audience, potentially leading to new customers. Another effective tactic involves creating exceptional customer experiences. When customers have a positive experience with a brand, they are more likely to share their satisfaction with others. Companies can achieve this by providing exceptional customer service, personalized interactions, and going above and beyond to exceed customer expectations. Positive testimonials and reviews from these satisfied customers can then be shared online or in offline conversations, fostering positive word-of-mouth advertising. Companies can also take advantage of social media to amplify word-of-mouth advertising. By encouraging customers to share their experiences and opinions on social platforms, companies can greatly extend their reach and engage with a larger audience. This can be done by running social media contests, offering incentives for sharing, or creating shareable content that sparks conversations. Engaging with customers on social media and responding to their comments and inquiries can further foster positive word-of-mouth advertising. Incentivizing referrals is another commonly used tactic. By offering rewards, discounts, or exclusive deals to customers who refer their friends or family, companies can motivate their existing customers to actively promote their brand. This not only helps to generate new leads but also strengthens customer loyalty and increases the chances of repeat business. Overall, word-of-mouth advertising tactics aim to harness the power of personal recommendations by creating positive experiences, leveraging influencers, utilizing social media, and incentivizing referrals. By implementing these strategies, companies can effectively boost their brand's reputation, reach, and customer acquisition without relying solely on traditional advertising methods.

Word-Of-Mouth Advertising

A short formal definition of word-of-mouth advertising in the context of advertisement is: Word-of-mouth advertising refers to the process of individuals spontaneously spreading information, recommendations, or opinions about a product, service, or brand to others within their social network. Unlike traditional forms of advertising, word-of-mouth advertising relies on the organic and genuine communication between individuals, without any direct involvement or control from the brand or company.